THE CONVICTION FACTORY

THE CONVICTION FACTORY

THE COLLAPSE OF AMERICA'S CRIMINAL COURTS

By Roger I. Roots

ISBN: 1492928895
ISBN 13: 9781492928898
Livingston, Montana: Lysander Spooner University Press

CONTENTS

ACKNOWLEDGEMENTS

This book is the product of at least 15 years of research and writing on criminal procedure issues. Some of these writings began during my law school years at Roger Williams University in Bristol, Rhode Island. In fact, a good portion of Chapter Three is a republication of my first published law review article, "If It's Not a Runaway, It's Not a Real Grand Jury," 33 *Creighton Law Review* 821-42 (2000), which began as a term paper in a seminar course at RWU. Other chapters in this book were previously published as articles in law journals, including "Are Cops Constitutional?" 11 *Seton Hall Constitutional Law Journal* 685-757 (2001), "The Rise and Fall of the American Jury," 8 *Seton Hall Circuit Review* 1 (2011), "Grand Juries Gone Wrong," 14 *Richmond Journal of Law & Public Interest* 331 (2012), and "The Originalist Case For the Fourth Amendment Exclusionary Rule," 45 *Gonzaga Law Review* 1-66 (2009). I am grateful to all of the law student editors who offered comments, questions and suggestions regarding these articles, and to all of the legal commentators who have offered their observations over the years.

I was an unusual student in the institutions of higher learning I attended, and I am an unconventional professor and lecturer on these topics today. Some of the insights I have offered and the opinions I have written are also unusual, and contradict conventional wisdom in academia. I have occasionally met with fierce resistance in academic and professional circles. But I have been protected and defended in these institutions by various scholars and mentors along the way, and I owe them great debts of gratitude. Chief among my defenders in the UNLV Sociology Department was the late Dr. Frederick Preston, my dissertation committee chair, who passed away in 2009.

I also owe a great debt to Rhode Island Supreme Court Justice Maureen McKenna Goldberg, for whom I interned as a student clerk during my final year of law school. Without Dr. Preston's assistance and guidance I would never have been awarded my Ph.D. from UNLV; and without Justice Goldberg I would never have been admitted to the Rhode Island bar.

Roger I. Roots

There were many others along the way. Professors Hans-Hermann Hoppe, Andy Fontana and David Dickins at UNLV. Jon Roland at the Constitution Society. The good folks at the Fully Informed Jury Association. Some (but not all) of the luminaries at the Federalist Society.

I must also thank my favorite clients, some of whom doubled as proof-readers and discussants. Looming high above these is the misanthropic sage of Aquidneck Island, Duane Horton, who occasionally paid for my legal services with much better proofreading. Then there is the indefatigable Rudy Stanko—a modern John Lilburne—who taught me to challenge every artifice of the modern prosecutorial state. Frank McLain, Curtis Richardson, Bill Stegmeier, Erwin Spruth and David Hergert have also guided my insights. I have many law school buddies who also deserve great thanks, and chief among these are Christopher Friel, who saw me through four years of struggle on the way to my law license, and Alberto Aponte Cardona, who briefly rented me my first law office (which doubled as my apartment). I must also thank Dave Milak of the Sacred Mysteries Bookstore and all my climbing and running buddies such as Randy Oostema, Robert Douglas, Jack Green, Kyle McKenzie, Leigh Holleman, John Dudas, Darryl Baker and Emily Rahn.

Like many grad students and traveling professors before me, I have lived on very limited income during this period. I have slept on floors, in cars and on the ground, gone months without plumbing and refrigeration while building a house, run a law practice out of a Nissan pickup, and occasionally bunked in hostels and on clients' couches. To everyone who ever gave me solace and shelter, thank you.

Above all who deserve thanks are my long-suffering parents in Big Timber, Montana.

PREFACE

Few observers of American life and culture could have predicted a century ago that the United States would become the world's leader in criminal punishment. Yet today much of what America is can be defined by its criminal justice system. Not only does the U.S. contain the earth's most populous prison systems; but America's contemporary incarceration rate is probably the highest ever recorded in any society in human history.[1] More than 2.3 million human beings are currently housed in the country's many thousands of prisons and jails. [2] Even more startling: some 13 million Americans—about 5 percent of the adult population—are arrested and placed in handcuffs annually. When the 4.9 million Americans on probation or parole[3] are added to the numbers of Americans incarcerated, something like 3.1 percent of U.S. adults (or almost 6 percent of adult males) are in one form of government custody or another at all times.[4]

This expansive net of governmental control represents a remarkable change from the America of the past. At the time of Tocqueville's observations of America (in the 1830s), "the means available to the authorities for the discovery of crimes and arrest of criminals [were] few,"[5] yet Tocqueville doubted "whether in any other country crime so seldom escape[d] punishment."[6] For most of American history, people handled most crimes informally, and criminal courts were something of a last resort. Nothing struck a European traveler in America, wrote Tocqueville, more than the absence of government in the streets.[7]

It is widely recognized that this transformation has come about through an increase in criminal laws, criminal sentences and police machinery in the streets. But it is not so well understood that there has been a gradual relaxation of procedural safeguards for criminal defendants in America's courts. As American history has developed, America's judges have increasingly favored prosecutors over defendants, and the country's rules of court procedure have increasingly offered greater advantages to the government.

It seems undeniable that the American people themselves have become more punitive. Jury conviction rates in trials in the nineteenth century were under 40 percent in most American jurisdictions. They did not rise above fifty percent until the middle of the twentieth century. Today, however, conviction rates are well above ninety percent in most American jurisdictions (when guilty pleas are included with trial verdicts).

But the zeal of Americans to punish those who break the rules has been eclipsed by the zeal of America's judges and lawyers for establishing procedures making it easier to do so.

Rulings in America's courtrooms have produced a landscape in which Americans are the most surveilled people on earth. Police officers in America's largest cities routinely stop, frisk and force Americans—mostly males of the lowest classes—to stand with hands against walls or drop prone onto sidewalks as officers rifle through their pockets and bags. Americans are also increasingly subject to armed stops on roadways and invasive searches of vehicles. Roadside strip searches and cavity searches without warrant have been reported in several jurisdictions.

I was thrown into the world of criminal justice as a teenager during the 1980s, when I hitchhiked across the United States and began to encounter police officers for the first time. When I was 19 I got into an argument with a Florida State Trooper and held my arms in front of my face as the officer beat me with a steel flashlight. I was subsequently convicted of "resisting arrest with violence." I began my adult life as both a high school dropout and a convicted felon.

When I was 22 years old I briefly attended a community college in Wyoming (I had earned a G.E.D. by then) where I gave a somewhat comedic classroom speech in a communications class on the topic of how to build homemade firearms out of household materials. I showed my fellow classmates several visual aids, including a model that I had fashioned from pieces of steel pipe, duct tape and a chunk of wood. After my instructor reported the incident to the school's administrators, my campus apartment was raided without warrant and I was federally indicted for "possession of an unregistered firearm" and being a felon in possession of firearms.

Like so many other Americans, I accepted a plea deal in which I pled guilty to one count (possessing an unregistered firearm which lacked a five-dollar federal tax stamp) in exchange for the government's dropping of two other firearm possession counts. I was sentenced to 20 months in federal prison.

These experiences reverberated across every dimension of my life. By my mid twenties I was a hardened hater of the federal government and an extreme racist. I read the writings of Hitler, William Gayley Simpson and William Pierce. My friends and associates were mostly white supremacists like myself. My encounters with the enforcement agents of the state were uniformly hostile.

The years that followed were cruel years. I lost job opportunities. Girlfriends left me when they discovered my views and my background. But I managed to finish college with high honors at Montana State University, Billings and to get accepted into the Roger Williams University School of Law in Bristol, Rhode Island. It was in law school where I discovered my interest in unraveling the mysteries of constitutional law. I was a voracious reader and spent many hours in the school law library and the other great libraries of the northeast.

When I applied for the Rhode Island bar in 1999, my bar application was an inch thick with explanations for my many mistakes. The clerk who accepted it told me it was probably the heaviest bar application ever filed in Rhode Island. Although I passed the bar exam on my first try, the State Supreme Court denied my application on account of my criminal record and my despicable character. I found myself thrown back out into the heartless world of poverty and underemployment. For a time I supported myself as a junkyard mechanic, a construction worker and a telemarketer.

In 2001 I was accepted into a Ph.D. program in Sociology at the University of Nevada, Las Vegas where I returned to my life of reading and late nights in libraries. I was also employed as a teaching assistant, and for the first time I was trusted to be a teacher of others. I relished it. By my early thirties I had abandoned my hatred of blacks and Jews and had come to view them as sharing with me a common struggle against the state. I increasingly saw the world through the eyes of a pure libertarian. Indeed, my loathing for the government had been transferred to all governments, everywhere, and at every period of history. I revered, however, the great principles of liberty that had fueled the American Revolution and defined the American Founding in the late eighteenth century.

I performed hundreds of hours of volunteer work and filed another—even thicker—Rhode Island bar application in 2003. It was granted four years after my first application was denied. In subsequent years I have sat at defense

Roger I. Roots

tables next to clients facing the prospect of many years of incarceration. I have often found myself returning—in a suit and tie—to correctional institutions to visit clients. I've even represented prisoners held at some of the same facilities where I myself was formerly imprisoned.

As I write these words I am an assistant professor of criminal justice at one of America's great historically black colleges. I still practice law occasionally, and, like most criminal defense lawyers, I revel in rare and slight victories while cursing the enormity of America's slide into prosecutorial supremacy. In theory, criminal convictions are supposed to be more difficult to obtain than civil judgments. Yet court rules have become so lopsided that the government seems to obtain convictions almost effortlessly.

At its heart, this is a book about criminal procedure: the esoteric rules of operation recognized in America's criminal justice system. As I show in the pages that follow, a steady stream of government-favoring alterations in court practices has voided much of the adversarial model of justice that was handed down by America's constitutional Framers. For the most part these alterations have been imposed by judges rather than legislators.

Today's criminal litigation may seem slow and inefficient to outsiders. But insiders know that the outcome of the vast majority of criminal cases— conviction and punishment—is mostly predetermined. Most felony cases are disposed of by only two or three separate court appearances: an arraignment hearing (in which the defendant initially pleads not guilty), a change-of-plea hearing (in which the defendant changes his plea to guilty), and a sentencing hearing. Today these hearings are not materially distinguishable from defendant to defendant. Occasionally two or more of these hearings may be combined, and in misdemeanor cases, the general practice in most jurisdictions is to hold all proceedings in one fell swoop: an "arraignment" (or at least a brief introduction of the charges), the acceptance of a quick guilty plea, and the issuance of a sentence on the spot. To be sure, many cases still have other types of hearings, including bail hearings, suppression hearings or preliminary hearings (in states that allow felonies to be prosecuted without grand jury indictments). But the vast technicalities that most people attribute to the American justice system are rarely given the full breath of life.

In practice, most cases involve an overworked public defender who expends most of his defense efforts in each case negotiating with the prosecutor over his client's *sentence*. Trials have become almost nonexistent. To understand this phenomenon, one must go beyond law into the realm of sociology. Criminal procedure has been given over to what Max Weber called rationalization: the sociological law that all perpetual systems of human interaction become more efficient over time. American criminal justice has been transformed into something of a factory process.[8]

The American bar and bench have collectively forgotten the history behind our system of procedural rights, a story as fascinating as any mystery or adventure saga. It is the story of men chained to dungeon walls and of royal officers tearing apart the city of London in search of the printers of pamphlets. It is the story of Joan of Arc raped or assaulted in dungeons and burned at the stake after being compelled to sign a confession she couldn't read. It is the story of Algernon Sidney's denunciation of his trial from his gallows, and of jurors locked up for refusing to deliver guilty verdicts against William Penn and William Mead. Of John Lilburne's refusal to take the oath before the Star Chamber, and John Wilkes' protests as his personal papers were bagged up pursuant to a general warrant. Of young men pulled from train cars and accused of crimes that never occurred, and a king beheaded after a summary trial. It is the story of accused witches in Salem Colony condemned to die by the testimony of four-year-old girls.

We have also forgotten how closely linked criminal procedure is to general prosperity. For generations after America's Founding, basic due process provided a groundwork for the development of the most prosperous and powerful nations on earth: those associated with the British Common Law. America's industry could thrive, America's workers could prosper, America's investors could expect profitable returns, and American writing and culture could flourish because the rule of law protected individual interests and property from the government. Law provided the means by which even the lowest among the American people were able to rise to wealth and prominence.[9]

In this book I offer a full-throated defense of the adversarial model of justice, with its emphasis on distrust of the state and upon the obstructive power of common citizenry. It is long past time to confront the bogus pseudohistory of the false "originalists" and fake "strict constructionists" who have taken over the bar and bench.

Roger Roots, Hawkins, Texas 2014

Introduction

ADVERSARIAL JUSTICE

"The history of liberty has largely been the history of the observance of procedural safeguards." U. S. Supreme Court Justice Felix Frankfurter, <u>McNabb v. United States</u>, 1943.

"[i]llegitimate and unconstitutional practices get their first footing by silent approaches and slight deviations from legal modes of procedure." <u>Boyd v. United States</u>, 116 U.S. 635 (1886).

"[T]he best and true interest of the people is to be found in a rigid adherence to those rules which preserve the fairness of criminal prosecutions in every stage." Chief Justice John Marshall, in <u>United States v. Aaron Burr</u>, Case No. 14,692c, 25 F.Cas. 27, 29 (C.C.D.Va. May 28, 1807).

There is an age-old debate in the criminal justice system about whether the system's highest aim is the determination of truth or the production of justice in some other sense. American students learn of this debate in the contours of comparisons between the adversarial justice model on display in the vestiges of the British Empire with the "inquisitorial" or civil law models found in continental and eastern Europe and elsewhere in the world.[10] The adversarial, or common law tradition pits the prosecution against the defendant on a level playing field, with a judge acting as something of an impartial referee and a jury of the defendant's peers (or at least one composed of common citizens) having the final say in whether the government can punish the defendant. By contrast, the civil law, or inquisitorial, tradition offers authorities a broader array of investigative powers to determine a defendant's guilt.

American criminal justice, having descended from the English common law, is based upon the adversarial tradition. This model is grounded in distrust and suspicion of government.[11] Indeed, its presumption of innocence, if stated differently, is a presumption that the government is wrong and that its prosecution is meritless or abusive. "Unlike European systems of justice, dominated by judge and prosecution," writes American crime historian Roger Lane, "in ours the parties are not even supposed to be engaged in an impartial search for the truth."[12] And when the truth is unknown, unproven or unknowable, the result must be acquittal.[13] Judges are to act as passive and disinterested referees. Moreover, by inserting the will of common laymen, the adversarial system allows for the outright obstruction of the state regardless of the evidence.

By contrast, the vast majority of countries on earth use some form of inquisitorial courts to adjudicate criminal guilt and punishment. In such courts the deciders are themselves government agents. Proceedings may be in secret. Judges act along with prosecutors to sift through evidence and arguments in order to decide guilt or innocence. Inquisitorial justice eschews the input of commoners and looks to the supposed greater trustworthiness of respected state functionaries.

"The essence of inquisitorial proceedings," writes Jenny McEwan, "is that the state *is* interested in the outcome and wishes an investigator to discover as many relevant facts as possible."[14] Rather than a presumption of innocence, inquisitorial investigations stem from a presumption that a crime has been committed.[15] "The court itself will pursue facts, and avail itself of any sources," as judges "are expected to arrive at the truth by their own exertions."[16] The parties generally have no power to prevent the inquisitorial judge from seeing any desired item of evidence.[17] Inquisitorial judges may at times show leniency to defendants or criticize the government, but they risk sanction or punishment themselves if they are seen as outright nullifiers of authority.[18]

And although acquittal rates have declined considerably in the American system over the past century, American defendants are still more likely to be acquitted than defendants in inquisitorial regimes. According to Professor Mike P.H. Chu, the average acquittal rate in inquisitorial systems is 2.4 percent compared to an 11-percent acquittal rate (for those who take charges to trial) in adversarial systems in comparable years.[19]

Even though the U.S. can no longer be considered a strictly adversarial system, some 69 percent of defendants who plead not guilty are acquitted of at least some of the accusations against them, or have at least some counts dismissed.[20] In Britain during 1994, some 42 percent of the 22.8 percent of defendants who did not plead guilty were either partially or fully acquitted or exonerated.[21] According to Chu:

> These figures can be contrasted to those of Japan that has an inquisitorial system. During 1992, a total of 3,886 out of 55,487 defendants pleaded not guilty (7%). Out of the 3,886 defendants pleading not guilty, only 3.8% were found innocent or partly not guilty. Thus, acquittal rates in Japan are still significantly lower when compared with those in both Britain and the United States.

Similar findings can be culled from acquittal rates in American trials when jury verdicts are compared to judge verdicts. According to Norman J. Finkel, research into 3,500 cases during the late 1960s revealed a 78 percent agreement between judge and jury verdicts: Of the 22 percent of cases where judge and jury disagreed, 19 percent were cases in which the judge convicted but the jury acquitted, while in only 3 percent of the cases did the judge acquit while the jury convicted.[22] This 16 percent "net leniency effect" of juries (or something close to it) appears to be consistent over the last few decades, even as American judges have increasingly sought to suppress jury independence.[23]

Not only do inquisitorial systems produce lower acquittal rates (or, said differently, higher conviction rates). They produce justice that is somewhat more notoriously political.[24] When inquisitorial systems err, they tend to err on the side of the state. Many inquisitorial systems do not even presume innocence, and most do not recognize any right to remain silent.[25] Evidence unlawfully seized or even stolen by authorities may be admitted and considered. Hearsay, privileged or even secret evidence may be introduced. The Soviet Russian justice system presumed guilt whenever a prosecutor lodged a criminal complaint.[26] When there were doubts about a defendant's guilt, prosecutors had "repeated chances to prove it."[27] China, a notorious land of "swift arrests and convictions,"[28] has reported acquittal rates at or below one percent in recent years.[29] Defendants may be convicted in closed proceedings, denied counsel and made to face trial without an opportunity to review the evidence.[30] In Cuba an indictment is tantamount to conviction and defense lawyers are taught to guide clients toward rehabilitation rather than argue a client's innocence.[31] In Iran a religious judge sitting for one term may sentence hundreds of defendants to death without evidence or even guiding principles.[32]

When the winds of public outrage or media scrutiny become critical of findings or proceedings, inquisitorial courts are known to change outcomes or even to change verdicts.[33] Above all else, inquisitorial systems allow the state greater protection from dissidents or critics who threaten the state's legitimacy.[34]

Many of the most significant procedures used in American adversarial courts grew in response to abuses by the British monarchies of the sixteenth through the eighteenth centuries. In their zeal to suppress and punish Puritans and radical Protestants, the Stuart monarchists of the early 1600s established "Star Chamber" court proceedings, utilizing procedures employed for centuries by Inquisitors in Spain and other countries on the European continent. In Star Chamber proceedings, "[t]here was no jury; the suspect was not allowed to cross-examine or, in some cases, even to see the witnesses against him," and he "might be tortured to extract evidence."[35] Even the accusations were sometimes secret and defendants were given no notice of the substance of the charges.[36] Possible sentences included death, imprisonment, exile and mutilation. Among the Star Chamber's most frequent cases were prosecutions for "criminal libel," by which the advocacy of Puritan ideology was equated with treason.[37]

Star Chamber proceedings had jurisdiction concurrent with common law courts but focused on political crimes. There was no resort to juries in the Star Chamber, as "[t]he Star Chamber offered the government a convenient forum for prosecuting sedition and ecclesiastical offences, when juries might not cooperate."[38] But by punishing jurors who were considered to have delivered "perverse verdicts" in common law courts, the Star Chamber courts "controlled all the justice of the kingdom."[39] Verdicts against the wishes of the king were enough to create fear in the heart of every juror that he might be prosecuted before the Star Chamber.[40]

The Star Chamber generated such a backlash that it helped fuel an English Civil War between Parliament and the forces of the Crown.[41] Hundreds were killed and King Charles 1 was captured and himself tried for treason before Parliament. The procedures used were similar to the inquisitorial procedures the King had sanctioned in the Star Chamber. Turnabout perhaps being fair play, King Charles was found guilty and beheaded in public in 1649.[42]

Libertarian movements in the English criminal justice system recurred over time. In 1762 British authorities issued a general warrant to identify and arrest the author of a pamphlet entitled *North Briton No. 45*. More than forty London printers were arrested and interrogated before authorities descended on the home of John Wilkes, a member of the House of Commons. Wilkes' personal books and papers were bagged up and he was taken to the Tower of London. The events led to mass demonstrations across Britain.

Wilkes became a popular hero and the accidental leader of an international libertarian movement. American colonists named streets, counties and cities for him (for example, Wilkes-Barre, Pennsylvania) and for Lord Camden, the libertarian British judge who later ruled that general warrants were invalid.[43] Precedents were established (or reestablished) which required that search warrants must state with specificity the names, descriptions and places of persons and things to be searched or seized. The Fourth Amendment is largely an extension of such precedents.

When the House of Commons refused to seat Wilkes after Wilkes won a Parliamentary election, London mobs rioted through the streets of London, even pushing into the courtyard of the Royal palace where, according to historian Arthur Cash, "they performed a pantomime of beheading the king."[44] On occasions when Wilkes was transported out of prison for court appearances, crowds intercepted and broke him out of the coaches in which he was held.[45] Later, rioting mobs attacked and demolished the chariot of Wilkes' prosecutor during its procession through the streets. Mobs brought stuffed figures representing King's ministers such as Lord Halifax (who had signed the general warrant under which Wilkes was arrested) into the street where the effigies were subjected to "solemn mock trials and then beheaded."[46]

These events are chronicled in Professor Cash's *John Wilkes: The Scandalous Father of Civil Liberty* (2006).[47] As Cash recounts, a cultural commitment to adversarial procedures and civil liberties permeated Anglo-American society by the end of the eighteenth century. And if anything, the American colonists were more demanding of liberty than their British counterparts. The highest judge in Massachusetts colony, Thomas Hutchinson, found that his mansion had been chopped to pieces by a hatchet-wielding mob after Hutchinson ruled in favor of the onerous Stamp Act.[48]

Protections for liberty were on the lips of seemingly almost everyone who spoke English during the late 1700s. And the distinctions between the British adversarial system and inquisitorial justice on display in Europe's other empires had never been more stark. An unnamed Frenchman of the late eighteenth century published his observations of the British justice system in James Boswell's famous *The Scots* magazine:

> Nothing is more astonishing than the mildness and humanity with which criminals are here treated, whether they be thieves, murderers, or incendiaries. Even if their guilt is evident, the bar, the jury, and the judges, all seem to conspire for their acquittal. They search the indictment for some trifling fault that may render it equivocal; a false surname, an indeterminate date, a single letter omitted; all these are fatal to the process, and will immediately put an end to it. The counsel defend the culprit with zeal, and the witnesses against him are questioned with much strictness, and sometimes with much severity. His own confession is never demanded, and he can be convicted by the evidence of credible witnesses alone. It is repugnant to human nature to see a man bear testimony against himself; and this philosophical maxim affords a strange contrast to the practice of those tribunals of which torture is the grand resource. When all the evidence is ended, it is permitted the accused to make his defence; and the greatest attention is paid to everything he says. If he is found guilty, a judge announces to him the punishment which the law inflicts on his offence, in a speech which, so far from being composed of reproachful and reviling words, is generally filled with tender and compassionate expressions.[49]

Contrast this courtroom environment with that of France during roughly the same period. The same edition of Boswell's The *Scots* contained a description of the procedure available to the inmates of Paris's famed Bastille. Prisoners were confined there "many weeks" before being "interrogated in the council-hall."[50] Upon their appearance in court, French defendants were interrogated with cunning tricks, outright lies and false promises of potential liberty in the event of confession. "The confession of the prisoner, however, far from operating his liberation, is sure to induce new interrogatories, to rivet still faster his own shackles, and most likely to endanger some of his friends or relations, at the same time that it increases his own misery by new acts of rigour."[51]

"Judges in eighteenth-century France," wrote Judith K. Schafer, "were instruments of the crown and considered part of the prosecution team. Indeed, it was a French judge's duty to secure convictions. French law placed the burden of proof on the accused to prove innocence, not on the state to establish guilt."[52] As constitutional historian Leonard Levy detailed in *The Palladium of Justice* (1999), the French and English systems were different in their very foundations.

> One system presumed the guilt of the accused; the other, requiring the prosecution to prove its case to a jury, did not. The one forced the accused to submit to a self-incriminatory oath; the other did not even permit the accused to give sworn testimony if he wanted to. One tried the accused by secret interrogatories, the other by public evidence. One was an official prosecution by the judge; the other made the trial an oral combat before a jury of the accused's peers. With the public watching, the crown's attorney prosecuting, and the judge basically passive. One empowered the judge to decide the question of guilt or innocence, while the other permitted a jury to control the verdict. One routinely used torture; the other regarded it as illegal. . . . . One, not recognizing the concept of double jeopardy, retried a suspect indefinitely, while the other would place no one in jeopardy more than once for the same offense . . . . Finally, one was cruel and arbitrary; the other was potentially fair and just, especially because a jury's verdict controlled the outcome.[53]

Britain found that its relaxed system of common law boosted its fortunes around the globe while France and Spain struggled under their more state-friendly legal systems by the nineteenth century. When English forces won out over the French and Spanish in most of the North American east coast, the English libertarian tradition followed the British victories.

For more than two centuries, English individualism won out over French and Spanish authoritarianism and paternalism.[54]

British Americans were among the freest people on earth, with low rates of taxation and low levels of government intrusion in their lives. But during the buildup to the American Revolution, Americans argued that their mother country was depriving them of their fundamental rights as Englishmen. When Ben Franklin, John Adams, and the other American Founding Fathers met in New York and Philadelphia to discuss their grievances, they often invoked the protections of the English Common law and demanded that their natural rights to such protections be recognized.[55]

America's Founding documents are heavily weighted with themes of criminal procedure. Among the primary grievances enumerated in the Declaration of Independence were the Crown's use of inquisitorial justice ("mock trials") and its denial of trial by jury for some colonists. Indeed, fifteen of twenty-six distinct guarantees in the first eight amendments of the Bill of Rights relate directly to criminal procedure.[56]

Chapter One

THE CHALLENGE TO ADVERSARIAL JUSTICE

The two centuries that followed the enactment of the American Bill of Rights saw a long series of departures from the adversarial paradigm. Although America had no intrinsic aristocracy, lawyers and judges emerged to serve as something of a substitute. It wasn't long before judges began to grumble at their status as neutral referees and to look with envy at the greater powers associated with the "truth"-determining inquisitors of continental Europe. American judges also chaffed under the superior role in the criminal process played by uneducated laymen serving on juries and grand juries.

By the dawn of the twentieth century, some of the highest-ranking figures in America's legal profession began to voice angry criticisms of the adversarial model. In an influential 1906 speech before the American Bar Association that was to define generations of legal thinking, Harvard Law School Dean Roscoe Pound condemned America's adversarial system as based on the "sporting theory of justice."[57] Pound criticized "sensational cross-examinations . . ., the "exertion to 'get error into the record' rather than dispose of controversies, and the "extravagant power of juries."[58] Pound's published lecture was widely circulated and is now considered by some to be "the most influential paper ever written by an American legal scholar."[59]

Judge Learned Hand, who served as chief judge of the U.S. Second Circuit Court of Appeals for many years and authored more than 2,000 legal opinions, wrote in 1923 that American court procedures had for too long been "haunted by the ghost of the innocent man convicted."[60] "It is an unreal dream," concluded Hand. "What we need to fear is the archaic formalism and the watery sentiment that obstructs, delays, and defeats the prosecution of crime."[61]

By the mid-twentieth century, such attacks on adversarial court procedures had become an industry. Generations of lawyers scored seats on high courts, tenure at law schools and other professional accolades by attacking the very system of procedure that had been so hard won in the tumultuous seventeenth and eighteenth centuries.[62] In 1969, antipathy toward adversarial process landed squarely on the U.S. Supreme Court in the form of Chief Justice Warren E. Burger. Burger was selected for the Chief Justiceship by President Nixon after Burger gave a speech criticizing the American Fifth Amendment right to remain silent and suggesting that courts in Scandinavian countries performed better by going "swiftly, efficiently and directly to the question of whether the accused is guilty."[63] Thereafter Nixon presented Burger—somewhat ridiculously—as a "strict constructionist" of the United States Constitution.[64]

As Chief Justice of the Supreme Court from 1969 to 1986, Burger peppered his rulings and opinions with the theme that the primary pur-pose of the justice system was the discovery of truth and the punishment of the guilty. Accordingly, Burger viewed rules of evidence or procedure which misdirected court resources to protect the "guilty" from punishment as unnecessary impediments.[65] Burger also condemned the high costs and alleged inefficiency of the jury system.[66] "The entire legal profession," wrote Burger in 1984, had "become so mesmerized with the stimulation of the courtroom contest, that we tend to forget that we ought to be healers of conflict ... Trial by adversarial contest must in time go the way of the ancient trial by battle and blood ... Our system has become too costly, too painful, too destructive, too inefficient for truly civilized people."[67]

Burger repeatedly sought to link zealous defense advocacy with unprofessionalism and to paint defense lawyers who too energetically defended "guilty" clients as unethical.[68] Burger is known to have sought the disbarment of a law professor who disagreed with him regarding the adversarial process. Burger may even have used deception to try to get the professor fired from teaching.[69]

Burger opposed the Fourth Amendment exclusionary rule, writing that exclusion of "evidence of undoubted reliability and probative value" merely because it was seized illegally was "an unworkable and irrational concept of law."[70] In Burger's view, federal law should change to accept unlawfully-seized evidence against criminal defendants. In his spare time, Burger authored law review articles and gave speeches attacking the adversarial system.[71]

By the late twentieth century, the American bar and bench was overpopulated with voices repeating the common theme that criminal defense lawyers, acting as overzealous advocates, had ignored the search for "truth" as the supposed hallmark of the profession. [72] Critics of the adversarial model pointed to the way that its rules of evidence "conceal" evidence and contain "truth-defeating devices"—devices that allow as many as a quarter of "guilty"

10

offenders to escape conviction.[73] Condemnation of the exclusionary rule, the privilege against self-incrimination and other rules of evidence became widespread by the end of the Burger Court era.

A 1996 best-seller by New York State Supreme Court Judge Harold Rothwax, entitled *Guilty,* echoed the same themes perfected by Pound, Hand and Burger. Judge Rothwax proclaimed that "criminals and defense attorneys hide behind a morass of poorly conceived statues, procedures, and technicalities that keeps them from resolving the paramount question at hand: Did the accused commit the crime?"[74] Another critic, former Los Angeles trial judge Burton Katz, even suggested that the adversarial system is downright *immoral*:

> A system that exalts a criminal's rights over the victim's, procedure over substance, and adversarial supremacy over the quest for truth and justice is on the verge of moral bankruptcy.[75]

"LAW AND ORDER ORIGINALISM"

The drive to reimpose inquisitorialism has been especially potent since the 1990s, as waves of self-styled "originalist" legal scholars have taken center stage at American law schools and on many of America's high courts.[76] Claiming to construe the Constitution "as it was originally understood by the framers and ratifiers" (in the words of Judge Robert Bork) "originalist" scholars have enjoyed great success in painting the Constitution's framers and ratifiers as tough-on-crime conservatives like themselves.[77] In Bork's "originalist" vision, the Constitution enshrined no rights to privacy, offered no allowance for juries to acquit if the prosecution establishes the violation of a statute, and recognized no substantive individual rights in addition to those specifically enumerated in the Bill of Rights (despite the Ninth Amendment's indication that it did so).

Some originalists have even claimed that the Bill of Rights was never intended as a protection for "the guilty" at all, but rather was intended as a means to protect the innocent while ensuring punishment for the guilty. Yale Law Professor Akhil Amar, for example, has suggested that it it a "commonsensical point" that "the essence of our Constitution's rules about criminal procedure" is that they "seek[ ] to protect the innocent" and that "lawbreaking, as such, is entitled to no legitimate expectation of privacy." [78] Judge Richard Posner has stated that constitutional provisions such as the Fourth Amendment were not designed to protect the interest of a criminal in avoiding punishment for his crime.[79]

But as a number of constitutional researchers have pointed out, this brand of "law and order originalism" (coined by Professor Thomas Davies of the University of Tennessee) [80]—at least as it regards issues of criminal justice[81]—is simply false.[82] Those who debated the various provisions of the Bill of Rights regarded the state not as a benevolent protector, but with suspicion and disdain.[83] Constitutional criminal procedure was designed to thwart the state at strategic points, sometimes in circumstances where agents of the state most desire evidence and information. Presumption of innocence, speedy trial provisions, requirements of strict and explicit charging, and double jeopardy clauses in early constitutions acted as bars to prosecutions even where the state's view of guilt was unchallenged.

Many of the procedural protections enunciated in the Bill of Rights are lineal descendants of protections that developed during the Inquisition era when the Catholic Church pursued alleged heretics with savage zeal.[84] Silence rights—and the exclusionary rules that developed to protect those rights at trials and other proceedings—were established as shields to protect "the guilty" from government and the Church.[85]

Some of the assertions of the faux originalists, such as Bork's proclamations about jury nullification,[86] are so outlandishly false that they collapse under the most superficial examination[87] (see Chapter 5). Trial by jury originally functioned not as a mere fact-finding device but also as a fundamental check on the power of government and a means to obstruct unwarranted government prosecutions of "guilty" offenders.[88] In the Founders' law practice, juries and not judges had the final say in the determination of guilt.[89] Early American juries can and often did issue not-guilty verdicts if they disagreed with the laws in question, and common people understood that jury duty included the duty to veto the application of bad laws. The right to a jury trial itself, by constitutional design, is a means for defeating "the truth" in some cases.[90]

THE IMPACT OF NONADVERSARIAL THINKING

It is difficult to overestimate the impact that this anti-adversarial thinking has had on criminal procedure during the past several decades. Today's rules of procedure reward even the most loathsome snitch so long as his acts of betrayal assist the prosecution and harm the defense.[91] Filing deadlines and pleading requirements now overtly favor the prosecution.[92] The government has become increasingly able to introduce evidence it has taken without warrant or stolen. The protections of the Fourth, Fifth and Sixth Amendments have been gradually softened if not eviscerated in many circumstances.

Several detailed studies of Supreme Court decisions regarding the Fourth Amendment have found that the Court in recent years has consistently interpreted the Amendment so as to favor the government. Sometimes the Court has established and then quickly altered rules in a manner that empowers the government.[93] Such was the level of pro-prosecution bias on the Supreme Court during the 1980s[94] that Justice Brennan declared that the Court's jurisprudence had gone "beyond a mere philosophic inclination to facilitate criminal prosecution" and appeared to be acting as "an arm of the prosecution."[95] The grand pageant of legal decisions of the last fifty years has overwhelmingly favored the state over the individual. At almost every turn there is now a double standard applied in favor of the state.[96]

In 2009, noted civil rights lawyer Harvey A. Silverglate authored an important book entitled *Three Felonies A Day*.[97] Silverglate astounded readers with the pronouncement that the criminal law has become so broad, complicated, confusing and ambiguous that each of us—if we are normal Americans—probably commit something like three felonies a day without realizing it. Any federal prosecutor, suggested Silverglate, could prosecute and imprison any of us if he chose, using vague, "accordion-like criminal statutes" that have been enacted by Congress in recent decades.

Few observers can argue with Silverglate's thesis. The once-libertarian America, the nation where freedom flowered like nowhere else, has become something of a technocratic police state by the twenty-first century, and lawmakers deserve a good bulk of the blame.

But more blame must be laid at the feet of the legal profession and its most powerful subgroup, the judiciary. For the most part, the vast codes of intrusive laws enacted by Congress have been met with passive approval by the judiciary. The courts have overwhelmingly approved, ratified and sustained the assaults upon liberty and property made by the executive and legislative branches.

The modern courtroom focus on questions of guilt or innocence— as opposed to questions about the overreach of criminal statutes, the confusing and ambiguous wording of laws, the selectiveness, vindictiveness or abusiveness of prosecutions, or the expanding reach of authoritarian law enforcement—has fundamentally transformed the nature of American criminal justice. Overshadowing all other alterations in criminal procedure have been changes in the scope of trial by jury. Criminal procedure has evolved so that judges regularly prohibit defendants from even arguing their innocence at trial if their arguments might tend to call the jury's attention to the merits or propriety of relevant statutes.[98] Many judges exert great efforts to conceal from juries the fact that juries have the power to consider whether a law is being applied improperly or oppressively.

Judges have relegated juries and grand juries to roles of servants rather than independent bodies with power to check the government. For decades, federal judges have been in the habit of disregarding jury acuittals and using sentencing guidelines to conceptually convict and punish defendants for crimes of which juries acquitted them. In fact, since 1986 the Federal Sentencing Guidelines have required judges to look at all charged conduct and increase sentences if a mere preponderance of the evidence suggests guilt on acquitted charges.[99] Thus a defendant who was *acquitted* by a jury of ten counts of trafficking cocaine but convicted of one count of mere possession of cocaine could find himself sentenced by a judge to a long prison sentence as if he had been convicted of every trafficking count.

In the landmark 2005 decision in *United States v. Booker*, this embarrassing problem led the Supreme Court to declare the entire Federal Sentencing Guidelines to be advisory rather than mandatory.[100] But even after the *Booker* decision, federal judges continue to use acquitted conduct to boost a defendant's sentence if a jury convicts a defendant of so much as a single minor count.[101] Obviously such sentencing practices incentivize prosecutors to file multicount indictments.

HABEAS CORPUS LAW

The influence of Chief Justice Burger and other anti-adversarialists has been especially strong in the area of habeas corpus law.[102] In 1976, the Supreme Court ruled in *Stone v. Powell* that state prisoners convicted by the introduction of illegally-seized evidence could not gain habeas corpus review in federal courts if they had an opportunity to litigate a challenge to the introduction of such evidence in their state proceedings. The ruling was a major step back from the Fourth Amendment exclusionary rule as well as the protections of habeas corpus. "Perhaps the most insidious element in the majority opinion in *Stone v. Powell*," according to Professor Emanuel Margolis, "is its emphasis on the concept—nowhere supported in the Constitution or the English common law—that resort to habeas corpus should be limited primarily to protect the innocent."[103] Indeed, the Court went well beyond the scope of the issues in *Stone* and pronounced that the "central concern in a criminal proceeding" is "the ultimate question of guilt or innocence . . ."[104] Chief Justice Burger, concurring, decried the rejection of "trustworthy evidence of guilt, at the expense of setting obviously guilty criminals free to ply their trade."[105]

THE INCREDIBLE SHRINKING BILL OF RIGHTS

Since the 1980s, the Supreme Court and other appellate courts have carved deep exceptions to the rights of defendants to resist unlawful arrests, as well as to refuse to provide blood, tissue, voice, fingerprints, and photographs.[106] Although the transformation of the law in these ways was not always smooth, and some of the decisions jettisoning these rights were by split decision,[107] they are now accepted as black-letter law.[108]

Today's state and federal courts employ balancing tests where bright-line rules of procedure once prevailed.[109] By proclaiming that a right is merely an interest to be balanced against the state's interest in fighting crime, such courts effectively subdue the Bill of Rights in a manner that is barely recognized.[110] Balancing tests generally allow appellate courts to defer to trial judges, who in turn defer to the decisions of police in matters of crime-fighting. The use of balancing tests means that government almost never crosses a bright line.

In Amy Bach's 2009 book *Ordinary Injustice*,[111] Bach documented the operation of American courtrooms where practices favoring prosecutors have been in place for so long that they are a part of regional court culture and tradition. Judges in some of these jurisdictions routinely impose heavy pre-trial bails on most defendants as a matter of course, causing most defendants to plead guilty in order to win release. The routine operation of such courts pits virtually every player in the courtroom—from the court clerks to the bailiffs—against a lone defendant (or a defendant accompanied by a harried and apologetic lawyer playing the role of groveling bitch). As Bach reports, when an occasional defendant dares to defend himself by proclaiming his innocence, the practitioners in these courthouses generally act in concert to teach him the lesson that cooperating with the prosecution is more rewarding than resistance.

This is the way criminal justice is actually experienced in the lives of millions of Americans today. And it bears little relationship to the adversarial design intended by those who carved the contours of the system two centuries ago. Today's massive criminal justice apparatus moves without much resistance in almost every direction. Increasingly, the American system is 'adversarial' in name only, as it operates upon a tilted playing field upon which government holds an immense advantage.[112] Government-centered, inquisitorial procedures now dispose of the vast majority of American criminal cases, as some 90 percent are resolved by plea bargaining. Other mechanisms such as probation (unknown at the time of America's Founding)[113] and various innovations such as "drug courts" which direct defendants to waive most of their essential rights have become increasingly prevalent.[114]

INQUISITORIALISM'S CONFUSING RELATIONSHIP WITH "THE TRUTH"

Nothing in this book should suggest that criminal procedure has developed along a straight trajectory or that procedures in the past were better in all respects than procedures of today. The river of legal history is an unsteady flow, with many wide bends, stops and starts and overcorrections. But reflection requires generalization, and we should calmly and rationally assess the costs and benefits of America's original adversarial system before we abandon it or adopt another. If inquisitorial justice systems—those that trust governmental authorities as deciders and in which judges are aligned with the prosecution—really are superior to adversarial systems in the accuracy of their assessments, this superior accuracy should be discernible.

Yet for all their vaunted focus on truth-seeking, inquisitorial proceedings invariably empower the state to *conceal* facts from the public as much as to discover them. "Blue ribbon" government panels of deciders appeal to the public's *trust* in the outcomes; but their actual work falls short of producing accurate adjudications in many cases. Perhaps the quintessential illustration of this is the Warren Commission and its Report which purported to investigate the assassination of U.S. President John F. Kennedy. The Johnson Administration—well knowing there were dark secrets undergirding the 1963 assassination—opted to stage a wholly inquisitorial farce, led by a blue-ribbon commission of high-ranking government officials, to investigate the matter. Although the Commission was named for Chief Justice Earl Warren, its most active member was Allen Dulles, the former director of the body most suspected of being involved in Kennedy's assassination, the Central Intelligence Agency.[115] The Commission's process focused on sifting through reports and statements written by FBI agents and Dallas Police investigators, and allowed for very little cross-examination. All but one hearing was in secret.[116]

The Commission's final report proclaimed that a single crazed gunman,

Lee Harvey Oswald, assassinated President Kennedy with a rifle from a sixth-floor window. Yet the majority of witnesses on the ground had said the shots that killed Kennedy came from another location.[117] The Warren Commission erected the tallest piles of superfluous evidence, including many pages of speeches. Yet some of the most important evidence—such as photographs taken from the most important angles and known to be in the government's possession—were not referenced or published.[118] Constitutional Lawyer Mark Lane saw the Warren investigation and its final report as a mere "brief for the prosecution" whose legitimacy would have been shattered if subjected to adversarial testing.[119] According to Lane:

> The Commission reviewed the testimony of 552 witnesses. Some of the testimony was inconsistent with other testimony . . . and it was necessary for the Commission to evolve a standard for assessing it. I believe it did so: testimony compatible with the theory of Oswald as the lone assassin was accepted, even when incredible, while incompatible testimony, no matter how credible, was rejected.[120]

Such is the manner in which inquiries can be directed toward a state-favored "truth" in proceedings without juries, without cross-examination, without a level playing field for accuser and accused, and without the presumption of innocence.

Chapter Two

GRAND JURIES GONE WRONG[121]

The Fifth Amendment to the United States Constitution requires that "[n]o person shall be held to answer for a capital, or otherwise infamous crime, unless on a presentment or indictment of a Grand Jury."[122] The requirement that no citizen could face a felony prosecution unless a group of his fellow countrymen vote to allow such a prosecution was one of the foremost protections in Anglo-American adversarial procedure. The lawyers of the eighteenth and nineteenth centuries considered this protection "a bulwark against oppression."[123] Even if "a man were to commit a capital offense in the face of all the judges of England," said the great British lawyer Thomas Erskine, "their united authority could not put him upon his trial; they could file no complaint against him, even upon the records of the supreme criminal court." Only a group of lay citizens acting as grand jurors could arraign him as a suspect, "and in their discretion," said Erskine to all the judges of the King's Bench, the grand jurors "might likewise finally discharge him, by throwing out the bill, with the names of all your lordships as witnesses on the back of it."[124]

Grand juries of the eighteenth century usually consisted of twenty-three people acting in secret who were able to investigate both on their own or upon the recommendations of a prosecutor.[125] Like trial juries, grand juries offered a separation of power in the justice system whereby the system's most significant determination, the decision to charge an individual with a serious (or "infamous") offense,[126] was left in the hands of common citizenry rather than the agents of government. The grand jury requirement was an important check upon both judges and prosecutors. Grand jurors also had independent power to issue public accusations and reports without the permission of governmental authorities.

The grand jury originated in the mists of early English common law.[127] The institution's 900-year history[128] makes it one of the oldest elements of Anglo-American criminal procedure.[129] The grand jury is older than Anglo-American democracy, older than professional prosecution, older than professional law enforcement, older than codified law,[130] and even older than trial by jury itself.

"Anglo Saxon liberty," wrote Justice Harlan in 1883, "would, perhaps, have perished long before the adoption of our Constitution, had it been in the power of government to put the subject on trial for his life whenever a justice of the peace, holding his office at the will of the Crown, should certify that he had committed a capital crime."[131]

The grand jury is first known to have existed in 1166, when the Norman kings of England required answers from local representatives concerning royal property rights.[132] In 1215 the Magna Carta provided that individuals had the right to go before a grand jury to be charged with their crimes. As trial by a jury of twelve replaced trial by ordeal, the grand jury became a body of twelve to twenty-three men, which is closer to the way it is set up today, acting as ombudsmen between the King's officials and royal subjects.

In addition to its traditional role of screening criminal cases for prosecution, common law grand juries had the power to investigate public officials without governmental influence or permission.[133] This allowed grand juries to serve a vital function of oversight upon the government.[134]

Crossing the Atlantic Ocean with the first English colonists, the grand jury became entrenched in the American justice system. But in America, grand juries were even more independent than their English counterparts. In fact American grand juries originated as something of a defense against the monarchy and were crucibles of dissent against the Crown. American grand juries were more than initiators of prosecutions; "in several of the colonies," write legal scholars Frankel and Naftalis, grand juries acted "as spokes-men for the people . . . and vehicles for complaints against officialdom."[135] American grand juries initiated prosecutions against corrupt agents of the government, often in response to complaints from individuals.[136]

The actions of grand juries figured prominently in the beginnings of the American Revolution. In 1765, a Boston grand jury refused to indict local colonists who had led riots against the Stamp Act.[137] Four years later, a Boston grand jury indicted some British soldiers located within the city boundaries for alleged crimes against the colonists, but refused to treat certain colonists who had been charged by the British authorities for inciting desertion in a like manner.[138] A Philadelphia grand jury condemned the use of the tea tax to compensate the British officials, encouraged a rejection of all British goods, and called for organization with other colonies to demand redress of grievances.[139]

As tensions with Parliament and the Crown increased, colonial grand juries encouraged individuals to support the effort of independence.[140] "In some instances," according to legal historians, "the calls to arms were sounded by the grand jurors themselves; in others, the sparks came from patriotic oratory by the presiding judges in their charges to the grand jury."[141] The public proclamations of these grand juries were often circulated in local and national newspapers in an effort to "fuel the revolutionary fire."[142]

Thus was the grand jury enshrined in America's constitutional criminal procedure. It was an antigovernment institution with power to confront, to stop and to denounce the state, its prosecutors and all its armies and officers. One Framer, James Wilson, stated that "All the operations of government, and of its ministers and officers, are within the compass of [grand jurors'] view and research."[143]

Early American grand juries often acted on their own initiative in the face of opposition from a district attorney. It was just such a grand jury that probed and "toppled the notorious Boss Tweed and his cronies" in New York City in 1872. Without the prosecutor's assistance, the Tweed grand jury independently carried out its own investigation in a district that had otherwise been very loyal to Tweed.[144]

In 1902, a Minneapolis grand jury on its own initiative hired private detectives and collected enough evidence to indict the mayor and force the police chief to resign. This same grand jury virtually governed the city until a new administration could be hired. Similar events occurred in San Francisco five years later, when a grand jury indicted the mayor and replaced him.[145]

Procedures used in grand jury investigations during America's first century differed in significant ways from procedures used today. Prior to the mid-nineteenth century, grand juries did not allow government prosecutors to prepare investigations for them.[146] In fact, the common law known to the nation's Founders forbade government prosecutors from venturing into grand jury proceedings at all unless a grand jury desired to speak to one.[147] The Albany, New York Supreme Court was explicit in an untitled decision in 1827: "The district attorney ought not to attend the grand jury for the purpose of examining witnesses, nor for any other purpose, except to advise them upon any question which they may put to him."[148]

The most famous grand jury case known to the Framers (the 1681 English case of Stephen Colledge and the First Earl of Shaftesbury) was explicit in its denunciation of prosecution or defense lawyers seeking to lecture grand juries on the law:

> I know not how long the practice in that matter of admitting counsel to a grand-jury hath been; I am sure it is a very unjustifiable and unsufferable one. If the grand jury have a doubt in point of law, they ought to have recourse to the court, and that publicly, and not privately, *and not to rely on the private opinion of counsel, especially of the king's counsel,* who are, or at least behave themselves as if they were parties.[149]

How did grand juries operate without the presence of a government prosecutor in their midst? For the most part, they conducted business in a closed courtroom or in a closed chamber adjacent to a public courtroom,[150] referring any legal questions to the judge who swore them in.[151] If the grand jury required the services of a district attorney, or wanted to inform a government attorney of evidence, they would hold proceedings in a public courtroom, out in the open, and allow the prosecutor to attend.[152]

In cases where grand juries identified an indictable offense, "the grand jury could not compel prosecution on its own initiative without the concurrence of the executive but could nonetheless use presentments and other reports to publicize to the people any suspicious executive decisions to decline prosecution."[153]

When former Vice President Aaron Burr was investigated by a federal grand jury in Kentucky, the United States Attorney for the district sought to "attend the grand jury in their room."[154] This motion—considered "novel and unprecedented" under the grand jury practice of the founding period—was denied.[155] Under the English jurisprudence that preceded the American ratification debates, grand jurors who allowed a prosecutor into the grand jury room were considered to have violated their oaths as grand jurors.[156]

The first American cases that allowed a government attorney of any kind to be present amidst grand juries apparently occurred around the 1820s, although this author has failed to find any published court ruling allowing the practice prior to 1832.[157] In England, the first known case arose in 1794, after the American colonies had split away from the Crown.[158] The presence of prosecuting attorneys was initially allowed when grand juries sought out such lawyers to assist them in drafting legal documents.[159] The practice of government attorneys regularly addressing grand jurors crept into grand jury practice during the mid-1800s, as prosecutors graduated from drafting documents to pure advocacy before grand juries.[160] Gradually, American practice evolved to allow government lawyers' presence to answer legal questions, and later to question witnesses.[161]

When the position of government prosecutor first took hold in the American colonies,[162] grand juries and district attorneys existed in something of an awkward cooperation. By the 1830s, "[a]n indictment [was] usually in the first instance framed by the officers of the government," wrote Joseph Story in his *Commentaries on the Constitution*, "and laid before the grand jury."[163] The grand jury would then hear evidence outside the presence of the government and, "if they are of opinion, that the indictment is groundless, or not supported by evidence, they used formerly to endorse on the back of the bill, "ignoramus" or we know nothing of it."[164] "If the grand jury are satisfied of the truth of the accusation, then they write on the back of the bill, 'a true bill.'"[165]

As the law became more confusing and complicated, the case law gradually allowed government lawyers in the midst of grand juries to advise the jurors.[166] By the beginning of the twentieth century, "[it was] the general custom . . . in all jurisdictions to permit the district attorney to attend the grand jury."[167] The great grand jury scholar George J. Edwards wrote in 1906 that "the tendency of the modern cases is to hold that it is the 'right' of the district attorney to be present to examine the witnesses and conduct the case for the government."[168]

In 1946, the drafters of the Federal Rules made this change permanent with Rule 6(d)'s mandate that "[a]ttorneys for the government . . . *may be present* while the grand jury is in session."[169] Grand juries went from having the right to have prosecutors help them with investigations to having prosecutors forced on them. [170] The grand jury's historic power to bar prosecutors from its investigations[171] was lost.

THE LOST PRESENTMENT POWER OF GRAND JURIES

A similar story can be told about the power of grand jurors to issue presentments. The Fifth Amendment to the United States Constitution requires that no person shall be held to answer for a capital or otherwise infamous crime except by a *presentment* or indictment of a grand jury.[172] What all authorities recognize as a "presentment," however, has been written out of the law and is forbidden under the current Federal Rules of Criminal Procedure.[173]

A presentment is a grand jury communication to the public concerning the grand jury's investigation. In early American common law, the presentment was a customary way for grand juries to express grievances against government or to accuse public employees or officials of misconduct.[174] A presentment was generally drafted from the knowledge and findings of the jurors themselves, rather than a prosecutor, and signed individually by each juror who agreed with it. A presentment stood public with or without approval of a prosecutor or court.

While an indictment was normally thought to be invalid without the signature of a prosecutor, a presentment required no formal assent by any entity other than the grand jurors themselves. In some early American jurisdictions, a presentment was thought to mandate a district attorney to initiate a prosecution.[175]

According to Professor Lester B. Orfield, who served as a member of the Advisory Committee on Rules of Criminal Procedure, the drafters of Rule 6 consciously decided that the term "presentment" should not be used in the Rules— even though the term appears in the Constitution.[176] "Retention," wrote Orfield, "might encourage the use of the 'run-away' grand jury as the grand jury could act from their own knowledge or observation and not only from charges made by the United States attorney."[177]

Professor Lester B. Orfield's history of the drafting of Rule 6, recounted both in the Federal Rules of Decisions and the multi-volume treatise that bears his name, includes the cryptic comment: "It has become the practice for the United States Attorney to attend grand jury hearings, hence the use of presentments has been abandoned."[178] The connection between the presence of the United States Attorney in the grand jury room and the grand jury's loss of presentment power was thus so close in Orfield's mind that one represented the cause or the reason of the other.

Thus, Rule 6 represented a monumental — and deliberate — change of grand jury practice.[179] Hundreds of years of grand jury jurisprudence was overthrown by codification. While nothing in Rule 6 explicitly precludes a federal grand jury from returning a presentment,[180] today's federal courts keep grand juries from doing so by broadly interpreting the *secrecy* require-ments of the Rules,[181] which prohibit grand jurors from disclosing "matters occurring" before the grand jury.[182] Today if a grand jury seeks to release its findings without government approval (as was the right of grand jurors in all American jurisdictions until the twentieth century) the grand jurors are accused of being in contempt of court for exposing "matters occurring" in grand jury proceedings.[183]

Because federal grand jurors are now forbidden from issuing presentments, they are also prevented from publicly exonerating a suspect. The 1806 Mississippi Territorial grand jury that pronounced that "Aaron Burr *has not been guilty of any crime or misdemeanor* against the laws of the United States or of this Territory" would be prohibited from doing so under today's rules.[184] Nor are today's grand jurors allowed to publicize the government's violations of civil liberties. The same [Aaron Burr] grand jury presentment declared that the arrests of Burr and his co-travelers had been made "without warrant, and . . . without other lawful authority," and represented a "grievance destructive of personal liberty."[185] In resounding condemnation, the grand jury proclaimed that Burr's pursuers and prosecutors were "the enemies of our glorious Constitution."[186] Such a bold attack on the prosecution would be unimaginable today, and would likely result in contempt charges against the grand jurors.

THE CHANGING APPLICATION OF GRAND JURY SECRECY

The alterations of grand jury practice discussed above could not have occurred if the courts had not slowly altered the way that rules of grand jury secrecy are applied and enforced. The application of grand jury secrecy in modern courts is fundamentally different from the way secrecy worked under the common law. When the Fifth Amendment grand jury clause was ratified in 1791, secrecy was a power of grand jurors—a right to investigate on their own in defiance of the state. This right was first widely recognized in England as early as 1681, in the case of *the Earl of Shaftesbury and Steven Colledge*, when the King of England and his royal prosecutors sought to prosecute the King's political and religious rivals for high treason. The King and royal prosecutors demanded that the grand jury proceeding be held in public. The grand jury refused, finally succeeding in questioning witnesses in secret outside the presence of royal prosecutors. After hearing the evidence, the grand jury refused to indict.[187] "With the shroud of secrecy came independence from the King."[188]

A review of American history reveals that grand juries of the Framers' era were secret only in their taking of evidence (if the grand jurors so choose) and internal deliberations.[189] An indicted defendant generally had a right to know the identities of those who testified, and in many jurisdictions, all bills issued by grand juries generally had to list the names of all witnesses who appeared on the face or the back of the bills.[190] The public had wide access to grand juries and could scrutinize everything from their composition to their political biases.[191] Thomas Jefferson wrote in 1793 that "our judges are in the habit of printing their [grand jury] charges in the newspapers."[192]

By the turn of the twentieth century, according to one commentator, "with the prosecutor inside the grand jury room, the purposes of grand jury secrecy were no longer apparent."[193] While originally intended to serve the investigatory function of the grand jury,[194] secrecy is now used to conceal from the public that which the government desires the public not see. "It is sadly ironic," wrote Judge Campbell, "that the secrecy of the grand jury, the original source of its independence . . . has through the passage of time been transformed into a shield of the prosecutor, immunizing him from public scrutiny and responsibility for his conduct."[195]

Today's grand jury practice turns the power of secrecy on its head: grand jury secrecy has become a shield for prosecutorial abuse.[196] Today's grand jurors are warned by prosecutors and judges that they must keep government manipulation secret or face prosecution. Modern courts have even invented and sustained a false history of grand jury secrecy to obscure its original purposes.[197] This transformation has scarcely been noticed by the so-called originalists who dominate today's legal scholarship and jurisprudence.

THE TAMING OF GRAND JURIES DURING THE TWENTIETH CENTURY

Beginning about 1910 or so, grand juries ceased to operate as independently as they had in the past. As the grand jury slowly lost its full historic purpose, grand juries became resigned to a minute corner of the American justice system. American grand juries ceased to initiate their own investigations. "Dramatic, sometimes violent confrontations between grand juries and prosecutors, politicians, legislatures, even within the grand juries themselves, became largely things of the past by about the 1930's."[198]

"Today, the grand jury is the total captive of the prosecutor," wrote one Illinois district judge, "who, if he is candid, will concede that he can indict anybody, at any time, for almost anything, before any grand jury."[199] Supreme Court Justice William Douglas wrote in 1973 that it was "common knowledge that the grand jury, having been conceived as a bulwark between the citizen and the Government, is now a tool of the Executive."[200]

Today, critics are nearly unanimous in describing the alleged oversight function of modern grand juries as essentially a tragic sham.[201] The ongoing national disgrace that is contemporary federal grand jury practice has attracted the attention of scholars for several decades.[202] Legal scholarship is disjointed and in disagreement over many points of law; but the assessment that the federal grand jury system has collapsed is held universally.[203] Scholars and professionals quibble only over what to call this procedural step. A "rubber stamp,"[204] a "handmaiden" of prosecutors,[205] a "kangaroo" proceeding,[206] a "mockery,"[207] a "charade,"[208] a "lap dog,"[209] "a tool" of prosecutors,[210] or simply "puppetry"[211] have all been suggested.[212]

Suspicions that the grand jury process provides no real protection for criminal suspects are borne out by rates of agreement between grand juries and prosecutors. Federal "indictment rates" greater than 99 percent have been reported in some years.[213] In 2001, federal grand juries declined to indict in only 21 cases nationwide.[214] "These numbers suggest that, whatever the reason, the federal grand jury now exercises very little power as a shield between the government and its citizens."[215]

But despite the ubiquity of scholarly condemnation of present grand jury practice, reformers have failed to do anything that decreases the pow-ers of prosecutors in grand jury chambers. Indeed, the only material grand jury reforms in recent decades have *increased* the government's power over grand juries.[216] The 2001 USA PATRIOT Act,[217] for example, granted greater latitude to government attorneys to make use of grand juries over district lines, and to share grand jury testimony with government attorneys from different agencies.[218]

The judicial branch has likewise assisted more than hindered prosecutors in their grand jury dominance. As Gregory T. Fouts noted in a 2004 law review article, modern judges pay lip service to grand jury independence "while acquiescing in actions that severely curtail that independence."[219] One federal judge testified before a congressional subcommittee that he saw his own role as an *assistant to the government* in building cases before grand juries.[220] U.S. Attorneys "need the right," stated Judge Edward Becker, "to disclose grand jury material to those who would assist them."[221]

Anecdotal evidence suggests that the numbers of false accusations, exaggerated prosecutions, and wrongful convictions of innocent persons in federal court have grown substantially since the 1970s.[222] Evidence also indicates that prosecutions in the United States have generally become more trivial and frivolous over time.[223] While there are many reasons for this trend, the collapse of the grand jury as a check on the Justice Department must surely shoulder much of the blame.

It is not at this point easy to imagine how federal grand jury practice could be more favorable to the government.[224] Today's federal prosecutors have blanket immunity from accountability for most of their misconduct and are often able to sustain indictments even where the indictments have been produced by unlawful procedures.[225] Concurrently, federal prosecutors are in good position to prosecute witnesses and grand jurors for trivial violations of the Rules.[226] When an occasional grand juror complains, prosecutors can and do threaten the recalcitrant grand juror with federal prosecution, and the federal courts offer little or no solace to the juror.[227] In complex cases involving multiple defendants, federal prosecutors manipulate and control the entirety of grand jury decision-making by selectively rewarding snitching witnesses, targeting others, and directing plea negotiations behind the scenes. Even when the grand jurors themselves do no investigation at all, prosecutors use the grand juries' broad subpoena powers to ferret out evidence unobtainable by the prosecutors' own search and seizure powers. Finally, prosecutors use the grand jury as a pretrial sounding board before which to practice the delivery of their case, discovering its strengths and weaknesses before trial.[228]

Chapter Three

THE EXPANSION OF THE CRIMINAL LAW

Today, some 40 to 75 percent of dockets in most courts of general jurisdiction are taken up by criminal cases.[229] This is sharply contrasted with American court dockets prior to the Civil War, in which criminal cases generally constituted fewer than fifteen percent of total court cases. The change in federal court has been even more pronounced. Federal courts had little or no criminal jurisdiction during America's first century; but they now produce dockets in which some 20 percent or more of new filings are criminal cases. Since the founding of the United States in 1789, the criminal law has taken an increasing share of the overall court dockets in most jurisdictions. The table below illustrates this startling trend.

CRIMINAL CASES AS A PERCENTAGE OF TOTAL DOCKET

Alabama Reports, random selected antebellum (pre-Civil War) volumes*	6.58
Delaware Reports, random selected antebellum volumes*	1.13
Johnson's Connecticut trial notebooks, 1770s*	2.63
Daniel Boorstin's 3-volume Delaware cases, drawn from antebellum trial lawyer notebooks*	22.3
Georgia Reports, random selected antebellum volumes*	9.9
Illinois Reports, random selected antebellum volumes*	8.1
Indiana Reports, random selected antebellum volumes*	9.5
Maryland Reports, random selected antebellum volumes*	10.6
North Carolina Reports, random selected antebellum volumes*	13.17
Ohio Reports, random selected antebellum volumes*	14.4
South Carolina Reports, random selected antebellum volumes*	12.7
Virginia Reports, random selected antebellum volumes*	11.1
First 15 volumes of West's Atlantic Reporter, beginning 1885*	2.7
First 15 volumes of West's Pacific Reporter, beginning 1885*	5.3
U.S. District Courts, 2001, new filings	19.5

Roger I. Roots

U.S. District Courts, 2002, new filings	19.6
U.S. District Courts, 2003, new filings	21.8
Pennsylvania Appellate Courts, 2004	56.6
Texas Trial Courts, 2004, new filings	70.4
Kentucky Supreme Court, 2004	65.0

These figures were gained as something of a byproduct of other research I conducted in various law libraries between 1999 and 2012. Usually my method was to pull numbers of old law books from shelves and examine their tables of contents and indexes for cases with "State," "Commonwealth," "Territory" or "People" in the title. (Some follow up research, consisting of examinations of the criminal cases in the volumes, also ensued.) While this method was far from perfect, it provided a good summary sketch for purposes of comparison between periods and jurisdictions. Unfortunately I am unaware of any more systematically-generated data regarding the percentages of criminal cases among early American case reporters.

The numbers don't lie. Over the course of American history, criminal litigation has expanded farther and faster than civil litigation. Activities in today's court rooms have increasingly been taken up by governmental accusations against private individuals. Prosecutors—who barely existed in the courtrooms of early America—are now the dominant players in American law.

Today it is easy to find writings and voices calling for "tort reform" in the civil docket and decrying the alleged explosion of abusive lawsuits and plaintiffs' lawyers. Large, well-financed organizations exist whose purpose is to stem the tide of civil tort filings. Over the past generation, such movements have achieved successes in many jurisdictions, as policymakers have enacted monetary caps on civil damages and other tort reforms.

Yet the explosion of civil litigation pales in comparison to the explosion of criminal litigation during American history. And not only have criminal filings *not* been capped or limited; the rules of procedure have been slowly altered to incentivize the filing of more criminal prosecutions. For example, the filing fees for civil cases can be prohibitive, yet no court that I'm aware of even charges a filing fee to docket a criminal case. Government is a privileged filer, with greater time and filing privileges than any other party. The Federal Rules of Procedure give government prosecutors twice or three times as much time

30

as nongovernmental parties to file and respond to briefs and other documents and pleadings.[230] The Rules also allow the government to file amicus-curiae briefs "without the consent of the parties or leave of court" while "[a]ny other amicus curiae may file a brief only "by leave of court or if the brief states that all parties have consented to its filing."[231]

There are dozens of published appellate court opinions in which learned judges warn that if they were to give credit to a particular defendant's argument, "floodgates" of litigation would be opened.[232] Yet many of the same judges have ruled in ways that have given the green light to prosecutors to flood court dockets with innovative and ever-more-trivial prosecutions. While judges have invented and applied rules that stop, thwart, prevent, and limit appeals and countersuits by criminal defendants, they have applied no meaningful brakes to the actions of prosecutors.

Not only are criminal cases much more prevalent today than two hundred years ago. Today's criminal indictments are also different from the indictments of the eighteenth and nineteenth centuries. Because lay citizen grand jurors— nonlawyers—wrote up most serious criminal charges in early America, criminal cases were almost self-limited in terms of length and complexity. The takeover of the grand jury system by government prosecutors has led to an explosion in lengthy and complicated indictments. Arguably, this phenomenon has also incentivized lawmakers to enact increasingly lengthy and complicated criminal laws. Like most of the trends discussed in this book, these trends overwhelmingly benefit the government.

The vast majority of criminal indictments filed in the 1700s and 1800s accused a single defendant of a single offense.[233] Such indictments were not only limited by the requirement that lay grand jurors draft them (or at least direct and oversee their drafting). They were also limited by the nature of criminal laws themselves, which, even if enacted as statutes, were often so simple and widely known that they were not even codified. Many criminal laws were found only in the common law, meaning they had not been enacted by legislatures but had been handed down over the generations in the pages of judicial rulings.

A codification movement thrived among legislators and lawyers throughout the late 1800s. By the twentieth century, most jurisdictions had changed the way they published new statutes so that the statutes were arranged topically and easily indexed. Today every jurisdiction has a "criminal code" that catalogs its recognized crimes. The federal criminal code has become so vast that even committees of Congress cannot determine precisely how many federal criminal laws now exist. This is because many criminal laws are enacted with so many clauses and subsections cross-referencing other laws that the numbers of possible permutations are unknowable. Almost anyone can be indicted for a prisonable felony at any time.

Studies of the impacts of complicated indictments show that such indictments greatly increase the likelihood of success for the government. Criminal defendants who are tried on a single count are convicted by juries about two-thirds of the time.[234] Thus, some 33 to 35 percent are acquitted. But for those tried on more than one count, remarks Professor Andrew Leopold, "the story is gloomier." The most comprehensive study of this phenomenon found that "as more counts were added the defendant was more likely to be convicted of something."[235] Even more significantly, "as more counts were added, defendants were also more likely to be convicted of the most serious charge against them."[236]

Here we have a concrete example of how alterations in the basic staging of a criminal case can significantly improve the government's chances of gaining a conviction. "A defendant who is guilty of one charge but innocent of another may find it difficult to present separate defenses to separate charges, particularly if he wants to take the stand on the second count but not the first," writes Leopold.[237] "More significantly, a jury considering an innocent defendant charged with multiple counts may infer a criminal disposition" and convict out of an assumption that the accumulation of so many accusations—even if based on only limited evidence in each case— must designate a guilty character.[238]

More simply stated, cases that are more complicated usually favor the prosecution and disfavor defendants. By stacking an indictment with multitudinous counts and roping in other defendants, the government can more easily convict almost anyone. And the use of multi-count and multi-defendant indictments has exploded over the past half-century. Using such indictments, prosecutors can convict as many defendants as possible of as many counts as possible in as few separate trials as possible.

Once again, our story finds that judges and not legislators or prosecutors deserve most of the blame for this trend. At one time there were precedents in many jurisdictions forbidding prosecutors from piling on counts in a single prosecution. For example, the Iowa Supreme Court held in 1881 that an indictment must state but a single offense.[239] But when faced with the emerging onslaught of multi-count, multi-defendant prosecutions during the early twentieth century, judges shrank rather than muster the courage to face down ambitious prosecutors.

In 1936, a federal judge in Texas wrote that "[t]here was a time when the nicety of pleading demanded an avoidance of so-called multiplicity or duplicity. I would not like to say that that time has wholly disappeared, but I do say that felonies and misdemeanors may now be joined."[240] "Frequently the courts have determined that a conspiracy may be charged in the same indictment with the main case," he continued.[241] "[A]nd the doctrine seems to go so far that the old cases, which denied the right to convict on a conspiracy charge when the conspiracy had already ripened or merged into the actual fact, seem to have been superseded by a more modern and sensible rule."[242] Although the court considered imposing a rule to pro-hibit prosecutors from piling on counts, the court ultimately ruled that a "sovereignty may plead in as many forms as the law justifies, in order to be sure to anticipate the defenses of the accused."[243]

The 1930s seem to have been a turning point in this area of procedural law. Progressive-Era advocacy for more trust in government had ripened into Depression-Era judicial passivity toward the executive branch. A 1936 state indictment against Charles "Lucky" Luciano, the father of modern organized crime, ran to 90 counts.[244] Convictions stemming from this complicated prosecution were upheld on appeal. The "floodgates" of criminal litigation were opening.

Judge Robert Inch of the Eastern U.S. District of New York (which covers the busy districts of Brooklyn, Queens and Long Island) confronted an early prototype of today's mega-indictments as early as 1934. Before him were three indictments charging dozens of defendants with dozens of mail and securities fraud charges. "[T]his is not the ordinary application that usually confronts the court in criminal cause," wrote Inch.[245] The indictments related to "a most complicated and involved business situation . . . covering thousands of transactions, all of which, presumably, is to be eventually submitted to a jury of twelve laymen for their verdict."[246]

But Judge Inch was at pains to find a way to declare the indictments invalid. Instead, he went down the easy path that has become customary for modern judges. "The 'high spots' in this indictment," wrote Inch, "appear to be the claims that the defendants fraudulently 'reappraised' assets of the companies so as to show a higher but fictitious value."[247] Inch granted defense requests for bills of certain particulars, upon grounds that the multifaceted charges were "likely to cause great difficulty in preparing a defense":[248]

> I have commented on this at this time for the purpose of indicating that this indictment, while possibly sufficient for prosecution, as to which I make no comment, nevertheless, is largely a "blanket charge" as to a most complex and extensive series of transactions covering a considerable time, and made by large and very active corporations.[249]

Here was an opportunity for a judge to place limits upon prosecutorial overreaching. Yet this insightful judge, as so many judges would do in the future, did nothing but attempt to force the prosecution to cough up various details of its accusations such as the names of the defrauded. Today it is unlikely if a federal judge would even award a defendant that much.

Thus we see, again and again in the past century when courts were confronted with burdensome, onerous, complicated charging instruments, they took the easy path rather than place reasonable limits on indictments or force prosecutors to face meaningful grand jury oversight.

A few hours in a law library will substantiate the growth of multi-count and multi-defendant prosecutions over the past century. Today, roughly half of trial defendants are charged with more than one count, and a third are tried jointly with codefendants.[250] Indictments running to more than 50 pages and containing 80 counts or more are not unusual in federal court and in many state courts.[251] Some indictments are now so complicated that they begin with lengthy indexes or tables of contents. Prosecutors know that almost no one facing a dozen counts can beat all of them, and that a larger number of counts increases by magnitudes the likelihood that defendants will plead guilty to one or more charges in exchange for the dismissal of other counts.

There are rules of procedure which allow judges to dismember criminal cases by separating defendants or counts into separate cases (e.g., Federal Rule of Criminal Procedure 14). But federal judges are reluctant to parcel big indictments into multiple cases, perhaps out of an unstated desire to conserve *their own* time and resources. Because most cases end in plea deals, and lengthy multi-count indictments help generate plea deals, judges may believe (almost certainly correctly) that splitting a big case into multiple smaller cases will increase the likelihood of trial, which means more work for the judges. Courts have denied defendants' motions to sever even in cases of more than fifty counts and numerous defendants.[252]

There are cases (mostly from decades ago) where courts held that a complicated prosecution overwhelmed a jury's ability to deliberate.[253] But with each passing decade, the burden of multi-count, lengthy criminal indictments grows more crippling. When defendants request that counts be divided into separate cases, trial judges need only point to the body of previous lengthy indictments as precedents.[254] "In reaching our determination that appellants were not unduly prejudiced by the length and complexity of the joint trial," wrote the U.S. Eleventh Circuit in 1982, "we are guided by recent cases of similar magnitude that have rejected the same argument."[255]

The courts even use the length and complexity of government charging instruments—which the courts' own rulings invite and incentivize— as grounds for ruling against defendants' motions for bills of particulars. How can defendants need more information to defend themselves, judges sometimes ask, when the many pages of the indictments provide so much information?[256]

When it becomes clear that a defendant insists on his innocence and intends to take accusations to trial, prosecutors are known to double down on their allegations and file lengthened, "superseding" indictments, usually adding more pages of accusations. Although there are a small handful of U.S. Supreme Court decisions that proclaim that it is forbidden to punish a defendant for insisting on his rights, judges almost never enforce such rules in practice. Judges share with prosecutors, after all, an interest in compelling defendants to spare them the work of putting on trials and to end cases by guilty pleas.

When prosecutors file superseding indictments, judges shockingly allow prosecutors to try defendants according to any one or a combination of the indictments on file in a case. At trial, prosecutors may pick and choose accusations from among numerous indictments, so that defendants may not even know what charges to prepare for at trial. "[T]he government may elect to proceed on any pending indictment,"[257] wrote the U.S. Ninth Circuit in a recent opinion, "whether it is the most recently returned superseding indictment or a prior indictment."[258]

In rare cases where defendants refuse to plead guilty, trials of such indictments can be ridiculously prolonged and confusing. The *New York*

Times reported in 1990 that the longest trial in American history was the trial of a nursery school operator charged with 65 counts of child abuse.[259] The trial lasted 30 months and ended in a verdict of not guilty on 52 counts and deadlocks on 13 others.[260] The 1988 trial of 20 alleged members of the Lucchese crime family of New Jersey *in which the defense quickly rested without calling a single witness* lasted 21 months before a federal jury acquitted the defendants on all 77 counts.[261] A single prosecution witness had spent several months on the stand.[262] A trial of ex-Oakland cops lasted a year and produced a jury that deliberated for four months. (The jury acquitted on 8 counts and were unable to reach a verdict on the remaining 27 counts.)[263]

Convictions on multiple counts tend to produce appeals with an almost infinitesimally small chance that an entire case will be reversed. In such cases, appellate courts often must review hundreds or even thousands of pages of trial records. Such trial records are more likely than records of simpler cases to register split verdicts, in which juries have convicted defendants of at least some offenses while acquitting them of others. Ironically, such split verdicts are then considered to be proof on appeal that the trials of such indictments were not overburdened by complexity.[264]

There are rules of appellate procedure which limit briefs on appeal from being much over 30 pages in length (now giving way to word-count limitations which may allow slightly higher page counts). One may often hear judges gripe about the length of lawyers' appellate briefs. Yet there are no rules limiting the lengths of indictments. Defense appeals are saddled with limitations of pleading that prosecutors are not.

THE LOSS OF THE RIGHT TO SPEEDY TRIAL

There are other ways that judges have incentivized prosecutors to file more criminal charges and to launch more complicated criminal prosecutions. For example, judges have virtually gutted the Speedy Trial Clause of the Sixth Amendment, a constitutional provision that originally acted as something of a brake on the charging decisions of prosecutors. Generally speaking, a prosecutor in the early Republic had to try his case within sixty days of filing criminal charges. This was an ancient protection enunciated in the Magna Charta and probably predating it. Under the Clause's original meaning, prosecutors would have been reluctant to bring complex or multitudinous charges. But the speedy-trial requirement has been rendered almost impotent by modern judges and lawmakers.

The Speedy Trial Act of 1974[265]—passed by Congress in order to construe the Sixth Amendment right—allows the suspension of the right to a speedy trial upon the mere declaration by a judge that a case is "complex." Federal judges have not only upheld this Act; they have enthusiastically pronounced hundreds of cases to be complex for purposes of evading the Speedy Trial clock.[266] But the same judges who pronounce a case "complex" for purposes of getting around defendants' speedy trial rights will generally pronounce the same cases to be *not so complex* as to require separation of counts or other limitations upon the prosecution.

Judges have also shifted other legal standards to accommodate prosecutors' lust for expansive accusations. It was once a rule in most jurisdictions that jurors had to stay together throughout the entirety of their deliberations until they came to a verdict. "Anciently, the utmost rigor and strictness was observed," wrote the New York Supreme Court of Judicature in 1825,[267] "in keeping the jury together, and when once charged with a cause, they never could be discharged till they had agreed upon their verdict; but the practice has been much relaxed in modern times in both these particulars."[268] As criminal cases grew exceedingly long and counts began to multiply, the "rigor and strictness" of jury deliberations were abandoned. Today jurors are generally allowed to go home each night before reaching a verdict.

So: the story of criminal litigation over the course of American history is: (1) criminal accusations and cases have exploded both in number and as a proportion of overall litigation in most American jurisdictions, (2) criminal indictments have also exploded in average length and complexity, as rates of multi-count and multi-defendant prosecutions have increased significantly, and (3) judges have tended to accommodate rather than limit this growing number, proportion and complexity by means of eviscerating certain constitutional and legal principles that formerly acted as barriers to expansive and complicated criminal prosecutions.

As the government has become more powerful and well-funded, the percentage of "wins" for defendants has steadily decreased. Today, conviction rates in most jurisdictions hover around 95 percent. Only 50 years ago, conviction rates were closer to 60 percent. Fifty years before that, government prosecutors generally lost more cases than they won. There are many reasons for this rise in conviction rates, including the increased use of jury instructions which obscure jurors' rights to nullify prosecutions by judging both the law and the facts, and jury selection procedures which bar persons with criminal records from serving on juries (and which thus exclude increasingly larger proportions of the male population which would most identify as peers of most defendants). But the increased complexity of modern criminal indictments must surely account for some of the increase in American conviction rates.

Chapter Four

ARE COPS CONSTITUTIONAL?[269]

Police work is often lionized by jurists and scholars who claim to employ "textualist," "strict constructionist" and "originalist" methods of constitutional interpretation. Yet professional police were unknown to the United States in 1789, and first appeared in America almost a half-century after the Constitution's ratification. The Framers contemplated law enforcement as the duty of mostly private citizens, along with a few constables and sheriffs who could be called upon when necessary. Modern policing is in many ways inconsistent with the original intent of America's founding documents. The growth of modern policing has substantially empowered the state in a way the Framers would regard as abhorrent to their foremost principles.

Uniformed police officers are the most visible element of America's criminal justice system. Their numbers have grown exponentially over the past century and now stand at hundreds of thousands nationwide.[270] Police expenses account for the largest segment of most municipal budgets and generally dwarf expenses for fire, trash, and sewer services.[271]2 Neither casual observers nor learned authorities regard the sight of hundreds of armed, uniformed state agents on America's roads and street corners as anything peculiar — let alone invalid or unconstitutional.

Yet the dissident English colonists who framed the United States Constitution would have seen this modern 'police state' as alien to their foremost principles. Under the criminal justice model known to the Framers, professional police officers were unknown.[272] The general public had broad law enforcement powers and only the executive functions of the law (e.g., the execution of writs, warrants and orders) were performed by constables or sheriffs (who might call upon members of the community for assistance).[273] Initiation and investigation of criminal cases was the nearly exclusive province of private persons.

At the time of the Constitution's ratification, most sheriffs and constables served without pay.[274] Most of their duties involved *civil* executions rather than criminal law enforcement. The courts of that period were venues for private litigation — whether civil or criminal — and the state was rarely a party. Professional police as we know them today originated in American cities during the second quarter of the nineteenth century, when municipal governments drafted citizens to maintain order.[275] The role of these "nightly watch" officers gradually grew to encompass the catching of criminals, which had formerly been the responsibility of individual citizens.[276]

While this historical disconnect is widely known by criminal justice historians, rarely has it been juxtaposed against the Constitution and the Constitution's imposed scheme of criminal justice.[277] "Originalist" scholars of the Constitution have tended to be supportive, rather than critical of modern policing.[278] However, modern policing violates the Framers' most firmly held conceptions of criminal justice.

The modern police-driven model of law enforcement helps sustain a playing field that is fundamentally uneven. Modern police act as an army of assistants for state prosecutors and gather evidence solely with an eye toward the state's interests. Police seal off crime scenes from the purview of defense investigators, act as witnesses of convenience for the state in courts of law, and instigate a substantial amount of criminal activity under the guise of crime fighting. Additionally, police enforce social class norms and act as tools of empowerment for favored interest groups to the disadvantage of others.[279] Police are also a political force that constantly lobbies for increased state power and decreased constitutional liberty for American citizens.

THE CONSTITUTIONAL TEXT

The Constitution contains no explicit provisions for criminal law enforcement.[280] Nor did the constitutions of any of the several states contain such provisions at the time of the Founding.[281] Early constitutions enunciated the intention that law enforcement was a universal duty that each person owed to the community, rather than a power of the government.[282] Founding-era constitutions addressed law enforcement from the standpoint of individual liberties and placed explicit barriers upon the state.[283]

PRIVATE PROSECUTORS

For decades before and after the Revolution, the adjudication of criminals in America was governed primarily by the rule of private prosecution: (1) victims of serious crimes approached a community grand jury, (2) the grand jury investigated the matter and issued an indictment only if it concluded that a crime should be charged, and (3) the victim himself or his representative (generally an attorney but sometimes a state attorney general) prosecuted the defendant before a petit jury of twelve men.[284]15 Criminal actions were only a step away from civil actions — the only material difference being that criminal claims ostensibly involved an interest of the public at large as well as the victim.[285]16 Private prosecutors acted under authority of the people and in the name of the state — but for their own vindication.[286]17 The very term "prosecutor" meant criminal plaintiff and implied a private person.[287]18 A government prosecutor was referred to as an attorney general and was a rare phenomenon in criminal cases at the time of the nation's founding.[288] When a private individual prosecuted an action in the name of the state, the attorney general was required to allow the prosecutor to use his name — even if the attorney general himself did not approve of the action.[289]

Private prosecution meant that criminal cases were for the most part limited by the need of crime victims for vindication.[290] Crime victims held the keys to a potential defendant's fate and often negotiated the settlement of criminal cases.[291] After a case was initiated in the name of the people, however, private prosecutors were prohibited from withdrawing the action pursuant to private agreement with the defendant.[292] Court intervention was occasionally required to compel injured crime victims to appear against offenders in court and "not to make bargains to allow [defendants] to escape conviction, if they ... repair the injury."[293]

Grand jurors often acted as the detectives of the period. They conducted their investigations in the manner of neighborhood sleuths, dispersing throughout the community to question people about their knowledge of crimes.[294] They could act on the testimony of one of their own members, or even on information known to grand jurors before the grand jury convened.[295] They might never have contact with a government prosecutor or any other officer of the executive branch.[296]

Colonial grand juries also occasionally served an important law enforcement need by account of their sheer numbers. In the early 1700s, grand jurors were sometimes called upon to make arrests in cases where suspects were armed and in large numbers.[297] A lone sheriff or deputy had reason to fear even approaching a large group "without danger of his life or having his bones broken."[298]29 When a sheriff was unable to execute a warrant or perform an execution, he could call upon a posse of citizens to assist him.[299] The availability of the posse comitatus meant that a sheriffs resources were essentially unlimited.[300]

LAW ENFORCEMENT AS A UNIVERSAL DUTY

Law enforcement in the Founders' time was a duty of every citizen.[301] Citizens were expected to be armed and equipped to chase suspects on foot, on horse, or with wagon whenever summoned. And when called upon to enforce the laws of the state, citizens were to respond "not faintly and with lagging steps, but honestly and bravely and with whatever implements and facilities [were] convenient and at hand."[302] Any person could act in the capacity of a constable without being one,[303] and when summoned by a law enforcement officer, a private person became a temporary member of the police department.[304] The law also presumed that any person acting in his public capacity as an officer was rightfully appointed.[305]

Laws in virtually every state still require citizens to aid in capturing escaped prisoners, arresting criminal suspects, and executing legal process. The duty of citizens to enforce the law was and is a constitutional one. Many early state constitutions purported to bind citizens into a universal obligation to perform law enforcement functions, yet evinced no mention of any state power to carry out those same functions.[306] But the law enforcement duties of the citizenry are now a long-forgotten remnant of the Framers' era. By the 1960s, only twelve percent of the public claimed to have ever personally acted to combat crime.[307]

The Founders could not have envisioned 'police' officers as we know them today. The term "police" had a slightly different meaning at the time of the Founding.[308] It was generally used as a verb and meant to watch over or monitor the public health and safety.[309] In Louisiana, "police juries" were local governing bodies similar to county boards in other states.[310] Only in the mid-nineteenth century did the term 'police' begin to take on the persona of a uniformed state law enforcer.[311] The term first crept into Supreme Court jurisprudence even later.[312]

Prior to the 1850s, rugged individualism and self-reliance were the touchstones of American law, culture, and industry. Although a puritan cultural and legal ethic pervaded their society, Americans had great toleration for victimless misconduct.[313] Traffic disputes were resolved through personal negotiation and common law tort principles, rather than driver licenses and armed police patrol.[314] Agents of the state did not exist for the protection of the individual citizen. The night watch of early American cities concerned itself primarily with the danger of fire, and watchmen were often afraid to enter some of the most notorious neighborhoods of cities like Boston.[315]

At the time of Tocqueville's observations (in the 1830s), "the means available to the authorities for the discovery of crimes and arrest of criminals [were] few,"[316] yet Tocqueville doubted "whether in any other country crime so seldom escapes punishment."[317] Citizens handled most crimes informally, forming committees to catch criminals and hand them over to the courts.[318] Private mobs in early America dealt with larger threats to public safety and welfare, such as houses of ill fame.[319] Nothing struck a European traveler in America, wrote Tocqueville, more than the absence of government in the streets.[320]

Formal criminal justice institutions dealt only with the most severe crimes. Misdemeanor offenses had to be dealt with by the private citizen on the private citizen's own terms. "The farther back the [crime rate] figures go," according to historian Roger Lane, "the higher is the relative proportion of serious crimes."[321] In other words, before the advent of professional policing, fewer crimes — and only the most serious crimes — were brought to the attention of the courts.

After the 1850s, cities in the northeastern United States gradually acquired more uniformed patrol officers. The criminal justice model of the Framers' era grew less recognizable. The growth of police units reflected a "change in attitude" more than worsening crime rates.[322] Americans became less tolerant of violence in their streets and demanded higher standards of conduct. Offenses which had formerly earned two-year sentences were now punished by three to four years or more in a state penitentiary.[323]

POLICE AS SOCIAL WORKERS

Few of the duties of Founding-era sheriffs involved criminal law enforcement. Instead, civil executions, attachments and confinements dominated their work.[324] When professional police units first arrived on the American scene, they functioned primarily as protectors of public safety, health and welfare. This role followed the bobbie model developed in England in the 1830s by the father of professional policing, Sir Robert Peel.[325] Early police agencies provided a vast array of municipal services, including keeping traffic thoroughfares clear. Boston police made 30,681 arrests during one fiscal year in the 1880s, but in the same year reported 1,472 accidents, secured 2,461 buildings found open, reported thousands of dangerous and defective streets, sidewalks, chimneys, drains, sewers and hydrants, tended to 169 corpses, assisted 148 intoxicated persons, located 1,572 lost children, reported 228 missing (but only 151 found) persons, res-cued seven persons from drowning, assisted nearly 2,000 sick, injured, and insane persons, found 311 stray horse teams, and removed more than fifty thousand street obstructions.[326]

Police were a "kind of catchall or residual welfare agency,"[327] a lawful extension of actual state 'police powers.'[328] In the Old West, police were a sanitation and repair workforce more than a corps of crime-fighting gun-slingers. Sheriff Wyatt Earp of OK Corral fame, for example, repaired boardwalks as part of his duties.[329]

THE WAR ON CRIME

Toward the end of the nineteenth century, police forces took on a brave new role: crime-fighting. The goal of maintaining public order became secondary to chasing lawbreakers. The police cultivated a perception that they were public heroes who "fought crime" in a general sense.

The 1920s saw the rise of the profession's second father — or perhaps its wicked stepfather — J. Edgar Hoover.[330] Hoover's Federal Bureau of Investigation (FBI) came to epitomize the police profession in its sleuth and intelligence-gathering role. FBI agents infiltrated mobster organizations, intercepted communications between suspected criminals, and gathered intelligence for both law enforcement and political purposes.

This new view of police as soldiers locked in combat against crime caught on quickly.[331] The FBI led local police to develop integrated reposito-ries of fingerprint, criminal, and fraudulent check records. The FBI also took over the gathering of crime statistics (theretofore gathered by a private association),[332] and went to war against "Public Enemy Number One" and others on their "Ten Most Wanted" list.[333] Popular culture began to see police as a "thin blue line," that "serves and protects" civilized society from chaos and lawlessness.[334]

THE ABSENCE OF CONSTITUTIONAL CRIME-FIGHTING POWER

But the constitutions of the Founding Era gave no hint of any thin blue line. Nothing in their texts enunciated any governmental power to "fight crime" at all. "Crime-fighting" was intended as the domain of individuals touched by crime. The original design under the American legal order was to restore a semblance of private justice. The courts were a mere forum, or avenue, for private persons to attain justice from a malfeasor.[335] The slow alteration of the criminal courts into a venue only for the government's claims against private persons turned the very spirit of the Founders' model on its head.

To suggest that modern policing is extraconstitutional is not to imply that every aspect of police work is constitutionally improper.[336] Rather, it is to say that the totality and effect of modern policing negates the meaning and purpose of certain constitutional protections the Framers intended to protect and carry forward to future generations.

Americans today, for example, are far more vulnerable to invasive searches and seizures by the state than were the Americans of 1791. The Framers lived in an era in which much less of the world was in "plain view" of the government and a "stop and frisk" would have been rare indeed.[337] The totality of modern policing also places pedestrian and vehicle travel at the mercy of the state, a development the Framers would have almost cer-tainly never sanctioned. These infringements result not from a single aspect of modern polic-ing, but from the whole of modern policing's control over large domains of private life that were once "policed" by private citizens.

THE DEVELOPMENT OF DISTINCTIONS

The treatment of law enforcement in the courts shows that the law of crime control has changed monumentally over the past two centuries. Under the common law, there was no difference whatsoever between the privileges, immunities, and powers of constables and those of private citizens. Constables were literally and figuratively clothed in the same garments as everyone else and faced the same liabilities — civil and criminal — as everyone else under identical circumstances. Two centuries of jurisprudence, however, have recast the power relationships of these two roles dramatically.

Perhaps the first distinction between the rights of citizen and constabulary came in the form of increased power to arrest. Early in the history of polic-ing, courts held that an officer could arrest if he had reasonable belief both in the commission of a felony and in the guilt of the arrestee.[338] This repre-sented a marginal yet important distinction from the rights of a private person, who could arrest only if a felony had actually been committed.[339] It remains somewhat of a mystery, however, where this distinction was first drawn.[340] Scrutiny of the distinction suggests it arose in England in 1827 — more than a generation after ratification of the Bill of Rights in the United States.[341]

Moreover, the distinction was illegitimate from its birth, being a bastardization of an earlier rule allowing constables to arrest upon transmission of reasonably reliable information from a third person.[342] The earlier rule made perfect sense when many arrests were executed by private persons. "Authority" was a narrow defense available only to those who met the highest standard of accuracy.[343] But when Americans began to delegate their law enforcement duties to professionals, the law relaxed to allow police to execute warrantless felony arrests upon information received from third parties. Constables could not be required to be "right" all of the time, so the rule of strict liability for false arrest was lost.

The tradeoff has had the effect of depriving Americans of certainty in the executions of warrantless arrests. Judges now consider only the question of whether there was reasonable ground to suspect an arrestee, rather than whether the arrestee was guilty of any crime. This loss of certainty, when combined with greater deference to the state in most law enforcement matters, has essentially reversed the original intent and purpose of American law enforcement that the state act against stern limitations and at its own peril. Because arrest has become the near exclusive province of professional police, Americans have fewer assurances that they are free from unreasonable arrests.

Distinctions between the privileges of citizens and police officers grew more rapidly in the twentieth century. State and federal lawmakers enshrined police officers with expansive immunities from firearm laws[344] and from laws regulating the use of equipment such as radio scanners, body armor, and infrared scopes.[345] Legislatures also exempted police from toll road charges,[346] granted police confidential telephone numbers and auto registration,[347] and even exempted police from fireworks regulations.[348] Police are also protected by other statutory immunities and protections, such as mandatory death sentences for defendants who murder them,[349] reimbursement of moving expenses when officers receive threats to their lives,[350] and even special protections from assailants infected with the AIDS virus.[351] Officers who illegally eavesdrop, wiretap, or intrude upon privacy are protected by a statutory (as well as case law) "good faith" defense,[352] while private citizens who do so face up to five years in prison.[353] The tendency of legislatures to equip police with ever-expanding rights, privileges and powers has, if anything, been strengthened rather than limited by the courts.[354]

But this growing power differential contravenes the principles of equal citizenship that dominated America's founding. The great principle of the American Revolution was, after all, the doctrine of limited government.[355] Advocates of the Bill of Rights saw the chief danger of government as the inherently aristocratic and disparate power of government authority.[356] Founding-era constitutions enunciated the principle that all men are "equally free" and that all government is derived from the people.[357]

RESISTING ARREST

Nothing illustrates the modern disparity between the rights and powers of police and citizen as much as the modern law of resisting arrest. At the time of the nation's founding, any citizen was privileged to resist arrest if, for example, probable cause for arrest did not exist or the arresting person could not produce a valid arrest warrant where one was needed.[358] As recently as one hundred years ago, but with a tone that seems as if from some other, more distant age, the United States Supreme Court held that it was permissible (or at least defensible) to shoot an officer who displays a gun with intent to commit a warrantless arrest based on insufficient cause.[359] Officers who executed an arrest without proper warrant were themselves considered trespassers, and any trespassee had a right to violently resist (or even assault and batter) an officer to evade such arrest.[360]

Well into the twentieth century, violent resistance was considered a lawful remedy for Fourth Amendment violations.[361] Even third-party intermeddlers were privileged to forcibly liberate wrongly arrested persons from unlawful custody.[362] The doctrine of non-resistance against unlawful government action was harshly condemned at the constitutional conventions of the 1780s, and both the Maryland and New Hampshire constitutions contained provisions denouncing nonresistance as "absurd, slavish, and destructive of the good and happiness of mankind."[363]

By the 1980s, however, many if not most states had (1) eliminated the common law right of resistance,[364] (2) criminalized the resistance of any officer acting in his official capacity,[365] (3) eliminated the requirement that an arresting officer present his warrant at the scene,[366] and (4) drastically decreased the number and types of arrests for which a warrant is required.[367] Although some state courts have balked at this march toward efficiency in favor of the state,[368] none require the level of protection known to the Framers.[369]

But the right to resist unlawful arrest can be considered a constitutional one. It stems from the right of every person to his bodily integrity and liberty of movement, among the most fundamental of all rights.[370] Substantive due process principles require that the government interfere with such a right only to further a compelling state interest[371]— and the power to arrest the citizenry unlawfully can hardly be characterized as a compelling state interest.[372] Thus, the advent of professional policing has endangered important rights of the American people.

The changing balance of power between police and private citizens is illustrated by the power of modern police to use violence against the population.[373] As professional policing became more prevalent in the twentieth century, police use of deadly force went largely without clearly delineated guidelines (outside of general tort law).[374] Until the 1970s, police officers shot and killed fleeing suspects (both armed and unarmed) at their own discretion or according to very general department oral poli-cies.[375] Officers in some jurisdictions made it their regular practice to shoot at speeding motorists who refused orders to halt.[376] More than one officer tried for murder in such cases — along with fellow police who urged dis-missals — argued that such killings were in the discharge of official duties.[377] Departments that adopted written guidelines invariably did so in response to outcries following questionable shootings.[378] Prior to 1985, police were given near total discretion to fire on the public wherever officers suspected that a fleeing person had committed a felony.[379] More than 200 people were shot and killed by police in Philadelphia alone between 1970 and 1983.[380]

In 1985, the United States Supreme Court purported to stop this carnage by invalidating the use of deadly force to apprehend unarmed, nonviolent suspects.[381] *Tennessee v. Garner*[382] involved the police killing of an unarmed juvenile burglary suspect who, if apprehended alive, would likely have been sentenced to probation.[383] The Court limited police use of deadly force to cases of self defense or defense of others.[384]

As a practical matter, however, the *Garner* rule is much less stringent. Because federal civil rights actions inevitably turn not on a strict constitutional rule (such as the *Garner* rule), but on the perception of a defendant officer, officers enjoy a litigation advantage over all other parties.[385] In no reported case has a judge or jury held an officer liable who used deadly force where a mere "reasonable" belief that human life was in imminent danger existed.[386] Some lower courts have interpreted *Garner* to permit deadly force even where suspects pose no immediate and direct threat of death or serious injury to others.[387] The U.S. Ninth Circuit Court of Appeals recently denied the criminal liability of an agent who shot and killed an innocent person to prevent another person from retreating to "take up a defensive position," drawing criticism from Judge Kozinski that the court had adopted the "007 standard" for police shootings.[388]

Untold dozens, if not hundreds, of Americans have been shot in the back while fleeing police, even after the *Garner* decision. Police have shot and killed suspects who did nothing more than make a move,[389] reach for their identification too quickly,[390] reach into a jacket or pocket,[391] "make a motion" of going for a gun,[392] turn either toward or away from officers,[393] 'pull away' from an officer as an officer opened a car door,[394] rub their eyes and stumble forward after a mace attack,[395] or allegedly lunge with a knife,[396] a hatchet,[397] or a ballpoint pen.[398] Cops have also been known to open fire on and kill persons who brandished or refused to drop virtually any hand-held object—a Jack Daniel's whiskey bottle,[399] a metal rod,[400] a wooden stick,[401] a kitchen knife (even while eating dinner),[402] a screwdriver,[403] a rake[404]— or even refused an order to raise their hands.[405]

Cops who shoot an individual holding a shiny object that can be said to resemble a gun—such as a cash box,[406] a shiny silver pen,[407] a TV remote control,[408] or even a can opener[409]—are especially likely to avoid liability. In line with this defense, police officers nationwide have been caught planting weapons on their victims in order to make shootings look like self defense.[410] In one of the more egregious examples ever proven in court, Houston police were found during the 1980s to have utilized an unofficial policy of planting guns on victims of police violence.[411] Seventy-five to eighty percent of all Houston officers apparently carried "throw-down" weapons for such purposes.[412] Only the dogged persistence of aggrieved relatives and the first-hand testimony of intrepid witnesses unraveled the police cover-up of the policy.[413]

Resisting arrest, defending oneself, or fleeing may also place an American in danger of being killed by police.[414] Although the law clearly classifies such killings as unlawful, police are rarely made to account for such conduct in court.[415] Only where the claimed imminent threat seems too contrived—such as where an officer opened fire to defend himself from a pair of fingernail clippers[416]— or where abundant evidence of a police cover-up exists, will courts uphold damage awards against police officers who shoot civilians.[417]

As Professor Peter L. Davis points out, there is no good reason why police should not be liable criminally for their violations of the criminal code, just as other Americans would expect to be (and, indeed, as the constables of the Founding Era often were).[418] Yet in modern criminal courts, police tend to be more bulletproof than the Kevlar vests they wear on the job. Remember that the district attorneys responsible for prosecuting police for their crimes are the same district attorneys who must defend those officers in civil cases involving the same facts.[419] Under the Framers' common law, this conflict of interest did not arise at all because a citizen grand jury— independent from the state attorney general— brought charges against a criminal officer, and the officer's victim prosecuted the matter before a petit jury. But the modern model of law enforcement provides no real remedy, and no ready outlet for the law to work effectively against police criminals. Indeed, modern policing acts as an obstruction of justice with regard to police criminality.

The bloodstained record of shootings, beatings, tortures and mayhem by American police against the populace is too voluminous to be recounted in a single book chapter.[420] At least 2,000 Americans have been killed at the hands of law enforcement since 1990.[421] Some one-fourth of these killings — about fifty per year—are alleged by some authorities to be in the nature of murders.[422] Yet only a handful have led to indictment, conviction and incarceration.[423] This is true even though most police killings involve victims who were unarmed or committed no crime.[424]

Killings by police seem as likely as killings by death-row murderers to demonstrate extreme brutality or depravity. Police often fire a dozen or more bullets at a victim where one or two would stop the individual.[425] Such indicia of viciousness and ferocity would qualify as aggravating factors justifying the death penalty for a civilian murderer under the criminal laws of most states.[426]

From the earliest arrival of professional policing upon America's shores, police severely taxed both the largess and the liberties of the citizenry.[427] In early municipal police departments, cops tortured, harassed and arrested thousands of Americans for vagrancy, loitering, and similar "crimes," or detained them on mere "suspicion."[428] Where evidence was insufficient to close a case, police tortured suspects into confessing to crimes they did not commit.[429] In the name of law enforcement, police became professional lawbreakers, "constantly breaking in upon common law and ... statute law."[430] In 1903 a former New York City police commissioner remarked that he had seen "a dreary procession of citizens with broken heads and bruised bodies against few of whom was violence needed to affect an arrest.... The police are practically above the law."[431]

THE SAFETY OF THE POLICE PROFESSION

Defenders of police violence often cite the dangerous nature of police work, claiming the police occupation is filled with risks to life and health. Police training itself — especially elite SWAT-type or paramilitary training that many officers crave — reinforces the "dangerousness" of police work in the officers' own minds.[432] There is some truth to this perception, in that around one hundred officers are feloniously killed in the line of duty each year in the United States.[433]

But police work's billing as a dangerous profession plummets in credibility when viewed from a broader perspective. Homicide, after all, is the second leading cause of death on the job for all American workers.[434] The taxicab industry suffers homicide rates almost six times higher than the police and detective industry.[435] A police officer's death on the job is almost as likely to be from an accident as from homicide.[436] When overall rates of injury and death on the job are examined, policing barely ranks at all. The highest rates of fatal workplace injuries occur in the mining and construction industries, with transportation, manufacturing and agriculture following close behind.[437] Fully 98 percent of all fatal workplace injuries occur in the civilian labor force.[438]

Moreover, police work is generously rewarded in terms of financial, pension and other benefits, not to mention prestige. Police salaries may exceed $100,000 annually plus generous health insurance and pension plans—placing police in the very highest percentiles of American workers in terms of compensation.[439] The founding generation would have been utterly astonished by such a transfer of wealth to professional law enforcers.[440] This reality of police safety, security and comfort is one of the best-kept secrets in American labor.

In all, it is questionable whether modern policing actually decreases the level of bloodshed on American streets. Police often bring mayhem, confusion and violence wherever they are called.[441] Approximately one-third of the people killed in high-speed police car chases (which are often unnecessarily

51

escalated by police) are innocent bystanders.[442] Cops occasionally prevent
rather than execute rescues.[443] "Police practices" ranked as the number one
cause of violent urban riots of the 1960s.[444] Indeed, police actively participated
in or even initiated some of the nation's worst riots.[445] During the infamous
Chicago Police Riot during the Democratic National Convention in 1968,
police physically attacked 63 newsmen and indiscriminately beat and clubbed
numerous innocent bystanders.[446]

PROFESSIONALISM?
    If the modern model of cop-driven criminal justice has any defense at all,
it is its "professionalism." Private law enforcement of the type intended by the
Framers was supposedly more inclined toward lax and arbitrary enforcement
than professional officers who are sworn to uphold the law.[447] Upon scrutiny,
however, the claim that professional police are more reliable, less arbitrary,
and more capable of objective law enforcement than private law enforcers is
drastically undermined.
    In the absence of police troops to enforce the law, the early criminal justice
system was hardly as hobbled and impotent as conventional wisdom suggests.
Private watch groups and broad-based advocacy groups existed to enforce
laws and track criminals among jurisdictions. Thousands of local antihors-
ethief associations and countless 'detecting societies' sprang up to answer the
call of crime victims in the nineteenth century.[448] In Maine, the "Penobscot
Temperance League" hired detectives to investigate and initi-ate criminal
cases against illegal liquor traffickers.[449] In the 1870s a private group called the
Society for the Suppression of Vice became so zealous in garnering prosecutions of the immoral that it was accused in 1878 of coercing a defendant into
mailing birth control information in violation of federal statutes,[450] one of the
earliest known instances of conduct that later became defined as entrapment.
Although some of these private crime-fighting groups were invested with limited state law enforcement powers,[451] they were not police officers in the modern sense and received no remuneration.
    Such volunteer nonprofessionals continue to aid law enforcement as aux-
iliary officers in many American communities.[452] Additionally, private organizations affiliated with regional chambers of commerce, neighbor-hood watch
and other citizens' groups continue to play a substantial — though underappre-
ciated — role in fighting crime.[453] America also has a long history of outright

vigilante justice, although such vigilantism has been exaggerated both in its sordidness[454] and in its scope.[455]

Moreover, government-operated policing is hardly a monopoly even today, neither in maintaining order nor over matters of expertise and intelligence-gathering.[456] There are three times more private security guards than public police officers and even activities such as guarding government buildings (including police stations) and forensic analysis are now done by private security personnel.[457]

The chief selling point for professional policing seems to be the idea that sworn government agents are more competent crime solvers than grand juries, private prosecutors, and unpaid volunteers. But this claim disintegrates when the realities of police personnel are considered. In 1998, for example, forty percent of graduating recruits of the Washington, D.C. police academy failed the comprehensive exam required for employment on the force and were described as "practically illiterate" and "borderline-retarded."[458] As a practical matter, police are more dependent upon the public than the public is dependent upon police.[459]

Cops rely on the public for a very high percentage of their investigation clearances. As the rate of crimes committed by strangers increases, the rate of clearance by the police invariably declines.[460] Roughly two-thirds of major robbery and burglary arrests occur solely because a witness can identify the offender, the offender is caught at or near the crime scene, or the offender leaves evidence at the scene.[461] In contrast, where a suspect cannot be identified in such ways, odds are high that the crime will go unsolved.[462]

Studies show that as government policing has taken over criminal investigations, the rates of clearance for murder investigations have actually gone down. For more than three decades—while police units have expanded greatly in size, power and jurisdiction—the gap between the number of homicides in the United States and the number of cases solved has widened by almost twenty percent.[463] Today, almost three in ten homicides go unsolved.[464]

DNA EVIDENCE ILLUSTRATES FALLIBILITY OF POLICE

Moreover, a surprisingly high number of police conclusions are simply wrong. Since 1963, at least 381 murder convictions have been reversed because of police or prosecutorial misconduct.[465] In the 25-year period following the Supreme Court's ruling in *Gregg v. Georgia*[466] reaffirming the use of capital punishment, one innocent person has been freed from death row for every seven who have been executed.[467] In Illinois, Thirteen men have been freed from death row since 1977 after proving their innocence—more than the twelve who were actually put to death over the same period. Governor George Ryan finally ordered a moratorium on executions until the death penalty system could be revamped,[468] referring to the death penalty system as "fraught with error."

Yet death penalty cases are afforded far more due process and scrutiny of evidence than noncapital cases. If anything, the error rate of police in noncapital cases is likely substantially higher. Governor Ryan's words would seem to apply doubly to the entire system of police-driven investigation.

The advent of DNA analysis in the courtrooms of the 1990s greatly accelerated the rate at which police errors have been proven in court, even while avenues for defendants' appeals have been systematically cut off by Congress and state legislatures.[469] DNA testing before trial has exonerated at least 5000 prime suspects who would likely have otherwise been tried on other police evidence.[470] Often, exculpatory DNA revelations have come in cases where other police-generated evidence was irreconcilable, suggesting falsification of evidence or other police misconduct.[471] The sheer number of wrongly accused persons freed by DNA evidence makes it beyond dispute that police investigations are far less trustworthy than the public would like to believe.[472]

Even more unjustified is the notion that a justice system powered by professional police possesses higher levels of integrity, trustworthiness and credibility than the criminal justice model intended by the Framers. Within the criminal justice system, cops are regarded as little more than professional witnesses of convenience, if not professional perjurers, for the prosecution.[473] Almost no authority credits police with high levels of honesty. Indeed, the daily work of cops requires strategic lying as part of the job description.[474] Cops lie about the strength of their evidence in order to obtain confessions,[475] about giving Miranda warnings to arrestees when on the witness stand,[476] and even about substantive evidence when criminal cases need more support. Cops throughout the United States have been caught fabricating, planting and manipulating evidence to obtain convictions where cases would otherwise be very weak.[477]

Some authorities regard police perjury as so rampant that it can be considered a "subcultural norm rather than an individual aberration" of police officers.[478] Large-scale investigations of police units in virtually every major American city have documented massive evidence tampering, abuse of the arresting power, and discriminatory enforcement of laws according to race, ethnicity, gender, and socioeconomic status. Recent allegations in Los Angeles charge that dozens of officers abused their authority by open-ing fire on unarmed suspects, planting evidence, dealing illegal drugs, or framing some 200 innocent people.[479] More than a hundred prosecutions had to be dismissed in Chicago in 1997 due to similar police misconduct.[480] During the infamous "French connection" case of the 1970s, New York City narcotics detectives were caught diverting 188 pounds of heroin and 31 pounds of cocaine for their own use, making the City's Special Investigating Unit the largest heroin and cocaine dealer in the city.[481]

Police criminality was so acute in New Orleans during the 1980s and 1990s that people were afraid to report crimes for fear that corrupt officers would retaliate or tip off organized crime figures. One New Orleans officer was convicted of ordering the execution of a witness who reported him to the internal affairs unit for allegedly pistol-whipping a teenager.[482] Thirty-six Washington, D.C. officers were indicted on charges such as drug dealing, sex-ual assault, murder, sodomy and kidnapping in 1992.[483]

In Detroit, repeated corruption allegations have seen a number of low- and high-ranking officers go to prison for drug trafficking, hiring hit men, provid-ing drug protection, and looting informant funds.[484] Police burglary rings have been uncovered in several cities.[485]

Patterns of police abuse tend to repeat themselves in major American cities despite endless attempts at reform.[486] New York City police, for exam-ple, have been the subject of dozens of wide-ranging corruption probes over the past hundred years[487] yet continue to generate corruption allegations.[488] Police exhibit unique levels of occupational solidarity.[489] Review boards and internal affairs commissions inevitably fail to penetrate police loyalty and find resistance from every rank.[490] Cops inevitably form an isolated authoritarian subculture that is both cynical toward the rule of law and disrespectful of the rights of fellow citizens.[491] The code of internal favoritism that holds police together may more aptly be described as syndicalism rather than professional-ism. Historically, urban police "collected" from local businesses.[492] Today, a more subtle brand of racketeering prevails, whereby police assist those busi-nesses which provide support for police and under-mine businesses which are perceived as antagonistic to police interests. This same shakedown also applies to newspaper editors and politicians.[493]

Even at the federal level, where national investigators presume to police corruption and oversee local departments, favoritism toward the police role is rampant. In 1992, for example, the federal government filed criminal charges in only 27 cases of police criminality.[494] A federal statute criminalizing violations of the Fourth Amendment has never been enforced even a single time, although it has been a part of the U.S. Code since 1921.[495] Throughout the 1980s and '90s, the FBI Crime Laboratory actively abetted the misconduct of local police departments by misrepresenting forensic evidence to bolster police cases against defendants.[496]

COPS NOT COST-EFFECTIVE DETERRENT

In terms of pure economic returns, police are a surprisingly poor public investment. Typical urban police work is very expensive because police see a primary part of their role as intervention for its own sake — poking, prodding and questioning the public in hope of turning up evidence of wrongdoing. Toward this end, police spin quick U-turns, drive slowly and menacingly down alleyways, reverse direction to track suspected scofflaws, and conduct sidewalk pat-down searches of potential criminals absent clear indicia of potential criminality.[497] Studies indicate, however, that such tactics are essentially worthless in the war on crime. One experiment found that when police do not 'cruise' but simply respond to dispatched calls, crime rates are completely unaffected.[498]

Thus the very aspect of modern policing that the public view as most effective — the creation of a 'police presence'— is in fact a monstrous waste of public resources.[499] Similarly, the history of America's expenditures in the war on drugs provides little support for the proposition that money spent on policing yields positive returns.[500] University of Chicago professor John Lott has found that while hiring police can reduce crime rates, the net benefit of hiring an additional officer is about a quarter of the benefit from arming the public with an equivalent dollar amount of concealed handguns.[501]

POLICE AS A STANDING ARMY

It is largely forgotten that the war for American independence was initiated in large part by the British Crown's practice of using troops to police civilians in Boston and other cities.[502] Professional soldiers used in the same ways as modern police were among the primary grievances enunciated by Jefferson in the Declaration of Independence. ("[George III] has kept among us standing armies"; "He has affected to render the military independent of and superior to the civil power"; "protecting them, by a mock trial....").[503] Thomas Jefferson proclaimed that although Parliament was supreme in its jurisdiction to make laws, "his majesty has no right to land a single armed man on our shores" to enforce unpopular laws.[504] James Warren said that the troops in Boston were there on an unconstitutional mission because their role was not military but rather to enforce "obedience to Acts which, upon fair examination, appeared to be unjust and unconstitutional."[505] Colonial pamphleteer Nicholas Ray charged that Americans did not have "an Enemy worth Notice within 3000 Miles of them."[506] "[T]he troops of George the III have cross'd the wide atlantick, not to engage an enemy," charged John Hancock, but to assist constitutional traitors "in trampling on the rights and liberties of [the King's] most loyal subjects ..."[507]

The use of soldiers to enforce law had a long and sullied history in England and by the mid-1700s were considered a violation of the fundamental rights of Englishmen.[508] The Crown's response to London's Gordon Riots of 1780 — roughly contemporary to the cultural backdrop of America's Revolution — brought on an immense popular backlash at the use of guards to maintain public order.[509] "[D]eep, uncompromising oppo-sition to the maintenance of a semimilitary professional force in civilian life" remained integral to Anglo-Saxon legal culture for another half century.[510]

Englishmen of the Founding era, both in England and its colonies, regarded professional police as an "alien, continental device for maintaining a tyranni-cal form of Government."[511] Professor John Phillip Reid has pointed out that few of the rights of Englishmen "were better known to the general public than the right to be free of standing armies."[512] "Standing armies," according to one New Hampshire correspondent, "have ever proved destructive to the Liberties of a People, and where they are suffered, neither Life nor Property are secure."[513]

If pressed, modern police defenders would have difficulty demonstrating a single material difference between the standing armies the Founders saw as so abhorrent and America's modern police forces.[514] Indeed, even the distinctions between modern police and actual military troops have blurred in the wake of

America's modern crime war.[515] Ninety percent of American cities now have active special weapons and tactics (SWAT) teams, using such commando-style forces to do "high risk warrant work" and even routine police duties.[516] Such units are often instructed by active and retired United States military personnel.[517]

In Fresno, California, a SWAT unit equipped with battering rams, chemical agents, fully automatic submachine guns, and 'flashbang' grenades roams full-time on routine patrol.[518] According to criminologist Peter Kraska, such military policing has never been seen on such a scale in American history, "where SWAT teams routinely break through a door, subdue all the occupants, and search the premises for drugs, cash and weapons."[519] In high-crime or problem areas, police paramilitary units may militarily engage an entire neighborhood, stopping "anything that moves" or surrounding suspicious homes with machine guns openly displayed.[520]

Much of the importance of the standing-army debates at the ratification conventions has been overlooked or misinterpreted by modern scholars. Opponents of the right to bear arms, for example, have occasionally cited the standing-army debates to support the proposition that the Framers intended the Second Amendment to protect the power of states to form militias.[521] Although this argument has been greatly discredited,[522] it has helped illuminate the intense distrust that the Framers manifested toward occupational standing armies. The standing army the Framers most feared was a soldiery conducting law enforcement operations in the manner of King George's occupation troops — like the armies of police officers that now patrol the American landscape.

THE SECOND AMENDMENT

The actual intent of the Second Amendment — that it protect a right of people to maintain the means of violently checking the power of government — has been all but lost in modern American society.[523] Modern policing's increasing monopoly on firepower tends to undermine the Framers' intent that the whole people be armed, equipped, and empowered to resist the state. Many police organizations lobby incessantly for gun control, even though the criminological literature yields scant empirical support for general gun control as a crime-prevention measure.[524]

Nor is there much legitimacy to the claim that professional police are more accurate or responsible with firearms than the armed citizenry intended by the

Framers. To this day, civilians shoot and kill at least twice as many criminals as police do every year,[525] and their 'error rate' is several times lower.[526] In a government study of handgun battles that lead to officer injuries, it was found that police who fired upon their killers were less than half as accurate as their civilian, nonprofessional, assailants.[527]

Moreover, police seem hardly less likely to misuse firearms than the general public.[528] In New York City, where private possession of handguns has been virtually eliminated for most civilians, problems with off-duty police misusing firearms have repeatedly surfaced.[529] Los Angeles police have been found to fire their weapons inappropriately in seventy-five percent of cases.[530] Between early 1989 and late 1992, more than one out of every seven shots fired by Washington, D.C. police officers was fired accidentally.[531]

THE THIRD AMENDMENT

Although standing armies were not specifically barred by the final version of the Constitution's text, some authorities have pointed to the Third Amendment[532] as a likely fount for such a conceptual proposition.[533] Additionally, the Amendment's proscription of quartering troops in homes might well have been interpreted as a general anti-search and seizure principle if the Fourth Amendment had never been enacted. The Third Amendment was inspired by sentiments quite similar to those that led to passage of the Second and Fourth Amendments, rather than fear of military operations. Writing in the 1830s, Justice Story regarded the Third Amendment as a security that "a man's house shall be his own castle, privileged against all civil and military intrusion."[534]

The criminal procedure concerns that dominated the minds of the Framers of the Bill of Rights were created not only before the Revolution but also after it. In the five years following British surrender, the independent states vied against each other for commercial advantage, debt relief, and land claims. Conflict was especially fierce between the rival settlers of Pennsylvania and Connecticut on lands in the west claimed simultaneously by both states.[535] Both states sent partisan magistrates and troops into the region, and each faction claimed authority to remove claimants of the rival state.[536] Magistrates occasionally ordered arrest without warrant, turned people out of their homes, and even ordered submission to the quartering of troops in homes.[537] In 1784, a Pennsylvania grand jury indicted one such magistrate and forty others for abuse of their authority.[538] Many agents had to be arrested before the troubles finally ended in 1788 — the very moment when the Constitution was undergoing its ratification debates.[539] These troubles, and not memories of life under the Crown, were fresh in the minds of the Framers who proposed and ratified the Bill of Rights.

The Third Amendment's proscription of soldiers quartered in private homes addressed a very real domestic concern about the abuse of state authority in 1791. This same fear of an omnipresent and all-controlling government is hardly unfounded in modern America. Indeed, the very evils the Framers sought to remedy with the entire Bill of Rights—the lack of security from governmental growth, control and power—have come back to haunt modern Americans like never before.[540]

THE RIGHT TO BE LEFT ALONE

The 'police state' known by modern Americans would be seen as quite tyrannical to the Framers who ratified the Constitution. If, as Justice Brandeis suggested, the right to be left alone is the most important underlying principle of the Constitution,[541] the cop-driven model of criminal justice is anathemic to American constitutional principles. Today a vast and omnipotent army of insurgents patrols the American landscape in place of grand juries, private prosecutors, and the occasional constable. This immense soldiery is forever at the beck and call of whatever social forces rule the day, or even the afternoon.[542]

THE FOURTH AMENDMENT

Now to the Fourth Amendment. The Amendment reads: "The right of the people to be secure in their persons, houses, papers, and effects, against unreasonable searches and seizures, shall not be violated, and no Warrants shall issue, but upon probable cause, supported by Oath or affirmation, and particularly describing the place to be searched, and the persons or things to be seized."[543] This protection was clearly regarded as one of the more important provisions of the Bill of Rights during debates in and out of Congress prior to ratification.[544] To this day, the Amendment is probably the most cited constitutional provision in challenges to police action.

The cold, hard reality, however, is that the interest protected by the amendment — security from certain types of searches and seizures — has been drastically scaled back since 1791. In saying this, I am mindful that there are those among the highest echelons of the bench and academy who claim that current Fourth Amendment law is more protective than the Framers intended.[545] Indeed, there are those claiming the mantles of textualism and originalism who would decrease Fourth Amendment rights even further.[546] The ever-influential Akhil Amar, for example, has argued that the Fourth Amendment's text does not really require warrants but merely lays out the evidentiary foundation required to obtain warrants.[547] Amar joins other "originalist" scholars who emphasize that the only requirement of the Fourth Amendment's first clause ("The right of the people to be secure in their persons, papers, and effects from unreasonable searches and seizures shall not be violated") is that all searches and seizures be "reasonable."[548]

The warrant requirement pronounced in many Supreme Court opinions, according to Amar, places an unnecessary burden upon law enforcement and should be abandoned for a rule Amar considers more workable — namely civil damages for unreasonable searches after the fact as determined by juries.

This type of "originalism" has appealed to more than one U.S. Supreme Court justice,[549] at least one state high court,[550] and various legal commentators.[551] Indeed, it has brought a perceivable shift to the Supreme Court's Fourth Amendment jurisprudence.[552] Even the U.S. Justice Department has adopted this argument as its own in briefs filed in the U.S. Supreme Court arguing for elimination of the warrant requirement.[553]

The problem with this line of interpretation is that it does not square with the original view of the Framers. Even the most cursory examination of history reveals that law enforcers of the Founding Era, whether private persons, sheriffs or constables, were obligated to procure warrants in many circumstances that modern courts do not require warrants.[554] The general rule that warrants were required for all searches and seizures except those involving circumstances of the utmost urgency seems so well settled at the time of ratification that it is difficult to imagine a scholar arguing otherwise.[555] But Professor Amar does. "Supporters of the warrant requirement," the professor writes, "have yet to find any cases" enunciating the warrant requirement before the Civil War.[556]

But there is an immense body of cases illustrating the warrant requirement as a fundamental understanding behind the Fourth Amendment. For example, in the 1814 case of *Grumon v. Raymond*, the Connecticut Supreme Court held both a constable, who executed an improper search warrant, and a justice of the peace who issued the warrant, civilly liable for trespass.[557] The court in

Grumon clearly stated that the invalidity of the search warrant left the search's legality "on no better ground than it would be if [the search had been pursuant to] no process."[558] Consider also the 1807 case of *Stoyel v. Lawrence*, holding a sheriff liable for executing a civil arrest warrant after the warrant's due date and declaring that the warrant "gave the officer no authority whatever, and, consequently, formed no defence";[559] or the 1763 Massachusetts case of *Rex v. Gay*, acquitting an arrestee for assaulting and beating a sheriff who arrested him pursuant to a facially invalid warrant;[560] or *Batchelder v. Whitcher*, holding an officer liable for ordering the seizure of hay by an unsealed warrant in 1838;[561] or *Conner v. Commonwealth*, in which the Pennsylvania Supreme Court concluded in 1810 that if the requirement of warrants based on probable cause could be waived merely to allow constables to more easily arrest criminals, "the constitution is a dead letter."[562]

Even the cases Amar cites for the proposition that search warrants were not required under antebellum Fourth Amendment jurisprudence do not squarely support such a proposition.[563] Most of them merely repeat the "warrant requirement" of the common law and find that their given facts fit within a common law exception.[564] Similarly, the cases Amar cites that interpret various Fourth-Amendment equivalents of state constitutions by no means indicate that Founding-era law enforcers could freely search and seize without warrant wherever it was "reasonable" to do so.[565]

WARRANTS A FLOOR, NOT A CEILING

Under Founding-era common law, warrants were often considered as much a constitutional floor as a ceiling. Warrants did provide a defense for constables in most trespass suits, but were not good enough to immunize officials from liability for some unreasonable searches or seizures.[566] The most often-cited English case known to the Framers who drafted the Fourth Amendment involved English constabulary who had acted pursuant to a search warrant but were nonetheless found civilly liable for stiff (punitive, actually) damages.[567]

For more than 150 years, it was considered *per se* unconstitutional for law enforcers to search and seize certain categories of objects, such as personal diaries or private papers, even with perfectly valid warrants.[568] Additionally, Fourth Amendment jurisprudence prohibited the government from seizing as evidence any personal property which was not contraband, even with a valid warrant.[569] The rationale for this "mere evidence" rule was that the interests of property owners were superior to those of the state and could not be overridden by mere evidentiary justifications.[570] This rule, like many other obstacles to police search and seizure power, was discarded in the second half of the twentieth century by a Supreme Court much less respectful of property rights than its predecessors.[571]

PRIVATE PERSONS AND THE FOURTH AMENDMENT

Under the Founders' Model, a private person like Josiah Butler, who lost twenty pounds of good pork under suspicious circumstances in 1787, could approach a justice of the peace and obtain a warrant to search the property of the suspected thief for the lost meat.[572] Private individuals applied for many or most of the warrants in the Founders' era and even conducted many of the arrests.[573] Even where sworn constables executed warrants, private persons often assisted them.[574] To avoid liability, however, searchers needed to secure a warrant before acting.[575] False arrest was subject to strict liability.[576]

The Founders contemplated the enforcement of the criminal law to be a duty of private individuals, and assumed that private law enforcers would represent their interests with private means. However, the Founders viewed private individuals executing law enforcement duties as "public authority" and thus intended for the Fourth and Fifth Amendments to apply to such individuals when acting in their law enforcement capacities.[577] Consequently, the Supreme Court's 1921 decision in *Burdeau v. McDowell*[578]— often cited for the proposition that the Fourth Amendment applies only to government agents — was almost certainly either wrongly decided or wrongly interpreted by later courts.[579]

Some of the earliest English interpretations of the freedom from search and seizure held the protection applicable to private citizens as much as or more so than government agents.[580] Massachusetts and Vermont were apparently the first states to require that search and arrest warrants be executed by sworn officers.[581] New Hampshire adopted the same rule in 1826, more than a generation after the Bill of Rights was ratified.[582] It is likely that some states allowed private persons to execute search warrants well into the nineteenth century.

Because many Founding-era arrests and searches were executed by private persons, and early constables needed the assistance of private persons to do their jobs, the Fourth Amendment was almost certainly intended for application to private individuals. *Burdeau* cited no previous authority for its proposition in 1921, and early American cases demonstrate an original intent that the Fourth Amendment apply to every searcher acting under color of law.[583] On the open seas, most enforcement of prize and piracy laws was done by "privateers" acting for their own gain but who were held accountable in court for their misconduct.[584] Later courts have taken this holding to mean that "a wrongful search or seizure conducted by a private party does not violate the Fourth Amendment."[585]

As explained earlier, early constables had powers no greater than those of other individuals, so they needed warrants before engaging in law enforcement activities beyond any citizen's authority. Like you or I, a constable would be thought outside the bounds of good etiquette (and well outside the law) were he to conduct an unconsented search of another's person, property or effects, and should — very reasonably — expect to be jailed, physically repulsed, or sued for such conduct.

A private person's only defense was the absolute correctness of his allegations. A person was liable if, for example, his complaint was too vague as to the address to be searched,[586] he misspelled the name of the accused in his complaint,[587] or he sought the execution of a warrant naming a "John Doe" as a target.[588]

This was the constitutional model secured to America by the Framers. The idea of police having special powers was only a seedling, alien to the scheme of ordered liberty and limited government created by the Constitution. Eventually, police interceded between private individuals and magistrates altogether, and today it is virtually unheard of for a private person to seek a search warrant from a magistrate.

Freedom from search and seizure has been retracting in favor of police ever since the ink was dry on the Bill of Rights. The Framers lived under a common law rule that required warrantless arrests be made only for felonies where no warrant could be immediately obtained.[589] By the early to mid-1800s, the rule had changed to allow warrantless arrests for all felonies regardless of whether a warrant could be obtained.[590] Early American courts also apparently allowed warrantless arrests for misdemeanor breaches of peace committed in the arrestor's presence. Toward the end of the nineteenth century, most state courts had changed to allow warrantless arrest for all crimes of any kind committed in an officer's presence, as well as for all felonies committed either within or without an officer's presence regardless of whether a warrant can be obtained.[591]

By the mid-1900s, arrest had become the almost-exclusive province of paid police, and their power to arrest opened even wider. A trend toward allowing police to arrest without warrant for all crimes committed even outside their presence has recently developed,[592] with little foreseeable court-imposed impediment.[593] Almost every American jurisdiction has legislated for the erosion of common law limitations with regard to domestic violence arrests and arrests for other high profile misdemeanors.[594]

Despite the Fourth Amendment, the Supreme Court has imposed almost no limits on warrantless arrest at all. Only forcibly entering a residence without warrant to arrest someone inside has been found to violate the Fourth Amendment.[595] Outside the home, modern police have been essentially licensed by the Court to arrest almost anyone at any time so long as probable cause exists.[596] The Supreme Court effectively buried the original purpose of warrantless arrest entirely in 1985, declaring that "[r]estraining police action until after probable cause is obtained... might... enable the suspect to flee in the interim."[597] Long forgotten is the fact that common law allowance for warrantless arrest was precipitated solely on an emergency rationale and allowed only to protect the public from immediate danger.[598]

The rationale for the felon exception to the warrant requirement in 1791, for example, was that a felony was any crime punishable by death, generally thought to be limited to only a handful of serious crimes.[599] Felons were considered "outlaws at war with society,"[600] and their apprehension without warrant qualified as one of the "exceptions justified by absolute necessity."[601] By the late twentieth century, however, thousands of crimes the Framers would have considered misdemeanors or no crime at all had been declared felonies and the rationale for immediate community action to apprehend "felons" had changed greatly.[602] The courts, however, have been slow to react to this far-reaching change.[603] In any case, the vast majority of arrests (seventy to eighty percent) are for misdemeanors,[604] which would have been proscribed without warrant under the Framers' law.

ORIGINALISTS CALL FOR CIVIL DAMAGES

Under Founding-era common law, citizens were generally able to sue and prevail against constables and sheriffs who trespassed upon their property and privacy.[605] Those who made false arrests in American colo-nial times were subject to strict liability—meaning they had no defense from suit. [606] Civil damages were often quite high.[607] Liability for officers was in many respects higher than for private persons. Sheriffs and deputies could be held liable for failing to arrest debtors for collection of debts[608] or to serve other process,[609] for allowing an imprisoned debtor to escape,[610] for failing to keep entrusted goods secure[611] or to deliver goods in custody at a proper time,[612] or for failing to keep faithful accounting and custody of property.[613] Sheriffs were also obligated to return writs within a specific time period, at pain of civil damages.[614] They were liable to debtors whose property was sold at sheriffs sales if proper advertisement procedures were not followed[615] and for negligently allowing other creditors to obtain priority interests on attached property.[616]

Law enforcers were liable for false imprisonment, even where they acted with court permission, if procedures were improper.[617] A deputy was liable for damages to an arrestee whom he arrested outside his jurisdiction.[618] Sheriffs were even liable if their deputies executed civil process in a rude and insolent manner.[619] When executing writs, sheriffs were liable for any unnecessary violence against innocent third persons who obstructed them.[620]

The Founders' law knew no "good faith" defense for law enforcers. Sheriffs and justices who executed arrests pursuant to invalid warrants were considered trespassers (as were any judges who granted invalid warrants). Any person was justified in resisting, or even battering, such officers.[621] Justices of the peace could be held liable for ordering imprisonment without taking proper steps.[622] Any party who sued out or issued process did so at his peril and was civilly responsible for unlawful writs (even if the executing officer acted in good faith).[623]

Nor did state authority provide the umbrella of indemnification that now protects public officers. Sheriffs of the nineteenth century often sought protection from liability by obtaining bonds from private sureties.[624] Their bonds were used to satisfy civil judgments against them while in office.[625] If the amount of their bonds was insufficient to satisfy judgments, sheriffs were liable personally.[626] It was not uncommon for a sheriff to find himself in jail as a debtor for failing to satisfy judgments against him.[627] Even punitive damages against officers—long disfavored by modern courts with regard to municipal liability—were deemed proper and normal under the law of the Framers.[628]

The uniformed police officers of the 1800s were generally introduced upon the American landscape by their oaths alone and without bonds.

Their municipal employers (hence, the taxpayers) were on the hook for their civil liabilities. Although courts tended to treat police identically to bonded officials,[629] their susceptibility to civil redress was much lower. This situation was very different from that of the constables of the early Republic who were personally liable for any lawless behavior. This change in the law of policing has had the effect of depriving Americans of remedies for Fourth Amendment (and other) violations.[630] The evil that now pervades criminal justice—swarms of officers unaccountable in court either criminally or civilly—was the very evil that the Founders sought to remedy in the late eighteenth century.[631]

DEVELOPMENT OF IMMUNITIES

Immunities follow duties, and duties placed upon police by lawmakers have exploded since 1791.[632] Immunities grew slowly, beginning with a slight deference to officer conduct so long as there was no bad faith, corruption, malice or "misbehavior,"[633] and ending with broad qualified immunity.[634] When the practice of professional policing arrived from England upon American shores (for the second time, actually, if we consider modern police to be akin to the "standing armies" of the Founders' generation), cases began to enunciate a general deference to police conduct, permit-ting that the actions of officers in carrying out their duties "not to be harshly judged."[635] Appellate courts began to reverse jury verdicts against officers upon new rules of law granting privileges unknown to private individuals.[636]

THE LOSS OF PROBABLE CAUSE, AND THE ONSET OF PROBABLE SUSPICION

Probable cause for the issuance of warrants has also become less strict.[637] The Supreme Court regarded hearsay evidence as insufficient to constitute probable cause for seventeen years in the first half of the twentieth century,[638] but has since given police free reign to construct probable cause in whatever way they deem proper. Instead of probability that a crime has been committed, the courts now require only some possibility, a relaxed standard that "robs [probable cause] of virtually all operative significance."[639] This watered-down "probable cause" for the issuance of ex parte warrants would have shocked the Founders.[640]

At common law, one could sue and recover damages from a private person who swore out a false or misleading search warrant affidavit.[641] In contrast, few modern officers will ever have to account for lies on warrant applications so long as they couch their "probable cause" in unprovables. "Anonymous citizen informants,"[642] material omissions and misrepresenta-tions,[643] irrelevant or prejudicial information,[644] and even outright falsities are now common fixtures of police-written search warrant applications.[645] For years, Boston police simply made up imaginary informants to justify searches and seizures.[646] Police themselves refer to the phenomenon as "testilying" — an aspect of normal police work regarded as "an open secret" among principle players of the criminal justice system.[647]

POLICE AND THE "AUTOMOBILE EXCEPTION"

The courts have been particularly unkind to Fourth Amendment protections in the context of motor vehicle travel. Since the 1920s, Fourth Amendment jurisprudence has allowed for a gaping and ever-widening exception to the warrant requirement with regard to the nation's roadways.[648] Today, police force untold millions of motorists off the roads each year to be searched or scrutinized without judicial warrant of any kind.[649] Any police officer can generally find some pretext to justify a stop of any automobile.[650] In effect, road travel itself is subject to a near total level of police control,[651] a phenomenon that would have confounded the Framers, who treated seizures of wagons, horses and buggies as subject to the same constraints as seizures of other property.[652]

The courts have laid down such a malleable latticework of exceptions in favor of modern police that virtually any cop worth his mettle can adjust his explanations for a search to qualify under one exception or another. When no exception applies, police simply lie about the facts.[653] "Judges regularly choose to accept even blatantly unbelievable police testimony." The practice on the streets has long been for police to follow their hunches, seek entrance at every door, and then attempt to justify searches after the fact.[654] Justice Robert Jackson observed in 1949 that many unlawful searches of homes and automobiles are never revealed to the courts or the public because the searches turn up nothing.[655]

THE FIFTH AMENDMENT

The Fifth Amendment prohibits the compulsion of self-incriminating testimony.[656] Various competing interpretations ebbed and flowed from this provision until 1966, when in *Miranda v. Arizona* the Supreme Court held that police are required to actually tell suspects about the Fifth and Sixth Amendments' protections before interrogating them.[657] The sheer volume of criticism by police organizations of the *Miranda* ruling over the next three decades indicates the strong state interest in keeping the Constitution's protections concealed from the American public.

Modern police interrogation could scarcely have been imagined by the Framers who met in Philadelphia in the late eighteenth century. Police tactics such as falsifying physical evidence, faking identification lineups, administering fake lie detector tests and falsifying laboratory reports to obtain confessions are methods developed by the professionals of the twentieth century.[658] Against such methods a modern suspect stands little chance of keeping his tongue. Like the exclusionary rule and the entrapment defense, the *Miranda* rule operates as an awkward leveling device between the rights of American citizens and their now-leviathanic government.

The police model of law enforcement tilts the entire system of criminal justice in favor of the state. The police are hardly neutral investigators, and work as an arm of the prosecutor's office.[659] Where police secure a crime scene for investigation, they in fact secure it for the prosecution alone and deny access to anyone other than the prosecution. A suspect or his defense attorneys often must obtain court permission to view the scene or search for evidence. Only such exculpatory evidence as by accident falls into the hands of the prosecution need be revealed to the suspect or defendant.[660] In cases where police misconduct is an issue, police use their monopoly over the crime scene to prepare the evidence to suit their version of events.[661]

ENTRAPMENT

Abandonment of victim-driven, mostly private prosecution has led to consequences the Framers could never have predicted and would likely never have sanctioned. Even in the most horrific examples of colonial criminal justice (and there were many), defendants were rarely if ever entrapped into criminal activity. The development of modern policing as an omnipotent power of the state, however, has necessitated the simultaneous development of complicated doctrines such as entrapment and "outrageous government conduct" as counterweights.

It was not until the late nineteenth century that any English or American case dealt with entrapment as a true defense to a criminal charge.[662] (The case law until then had been virtually devoid of police conduct issues altogether).[663] Beginning in 1880, English case law slowly became involved with phenomena such as state agents inducing suspects to sell without proper certificates,[664] persuading defendants to supply drugs to terminate pregnancy,[665] and enticing people to commit other victimless crimes. Dicta in some English cases expressed outrage that police might someday "be told to commit an offense themselves for the purpose of getting evidence against someone."[666] Police who commit such offenses, said one English court, "ought also to be convicted and punished, for the order of their superior would afford no defense."[667]

Entrapment did not arise as a defense in the United States until 1915, when the conduct of government officers for the first time brought the issue before the federal courts. In *Woo Wai v. United States*, the Ninth Circuit overturned a conviction of a defendant for illegally bringing Chinese persons into the United States upon evidence that government officers had induced the crime.[668] Growth in police numbers and "anti-crime" warfare was so rapid that in 1993, the Wyoming Supreme Court wrote that entrapment had "probably replaced ineffectiveness of defense counsel and challenged conduct of prosecutors as the most prevalent issues in current appeals."[669]

The growth of the use of entrapment by the state raises troubling questions about the nature and purposes of American government. Rather than "serving and protecting" the public, modern police often serve and protect the interests of the state against the liberties and interests of the people. A significant amount of police brutality, for example, seems aimed at mere philosophical, rather than physical, opposition. Police dominance over the civilian (rather than service to or protection of him) is the "only truly iron and inflexible rule" followed by police officers.[670] Thus, any person who defies police faces virtually certain negative repercussions, whether a ticket, a legal summons, an arrest, or a bullet.[671] One study found nearly half of all illegal force by police occurred in response to mere defiance of an officer rather than a physical threat.[672]

In the political sphere, police serve the interests of those in power against the rights of the public. New York police of the late nineteenth century were found by the New York legislature to have committed "almost every conceivable crime against the elective franchise," including arresting and brutalizing opposition-party voters, stuffing ballot boxes, and using "oppression, fraud, trickery [and] crime" to ensure the dominant party held the city.[673] In the twentieth century, J. Edgar Hoover's FBI agents burglarized hundreds of offices of law-abiding, left-wing political parties and organizations, "often with the active cooperation or tacit consent of local police."[674] The FBI has also spent thousands of man-hours surveiling and investigating writers, playwrights, directors and artists whose political views were deemed a threat to the interests of the ruling political establishment.[675]

Police today are a constant agent on behalf of governmental power. Both in the halls of legislatures and before the courts, police act as lobbyists against individual liberties.[676] Police organizations, funded by monies funneled directly from police wages, lobby incessantly against legisla-tive constraints on police conduct.[677] Police organizations also file amicus curie briefs in virtually every police procedure case that goes before the Supreme Court, often predicting dire consequences if the Court rules against them. In 2000, for example, the police lobby filed amicus briefs in favor of allowing police to stop and frisk persons upon anonymous tips, warning that if the Court ruled against them, "the consequence for law enforcement and the public could be increased assaults and perhaps even murders."[678]

Chapter Five

THE ORIGINALIST CASE FOR THE FOURTH AMENDMENT EXCLUSIONARY RULE[679]

The Fourth Amendment exclusionary rule has been the law of the land in all federal jurisdictions since 1914[680] and in all state jurisdictions since 1961.[681] Yet critics continue to question the rule's constitutional pedigree. Generations of conservative jurists and scholars have called for the rule's abolition on "originalist" grounds.[682] These scholars argue that the rule is of recent vintage,[683] unsupported in the Fourth Amendment's text, and disloyal to the Amendment's original intent.[684] In this paper, the author argues that exclusion is actually an ancient remedy, widely applied by courts in various contexts since the dawn of American history. Contrary to the writings of anti-exclusion scholars, the basic framework for the exclusionary rule was well established in the regular practices of Founding-era judges and lawyers. Indeed, the idea that exclusion or exclusion-like remedies were required by the search and seizure protections of the Founding period almost certainly predates by many years the earliest American holdings opposing exclusion.

Perhaps no criminal procedure topic has enjoyed as much fiery debate in legal scholarship as the Fourth Amendment exclusionary rule.[685] Exclusion— the rule requiring that evidence seized in violation of the Fourth Amendment[686] may not be used against a defendant in a subsequent criminal case—has been attacked for decades by police organizations, attorneys general, and conservative legal scholars. Opponents of the rule argue that exclusion benefits only criminals,[687] keeps juries from seeing and hearing "the truth,"[688] and sometimes allows "guilty" offenders to escape conviction.[689]

But by far, the most powerful rhetorical argument against the rule involves its origins. Anti-exclusion scholars allege that "for one hundred years after the passage of the Fourth Amendment, evidence of the defen-dant's guilt was never excluded just because it was obtained illegally."[690] Consequently, exclusion of wrongly seized evidence is said to have no constitutional foundation. According to Yale law professor Akhil Amar, "no state court ... ever excluded evidence in [the] first century" of American history,[691] and "nothing in the text, history, or structure of the Fourth Amendment" supports such a remedy.[692]

The claim that exclusion of illegally seized evidence represents a stark reversal of widespread Founding-era jurisprudence is one that has gone largely unchallenged.[693] This may be because the self-described social liberals, who generally support and promote the exclusionary rule, tend to eschew the cape of "originalism" and cede the originalist high ground to their "conservative," tough-on-crime opponents.[694] Yet as this paper will establish, the Fourth Amendment exclusionary rule is soundly based in the original understandings of the Constitution and the practices of the Founding period.

THE EXCLUSIONARY RULE IN CONTEMPORARY FOURTH AMENDMENT JURISPRUDENCE

The Fourth Amendment states that "the right of the people to be secure in their persons, houses, papers, and effects, against unreasonable searches and seizures" shall not be violated, and that "no Warrants shall issue" without sworn, particularized affirmations of probable cause. Although a number of jurists and scholars have suggested that exclusion is required by their reading of the Fourth Amendment, [695] most have declared that exclusion is not invoked by the plain language of the amendment. Thus, the applicability of the rule is said to be at the pleasure, or sufferance, of the nation's contemporary policy-makers, who may opt to abolish the rule when they please.[696]

The Supreme Court majority that imposed the rule on all American jurisdictions in 1961 did so because it viewed exclusion as required by either the Fourth Amendment or a union of the Fourth Amendment with the principles of the Fifth Amendment.[697] However, later Supreme Court opinions have tended to paint the rule as the application of a temporary cost-benefit analysis. Accordingly, the rule might be abolished when the costs and benefits are reevaluated.[698]

Criticisms of the rule have generated a steady advance against its application in recent years. [699] Members of Congress have repeatedly attempted to limit the rule and, occasionally, even to abolish it.[700] Some state judges have openly proclaimed that they are not bound by the exclusionary rule and have undertaken efforts to override the rule in state courts.[701] Moreover, at least four members of the contemporary Roberts Court have signaled that they would abolish the rule completely.[702]

This chapter will not delve deeply into the social costs or benefits of exclusion as many informed books and articles have.[703] Rather, it will address the specific question of whether the Framers of the Fourth Amendment envisioned its likely remedies to include exclusion of evidence obtained in its violation. To this question the answer must certainly be yes, in accordance with statements of Founding-era spokesmen and court rulings generated by American jurists during the first three generations after ratification. Such rulings either applied versions of exclusion (such as discharge of defendants) or voiced the opinion that unconstitutionally obtained evidence vitiated the criminal proceedings. The evidence supporting this conclusion is overwhelming, and contrary to claims by modern anti-exclusion scholars that "a strict nonexclusionary rule" prevailed in nineteenth-century jurisprudence, driven by "the common law courts' paramount concern with truth-seeking and punishing the guilty."[704]

As this chapter illustrates: (1) there were few or no published cases on search and seizure questions in most states prior to the late nineteenth century; (2) those published cases that do exist show that searches for physical evidence were very rare because criminal trial evidence was for the most part testimonial; (3) the only exception to this dearth of early published search and seizure decisions occurred in cases of warrantless or otherwise improper arrests of suspects; and (4) in these cases, early American courts did in fact apply the remedy of exclusion by discharging the suspects entirely. Moreover, (5) the "guilt" or "innocence" of an arrestee—though often undeterminable in any case—was irrelevant to the application of such exclusionary remedies. The originalist case for the Fourth Amendment exclusionary rule is further bolstered by (6) dicta in early court opinions and non-judicial texts indicating that exclusion was the appropriate remedy in cases of illegally seized physical evidence, and (7) the strong relationship between silence rights and search and seizure protections (hence, the "intimate relation"[705] between the Fourth Amendment and the Fifth Amendment exclusionary rule), which was recognized in pre-ratification publications discussing search and seizure issues in depth.

Having sifted through reams of antebellum documents, the author suggests that exclusion was not only considered by the Fourth Amendment's Framers, but that exclusion was almost certainly among the remedies for Fourth Amendment violations intended by the Amendment's Framers in 1791. In contrast to the claims of modern anti-exclusion scholars such as Professor

Amar,[706] almost everything in the "text, history, [and] structure of the Fourth Amendment" supports exclusionary remedies.[707]

The Anti-Exclusion Argument Conventional wisdom holds that exclusion of illegally seized evidence originated in 1886 with the U.S Supreme Court's decision in *Boyd v. United States*[708] and was imposed as a rule governing Fourth Amendment outcomes in all federal courts in 1914 with *Weeks v. United States*.[709] Prior to *Boyd*, it is alleged that no jurist ever voiced the suggestion that exclusion was required where government agents violated the Constitution to obtain evidence.

Professor Amar, one of the most outspoken critics of the exclusionary rule, has authored a number of books and articles attacking the Supreme Court's rulings in *Boyd* and *Weeks*.[710] A renowned constitutional scholar, Amar's self-styled "originalist" interpretation of the Fourth Amendment has been recited in a number of published court opinions.[711]

Amar's argument is essentially that the Founders merely intended that searches and seizures be "reasonable" (apparently as determined on a case-by-case basis).[712] Accordingly, those who contended they were searched or seized unreasonably could only sue in civil court, where warrants (which Amar claims were never required to search) could be used by police to defend themselves against such lawsuits.[713] Instead of excluding incriminating evidence from the trials of "guilty" defendants, according to this argument, the Founders merely intended to compensate "innocent" victims by allowing them to seek civil damages for their troubles. The "guilty," according to anti-exclusion scholars, had no remedy, either in their own criminal prosecutions or in any civil suit, because recovery would be prohibited by the reasonableness of an officer's actions, and the fact of guilt would categorize a seizure as reasonable by definition.

While some of Amar's generalizations have been discredited,[714] there is much in his critique to be taken seriously.[715] It is true, of course, that government agents who engaged in illegal searches and seizures in the early republic were held liable for civil damages with great regularity.[716] In general, these lawsuits were framed not as constitutional claims but as tort claims such as trespass, assault and battery, false imprisonment,[717] or malicious prosecution. Yet taking Amar's argument at face value essentially writes the Fourth Amendment out of the Constitution altogether, or reduces it to a "truism" in the model of the Supreme Court's occasional interpretations of the Ninth and Tenth Amendments.[718] Without a warrant requirement and an exclusionary rule, the Fourth Amendment becomes merely an awkwardly rewritten statement of the law of trespass, which exists in common law independent of the Constitution.[719]

Founding-era case reporters are indeed filled with civil court decisions stemming from wrongful searches and seizures, trespasses by law enforcers and false arrests.[720] But these published civil cases rarely indicate what pretrial or evidentiary rulings (if any) were made in their underlying criminal prosecutions (if any).[721] As demonstrated below, the absence of a large corpus of published criminal cases voicing exclusion-type holdings should not be read as indicating that civil suits were the sole remedy for search and seizure violations. In many cases, underlying criminal cases, which generally did not survive into publication, for reasons explained below, may have been dismissed due to applications of exclusion or exclusion-like remedies (such as pretrial discharge).

Criminal procedure in the United States has literally been transformed over the course of American history.[722] During the late eighteenth century, when the Constitution was debated and ratified, there were no professional police officers to enforce criminal laws. Criminal law enforcement was mostly the province of private citizens, who conducted investigations, made arrests and initiated complaints in criminal court. Constables and sheriffs were not salaried but instead paid by user fees.[723] When a crime was alleged, a sheriff or constable might be given a warrant to arrest a suspect and draw upon other citizens in a *posse comitatus* to assist him.[724]

At the time of the American Revolution, many criminal cases were privately prosecuted without government attorneys general.[725] The distinction between civil and criminal cases was still emerging, and most criminal accusations were simply controversies between private parties.[726] Citizen grand juries investigated and indicted suspected criminals without the assistance—or even the approval—of government prosecutors.[727] Searches and seizures by state officials were rare because the domain of the state was substantially smaller than it is today.[728] Usually, a private person would complain to a justice of the peace or a grand jury and occasionally accompany constables on the search if a warrant was issued.[729] When no constable was available, a justice or magistrate would deputize a private citizen to per-form executive duties such as searches and arrests.[730] Occasionally, private citizens served and executed their own search warrants after magistrates signed them.[731]

Professor Thomas Y. Davies, who has studied the origins of the Fourth Amendment for many years, reminds us that the criminal justice machinery in existence in the late 1700s and early 1800s did not employ government law enforcement agents on the general scale we know today.[732] Many searches and arrests were in fact executed by private citizens under the authority of warrants issued by regional magistrates or pursuant to state statutes or ancient common law principles.[733] Because the Bill of Rights was a restriction on government, the Founders probably did not foresee that the focus of Fourth Amendment violations would someday shift from judges and legislatures to (mostly private) law enforcers themselves.[734] Rather, legislatures and judges were viewed as the most likely violators of the Fourth Amendment (and its state corollaries).[735] According to Davies, this may account for the relatively late introduction of the issue of whether to exclude wrongly seized physical evidence into the jurisprudence of the criminal law.[736] Nonetheless, the broad principles upon which exclusion of physical evidence is grounded were certainly ever-present in the Founders' constructions of search and seizure protections.

FOURTH AMENDMENT REMEDIES IN THE CONSTITUTION'S TEXT

Every originalist analysis must, of necessity, begin with scrutiny of constitutional text. It is often said that the Fourth Amendment does not lay out or prescribe its own remedy.[737] However, scrutiny of the Constitution as a whole provides clues to the Framers' intended remedies. There are at least three sources of potential remedies that are explicit in the Constitution:

(1) the habeas corpus clause, article I, section 9, clause 2; (2) the Seventh Amendment right to civil jury trials—and its implication of civil remedies; and (3) the Fifth Amendment's description of an exclusionary rule in the context of self-incriminatory statements.[738]

The Federalist contains an enunciation of a fourth possibility: criminal charges against officials who violate the Constitution's search and seizure protections.[739] In Federalist No. 83, Alexander Hamilton (writing as Publius) indicated that "wilful abuses of a public authority [such as the aggressive revenue searches that the Framers were familiar with], to the oppression of the subject, and every species of official extortion," should be remedied by "indictment and punishment according to the circumstances of the case."[740] Scrutiny of early primary sources does indeed unearth cases in which authorities were criminally prosecuted for violating search and seizure standards.[741] In some cases, wrongful arrestors were charged with assault and battery upon arrestees.[742] In other cases, even magistrates and complainants were criminally prosecuted for violating the search and seizure rights of arrestees.[743]

It is noteworthy that Blackstone's *Commentaries*, published in the 1760s and read widely by the Framers, suggested that an appropriate remedy against officials who wrongfully seized persons and sent them to overseas penal colonies was the penalty of *praemunire,* the "incapacity to hold any office, without any possibility of pardon."[744] Blackstone wrote that lesser degrees of false imprisonment should be punished by criminal indictment, fines and imprisonment. These suggested remedies should be kept in mind when more recent scholars and jurists such as Chief Justice Warren Burger describe the exclusionary rule as a "drastic" remedy.[745]

The suggested remedies described above all further the aim of the Fourth Amendment that people be "secure" from the threat of unreasonable search and seizure. But the exclusionary rule is distinguishable from other collateral remedies in that it impedes or halts criminal prosecutions before illegally seized evidence can be used at a trial. Only exclusion—or exclusion-like remedies such as total discharge—truly "secures" people from illegal searches and seizures by restoring the *status quo ante.*[746]

Search and Seizure Remedies of the Founding Era are Difficult to Ascertain by Reading Case Law For a variety of reasons, the evidentiary rulings applied in the criminal courts of early America are difficult to know.[747] For one thing, the law of evidence itself was relatively new and in a stage of rapid development during the period.[748] According to Professor Frederick Schauer, "There was no systematic attempt to compile the various bits and pieces of evidentiary rulings into a distinct topic until well into the eighteenth century."[749] And it is often forgotten that judicial doctrines now taken for granted—such as, judicial review of legislation or stare decisis—were fledgling notions at the time of the Founding.[750]

Most state criminal cases of the period were overseen and disposed of by justices of the peace who did not preside over courts of record.[751] Even judgments and verdicts were recorded only haphazardly, and an offender could easily escape the shame of conviction in one community by relocating to another.[752]

Of course, it is from published case reports that modern legal researchers obtain most of their knowledge about rules of law and evidence that were applied in early American courts. But reports of pre-Revolutionary American appellate cases were virtually nonexistent in most of the American colonies.[753] More importantly, appellate courts of the late eighteenth and early nineteenth centuries often had little or no jurisdiction over criminal cases,[754] even where legal systems offered appellate review of civil cases.[755] Thus, appellate criminal opinions on evidentiary matters were rare even when decisions in criminal trial courts were otherwise recorded.[756] Of the paltry set of published criminal cases from the antebellum period dealing with evidence, the number with discernable search and seizure issues is smaller still.[757] And remember that the U.S. Supreme Court lacked general appellate jurisdiction over even federal criminal cases for almost the entire first century of the Bill of Rights.[758]

There is another reason for the paucity of early published cases involving the admission of unconstitutionally seized physical evidence: the fact that criminal prosecutions almost never utilized physical evidence at all. [759] Law enforcers of the early Republic rarely executed searches for physical property except when the property was alleged to be stolen, and then only for the purpose of returning it to its owner(s).[760]

Thus, almost nothing is easier for a scholar than to proclaim that a given evidentiary doctrine is not found in published criminal cases from the Founding period.[761] Yet consider the *hauteur* with which modern-day originalists assert a claim of early ubiquity for their "strict nonexclusionary rule" under the "common law":[762]

> Supporters of the exclusionary rule cannot point to a single major statement from the Founding—or even the antebellum or Reconstruction eras—supporting Fourth Amendment exclusion of evidence in a criminal trial.[763]

Not even a "single major statement" "supporting" Fourth Amendment exclusion? This is a challenge that deserves a response. As a preliminary matter, the seemingly broadly worded boast above is actually quite conditional. Every Fourth Amendment scholar recognizes that a vast majority of early recorded statements about the Fourth Amendment (or, in the broader sense, search and seizure law) involved arrest warrants or seizures of persons rather than search warrants or searches for physical evidence.[764] And even where early search warrants sought physical property, they almost always involved searches for stolen property—again, not to be used for "evidence" so much as to be returned to its rightful owner.[765] Moreover, the decision whether to exclude the ill-gotten gains of searches or seizures—both today and in the past—rarely occurs "in a criminal trial" but generally occurs in pretrial proceedings.

As shown below, major statements supporting the concept of Fourth Amendment exclusion and suggesting that such a remedy must naturally develop within the then-gestational law of evidence abound in writings and decisions of the Founding era, as well as in the antebellum and Reconstruction eras. Such statements can chiefly be categorized as accompaniments to a trio of jurisprudential doctrines that have long been lost to history (or consolidated into the modern exclusionary rule): (1) pretrial habeas corpus discharge as a search and seizure remedy, which has now been abolished, (2) the "mere evidence rule," which forbade searches for property owned by another person unless it was stolen or contraband (and has likewise been abolished) and (3) numerous evidentiary privileges that disqualified large amounts of early trial evidence, privileges which in some applications operated as exclusionary rules (and which have since been abolished or severely limited).

Consider the 1787 Connecticut Superior Court decision in *Frisbie v. Butler*. *Frisbie* was published in the first volume of the first case reporter ever printed in America.[766] It involved a search warrant issued upon the complaint of a private person (Butler) who lost "about twenty pounds of good pork" under suspicious circumstances. [767] Butler suspected Benjamin Frisbie of nearby Harwinton, but the search warrant was written out in very general terms.[768] It commanded another private person, John Birge, to accompany Butler and "search all suspected places and persons that the complainant thinks proper" until the pork was found and a suspect was made to "appear before some proper authority."[769] They arrested Frisbie "by virtue of this warrant" and "brought [him] before the [issuing] justice," who found him guilty of theft.[770]

On appeal by writ of error (there being no direct appeals from Connecticut criminal judgments at the time), Frisbie argued six grounds of illegal procedure - three of which involved flaws in the search warrant.[771] A unanimous panel of the Connecticut Superior Court [772] reversed Frisbie's conviction - apparently on grounds that the facts alleged did not rise to the level of theft: "The complaint ... contained no direct charge of theft, ... nor, indeed, does it appear to have been theft that [Frisbie] was even suspected of, but only a taking away of the plaintiff's property, which might amount to no more than a trespass."[773]

In dicta, the Court observed that the search warrant was "clearly illegal" because it did not specify the places to be searched or the person(s) to be seized.[774] "[Y]et, how far this vitiates the proceedings upon the arraignment, may be a question, which is not necessary now to determine."

By its own terms, the *Frisbie v. Butler* Court recognized that an illegal search warrant "vitiated" proceedings in a criminal case in 1787 (The only question was how much). Is this not a "major statement" "supporting" Fourth Amendment exclusion? Certainly, the *Frisbie* dicta contradict the assertions of modern anti-exclusionists that jurists of the Founding period considered a "doctrine of non-exclusion" as well settled. Indeed, the *Frisbie* case establishes that exclusion, or remedies similar to exclusion which "vitiate the proceedings upon the arraignment," were on the table for consideration at the time of the Fourth Amendment's ratification. *Frisbie* predated the first case generally cited as representing the "common law rule" of nonexclusion by more than a half century.[775]

Major statements supporting the Fourth Amendment exclusionary rule were much more than mere dicta; early courts did in fact exclude unconstitutionally seized persons from criminal actions. Dozens of early reported cases find judges imposing the ultimate exclusionary sanction: discharge.[776] Such discharges occurred both as applications of that powerful yet murky remedy known as habeas corpus as well as by impositions of courts' inherent powers to manage and dispose of matters improperly brought before them.[777]

An 1814 Connecticut case entitled *Grumon v. Raymond* illustrates the Founders' interpretation of search and seizure protections. *Grumon* involved a criminal complaint alleging a theft of goods and a search war-rant directing investigators to search "the premises of Aaron Hyatt ... and other suspected places, houses, stores or barns ... and also to search such persons as are suspected ... and arrest the person suspected" if the stolen goods were found.[778] The stolen goods were apparently located at Hyatt's store in Wilton, Connecticut, and five suspects were arrested and brought before the issuing justice. But the search warrant was clearly too general, and the prosecution apparently ended then and there as a consequence of the flawed warrant: "The persons arrested demurred to the complaint and warrant; and the justice adjudged the same to be insufficient, and taxed costs against the complainant."[779]

These stated facts leave many questions about the criminal proceedings unanswered. (The published *Grumon v. Raymond* opinion stemmed from an appeal of a civil judgment that followed the dismissal of the original criminal case.) However, we know that (1) both the physical evidence and the suspects were apparently discharged entirely when the illegality of the search warrant was recognized, (2) even though the recovered evidence was apparently the stolen property which was sought.[780] Moreover, (3) one of the arrestees successfully sued both the justice of the peace who issued the warrant and the constable who executed the warrant for trespass, and (4) Connecticut's highest court upheld a civil judgment against both the justice and the constable.[781] Thus, both exclusionary remedies and civil remedies were applied—and with much more force than the way they operate today.

Such extreme applications of exclusionary and civil remedies would be unimaginable in today's legal practice. But they clearly illustrate the remedies intended or sanctioned by the Founding generation. The Connecticut Supreme Court panel that upheld the civil judgment against the constable and justice was staffed by bona fide Founding Fathers such as Zephaniah Swift, who had been a member of the Connecticut legislature when it voted to approve the U.S. Constitution in 1788.[782] Justice Simeon Baldwin, also on the *Grumon* panel, was the son-in-law of Roger Sherman, a delegate to the federal Constitutional Convention of 1787 and the only man to sign all four of America's great Founding documents: the Articles of Association, the Declaration of Independence, the Articles of Confederation and the Constitution.[783] Another member of the panel, John Trumbull, had studied law under John Adams and attended the Continental Congress in Philadelphia.[784] Chief Justice Tapping Reeve founded the first proprietary law school in the United States, the Litchfield Law School in Litchfield, Connecticut, an institution that trained three future Supreme Court justices and future Vice Presidents Aaron Burr (Reeve's brother-in-law) and John C. Calhoun.[785] The attorney for the plaintiff in the *Grumon* case was Roger Minott Sherman, whose uncle was the Roger Sherman already mentioned.[786] If these justices and lawyers disagreed with the exclusionary remedies that were applied in the underlying criminal proceedings, or knew John Adams or Roger Sherman (both of whom were drafters of language that became parts of the Constitution, if not the Fourth Amendment)[787] to be of the opinion that "a strict nonexclusionary rule" required the admission of "all competent and probative evidence regardless of its source,"[788] the *Grumon* case would have provided a good opportunity to say or write so.

PRETRIAL WRITS OF HABEAS CORPUS

Lost in the modern discussion of Fourth Amendment remedies is the fact that one ancient remedy—the pretrial writ of habeas corpus—once operated as something of an exclusionary rule in search and seizure cases but has since been stripped of its Founding-era substance. Today we know habeas corpus as a narrow, post-conviction remedy applied mostly as a sentence-review mechanism.[789] But the Framers viewed habeas corpus as primarily a pretrial remedy that was often applied in search and seizure cases.[790] Two centuries of relentless legislative attacks upon the "Great Writ" have confined this remedy to an increasingly narrow corner.[791]

As Professor Amar himself acknowledges, habeas corpus was "the original Constitution's most explicit reference to remedies."[792] The habeas corpus clause—which appears in Article I of the Constitution and thus pre-ceded the Bill of Rights by two years—provided that "the Privilege of the Writ of Habeas Corpus shall not be suspended, unless when in Cases of Rebellion or Invasion the Public Safety may require it."[793] For generations prior to 1789, habeas corpus was the means for challenging unlawful detention procedures and demanding the release of inmates.[794] More importantly for our present discussion, habeas corpus operated as an antebellum exclusionary rule—except that it was more powerful than the modern exclusionary rule, which functions as a mere rule of evidence.

Under the common law, an inmate seized or held illegally could petition the nearest court for a writ of habeas corpus to release him.[795] In cases where the inmate had no access to a court, a friend or representative could step in and file such a petition.[796] A court receiving a habeas petition generally called an immediate hearing to inquire into the lawfulness of the inmate's custody.[797] Typically, the official having custody of the inmate would be called upon to bring the inmate before the court and explain the situation.[798] The merits of a criminal accusation—any issues relating to the guilt of the offender—were irrelevant to a habeas corpus proceeding.[799] If a court found a constitutional or legal violation regarding an inmate's custody, it could release the inmate from custody.[800]

In eighteenth-and early nineteenth-century American jurisdictions, someone who was improperly arrested, such as by unnecessary violence or an incomplete or invalid warrant, had the right to demand his release from incarceration via habeas corpus.[801] Thus, in 1796, only five years after the Fourth

Amendment became part of the Constitution, the North Carolina Supreme Court upheld the discharge of a debtor arrested pursuant to an illegal warrant.[802] Because the warrant in *Lutterloh v. Powell* did not specify that the debtor owed enough funds to qualify for arrest and detention (although he may have owed a sufficient amount), "the arrest was illegal, and releasing the Defendant in the warrant was proper and what [the trial judge] ought to have done."[803]

Surviving records suggest that such discharges were fairly routine although cases were reported only sporadically.[804] Persons were released, for example, when warrants failed to specify their names or the amount of their debts or were otherwise in improper form.[805] Discharge was also warranted if an arrest was executed outside the territorial jurisdiction where the arrest warrant had been issued. [806]

In 1812, the Supreme Court of Appeals of Virginia considered the case of a debtor arrested for debts without a proper warrant. [807] A defense attorney named Wickham argued that "the defendant is entitled to a writ of habeas corpus if there be no written warrant justifying his detention."[808] The Court held that without sufficient warrant of detention the debtor-prisoner was entitled to complete discharge.[809]

In *Jones v. Commonwealth*, an 1842 Virginia case, a suspect arrested and jailed for perjury pursuant to an invalid warrant challenged the seizure of his person.[810] A Virginia judge granted the writ, excluding the wrongfully seized person from custody based on the illegality of the warrant: "Whereupon, it appearing to the court that the said warrant had been illegally issued, and that [the suspect] was illegally detained in custody thereon, it was ordered that he be discharged out of the custody of [the constable] and that the said [constable] pay the costs ... ."[811] The defendant later succeeded in having the constable who arrested him, the magistrate who issued the warrant and the original complainant charged with criminal assault.[812]

Defects in warrants issued during the early nineteenth century generally justified the dismissal of all proceedings.[813] The Supreme Court of Alabama, in *Hemphill v. Coates* (1833), even struck down the application of a statute that purported to require adjudication of matters regardless of "defects or informality" of process.[814] Early American courts routinely discharged defendants arrested by authorities lacking proper paperwork, or who were arrested on charges for which the courts did not have jurisdiction.[815] There were also antebellum cases in which failure to introduce an arrest warrant at trial resulted in total discharge.[816]

If ever there were "major statements" supporting the proposition that the Founders intended and assumed that wrongly seized persons, papers and effects should be excluded from use by authorities in subsequent criminal prosecutions, they can be found in the first two Supreme Court cases ever to mention the Fourth Amendment. In the 1806 case of *Ex parte Burford*, the Supreme Court was asked to grant the release of a local scoundrel from incarceration via habeas corpus on grounds that the man had suffered a combination of constitutional improprieties.[817] Burford, who was apparently a vice merchant of some type in the District of Columbia,[818] was arrested pursuant to a warrant alleging he was "an evil doer and disturber of the peace" and demanding that he provide sureties or bond money before he was released.[819]

Because this case arose in the District of Columbia, where federal courts had jurisdiction, *Burford* provides a rare (and often overlooked) glimpse into how the Framers viewed the scope of the Fourth Amendment. The Marshall Court was "unanimously of opinion that the warrant of commitment was illegal for want of stating some good cause certain, supported by oath," and ordered Burford released.[820] It was the first Supreme Court decision ever to mention the Fourth Amendment, which the Court referred to as "the 6th article of the amendments."[821] While the written order in *Burford* can be interpreted in different ways, it must certainly be read as a major statement supporting the proposition that jurists of the Founding Era--indeed, the Founders themselves[822]-- regarded Fourth Amendment violations (at least in cases of wrongful seizures of persons) as meriting total exclusion from custody, regardless of the "guilt" of suspects.[823] At the very least, *Burford* mocks and refutes pronouncements of the more recent Roberts Court, in cases such as *Hudson v. Michigan*[824] and *Herring v. United States*,[825] that exclusion "has always been our last resort, not our first impulse."[826]

Barely a year after its decision in *Burford*, the Supreme Court briefly addressed the Fourth Amendment a second time in a case entitled *Ex parte Bollman*.[827] *Bollman* involved the contentious treason accusations by the Jefferson Administration against former Vice President Aaron Burr, following Burr's exploits in Louisiana Territory and the western frontier.[828] Modern legal scholars cite *Bollman* mostly for its narrow construction of treason and its broad construction of habeas corpus.[829] For our purposes, the majority opinion provides insight into the original intended remedies for Fourth Amendment violations.

The majority opinion, authored by Chief Justice Marshall, ordered two acquaintances of Burr (Bollman and Swartwout) released via writ of habeas corpus after examining the stated grounds for arresting the men for treason.[830] Marshall suggested that the stated evidence hardly rose to the level required to prove treason.[831]

Charles Lee, the attorney for Swartwout, specifically recited the Fourth Amendment in his argument that the arresting and charging instruments in the case "did not show probable cause."[832] Although the Court's ruling did not specifically invoke the Amendment in its order to discharge Bollman and Swartwout, Marshall's pronouncement that there was "want of precision in the description of the offense which might produce some difficulty in deciding what cases would come within it"[833] was a clear, plain and "major statement" supporting the Fourth Amendment exclusionary rule. It was the second pronouncement regarding the Fourth Amendment in Supreme Court history, and again it ordered the exclusion, or total discharge, of wrongly seized persons.[834]

Reasonable minds can quibble over the precise scope of the Fourth Amendment's treatment in *Burford* and *Bollman*.[835] At minimum, both cases support the proposition that the Founding Fathers (several of whom were on the very Supreme Court panels that considered the cases),[836] rather than rejecting exclusion and exclusion-like remedies, accepted and embraced them at their "first impulse." These cases illustrate that the faux originalism of modern anti-exclusionists is largely a projection of contemporary punitive and statist political views onto an invented past.

The idea that wrongful seizure of a person should merit discharge from prosecution, a notion which has been lost to constitutional history, was hardly confined to the halls of judges and lawyers. The first federal arrest of great notoriety in American history—that of former Vice President Aaron Burr for treason in 1807—resulted in a grand jury's public condemnation of Burr's warrantless arrest and the grand jury's refusal to indict Burr, in part, because Burr was arrested without warrant. Burr had been arrested under cloudy allegations that his independent explorations in what was then the western United States constituted a treasonous conspiracy to (in the words of one commentator) "seize New Orleans, attack Mexico, assume Montezuma's throne, add Louisiana to [Burr's] empire, and then add the North American states from the

Allegheny Mountains west."[837] President Jefferson, who was a hated rival of Burr after the contentious election of 1800, insisted upon the prosecution. [838]

A federal grand jury in the Mississippi Territory shrugged off attempts by the Jefferson Administration to indict Burr on charges relating to Burr's trip down the Mississippi River.[839] Furthermore, the grand jury declared that the arrests of Burr and his co-travelers had been made "without warrant, and ... without other lawful authority," and dismissed the entire matter. Burr's warrantless arrest and the illegal arrests of Burford, Bollman and Swartwout were the first notorious violations of the Fourth Amendment in American history. And voices of the period—from the highest judges in the country to the common citizenry—regarded these violations as meriting the application of exclusionary remedies.

As far as we know, Burford, Burr, Bollman and Swartwout never sued their arrestors in civil court. But the fact that they could have sued illustrates an important point. The record of such civil suits does not establish that a civil suit was the only remedy recognized by the Framers of the Fourth Amendment.[840] Many published civil cases may hide underlying exclusionary remedies in unpublished criminal cases.[841] In early civil suits where wrongful seizure or malicious prosecution was alleged, little was writ-ten of the underlying criminal cases. Most antebellum civil decisions involving trespass by authorities, false arrest or malicious prosecution offered only fleeting references to the criminal proceedings.[842] Thus, the very civil cases referenced by anti-exclusion scholars as supporting the supposed existence of a "strict nonexclusionary rule"[843] may also support the possibility of exclusion in the underlying criminal cases.[844] Again, this is much more than speculation; perhaps dozens of published antebellum civil suits over wrongful searches or seizures suggest that exclusionary remedies were applied in their underlying criminal proceedings.

Although modern anti-exclusionists insist that a "strict common law rule"[845] mandated that civil suits were the only remedy available to early search and seizure victims, [846] we know that nineteenth-century courts often applied multiple remedies for search and seizure violations. [847] During the American Civil War, after President Lincoln ordered the suspension of habeas corpus, a federal judge ruled in a case entitled *McCall v. McDowell* that a wrongfully imprisoned detainee could sue his captors even if habeas corpus was lawfully unavailable.[848] The court explicitly stated that, had the illegal detention occurred without the wartime suspension of habeas corpus, both remedies (habeas corpus and civil suit) would have applied: "The writ of habeas corpus is the remedy by which a party is enabled to obtain deliverance from a false imprisonment. Ordinarily, every one imprisoned without legal cause or warrant is entitled to this remedy...."[849]

In another Civil-War-era case, entitled *Griffin v. Wilcox*, the Indiana Supreme Court ruled that a wrongfully arrested person could sue his captors despite Lincoln's pronouncement that habeas corpus was suspended.[850] "Can Congress enact that the citizen shall have no redress for a violation of his rights, secured to him by ... amendments 4 and 5[?]," asked the Court.[851] The answer was no.[852]

Similarly, the U.S. Circuit Court for the District of Vermont, in an 1862 case entitled *Ex parte Field*, held that Vermont residents arrested without warrant were entitled to release via habeas corpus upon a showing that their Fourth Amendment rights were violated, despite the suspension orders issued by Congress and the President that applied to battlefield theaters.[853]

McCall, *Griffin* and *Field* all illustrate the nineteenth-century view that habeas corpus is inextricably linked to the Fourth Amendment as the Amendment's preferred remedy. Habeas corpus discharge—a form of exclusion by another name—was thought to be required under the Fourth Amendment.[854]

ANALOGIES BETWEEN HABEAS CORPUS AND EXCLUSION

The law of habeas corpus has been markedly scaled back in recent generations—even as increasing numbers of Americans have been prosecuted and imprisoned.[855] Prior to the Civil War, habeas corpus was invoked mostly to attack pretrial proceedings, and search and seizure issues were among the most common matters that were remedied by the Great Writ.

Consider how closely the early law of pretrial habeas corpus paralleled the modern doctrine of Fourth Amendment exclusion. Habeas corpus operated as a (1) collateral (separate from other issues in a case), (2) pretrial, (3) mechanism for reviewing seizures, with no consideration given to the merits of any criminal case-in-chief.[856] In fact, the procedural course of pretrial habeas corpus hearings was almost identical to the procedural course of modern evidence-suppression hearings. The legal practitioners of 1791 would probably feel quite at home in a twenty-first-century pretrial evidence-suppression hearing.

Roger I. Roots

Remember that the text of the Fourth Amendment draws no distinction between the treatment of persons and the treatment of "houses, papers, and effects."[857] Because the Founders viewed habeas corpus discharge as one of the remedies (along with civil suit) for wrongful searches and seizures of persons, they would logically have intended that exclusion be an appropriate remedy (along with civil suit) for wrongful searches and seizures of houses, papers and effects. What, after all, is exclusion if not an evidence-specific application of the principles of habeas corpus? As even Akhil Amar concedes, "Dismissal with prejudice is indeed an exclusionary rule of sorts."[858] Except that pretrial habeas corpus was a more powerful remedy than exclusion; it often mandated the end to an entire prosecution.

JUDGE WILKEY'S INADVERTENT ARGUMENT IN FAVOR OF FOUNDING-ERA EXCLUSION

It seems startling that any scholar might suggest that no Founding-era jurists ever thought to exclude wrongfully gained evidence when they clearly did exclude wrongfully arrested *individuals*. But many anti-exclusion scholars appear to be ignorant of such cases.

United States Judge Malcolm Richard Wilkey of the D.C. Circuit unknowingly conceded this point while arguing against the exclusionary rule in a 1978 *Judicature* article.[859] Wilkey claimed that "it makes no sense to argue that the admission of illegally seized evidence somehow signals the judiciary's condonation of the violation of rights when the judiciary's trial of an illegally seized person is not perceived as signaling such condonation."[860] "Why should there be an exclusionary rule for illegally seized evidence," asked Wilkey, "when there is no such exclusionary rule for illegally seized people?"[861] Wilkey cited the 1886 *Ker v. Illinois* decision[862] (holding that a defendant kidnapped in Peru and brought without warrant to Illinois had no right to release), the 1888 decision in *Mahon v. Justice*[863] (refusing to release a suspect illegally captured in West Virginia for trial in Kentucky), and the 1952 case of *Frisbie v. Collins* [864] (upholding forcible seizure of a defendant in Illinois for trial in Michigan) for support.[865]

But as already demonstrated, *Ker*, *Mahon* and *Frisbie* represented clear departures from the constitutional understandings of 1791.[866] The jurists who took seats on benches in the late nineteenth and early twentieth centuries were apparently oblivious to the rule of pretrial discharge that prevailed during the

Founding period. Judge Wilkey was echoing half-truths that had been mistakenly pronounced by generations of judges who preceded him. Justice Hugo Black, writing in *Frisbie v. Collins* in 1952, stated that "this Court has never departed from the rule announced in *Ker v. Illinois* ... ."[867] The Supreme Court, in *Adams v. New York* (the 1904 case often cited by anti-exclusionists as validating their view of exclusion as an orphaned, discredited remedy), cited *Ker* for the same points made by Judge Wilkey in 1978.[868] The 1886 *Ker* Court, for its part, had claimed that the illegality of a capture should not impact the merits of a prosecution. [869]

Of course, as already established, the holding in *Ker* was an abandonment of common law. [870] The rule announced in *Ker* was not even shared by all courts during the late 1800s. Only seven years before the *Ker* decision, the Michigan Supreme Court ordered the release of a prostitute after Detroit police arrested her without a warrant in circumstances requiring a warrant. [871] "It is the duty of all courts," wrote the Court, "to prevent good or bad citizens from being unlawfully molested."[872] In another decision in 1888, the Michigan Supreme Court ordered the discharge of a defendant arrested pursuant to an unsigned warrant. [873] A Kansas Supreme Court decision entitled *State v. Simmons*, in 1888, struck down the conviction of a defendant arrested by Kansas officers outside their jurisdiction in the state of Missouri.[874] The court wrote: "It would not be proper for the courts of this state to favor, or even to tolerate, breaches of the peace committed by their own officers in a sister state ... ."[875]

John E. Theuman entitled a 1983 A.L.R. article he authored on the topic, "*Modern Status of Rule Relating to Jurisdiction of State Court to Try Criminal Defendant Brought within Jurisdiction Illegally*."[876] But the very first A.L.R. article on the topic, published in the 1920s, cited cases announcing a doctrine contrary to that of the late nineteenth century.[877] Thus, although the 1886 *Ker* decision reflected the consensus of nondischarge that prevailed at that time (and forever after), it gave short shrift to an immense body of discharge cases, flowing backward in time to the releases of Burr, Bollman, Burford and beyond, wherein criminal defendants won release by showing that their Fourth Amendment (or respective jurisdictional search and seizure corollary) rights were violated.

Judge Wilkey's 1978 ruminations were not just historically inaccurate. When considered in light of the true history of pretrial habeas corpus, they greatly undermine a central argument of anti-exclusion scholars.[878] Therefore,

Roger I. Roots

Wilkey's question should be inverted and rephrased: Why would the Founders *not* have sanctioned an exclusionary rule for illegally seized physical evidence when they clearly sanctioned just such an exclusionary rule for illegally seized people?

These remarks may be extended even more boldly. The pretrial discharge of defendants who were improperly arrested represented the only "rule" of search and seizure remedies that was generally applied in criminal cases at the time the Fourth Amendment was proposed and ratified in the late 1700s. Thus, to the extent that there was any "common law rule" governing search and seizure remedy practices in the Founding period, *it was a rule of exclusion.* It seems axiomatic, therefore, that the Framers of the Fourth Amendment must have intended and anticipated that exclusion be applied to remedy all other Fourth Amendment violations.

EARLY PRIVILEGES TO RESIST ILLEGAL ARREST SUPPORT EXCLUSIONARY REMEDIES

The Founders lived in a period when even "guilty" people were privileged to use violence against government officials who forcefully violated their Fourth Amendment rights.[879] At the time of the nation's founding, any person was privileged to resist arrest if, for example, probable cause for arrest did not exist or the arresting person could not produce a valid arrest warrant where one was needed. Even fugitive criminals were entitled to use deadly force to resist violent arrests by law enforcement officers.[880]

Early American law also allowed third-party intermeddlers to "rescue" an arrestee from authorities by force—either during or after an improper arrest.[881] And if a rescuer killed a sheriff while freeing an arrestee from unlawful arrest, the rescuer was guilty of only manslaughter.[882] The 1820 South Carolina case of *City Council v. Payne* illustrates a common attitude among early Americans regarding search and seizure: a private citizen physically rescued a suspect from a city guard, vowing that "whilst he drew the breath of life, no guard should carry a citizen to the guard-house" with-out a warrant.[883] The rescuer (Payne) was convicted of obstructing an officer only because the officer had arrested the suspect pursuant to a recognized exception to the warrant requirement.[884]

This largely forgotten line of cases[885] illustrates the Founders' high regard for the protective technicalities of Fourth Amendment law. [886] Yet when

92

anti-exclusion scholars depict the Founding period, they consciously or sub-consciously replace the Founders' values with those drawn from the legal-cultural *milieu* of the present, with its leviathanic state institutions, massive public budgets and professional police forces. In the Founders' world, aggression by the state was presumed unlawful and could be justified only if there was strict adherence to prescribed procedures. [887] Entick's counsel argued this point in the famed English 1765 *Entick v. Carrington* case: "if a man be made an officer for a special purpose to arrest another, he must shew his authority; and if he refuses, it is not murder to kill him."[888] Such were the words the Framers contemplated as they debated and approved the Fourth Amendment. For a century afterward, citizens had the right to shoot to kill law enforcement authorities who employed violence to execute illegal arrests.[889]

Preventive remedies like exclusion—those that flow from the right to be free from government intrusion and interference, to refuse to submit to government demands, to shoot to kill when government authorities attempt illegal arrests with violent force, and to use violence to spring friends and neighbors wrongly seized by government agents—were enshrined in Founding-era criminal procedure.[890] Notions that government may trump the rights of the people, if acting in "good faith" or in furtherance of "truth-seeking" or "punishing the guilty," came much later. [891]

MERE EVIDENCE AND EXCLUSION

Another reason why we know that the Founders almost certainly intended that Fourth Amendment violations be remedied with exclusionary rules involves the Founders' conception of property rights. According to the original understanding of the Constitution's Framers, individual property rights trumped any interest the government had in property for use as mere evidence in court cases.[892] Because people held title to their property superior to that held by government officials, search warrants could be issued only for contraband or stolen property.[893] Personal property rightfully belonging to a defendant could never be taken from him without due process and then introduced at his criminal trial.

This rule—known as the "mere evidence rule"—existed for two centuries in Anglo-American jurisprudence.[894] It was voiced in history's greatest search and seizure decisions and restated in treatises published on both sides of the Atlantic.[895] The Supreme Court of the United States abandoned this rule in 1967.[896] For most of American history, however, the rule meant that an immense sphere of information could not be made known by the powers of government, no matter how urgent the state's claim of need.[897] Private diaries, for example, were considered off-limits to the state even if obtained by valid warrants stating probable cause.

The mere evidence rule has troubled some so-called originalists among today's scholars to no end. While acknowledging the mere evidence rule's existence in early American jurisprudence, such scholars simultaneously claim that the Founders sanctioned the admission of illegally seized property into evidence in order to convict people of crimes.[898] And while anti-exclusion scholars present their vision as consistent with the Framers' intent, they resort to decidedly non-originalist tactics to evade the mere evidence rule's implications vis-a-vis the modern exclusionary rule. Professor Amar, for example, sidesteps this dilemma by accusing the Framers of "property worship"[899] and saying that the mere evidence rule was just "silly."[900]

WILKES V. WOOD AND *ENTICK V. CARRINGTON*: PRECURSORS TO EXCLUSION?

The Founding-era basis for the Fourth Amendment exclusionary rule becomes plain when we examine the mere evidence rule in combination with the Founders' view of the right to remain silent against government demands. Consider the two most revered search and seizure cases known to the Framers of the American Constitution.

It is universally acknowledged that the British cases of *Wilkes v. Wood* in 1763 and *Entick v. Carrington* in 1765 were the most famous search and seizure cases known to the Framers of the Fourth Amendment.[901] The *Wilkes* case involved a wide-ranging investigation into the authorship of an anonymous pamphlet that harshly criticized the King and other high-ranking British officials. [902] London investigators questioned a number of printers in the city and quickly zeroed in on John Wilkes, a member of the House of Commons, as the author.[903] Wilkes's home was searched pursuant to a very general warrant.[904] A mountain of his papers were haphazardly bagged up and seized, including writings indicating Wilkes's guilt in the affair.[905] Wilkes was subsequently arrested and charged with seditious libel, a misdemeanor.[906]

Entick similarly involved an author of publications critical of the Crown and its officers. John Entick was an associate of Wilkes who authored and published a scathing political periodical known as *The Monitor*.[907] As in *Wilkes*, Entick's papers were bagged up and seized in a haphazard manner— yet pursuant to a more specific search warrant that at least named him and described the papers' location.

The *Wilkes* and *Entick* cases were of great renown in the American colonies.[908] Americans of the Founding period named several towns and counties for John Wilkes, including Wilkes-Barre, Pennsylvania; Wilkes County, Georgia; and Wilkes County, North Carolina.[909] Lord Camden, the judge who presided over the *Wilkes* and *Entick* cases and authored two of the "most famous search and seizure opinions in the history of Anglo-American law,"[910] was also honored by the naming of American cities such as Camden, New Jersey and Camden, South Carolina[911] (as well as Camden Yards, where the Baltimore Orioles play baseball).[912]

Because Wilkes and Entick successfully sued their searchers and seizers, *Wilkes v. Wood* and *Entick v. Carrington* are sometimes referenced by "law and order originalists"[913] as supporting the proposition that the Founding generation viewed civil litigation as the sole appropriate remedy for search and seizure violations.[914] But such a conclusion ignores language in both cases (especially in *Entick*) explicitly recognizing that the right to remain silent is implicated by the search and seizure of papers and other evidence.[915] "It is very certain that the law obligeth no man to accuse himself," wrote Lord Camden in *Entick*,[916] "and it should seem, that search for evidence is disallowed upon the same principle."[917] Thus, exclusion, the "same principle" applied in cases of compelled oral statements since time immemorial, should likewise be applied in cases of illegally taken writings and other evidence. "Nothing can be more unjust in itself," the *Wilkes* opinion proclaimed, "than that the proof of a man's guilt shall be extracted from his own bosom," in specific reference to the seizure of Wilkes' *papers*.[918]

Entick and *Wilkes* clearly propounded a rule depriving the state of any power to possess and use personal property taken illegally from crime suspects "to help forward their convictions."[919] There is no denying that the exclusion principle, *Entick*'s "same principle," was embedded in the Fourth Amendment from its beginning.[920] And for a hundred years thereafter, every court opting to deny exclusion either distinguished *Entick* or violated *Entick*'s stated principles. The 1841 *Commonwealth v. Dana* decision in Massachusetts, often cited by anti-exclusionists as representative of some vast jurisprudence of nonexclusion decisions, clearly distinguished its own holding from the exclusionary call of *Entick*.[921]

Entick and *Wilkes* were not the only sources suggesting the exclusion remedy among Founding-era documents. The most important pre-Founding pamphlets and letters addressing search and seizure topics also linked search and seizure protections with exclusion remedies. A widely circulated 1764 pamphlet by "Father of Candor," entitled *A Letter concerning libels, warrants, and the seizure of papers*, probably the most popular tract on the topic in England and the American Colonies, [922] made the connection throughout its pages. [923] Another widely published letter, *A Reply to the Defence of the Majority, on the Question Relating to General Warrants* by Sir William Meredith, published in 1764 (and sometimes circulated along with the "Father of Candor" pamphlet), drew the same legal conclusions:

> Of all those laws, under which we live and are protected, there is none more sacred than that law, which says, that no man shall be obliged to furnish evidence against himself. In felony, you may search for stolen goods, but not for other evidence against the thief. In treason, you may search for and seize papers, in order to discover treason, but cannot use those papers in evidence against the man in whose custody they are found. [924]

Not much support for the anti-exclusionists' notion of a "universal law against exclusion" there.[925] This exclusion-requiring conceptualization of the right to be secure from unreasonable searches and seizures was embedded in the Fourth Amendment from its inception.[926] And in 1886, *Entick*'s "same principle" language became formally enshrined in Fourth Amendment jurisprudence in the *Boyd v. United States* decision. In *Boyd*, the Supreme Court conceptually married the Fourth Amendment to the exclusionary remedy of the Fifth Amendment after finding the amendments were already in an "intimate relation."[927] From this union was born the exclusionary rule in its modern form. [928]

Because the *Fifth* Amendment's exclusionary remedy is explicit and unchallengeable ("No person ... shall be compelled in any criminal case to be a witness against himself"), anti-exclusion scholars recognize the danger to their position posed by any link between the Fourth and Fifth Amendments.[929]

Consequently, anti-exclusionists have been trying to divorce the pair for over a century, despite the clarity with which Founding-era sources linked silence rights to search and seizure protections. [930] And in their zeal to narrow and deaden the Fourth Amendment, the anti-exclusionists have likewise had to distort the history and intent of the Fifth Amendment as well—imaginatively claiming (as they must) that the Fifth Amendment privilege was intended to apply only to oral testimony, only to in-court testimony, only after a formal prosecution has begun, et cetera. Ultimately, this tortured and inaccurate view of the Bill of Rights seems remarkably activist despite the veil of "strict constructionism" that the anti-exclusionists cast over it.[931]

It is undeniable that the most widely circulated texts that discussed search and seizure law in any depth during the Founding period drew a clear connection between silence rights and search and seizure protections. Yet beginning in the first decade of the twentieth century, scholars such as John Wigmore began claiming that *Boyd*'s finding of an "intimate relation" between the Fourth and Fifth Amendments was based on a "radical fallacy."[932]

By the 1970s, Supreme Court Chief Justice Warren Burger and other anti-exclusionists were claiming that the two amendments (and their ancient doctrinal bases) were distinguishable on reliability grounds.[933] Burger included a paragraph in his 1976 *Stone v. Powell* concurrence suggesting that the Framers distinguished coerced oral statements from illegally seized physical evidence because coerced oral statements are "inherently dubious" while "the reliability of [physical evidence illegally seized] is beyond question."[934] Professor Amar has argued in several books and articles that *Boyd*'s "fusion" of the Fourth and Fifth Amendments was "a plain misreading" of both Amendments.[935] Sanford E. Pitler called the notion that the Fifth Amendment's exclusionary rule might apply to Fourth Amendment violations "the convergence theory" and pronounced that scholars and judges "almost universally rejected" the "theory" soon after *Boyd*.[936]

When these anti-exclusion writers do acknowledge the *Entick* "same principle" language, they employ various means to suggest that the Framers were not aware of or influenced by it. Amar repeatedly cites *Entick* as authoritative for several of his arguments, yet skips over *Entick*'s "same principle" language with palpable discomfort: "*Boyd* claimed roots in a landmark English case that followed *Wilkes v. Wood*, but [others] have shown that the murky dictum on which Boyd relied was most probably off point."[937]

Roger I. Roots

THE TROUBLING PRESENCE OF THE WORD "PAPERS"

There is also the troubling presence of the word *papers* in the Fourth Amendment ("persons, houses, papers, and effects"). The use of this word by the Framers can only support a connection between the Fourth Amendment and the compelled-witness prohibitions of the Fifth Amendment, its ancestors and progeny. Papers have little intrinsic value as property but may have immense evidentiary value because of the words written upon them. Indeed, their only true value to would-be searchers and seizers lies in their informational content.

It is through the word papers that the Fourth Amendment becomes conceptually linked with the word witness in the Fifth Amendment.[938] "Papers are the owner's goods and chattels; they are his dearest property; and are so far from enduring a seizure, that they will hardly bear an inspection," wrote Lord Camden, one of the most respected jurists in English history, in the *Entick* decision.[939] If the state allows its agents to rifle through people's personal papers, wrote Camden, "the secret cabinets and bureaus of every subject in this kingdom will be thrown open" to government inspection, and such a practice "would be subversive of all the comforts of society."[940] Camden noted that such a power is "unsupported by one single citation from any law book."[941] Later, in *Commonwealth v. Dana*, the court recognized that Camden's opinion displayed conclusively that "the right to search for and seize private papers is unknown to the common law." [942]

Yet the construction of the Fourth Amendment suggested by law-and-order originalists denies the special importance of papers that the Framers obviously intended.[943] According to Amar, the Fourth Amendment is only "about things—houses, papers, effects, stuff—but it is not about exclusion."[944] In contrast, Amar claims that "the Fifth Amendment is about exclusion in criminal cases—but only about excluding words, because they can be unreliable."[945] Amar reads several limitations into the Fourth and Fifth Amendments that the Amendments' Framers did not.

Law enforcement agents of the Founding period were barred entirely from searching for or seizing papers which were not themselves contraband. According to Professor Russell W. Galloway, at the time of the Founding, the constitutional bar on searching for or seizing papers was solidly grounded on three separate and distinct doctrines: the mere evidence rule; silence rights; and the prohibition against general warrants (which originally barred investigators from even perusing through papers to locate incriminating documents or statements).[946] Over the course of the twentieth century, each of these three doctrinal bases was undermined and then abandoned, and today the agents of government regularly search for and seize papers, records of conversations, and electronic writings with great regularity and often without warrants.

As Galloway showed in 1982, the Fourth Amendment's invocation of the word *papers* was meant to establish an outright ban on the seizure of personal papers, rather than a weaker requirement that authorities could seize papers only when reasonable.[947] Indeed, the 1765 *Entick* opinion plainly suggested the exclusionary rule that was recognized in *Boyd v. United States*: "Our law has provided no paper search in these cases to help forward the convictions."[948]

Privileges and Exclusion of Witnesses in Early American Criminal Trials All evidentiary privileges that keep information from the eyes of a trier of facts can be characterized as truth-suppressing devices.[949] Privileges such as the attorney-client, doctor-patient and spousal privilege, and—first and foremost—the privilege of silence in the face of government demands, are unquestionably mechanisms that impede "truth-seeking and punishing the guilty."[950] But if anything, such privileges were more numerous at the time of the Founding than they are now.[951] This alone casts doubt upon depictions of Founding-era evidence law promoted by modern anti-exclusionists.

In the late eighteenth and early nineteenth centuries, people were free from arrest while going to and coming from church,[952] while attending court,[953] and while going to and returning from election places.[954] Defendants arrested while holding such privileges were discharged upon a mere showing that their arrests occurred while they held them.[955] John Wilkes, the most famous victim of an illegal search and seizure known to the Founding Fathers, was released instantly from the Tower of London upon showing that he was privileged from arrest because he was a member of Parliament.[956]

The Speech and Debate Clause of the United States Constitution describes a privilege from arrest for Congressmen while making law and coming from or going to their legislative chambers.[957] Congress passed a statute in 1802 prohibiting the arrest of an active soldier for debt.[958] Such privileges differed from state to state, and sunsetted at different times in different locations. (And some, of course, still exist today.) But their very prevalence at the time of the Fourth Amendment's ratification mocks and defies the claims of modern anti-crime scholars who suggest that the Founders sanctioned the interception of any person or property at any time upon a showing of public necessity.

The same goes for the many testimonial privileges, which prevailed in court practice during the Founding period. Various evidentiary privileges, such as the spousal privilege, the attorney-client privilege and the priest-penitent privilege, have protected defendants from conviction for centuries.[959] These privileges operated because the law known to the Framers recognized values that were higher than the state's interest in "truth-seeking and punishing the guilty."[960] They were, in some respects, more powerful obstacles to the state than a defendant's right against compelled self-incrimination because that right can be lifted simply by granting immunity from prosecution to the speaker and issuing him a subpoena.[961] Relationship privileges, on the other hand, rest on privacy barriers that cannot be breached no matter how compelling the state's desire for evidence.

Trial practices of the nineteenth century often disqualified witnesses from testifying no matter how truthful their testimony might be. Blacks, Indians and other nonwhites were all excluded as witnesses in early American court practice.[962] Spouses of parties were also disqualified as witnesses.[963] The testimony of both criminal defendants and their accusers was excluded from early trials. "Conviction of crime, want of religious belief, and other marks of ill fame were held sufficient" during the Founding period to exclude witness testimony.[964] "Indeed," wrote Justice Sutherland, "the theory of the common law was to admit to the witness stand only those presumably honest, appreciating the sanctity of an oath, unaffected as a party by the result, and free from any of the temptations of interest."[965] Congress and the courts were busy eliminating these "competency" exclusionary rules throughout the late nineteenth and early twentieth centuries.[966] But as late as 1878 a defendant could not testify in his own defense in a criminal case,[967] and the Supreme Court was still dealing with whether defendants could call their own spouses to testify in their defense as recently as 1933.[968]

These lines of cases further rebut the claims of anti-exclusion scholars that "under the common law, a strict nonexclusionary rule required a court to admit all competent and probative evidence regardless of its source."[969] To the contrary, the evidentiary practices of the common law were riddled with seemingly nonsensical exclusionary rules regarding the competency of witnesses. While it is true that some of these rules were aimed at "truth-seeking" (e.g., the bar on convicted criminal or atheist testimony), others were extensions of patrician or discriminatory interests.[970] But more importantly, these archaic rules of witness competency allowed an immense realm of factual knowledge to evade exposure in criminal trials. All the powers of the state, even in the government's unceasing quest to "punish the guilty," could not pierce such rules. The all-seeing eye of the state is a modern invention, without sanction in the criminal justice practices of early America.

DID THE FOURTH AMENDMENT'S FRAMERS INTEND TO PROTECT ONLY THE INNOCENT?

What of the recurring claim that the Framers of the Bill of Rights intended that the Fourth Amendment apply only to "innocent" people? [971] According to this argument, justice "is, or should be, a truth-seeking process" and "the guilty" should never claim to be wrongly arrested or convicted.[972]

It is upon this set of assertions where anti-exclusion scholars are on their weakest footing.[973] Recall that most Founding-era search cases turned on a property rationale. The Founders generally viewed property rights as stemming from values that trump the power of the state to know all or punish all offenses against it. It was only in 1967, in *Warden v. Hayden*, that the Supreme Court announced for the first time that the "principle object of the Fourth Amendment is the protection of privacy rather than property,"[974] overturning at least five prior Supreme Court decisions[975] and discarding search and seizure limitations that had existed for two centuries.

When the Supreme Court imposed the exclusionary rule on all federal courts in *Weeks v. United States*, it did so because the evidence in question—certain papers relating to an illegal lottery—was owned by Weeks and not by the government.[976] Upon consideration of a motion by Weeks for the return of his illegally seized (stolen, actually) property, the Supreme Court recognized that exclusion was the only rule consistent with constitutional property rights.[977] Yet modern-day faux originalists claim the government has a constitutional power to retain such property in its quest to "punish the guilty."[978]

Given the Framers' interest in protecting property rights, it seems hardly revolutionary that they would have looked favorably upon search and seizure remedies that require investigators to immediately return illegally seized property to its rightful owners. As several scholars have pointed out, exclusion simply "restores the status quo ante," placing "both the State and the accused in the positions they would have been in had the Constitution not been violated - neither better nor worse."[979]

Judges have occasionally applied exclusionary remedies with just such simplicity. Consider the ruling of the Kentucky Supreme Court in *Youman v. Commonwealth* in 1920 where the Court reversed an order of the trial judge demanding that the sheriff pour the contraband whiskey into a sewer and ordered that the whiskey—contraband though it appeared to be—be returned to its owner.[980]

In this light, the position of anti-exclusion scholars—that the Framers would have sanctioned a criminal justice system allowing state actors to search for and take property from its owners without warrant or valid pro-cess and then retain it merely because the state asserts an evidentiary value in such property—seems quite dubious. The Founders' well-established distrust of the state exposes this assertion as highly unrealistic.[981]

Remember also that the most famous search and seizure case known to the Framers who enacted the Bill of Rights involved an unquestionably "guilty" offender,[982] John Wilkes of Parliament, who had authored anti-monarch pamphlets but nonetheless recovered damages from his illegal searchers and seizers.[983] Courts of the Founding and antebellum periods were not the voices for communitarian control or law and order that we know today. "Even guilty persons are entitled to the benefit of the laws and constitution," wrote Justice Spencer Roane of Virginia in 1814.[984] "It can never be the true understanding of those [constitutional] principles, that a general warrant[ ] is void where the party arrested is innocent, and valid if he be guilty."[985]

In all, the notion that the Framers viewed the Fourth Amendment as a protection only for the innocent seems remarkably foolish. [986] Those who debated the various provisions of the Bill of Rights regarded the state not as a benevolent protector, but with suspicion and disdain.[987] Constitutional criminal procedure was designed to thwart the state at strategic points, sometimes in circumstances where agents of the state most desire evidence and information. Presumption of innocence, speedy trial provisions, requirements of strict and explicit charging, and double jeopardy clauses in early constitutions acted as bars to prosecutions even where the state's view of "guilt" was unchallenged. Trial by jury originally functioned not only as a mere fact-finding device but also as a fundamental check on the power of government and a means to obstruct unwarranted government prosecutions of "guilty" offenders. [988]

Most of the procedural protections enunciated in the Bill of Rights are lineal descendants of protections that arose during the Inquisition era when the Catholic Church pursued alleged heretics with savage zeal.[989] Silence rights—and the exclusionary rules that developed to protect those rights at trials and other proceedings—were established as shields to protect "the guilty" from government and the Church. [990]

WIGMORE'S CONSTRUCTION OF A "COMMON LAW DOCTRINE OF NONEXCLUSION"

What about those nineteenth-century cases, which are often cited by anti-exclusion originalists, that admitted illegally seized evidence? These holdings should be assessed for what they are: isolated statements of the law that hardly represented the "universal law against exclusion," which Professor Amar and others have suggested prevailed across the United States in the mid-1800s.[991] Scrutiny of such citations reveals that only two jurisdictions, Massachusetts and New Hampshire, had adopted clear rules of nonexclusion by the time the Supreme Court decided *Boyd* in 1886.[992] These two jurisdictions were greatly outnumbered by jurisdictions with few or no criminal cases on their books regarding searches or seizures—except cases excluding illegally seized persons from custody, as already discussed.[993]

To understand the actual fabric of search and seizure jurisprudence during the nineteenth century, one must don the hat of a historiographer. Historiography is the study of history by means of scrutinizing the writings of historians rather than their underlying facts.[994] In the case of the exclusionary rule, a historiographical analysis invariably and inevitably directs and redirects scrutiny upon the writings of a single individual: the dean of evidence law, John Henry Wigmore.

Wigmore was the Akhil Amar of his day. He invested decades of effort into a personal war against the exclusionary rule. Wigmore's writings on the exclusionary rule began before the end of the nineteenth century and continued well into the twentieth. As dean of the Northwestern University School of Law and the author of America's foremost treatise on the law of evidence—which continues in print long after his death[995]—Wigmore was able to promote and foster a revisionist view of early American search and seizure law that greatly impacted the way future legal historians would think about the Fourth Amendment exclusionary rule.[996]

In Wigmore's narrative, the 1841 Massachusetts case of *Commonwealth v. Dana*, 43 Mass. (2 Met.) 329 (1841), was said to be representative of a vast jurisprudence, which sustained the admissibility of illegally seized evidence in state criminal trials.[997] But neither *Dana* nor any other precedent in any American jurisdiction at the time admitted illegally-seized evidence in criminal litigation.[998] The *Dana* court found that its search and seizure of lottery tickets and other evidence was legal and reasonable because "the warrant in [that] case [was] in conformity with all the requisites of the statute and the [Massachusetts] declaration of rights," and, thus, there was no need to consider the question of constitutional remedies.[999] However, the court offered the dicta that an illegal search was not "good reason for excluding the papers seized as evidence."[1000]

In 1858 the New Hampshire Supreme Court decided *State v. Flynn*,[1001] upholding the admission of testimony by an officer who had properly executed a valid search warrant and uncovered evidence of illegal liquor sales.[1002] The *Flynn* Court cited *Commonwealth v. Dana* as support for the proposition that "evidence ...will not be rejected because it has been either illegally or improperly obtained."[1003] The *Flynn* decision ultimately grew into New Hampshire's general rule that "the method by which" evidence is "obtained and produced before the court, even if illegal, does not affect [its] value as evidence."[1004]

But it was not until 31 years after the *Dana* decision that the dicta published in *Dana* became law with regard to physical evidence anywhere in the United States. In *Commonwealth v. Welsh*, an 1872 Massachusetts decision, the court upheld the admission into evidence of seized liquor in a criminal trial on grounds that "If the officer was guilty of any misconduct in his mode of serving the warrant, he may perhaps have rendered himself liable to an action, or indictment; but the fact that intoxicating liquors were found in the safe would not thereby be rendered incompetent as evidence." [1005]

Here we have what appears to be the first sighting of a "rule of nonexclusion" in any American jurisdiction, authored some four generations after ratification of the Bill of Rights. But such is the nature of stare decisis that a string of citations, built upon a weak foundation and following a particular doctrine in a single jurisdiction, can be seen as a bounty of authority within a few decades. [1006]

In 1886, however, when the U.S. Supreme Court delivered the *Boyd* decision (holding that compulsory production of private papers to establish a criminal charge is barred by the Fourth Amendment), there were probably only two decisions in the country—both from Massachusetts—that conflicted with the ruling.[1007] In 1897, the Georgia Supreme Court cited the *Dana/Welsh* citation string for the proposition that a rule of inclusion was "consistently adhered to" in Massachusetts.[1008] By 1909, the South Dakota Supreme Court was able to cite the same string (along with Georgia's ruling) as standing for the proposition that "the great weight of authority seems to be in favor of [inclusion of evidence], without regard to the manner in which it was obtained."[1009]

There were cases in other jurisdictions that went the other way on the same questions.[1010] But by the time of the first edition of Wigmore's *A Treatise on the System of Evidence in Trials at Common Law*, in 1904, Wigmore was able to rope together a formidable citation string, which he presented as evidence that *Boyd* represented an "unsatisfactory opinion"[1011] and a "dangerous heresy"[1012] against settled common law. Wigmore also began mixing the Massachusetts and New Hampshire citations with precedents that were barely on point and packing all of them into an ever-expanding footnote in his many books and essays.[1013] By the time of Wigmore's famed 1922 anti-exclusion article in the *ABA Journal*, his footnote had grown to cover parts of five pages and contained citations to more than 100 cases.[1014] Such a formidable wall of precedents supposedly showing *Boyd* to be "thoroughly incorrect in its historical assertions"[1015] ensured that all but *Boyd*'s most intrepid defenders would be dissuaded from checking Wigmore's citations, lest a week be lost in a law library.

But the devil is always in the details, and Wigmore's footnote contained much slimmer support for his claims than its length suggested. A large number of the cases cited by Wigmore, for example, merely distinguished the Supreme Court's *Boyd* or *Weeks* rules from their given facts and, thus, followed the rule of exclusion implicitly.[1016] Some of the cases announced exceptions to the exclusionary rule, such as the search-incident-to-arrest[1017] or consent exceptions,[1018] thus upholding exclusion by implication. One of Wigmore's cited cases involved a lawyer who expressed regret over voluntarily surrendering deed papers to a party in civil litigation without asserting a work-product privilege or other defense.[1019] Another case upheld the admission of a book of tax records over objections that the book did not state exact dates or precisely match an indictment.[1020] One involved litigation over a coroner making an unauthorized autopsy.[1021] Others were civil cases in which one party objected unsuccessfully to discovery violations.[1022] Many were simply cases where defendants unsuccessfully asserted a privilege or unsuccessfully objected to the admission of evidence on non-Fourth-Amendment grounds.[1023] Still others supported exclusion, and Wigmore cited to them as a concession.[1024]

Like an appellate brief written by a shrewd litigator, Wigmore's impressive-looking footnote concealed as much as it illuminated.[1025] In 1922, even after twenty years of researching the question, Wigmore could identify no law on the subject in more than one-quarter of the states.[1026] Wigmore misstated, deliberately it would seem, the holdings in some of the cases he cited.[1027] Some states cited by Wigmore (e.g., Maryland[1028] and Michigan[1029]) switched from recognizing an exclusionary rule to admit-ting illegally seized evidence in the wake of Wigmore's initial writings[1030]—contrary to Wigmore's assertion that "the heretical influence" of *Boyd* and *Weeks* was spreading "a contagion of sentimentality in some of the State Courts, induc-ing them to break loose from long-settled fundamentals."[1031] Significantly, some jurisdictions that switched from an exclusionary rule to an inclusionary rule even cited Wigmore's assertions among their grounds for doing so.[1032]

More significantly, only a small handful of Wigmore's cases were ren-dered prior to the 1886 *Boyd* decision, which anti-exclusionists claim defied the "universal law" of the nineteenth century.[1033] Even Massachusetts and New Hampshire had adopted their rules of nonexclusion fairly recently at the time of the *Boyd* decision and rather tepidly at first. Initially, their courts merely distinguished then-prevailing legal standards (e.g., those laid out in 1765 in *Entick v. Carrington*) or cited their own dicta or English cases that were not on-point.[1034] The law in the other states was unsettled, and in a state which Wilson Huhn describes as pre-decided.[1035]

Yet for generations after the first publication of Wigmore's writings, scholars have cited them for the proposition that some vast body of jurispru-dence of the nineteenth century recognized an inclusionary rule. Professor Amar, building on Wigmore's arguments, alleged the existence of a "universal law against exclusion," which supposedly prevailed in the mid-1800s.[1036] Yet Wigmore conceded that prior to the twentieth century, criminal defendants who "had occasion to invoke the Fourth Amendment" as a bar to seizure and admission of physical evidence were "limited in number."[1037] It was only with Prohibition and the government's drive to convict people of victimless crimes such as selling liquor that the Fourth Amendment "suddenly came into wide and frequent" application.[1038]

It must be recognized that with the exception of John Wigmore's writings, anti-exclusion scholarship was fairly sparse until the second half of the twentieth century.[1039] Most legal scholars of the late 1800s and early 1900s were far less likely than Wigmore to express the opinion that the exclusionary rule represented a radical revolution in criminal justice practices. Although today's anti-exclusionists regard Wigmore's assertions as representative of the scholarship of his day, Wigmore's bold procla-mations were in fact criticized at the time.[1040] Someone on the Michigan Supreme Court must have spent a few hours checking Wigmore's citations in preparation for a 1919 opinion. The Court, in *People v. Marxhausen*, cast a doubtful eye upon his assertions:

There has been some criticism of the *Boyd* Case by courts and writers, who have regarded it as not in accord with a long line of cases in state courts [citing Wigmore's principle cases].... .

We are impressed, however, that a careful consideration of the *Boyd* Case, in connection with the *Adams* Case and the decisions of the state courts, some of which are cited above, but many of which are not, taken in the light of what was said by the court in the *Weeks* Case, demonstrate that in the main the United States Supreme Court and the courts of last resort of the various states are in accord, and that the *Boyd* Case does not conflict, as its critics claim, with the holdings of the many state courts. [1041]

Consider also Osmond K. Fraenkel's 1921 critique: "the connection between the privilege against self-incrimination and the right to be free from unreasonable searches is much closer than the critics of the [*Boyd*] opinion [meaning Wigmore] concede."[1042] Fraenkel pointed out that the connection between the two principles was prominent in the pamphlets that accompanied the *Wilkes* and *Entick* cases, with which the Amendment's drafters and rati-fiers were familiar. [1043] Wigmore's contention that the Fourth Amendment was not intended to aid "the guilty"—now the stock-in-trade of all anti-exclusion scholarship—was also discredited by Wigmore's contemporaries.[1044]

As Justice Potter Stewart observed in a 1983 speech, none of the Supreme Court decisions credited with creating the exclusionary rule included much discussion about *whether* the exclusionary rule should exist.[1045] They assumed it should. Nor were there dissents in any of those cases in which any justice scolded his colleagues for abandoning a long-settled "common law rule of nonexclusion."[1046]

It was until the 1970s before any member of the Supreme Court wrote that the exclusionary rule represented a novel abandonment of long-standing nineteenth-century black-letter law. [1047] What the cases cited by Wigmore illustrate is not that exclusion was a radical departure from the settled law of the late nineteenth century, but that the law governing illegally seized physical evidence was unsettled and developing during the period. The sparse record of regional trial practices in the early republic yields scant basis to make any categorical statements about early evidentiary practices. And because appellate courts rarely ruled on criminal trial evidence decisions during the 1800s, there were no rules at all in many jurisdictions, other than the exclusion-implicating rules mandated by the law of pretrial habeas corpus and the mere-evidence doctrine. It was only after 1914 that some state appellate courts began ruling one way or the other on the specific question of whether to exclude wrongfully seized physical evidence, either following *Weeks* or declining to follow it. Many state jurisdictions had only a few binding search and seizure interpretations before *Mapp* closed off all nonexclusionary options in 1961.[1048]

Early American criminal evidentiary remedies went for the most part unrecorded and unreviewed. What we do know of such remedies supports, rather than undermines, the notion that early American judges applied exclusion where evidence was taken illegally by state actors. The very first U.S. Supreme Court decisions to consider the meaning of the Fourth Amendment ordered criminal defendants discharged before trial on Fourth Amendment grounds.[1049] The earliest Supreme Court decision to construe the Fourth Amendment's applicability to physical evidence applied an exclusionary rule.[1050] Pre-Founding statements by judges and commentators indicating that illegal seizure of evidence merited exclusion, or the vitiation of subsequent criminal prosecutions, brought no recorded challenge.[1051] By contrast, there was no known opposition to this position during the Founding period.

All of this means that exclusionary remedies were unquestionably among the originally intended remedies of the Fourth Amendment. Although modern-day anti-exclusion scholars claim that the Constitution's Founders lived in a world where exclusion of evidence on search or seizure grounds was unknown, or even that a rule of nonexclusion prevailed during the Founding and antebellum periods, the exact opposite is true. Late eighteenth-and early nineteenth-century courts routinely discharged victims of search and seizure violations from custody. The proposition that search and seizure protections were closely allied with silence rights (and hence exclusionary principles) is supported by a number of sources in the political and legal discourse of the Founding period. In contrast, court holdings that explicitly rejected the notion of Fourth Amendment (or state corollary) exclusion were rare phenomena in the American states prior to the U.S. Supreme Court's exclusion ruling in *Boyd v. United States* in 1886. Such holdings arose in only two state court systems, during a 40-year period from the 1850s to the 1890s. Moreover, the legal-historical record strongly supports the proposition that these two regional lines of pre-*Boyd* nonexclusion cases represented departures from the common law known to the Founding generation and their understandings of search and seizure provisions in the federal Constitution and early state constitutions.

Chapter Six

THE RISE AND FALL OF THE AMERICAN JURY[1052]

The Framers of the Federal Constitution considered trial by jury to be so important to individual liberty that they enshrined the right in no fewer than three provisions[1053] (four if you count the Fifth Amendment *Grand Jury* Clause[1054]):

"The Trial of all Crimes, except in Cases of Impeachment, shall be by Jury; and such Trial shall be held in the State where the said Crimes shall have been committed; but when not committed within any State, the Trial shall be at such Place or Places as the Congress may by Law have directed." **U.S. Constitution, Article III, Section II.**

"In all criminal prosecutions, the accused shall enjoy the right to a speedy and public trial, by an impartial jury of the State and district where in the crime shall have been committed, which district shall have been previously ascertained by law" **U.S. Constitution, Sixth Amendment.**

"In Suits at common law, where the value in controversy shall exceed twenty dollars, the right of trial by jury shall be preserved, and no fact tried by a jury, shall be otherwise reexamined in any Court of the United States, than according to the rules of the common law".
U.S. Constitution, Seventh Amendment.

Juries "were at the heart of the Bill of Rights" in 1791.[1055] Indeed, as Yale Law Professor Akhil Amar recounts, the entire debate at the Philadelphia convention over the necessity of a bill of rights "was triggered when George Mason [mentioned] . . . that 'no provision was yet made for juries in civil cases.'"[1056] Jury trial was so important to the ratification of the Constitution that five of six states that advanced amendments during their ratifying conventions included *two or more* jury-related proposals.[1057] Indeed, the *only* right secured in all state constitutions penned between 1776 and 1787 was the right to jury trial in criminal cases.[1058]

It can even be said that infringement upon the right to jury trial *instigated* the American Revolution.[1059] The Declaration of Independence condemned the Crown for "depriving us, in many cases, of the benefits of trial by jury" and "transporting us beyond Seas to be tried for pretended offenses," while protecting government officials "by a mock Trial" (*i.e.*, without local juries) for murders they committed against the colonists.[1060] The earlier revolutionary documents, such as the 1774 Declaration of Rights of the First Continental Congress and 1775 Declaration of the Causes and Necessity of Taking Up Arms,[1061] also invoked the denial of trial by jury as foremost among the grievances of the American colonists.[1062] John Adams' Braintree, Massachusetts Resolutions against the Stamp Act exclaimed that, "In [the admiralty courts hearing Stamp-Act prosecutions], one Judge presides alone!" and "No Juries have any Concern there!"[1063]

According to Supreme Court Justice Hugo Black, the British Crown's various efforts to deprive British subjects' right to jury trial between the fifteenth and seventeenth centuries may even have caused the colonization of North America by embittered Englishmen during that period.[1064] Thus, wrote Black, the denial of jury trial "led first to the colonization of this country, later to the war that won its independence, and, finally to the Bill of Rights."[1065]

THE PRESENT-DAY JURY IS A "SHADOW OF ITS FORMER SELF"

But the high regard in which the Framers held the right to jury trial has not been passed down to contemporary policymakers. The jury trial provisions of the Constitution—provisions which the Founders fought a bloody eight-year war against their own government to reestablish—have been increasingly marginalized and rendered impotent by the precedents underpinning contemporary American criminal procedure. As Amar writes, "the present-day jury is only a shadow of its former self."[1066] Today the right to jury trial has been (1) eliminated in the vast majority of criminal cases due to the ubiquitous practice of plea bargaining (which was unknown to the Framers of the original Constitution), (2) marginalized by confinement to only cases exposing defendants to more than six months imprisonment (a proposition at odds with the plain language of the Constitution),[1067] and (3) increasingly controlled through the elimination of juries of the vicinage, as federal trial practice has moved more federal criminal litigation into the largest metropolitan centers of federal court districts.[1068]

But by far the most profound limitation placed upon jury trials by modern practice involves the transformation of jurors from deciders of both the law and the facts into mere evaluators of facts. This seemingly subtle change has wrought drastic ramifications upon the development of the law during the past century.[1069] Indeed, it may be said that the elimination of the jury's traditional lawfinding role has paved the way for a wholesale enlargement of government in American personal affairs. Today's gargan-tuan criminal justice landscape, with its hundreds of penal institutions and expansive offender registries, could not have been possible but for the jury's decreased role as a check on the power of the state. And because juries are no longer allowed to openly cast votes against bad laws, the criminal codes of every American jurisdiction have exploded in length, triviality, and complexity.

As American history has progressed, Americans have looked with increasing trust toward the courts—especially the U.S. Supreme Court— as a primary protector of their constitutional liberties. This trust has been mostly betrayed.[1070] Moreover, even a cursory review of the original meanings behind the Constitution's jury provisions reveals that such trust in judges was never intended by the drafters of the Constitution.

The Framers viewed judges as equals to laymen with regard to knowledge of the law.[1071] Common citizens of early America were known to have been highly interested in and knowledgeable about legal issues. Nearly 2,500 copies of Blackstone's *Commentaries* were sold in the colonies in the ten years prior to the Revolution.[1072] Edmund Burke famously stated that "[i]n no other country perhaps in the world is the law so general a study."[1073] Many American court systems did not even require that judges be lawyers. [1074] "In several jurisdictions, lay judges presided in the courts long beyond the revolutionary period."[1075] A blacksmith served on the highest court in Rhode Island from 1814 to 1818.[1076] The chief justice of the same court from 1818 to 1826 was a farmer.[1077] In New Hampshire, ministers, merchants, and farmers served on the state supreme court in the early years of the Republic.[1078]

Early colonial judges worked mostly as administrators, providing a wide variety of clerical and routine municipal duties. According to Jack Rackove, one of the foremost authorities on the original intent of the Constitution:

When courts exercised their properly judicial (as opposed to adminis-trative) functions, *the decision-makers were juries.* The most striking feature of colonial justice was the bare modicum of author-ity that judges actually exercised. "Americans of the prerevolutionary period expected their judges to be automatons who mechanically applied immutable rules of law to the facts of each case . . . . The compe-tence of the jury *extended to matters of law and fact alike,* and juries used this authority freely. In cases tried before panels of judges, a jury might hear multiple explanations of the relevant law from judges speaking seriatim, as well as from the rival attorneys. It was then free to decide the case on any basis it chose, and though appeals could be taken from its decision, the devices that English judges could use to set unreasonable jury verdicts aside were left largely untapped in America. Only rarely were colonial juries lim-ited to reaching spe-cial verdicts in which they decided narrow ques-tions of fact, leaving the legal consequences of their findings to the bench; far more often they rendered general verdicts resolving questions of law and fact at once.[1079]

Even more significantly, judges were viewed as inherently suspicious.[1080] Judges were identified as being aligned with the intrusive state, and unlikely to challenge other government officials.[1081] "Judges, unincumbered by juries," wrote An Old Whig in 1787, "have been ever found much better friends to government than to the people. Such judges will always be more desirable than juries to . . . those who wish to enslave the people . . . ."[1082] "A Democratic Federalist," a pseudonymous writer in 1787, wrote that "a lordly court of jus-tice, [is] always ready to protect the officers of government against the weak and helpless citizen."[1083]

Corrupt and government-supremacist judges had been among the major grievances of the American Revolutionaries, and the court practices of early America had enshrined the Founders' general suspicion and distrust of judges as much as of government generally.[1084] "In ten of the thirteen col-onies, the sitting chief justice or his equivalent ultimately chose George III over George Washington" during the Revolution.[1085] After the Chief Justice of Massachusetts, Thomas Hutchinson, indiscriminately enforced provisions of the hated Stamp Act on American colonists, he went home one evening to find his home had been chopped to pieces by a hatchet-wielding mob.[1086] This and other attacks on early Tory judges reflected an intense and widespread anti-judge sentiment in early American law.[1087]

JURY NULLIFICATION SUGGESTED FROM CONSTITUTIONAL TEXT

The right to jury trial makes its entrance in the Constitution in Article III, Section 2.[1088] Article III, laid out only in only the barest of framework,[1089] is the section of the Constitution that creates the federal judiciary. Numerous scholars have suggested that the incongruous placement of the right within Article III was intended to impose a separation of powers in judicial adjudications similar to the division of the legislative branch into two chambers.[1090] "Analogies between legislatures and juries abounded" in the ratification debates.[1091] Juries composed of the people were the "lower judicial bench" in a bicameral judiciary, according to John Taylor, writing in 1814.[1092] As the "lower judicial bench," early jurors could both make and pass judgment on the law. "The judicial structure," noted Amar, "mirrored that of the legislature, with an upper house of greater stability and experience and a lower house to represent popular sentiment more directly."[1093]

The jury was to have an independent role of interpreting the Constitution which was to rival that of the judiciary.[1094] One could easily say that trial by jury was introduced in Article III as the most important limitation on the judicial branch of government.[1095] The fact that only a jury and not a judge could determine guilt reflected the Framers' intent that government operations against the populace be at the sufferance of the people at large rather than by the wisdom or divine right of rulers.[1096]

By contrast, there are _no_ provisions in Article III, or anywhere in the Constitution, that say that judges are to have the final power of interpreting the law. Article III speaks only of "the judicial Power" and says in Section 2 that juries—as much as or more than judges—wield this power in the "trial of all crimes."[1097] Indeed, both Federalists and Anti-Federalists intended that judges would not be the final arbiters of the meaning of laws. When Anti-Federalists criticized the proposed Constitution for granting too much power to untrustworthy judges,[1098] Federalists insisted that the Constitution would do no such thing.[1099] In *Federalist No. 78*, Hamilton assured critics that Article III would not "suppose a superiority of the judicial to the legislative power; it only supposes that *the power of the people is superior to both.*"[1100]

Roger I. Roots

The jury's true constitutional role—as a check on government rather than a mere evaluator of evidence—can also be seen in the centrality of jury power shown by the *non-jury* provisions of the Bill of Rights.[1101] The double jeopardy clause of the Fifth Amendment, for example, places in the jury's hands the ability not only to nullify a law's application but to effectively end the government's prosecutorial attack on a fellow countryman altogether. "[T]he hard core of the double-jeopardy clause is the absolute, unquestionable finality of a properly instructed jury's verdict of acquittal, even if this verdict is egregiously erroneous in the eyes of judges."[1102]

The double-jeopardy clause has two major aspects: it not only stops the government from pursuing another trial; it stops the legal system itself— with all its wise and learned lawyers and judges, and its armed bailiffs and marshals—from reconsidering the defendant's "guilt" in any *appeal* or appeal-like process.[1103] Thus, the jury represents a material obstruction to the power of judges and other government authorities.

Theophilus Parsons, first Chief Justice of Massachusetts, explained the power and eminence of juries this way in 1788:

[T]he people themselves have it in their power to resist usurpation, without being driven to an appeal to arms. An act of usurpation is not obligatory; it is not law; and any man may be justified in his resistance. Let him be considered a criminal by the general government, yet only his fellow citizens can convict him; they are his jury, and if they pronounce him innocent, not all the powers of Congress can hurt him; and innocent they certainly will pronounce him, if the supposed law he resisted was an act of usurpation.[1104]

The intent that juries be empowered to nullify usurpatious laws is also plainly indicated by the fact of the right to jury trial itself. Article III, Section 2 plainly states that "[t]he trial of all crimes . . . shall be by jury."[1105] The Sixth Amendment commands that "[i]n all criminal prosecutions, the accused shall enjoy the right . . . [to jury trial]."[1106] This right applies even to cases where evidence of factual "guilt" is overwhelming or unchallengeable.[1107] In a case where criminal acts are recorded by a dozen surveillance cameras, or where a hundred neutral and disinterested people saw the accused commit the crime, why offer him a jury trial at all? Or when a criminal defendant openly

116

admits under oath on the witness stand that he commit-ted every element of an offense, why grant him the right to be acquitted by a jury at all?[1108]

The answer lies in the Framer's fundamental distrust of government power, and ultimately, in the Framers' intention that jurors act as buffers between the government and their neighbors. The Framers saw the jury as "the ultimate check against a tyrannical government."[1109] By design, any defendant is enti-tled to a chance to be acquitted by a jury even where evidence of guilt is vast, insurmountable, and undisputed.[1110] As the Supreme Court wrote in *Gregg v. Georgia*, any legal system that would rob jurors of their discretion would be "totally alien to our notions of criminal justice."[1111]

The U.S. Supreme Court (and virtually all the highest courts in every state) have interpreted the right to jury trial to forbid special verdicts that require jurors to describe the reasons for their verdicts or to provide any information about their votes.[1112] This right of jurors to issue a "general verdict"—a myste-rious one- or two-word statement, with no record or account of what grounds the verdict was based on, or the degree of the jury's agreement—flows from the right of juries to deliberate in secret.[1113] Because no jury ever has to answer for its verdict after rendering it, jury nullification survives in the face of all governmental attempts to stamp it out. Juries have an inherent "veto power" that can be brought into use to protect a member of their community from any criminal prosecution.[1114]

THE HISTORICAL LANDSCAPE OF JURY NULLIFICATION IN EARLY AMERICA

All of this discussion yields the conclusion that the Constitution's Framers intended the provisions of the Constitution described above to enshrine the absolute power of juries to acquit a factually guilty defendant, and to deter-mine both the law and the facts in jury trials. That the Constitution's Framers intended jury trial to represent a check on government power rather than a mere fact-finding device is also resoundingly clear from the historical record.[1115] Early precedents allowed lawyers to make legal arguments to juries, and allowed juries to nullify unjust laws.[1116] The only Supreme Court Justice ever impeached, Samuel Chase, was impeached in part for giving a jury instruction suggesting a jury must follow a judge's instructions on the law.[1117]

The Constitution's Framers disagreed over many issues of criminal pro-cedure but were in uniform consensus that juries had constitutional power to decide both the law and the facts in their final determinations.[1118] In *Georgia v. Brailsford*,[1119] the first jury trial ever held before the Supreme Court, Chief Justice John Jay's jury instruction stated plainly that "you [the jury] have nevertheless a right to take upon yourselves to judge of both, and to determine the law as well as the fact in controversy."[1120] "[I]t is presumed, that juries are the best judges of fact; it is, on the other hand, presumable, that the courts are the best judges of the law. But still both objects are lawfully within your power of decision."[1121]

Even a casual glance at the statements of the Framers regarding jury independence yields a record that belies the later marginalization of juries as mere citizen factfinders.[1122] The Founders viewed jurors as participants in the political system no less than senators or congressional representatives.[1123] Some Framers suggested the jury "could function like a sitting constitutional convention, an authoritative interpreter of the meaning of constitutional documents."[1124] The Framers repeatedly spoke of juries as playing a role of spoiler in the judicial branch, protecting local citizens against arbitrary acts of government power.[1125]

In *The Complete Anti-Federalist*, The Federal Farmer declared that if judges tried to "subvert the laws, and change the forms of government," jurors had a right to "check them, by deciding against their opinions and determinations."[1126] "If the conduct of judges shall be severe and arbitrary, and tend to subvert the laws, and change the forms of government," the Federal Farmer continued, "the jury may check them, by deciding against their opinions and determinations, in similar cases."[1127] Tocqueville wrote in the 1830s that "[t]he jury is, above all, a political [and not merely a judicial] institution . . . . The jury is that portion of the nation to which the execution of the laws is entrusted, as the legislature is that part of the nation which makes the laws."[1128]

"Jury nullification," or rather, the right of jurors to check the power of government by acquitting a factually "guilty" defendant, was approved by all of America's foremost founding fathers. Amar notes that "the writings of some of the most eminent American lawyers of the age—Jefferson, Adams, Wilson, Iredell, and Kent, to mention just a few"—cast approval of the nullification right of juries.[1129] John Adams stated that "it would be an 'absurdity' for jurors to be required to accept the judge's view of the law, 'against their own opinion, judgment, and conscience.'"[1130]

Maryland delegate Luther Martin, one of the leaders of the Anti-Federalist revolt that led to the ratification of the Bill of Rights, observed that the jury trial provided a vital means of checking the ten-dencies in government toward tyranny.[1131] Trial by jury forced the government to bring its claims against a panel of common people before it could enforce unjust laws, said Martin. "It would be difficult," writes historian Saul Cornell, "to overstate the importance of trial by jury in the minds of Anti-Federalists like Cincinnatus [Arthur Lee] or Martin."[1132] Such voices ensured that the right to jury trial—as a true check on the power of government and not a mere fact-finding device—would enjoy the highest station among all of the principles of American constitutional law.

JURIES VERSUS JUDGES

The Framers and Founders were quite explicit that they viewed trial by jury as necessary to thwart and obstruct *judges*, not merely prosecutors with weak cases.[1133] Eldridge Gerry—an important Framer and delegate to the debates in Philadelphia who later refused to sign the Constitution because it did not contain a bill of rights[1134]—insisted that jury trials were necessary to guard against corrupt judges.[1135] Alexander Hamilton echoed this concern in *Federalist No. 83*, when he wrote that "[t]he strongest argument in its [trial by jury's] favour is, that it is a security against corruption." [1136] John Adams famously remarked that it was a juror's duty to "find the verdict according to his own best understanding, judgment and conscience, though in direct opposition to the direction of the court."[1137] One of the most articulate voices among the Anti-Federalists during the ratification period—the Federal Farmer[1138]—noted that the jury trial provisions of the proposed bill of rights were intended to "secure to the people at large, their just and rightful controul (sic) in the judicial department."[1139]

But if jurors were intended to control the "judicial department," the subsequent two centuries of jurisprudence have effectively divested them of their rightful control. In most American jurisdictions today, judges instruct juries that that they are required to follow the judge's interpretation of the law and "must find the defendant guilty" if the prosecution proves its case by proof beyond a reasonable doubt.[1140] Many judges will not even allow a defense attorney to argue for nullification (or even to inform jurors of their power to nullify) during closing arguments.[1141]

Roger I. Roots

This reversal of fortunes—the placement of judges' prerogatives above juries' interpretations of the law—has had major impacts on the development of American law. Today's fabric of criminal codes is both lengthier and more complicated than it would be if jurors were instructed of their right to nullify inequitable laws. This is because modern lawmakers no longer generally worry over whether their enactments can be sold to and understood by lay jurors. The ancient maxim that ignorance of the law is no excuse[1142] may have been workable in an era when it was at least conceptually possible to know what the law was. But today's criminal and regulatory statutes—with their many sections and subsections, their exception clauses and their complicated application provisions—make the law a great mystery even to the most learned legal scholars. Even the finely honed legal minds on the nation's highest courts regularly disagree over what the law is.[1143]

WHAT HAPPENED?
Any review of the historical record illustrates that the courtroom practice that prevailed before, during, and for generations after the founding of the United States allowed jurors to be informed of their power to defy legislatures, prosecutors and judges by acquitting defendants who were factually "guilty."[1144] This begs the question: when and where did the notion that juries may be restricted to deciding only issues of fact originate? Amar cites the 1851 case of *United States v. Morris*,[1145] in which the Federal Circuit Court of the District of Massachusetts prevented counsel from arguing the constitutionality of a statute to a jury on the ground that the jury had no right to decide law.[1146] Clayton Conrad cites the New Hampshire case of *Pierce v. State* (1843)[1147] as the first recorded case upholding the denial of a jury to openly determine the law.[1148] A Massachusetts decision limiting the rights of juries in 1845 closely followed upon the heels of *Pierce*.[1149]

It is evident from reading the writings of lawyers, judges, and commentators contemporary to the founding period, however, that the conceptual framework for the change was established well before the end of the eighteenth century.[1150] Jack Rackove states that by the mid-1700s, "a movement to restrict the law-finding power of juries and enlarge that of judges was well under way in England," and Americans were well aware and contemptuous of that movement.[1151] When John Adams wrote a rough draft of an essay on juries in his diary on February 12, 1771, he indicated that he was beginning to hear "[d]octrines, advanced for law, which if true, would render Juries a mere Ostentation and Pageantry and the Court absolute Judges of Law and Fact."[1152]

Supreme Court Justice Joseph Story began undermining (or at least criticizing) the power of juries to determine the law while sitting as a trial judge in a federal circuit case as early as 1835.[1153] Debate on the topic flourished during the latter half of the nineteenth century. This was the period when formal lawyers' bar associations were ascendant, and the practice of law was slowly transforming from a domain of laypersons and informal apprenticeships into a profession dominated by formally-educated attorneys.[1154]

There is a wise aphorism that hard cases make bad law.[1155] And like many other jurisprudential trends against Americans' liberties, the gradual loss of Americans' right to have juries of common people review the enactments and predations of the state occurred through a series of close votes, split decisions and accidents of legal history.[1156] In 1894, three murder defendants named Herman Sparf, Hans Hansen, and Thomas St. Clair stood trial in the U.S. District of Northern California for the bloody murder of a fellow mariner on the high seas. St. Clair seemed to have been the actual hatchet man, as a bloody hatchet was found beneath his bunk.[1157]

In June 1893, St. Clair was tried separately from the other two men. He sought "but one" jury instruction, an instruction on the law of manslaughter.[1158] However, St. Clair had been indicted for capital murder, and the trial judge refused to sanction a manslaughter instruction.[1159] A jury convicted St. Clair of murder and he was sentenced to death.[1160] On appeal in the U.S. Supreme Court, Justice Harlan turned away St. Clair's appeal on the grounds that "[t]he indictment contained but one charge, that of murder." [1161] "[W]hile the jury had the physical power to find him guilty of some lesser crime," concluded Justice Harlan, "[t]he verdict of 'Guilty' in this case will be interpreted as referring to the single offense specified in the indictment."[1162] The decision upholding St. Clair's conviction and death sentence was issued in May 1894. There were no dissents.[1163]

On the heels of the *St. Clair* trial, Sparf and Hansen stood trial in the same court in San Francisco, for the same offense. Knowing that St. Clair had already received the death penalty, Hansen and Sparf beefed up their own efforts to get the court to issue a manslaughter instruction to the jury. The trial judge refused a request by the defendants to instruct the jury that "the defendants may be convicted of murder, or manslaughter, or of an attempt to commit murder or manslaughter,"[1164] on grounds that the evidence did not suggest such an instruction.[1165] Later requests by the jury for clarification prompted the trial judge to repeat that the evidence gave rise to verdicts of either guilty or not guilty of murder only.[1166] The jury convicted both men of murder.[1167]

The *Sparf and Hansen* verdicts were problematic on several levels, not the least of which was the trial judge's instruction to the jury regarding determinations of facts (*i.e.,* what "the evidence" supposedly suggested). One cannot but conclude that the summary treatment of St. Clair only weeks earlier played upon the minds of both the trial judge and the members of the Supreme Court who considered the fate of Sparf and Hansen. This time, issues of jury prerogatives were emphasized in the briefs to the Supreme Court. And this time, the issue prompted an intense disagreement among the Justices. It appears that a vigorous effort was launched by Justices Gray and Shiras to overturn Sparf's and Hansen's convictions and perhaps even the *St. Clair* decision of seven months before.[1168] "Some of the members of this court, after much consideration and upon an extended review of the authorities," wrote Justice Harlan for the winning plurality, "are of opinion that the conclusion reached by this court is erroneous."[1169]

But Harlan's four-justice plurality won the day, with the assistance of Justice Jackson's mostly unexplained concurrence vote.[1170] The opinion that Justice Harlan authored bobbed and weaved through a fictional fabric of legal history, offering dicta that went far beyond the determination of the issues *Sparf* and *Hansen* presented. Having already ruled that the same trial court was excused for its heavy-handedness in the *St. Clair* trial, the *Sparf* quartet expounded on matters of constitutional theory and design. Much of what Harlan wrote was pure dicta, as the case could have been sustained based on existing precedents upholding judges' refusals to instruct juries regarding lesser-included offenses.[1171] But the plurality suggested that a strict line between judges and juries regarding issues of law and fact had always been universally recognized.[1172] The plurality suggested that much precedent regarding the rights of jurors was mistaken,[1173] that previous judges had not meant what they said, and that decades of case law on the subject had been otherwise misinterpreted.[1174] "A verdict of guilty of an offense less than the one charged would have been in flagrant disregard of all the proof, and in violation by the jury of their obligation to render a true verdict."[1175]

Justice Jackson's concurrence stated only that Jackson "concurs in the views herein expressed," and that the judgment of the lower court "is reversed as to Sparf, with directions for a new trial as to him."[1176] Justices Brewer and Brown dissented on grounds that certain confessions had been properly entered against Sparf.[1177] Justices Gray and Shiras dissented with a competing overview of the glorious history of jury nullification of unjust laws and the traditional judicial instructions that juries had such prerogatives.[1178] The confusing collection of opinions meant that Sparf's conviction was overturned; he was retried and acquitted in 1895.[1179] Hansen and St. Claire were hanged at San Quentin on October 18, 1895.[1180]

The *Sparf* case hardly stands for the proposition that judges need not instruct juries of their power to render a verdict against the evidence; in fact, the trial judge did tell the jury that it had such power.[1181] At most, *Sparf* can be said to stand for the proposition that a judge may tell a jury that in his own opinion, a verdict should confine itself to either guilty or not guilty to the charge under consideration. But there were those dozens of pages of dicta on the dichotomies and distinctions between law and fact and judge and jury.[1182] For generations afterward, judges have cited this four-vote opinion[1183] as support for the proposition that judges are not required to inform jurors of their power to judge both the law and the facts.

Some scholars and judges have even declared that the *Sparf* decision settled the supposed rule mandating that juries be deceived (or at least allowing them to be deceived).[1184] Yet jury instruction practices continue to vary widely from place to place,[1185] and some judges are known to give radically differing jury instructions when compared to fellow judges down the hallways in the same courthouses.[1186] Indeed, some judges refuse to instruct jurors regarding their nullification powers.[1187] The issue and its many variants recurs often in state and federal litigation.[1188]

In 1972, The Court of Appeals for the D.C. Circuit addressed the issue anew in a thirty-six-page split decision in *United States v. Dougherty*.[1189] Circuit Judges Leventhal and Adams voted not to overturn a conviction gained after a jury was not informed of its power to acquit against the evidence.[1190] Chief Judge Bazelon, one of the most influential federal judges in the country at the time, issued a strong dissent in favor of fully informing jurors.[1191] For forty years, the *Dougherty* split decision has reigned as something of the last word on the subject. More than 300 other court opinions have cited the case since 1972.[1192]

But the law is not nearly as settled in the minds of most legal commentators as it is suggested to be among some of the nation's judges. Indeed, the supposed judicial antipathy against fully informed juries finds only modest support in contemporary scholarly literature. American legal scholarship overwhelmingly supports the right (or "power") of juries to issue so-called nullification verdicts. Of approximately 100 published scholarly articles dedicated to the topic over the past decades, at least 80 argue that juries should be fully informed of their powers or that jury nullification verdicts contradicting the instructions of judges are generally beneficial to American society.[1193]

Only a couple dozen legal scholars over the decades have authored detailed articles in support of the current regime of jury disinformation.[1194] Many of those are aligned with the prosecution bar and the "tough on crime" judiciary. But a number of judges have written in favor of jury nullification and fully informed juries.[1195] Even more significantly, it seems that every full-length book that has ever been authored on the subject of jury history or jury practices has favored fully informed juries.[1196]

Today, the Supreme Court routinely authors grand pronouncements of the glories and benefits of jury trial. Yet, these invocations of jury trial as an "inestimable safeguard"[1197] against "judicial despotism,"[1198] "corrupt overzealous prosecutor[s]," and "a spirit of oppression and tyranny on the part of rulers"[1199] are belied by the Court's acquiescence to widespread court practices that purport to limit juries to questions of fact only. Review of facts, of course, rarely produces any fundamental obstacle or check upon the actions of government, and it does not "safeguard" security or "prevent oppression" to the degree suggested by such judicial pronouncements. Additionally, the theft of the jury's traditional right to review all questions of law and fact in criminal cases is rarely reconciled with certain Justices' repeated claim that they apply "originalist" approaches to construction of the Constitution's jury-trial provisions.[1200]

THE PROBLEM OF JURIES DECEIVED

While no scholar could argue that juries are without *power* to nullify laws and acquit factually "guilty" criminal defendants, many judges and prosecutors argue that juries have no *right to be informed* of their power.[1201] Thus, attempts to suppress jury nullification invariably take the shape of arguments that juries be uninformed or outright misinformed about their proper station in the justice system. Some American judges exhibit extreme hostility against juries acting as a check on government. It might be said that jury nullification impedes judges' natural self-interest in maintaining a *de facto* professional monopoly over legal interpretation.

According to jury scholar Andrew D. Leipold, many judges engaged in a tactical and strategic effort to expand their assumed monopoly in the century after the *Sparf v. United States* decision in 1895.[1202] "[T]he debate over nullification has remained surprisingly narrow," writes Leipold.[1203] "Most of the discussion has centered on whether juries should be encouraged to nullify, and in particular on whether they should be told by the judge that they have this power."[1204] "In extreme cases," writes Professor James Joseph Duane, "this judicial hostility even extends to dishonesty."[1205] As Chief Judge Bazelon correctly observed, current law on this topic is tantamount to a "deliberate lack of candor."[1206] In one especially outrageous case, the jury deliberated for hours in a criminal tax case before sending the judge a note asking what jury nullification stood for.[1207] The defendant was convicted shortly after the judge falsely told the jury that "[t]here is no such thing as valid jury nullification," and that they would violate their oath and the law if they did such a thing.[1208] Over a vigorous dissent, the Court of Appeals deemed the instruction proper and affirmed the conviction.[1209]

ARGUMENTS AGAINST FULLY INFORMED JURIES

The practice of deceiving jurors about their nullification powers could not occur but for a sort of mutual understanding among some judges that they must vigorously promote the notion that they (the judges) should maintain a monopoly over matters of constitutional and legal construction.[1210] As already discussed, however, the Framers of the Constitution never intended or foresaw such a monopoly.[1211] The arguments against allowing juries to be informed of their freedom to nullify generally fall into four categories:

(1) the "chaos" argument, or the argument that informed juries might make the law unstable or unpredictable, unlike judges who supposedly do not,[1212]

(2) the claim that juries should not be "mini-legislatures" and be allowed to disturb the sound and wise enactments of learned lawmakers,[1213] (3) the claim that professional lawyers and judges know better the meanings of constitutions

and laws than common people on juries, and (4) the argument that perceptive jurors already know about jury power or can figure it out during jury trials, and thus they need no instruction on the topic.[1214]

The claim that fully informed juries would bring chaos to the law is, of course, inconsistent with known history. Indeed, it is arguable that courts and the imposition of laws have never been more chaotic than they are right now.[1215] Oprah Winfrey was, after all, forced to face trial for defaming hamburgers in 1996.[1216] Schoolchildren have been arrested and/or criminally prosecuted in recent years for participating in food fights at their school cafeterias,[1217] bringing steak knives to school to prepare lunch,[1218] writing on their desks,[1219] and farting in class.[1220] A 12-year-old boy was recently arrested and taken into custody for opening a Christmas present too early.[1221] Four Americans were imprisoned (three for eight years) during the 1990s for innocently importing lobster tails in plastic bags instead of boxes in violation of a complicated federal statute.[1222] A 70-year-old woman was jailed in Orem, Utah for having a brown lawn.[1223] One could easily fill volumes with accounts of similarly selective, trivial, and capricious arrests and prosecutions over the past few years. The loss of the jury as an effective check on the power of the state has wrought a criminal justice system that is subject to few controls and bears little accountability.

Today's police and prosecutors have much more power than the Framers of the Constitution could have ever predicted. They arbitrarily can pursue—or not pursue—any American they select, based on virtually unreviewable criteria. Rewards and punishments in the criminal justice system are handed out utterly haphazardly, mostly in accordance with perceived loyalty to the state.[1224] The primary problems associated with contemporary American criminal justice are over-legislation, overuse of plea-bargaining, mass incarceration, and the growing threat of wrongful conviction. Each of these problems would surely fade if juries were more consistently informed of their lawful role as government spoilers in the court system.

The claim that juries are not supposed to act as "mini-legislatures" or to review the wise statutes of legislators has two answers. First, it is false, as the Framers of the Constitution intended juries to function as "mini-legislatures" in some cases.[1225] As already discussed, the right to jury trial in criminal cases was placed in Article III of the Constitution as the most important limitation upon the federal judiciary. Various Framers indicated that this placement was designed to shape the Judicial Branch into something of a two-tiered structure akin to the two-chambered structure of the Legislative Branch. Voices of the Founding Period indicated that juries were to "function like a sitting constitutional convention."[1226] Jefferson's famous quote that he "consider[ed] [trial by jury] as the only anchor ever yet imagined by man, by which a government can be held to the principles of its constitution" reveals the prevalent view among the Founders that juries were to share powers of constitutional interpretation with judges.[1227]

Second, the sea of statutes and rules the legislative branches of modern American jurisdictions (and sometimes by the executive branches) generate is hardly worthy of such deference. One could easily fill volumes with accounts of the imposition of oppressive, silly, and stupid laws over the past century.[1228] New Jersey still prohibits self-service gas stations by law.[1229] Many jurisdictions make it a criminal offense for automobilists to "cruise" repeatedly through a town's main street.[1230] Lists of stupid laws are frequent fare for comedians and games of trivia.[1231] It may be said that laws have increased in their levels of stupidity and cupidity as juries have become increasingly misinformed about their constitutional powers to nullify their effects.[1232] Many of today's enactments are thousands of pages in length, and most lawmakers do not even read them in their entirety before voting to approve them.[1233] In practice, today's statutes are written by teams of self-interested lobbyists, who may cunningly or even deceptively salt them with ignoble and corrupt features.[1234]

The claim that learned lawyers and judges know better the "true" meanings of statutes and constitutions than common people, even if accurate in a conceptual sense, violates the general rule that laws (especially criminal laws) are to be simple and easily understood by all. The Framers were resounding in their consensus on this proposition. The first volume of the *U.S. Reports* contains a discussion by Pennsylvania Anti-Federalist William Findley regarding the unfairness of laws being solely construed by lawyers and judges. "[E]very man," said Findley, "who possessed a competent share of common sense, and understood the rules of grammar, was able to determine on a bare perusal of the bill of rights and constitution. With these aids, he defied all the sophistry of the schools, and the jargon of the law . . ."[1235] "[I] t would be fatal indeed to the cause of liberty," he continued, "if it was once established, that the technical learning of a lawyer is necessary to comprehend the principles laid down in this great political compact between the people and their rulers."[1236]

The Constitution and the Bill of Rights were pronouncements of natural law, and each person had a right to his own interpretation. "Since natural law was thought to be accessible to the ordinary man, the theory invited each juror to inquire for himself whether a particular rule of law was consonant with principles of higher law."[1237] As Amar writes, the elimination of this one stage of review eliminates an important check on government. "[W]hoever could be obliged to obey a constitutional law, is justified in refusing to obey an unconstitutional act of the legislature," wrote James Wilson. [1238] "When a question, even of this delicate nature, occurs, every one who is called to act, has a right to judge . . ."[1239]

This principle, that the common citizenry rather than any aristocracy of elites were to hold the keys to understanding and interpreting the laws, was widely recognized among the Founding Generation. It was propounded by Federalists as well as Anti-Federalists, lawyers as well as non-lawyers. James Madison wrote in *Federalist No. 62* that "[i]t will be of little avail to the people, that the laws are made by men of their own choice, if the laws be so voluminous that they cannot be read, or so incoherent that they cannot be understood."[1240] Accordingly, jurors were to be the arbiters of legal meanings as much as the most learned jurists on the nation's highest benches. John Adams wrote in his diary in 1771 that "[t]he general Rules of Law and common Regulations of Society, under which ordinary Transactions arrange themselves, are well enough known to ordinary Jurors," as were the "great principles of the [British] Constitution."[1241]

Finally, there is the argument that jurors "already know" or can figure out their powers of nullification and that, therefore, no instruction on such matters is necessary. It was this claim upon which the 1972 *Dougherty* split decision in the D.C. Circuit was largely based, and the same notion has occasionally featured in other decisions. The *Dougherty* majority held that no instructions on nullification needed to be given to jurors because jurors at that time could read between the lines of various jury instructions and know they had the power to nullify.[1242] But as Professor Duane has pointed out, in the years since the *Dougherty* split decision, jury instruction practices in most courtrooms have become decidedly more deceptive, more punitive, and more "indefensible."[1243] During the 1970s, when *Dougherty* was decided, the common practice was for judges to use the word "must" only when instructing jurors to acquit when prosecutors fail to show proof beyond a reasonable doubt. In contrast, the word "should" was used when instructing jurors about their obligations when prosecutors prove their cases.[1244]

But today, many courts have switched to using "must" in both commands. "Contrary to the *Dougherty* court's assumption about what a criminal trial judge would 'never' do," writes Professor Duane, "the United States Judicial Conference has instructed federal judges to tell every criminal jury that 'if you are firmly convinced that the defendant is guilty of the crime charged, you *must* find him guilty.'"[1245] It might even be said that "must convict" jury instructions now prevail in the criminal courts.[1246]

One can scarcely imagine how juries could be further marginalized without abolishing them altogether. Today's juries are routinely ordered to convict when prosecutors prove their cases, in plain violation of the original intent of the Constitution's Framers. Although attempts have been made repeatedly to correct this problem through legislation, citizens' referenda, and court litigation, the contemporary bar and bench has erected an increasing array of barriers to such restorative reforms.

Under the Constitution's original intent, jurors were to act as a check against the power of government rather than as a mere fact-finding device. All of the principal Constitutional Framers, including Madison, Adams, Jefferson, Hamilton, and others, are on record stating that juries were meant to judge both the law and the facts in jury trials. The text of the Constitution itself virtually mandates this construction, with its Double Jeopardy Clause, its requirement that juries be available in "all" criminal cases and prosecutions, and its placement of trial by jury in criminal cases into the structural framework of the Judicial Branch as part of a bifurcated system of justice.

America's contemporary judges have not distinguished themselves as protectors of the people's liberties in the face of encroachments by the political branches of government. To this day, the United States Supreme Court has struck down as unconstitutional only approximately 150 federal statutes.[1247] As laws have multiplied and the predations of government lawyers have become more ambitious, courts have failed to erect material legal barriers to America's growing prison and police state. Never before have so many Americans faced the threat of prison for technical violations of so many nearly incomprehensible laws, and never have fully informed juries been more necessary.[1248]

CONCLUSION

The great German sociologist Max Weber, in his theory of rationalization, postulated that systems of continuing human interaction tend to gradually become more efficient as their mechanizations take on the attributes of a bureaucratic assembly line. Perhaps no area of American life demonstrates the potency of Weber's theory like America's criminal justice system. Indeed, numbers of trials have declined even though numbers of law schools, lawyers, criminal cases and prisons have increased significantly.[1249]

This great transformation in American criminal justice has occurred largely due to popular acceptance among the legal profession of a great modern myth: the myth that America's origins countenanced deductive inquisitorial justice systems that emphasize government "truth-seeking" rather than adversarial systems in which the assertions of the state are subjected to the suspicious scrutiny of judges, jurors and grand jurors. At its heart, this alteration is attributable to what Marc Galanter has called "a shift in ideology and practice among litigants, lawyers, and judges."[1250]

This book has touched on only a few areas of law and practice that illustrate this great transformation. In truth, America's descent into inquisitorialism can be seen not only in criminal litigation *per se* but in certain counterparts of the civil laws. To function properly, a system of justice must offer opportunities for victims of police and prosecutorial overzealousness to sue authorities and recover damages from them.[1251] But the availability of suits for false imprisonment, malicious prosecution, and trespasses by authorities have declined markedly since the Bill of Rights was enacted.

In the early1800s, a justice of the peace could be held liable for ordering imprisonment without taking proper steps.[1252] Any party who sued out or issued process did so at his peril and was civilly responsible for unlawful writs (even if the executing officer acted in good faith).[1253] In 1806, even the U.S. Supreme Court pronounced that justices who improperly allowed authorities to enter a person's house and take away his goods were liable for trespass.[1254] "The court and the officers are all trespassers," wrote the Supreme Court.[1255]

Such rulings would be unimaginable today. The judicial branch has cloaked itself in a vast net of immunity, and extended this immunity to the prosecution bar as well.[1256] While early American law constrained people from hastily making arrests or criminal accusations,[1257] today's criminal pro-cedure greatly incentivizes arrests and prosecutions. While early American law quickly awarded costs to defendants who were acquitted,[1258] today's legal landscape offers acquitted victims little but hurdles and landmines. The incentives and constraints have essentially been flipped upside down.

Again and again we return to the central problem of inquisitorial justice: its placement of decisionmaking power in the hands of elite government authorities. The American judiciary has, over the course of two centuries, assumed powers which the Framers intended to be reserved in the hands of jurors and grand jurors.

Consider the way modern judges discard suits against police officials for malicious prosecution and false imprisonment. In the nineteenth century, every American jurisdiction recognized that arrests and prosecutions that resulted in exonerations or dismissal could subject prosecutors or police to civil liability for false arrest (if warrantless) or malicious prosecution (if an arrest warrant had been issued). But during the twentieth century, police-friendly precedents displaced older precedents, to the point that judges began reserving the question of whether probable cause existed for themselves as a "legal" question.

In Rhode Island, for example, an unbroken chain of precedents extending for more than a century after the Founding required that the question of probable cause in such lawsuits be decided by a jury.[1259] Even where "[t]he facts [supporting probable cause] are practically undisputed," wrote the Rhode Island Supreme Court in 1938,[1260] the determination of whether probable cause existed or did not exist was a question for the jury in a subsequent trial for malicious prosecution. Remember that the most famous civil cases involving wrongful prosecution at the time of America's Founding—the cases of *Wilkes v. Wood, Entick v. Carrington* and *Money v. Leach*—gave the final determination of this question to juries.

But by the late twentieth century, judges in most American states had altered the law to allow judges to summarily dismiss lawsuits if they (the judges) determined that prosecuting officers had acted upon probable cause.[1261] Today's judges intercept and dismiss a high percentage of malicious-prosecution and false-arrest lawsuits before they go to civil trial. Consequently, police authorities are encouraged to make more questionable arrests and pursue more reckless prosecutions. In essence, the most important powers of adjudication and resolution in such matters have become vested in an oligarchy.

So: the history of America's criminal procedure from the birth of the Bill of Rights to the present shows that (1) there has been an increase in both the numbers and prevalence of criminal prosecutions over the course of American history, relative to the growth of population and to the civil docket. (2) As criminal laws have become more numerous and complicated, criminal prosecutions have tended to become more complex, with increased rates of multi-count and multi-defendant prosecutions. (3) American criminal prosecutions have increasingly been driven by armies of government officers and public prosecutors rather than (as the Framers of the Bill of Rights intended) by private lay citizen grand jurors. (4) Rulings by American judges have tended to incentivize prosecutions and expand the surveillance and enforcement powers of government agents.

Moreover, (5) conviction rates have gone up as judges have increasingly instructed jurors that they must follow judicial interpretations of the law and convict defendants whenever prosecutors prove a violation of a statute. (6) Appeals to outside courts—including via mechanisms such as *habeas corpus* or other writs—have become more hopeless. (7) Even the availability of civil remedies against the state appear to have declined as the legal culture has lurched toward the embrace of government supremacy.

---

1 The United States has the highest documented incarceration rate in the world (743 per 100,000 population), Russia has the second highest rate (577 per 100,000), followed by Rwanda (561 per 100,000). At year-end 2007 the United States had less than 5% of the world's population and 23.4% of the world's prison and jail population (adult inmates).

2 U.S. Department of Justice, Bureau of Justice Statistics, Press Release: U.S. Correctional Population Declined for Second Consecutive Year, Thursday, December 15, 2011. http://bjs.ojp.usdoj.gov/content/pub/press/ p10cpus10pr. cfm (accessed March 18, 2012).

3   Lauren E. Glaze, Correctional Population in the United States, 2010 (NCJ 236319).

4   *Id.*

5   ALEXIS DE TOCQUEVILLE, DEMOCRACY IN AMERICA 96 (J.P. Mayer ed., Harper Perennial Books 1988) (1848).

6   *Id.*

7   *Id.* at 72.

8   *See* Reinhard Bendix, Max Weber: an intellectual portrait (1977) (detailing Max Weber's theoretical considerations of bureaucratic organizational structures); From Max Weber: essays in sociology (edited and translated by Hans H. Gerth and C. Wright Mills) (1991) (reprinting translations of Max Weber's essays on bureaucracy and rationalization).

9   It is noteworthy that economic abundance and liberalization worldwide appear to be corresponsive to the acceptance of adversarial models of justice. China, for example, adopted adversarial reforms in its court system in 1996, and its economy has prospered markedly in the years since.

10   Professor Merryman attempts to organize the earth's legal traditions into three categories, civil law, common law, and socialist law. See John Henry Merryman, The Civil Law Tradition 1(1969). The socialist law tradition, according to this view, views "all law [as] an instrument of economic and social policy, and [common and civil law models as reflecting] a capitalistic, bourgeois, imperialist, exploitative society, economy and government." Id. At 4. But the socialist model seems to be mostly an innovation on civil law traditions, with perhaps a greater role for ideological navigation by governing authorities.

11   Roger Lane, Murder In America: A History 335 (1997) ("The revolutionary tradition reflected in the Bill of Rights is not to trust the state, that is, the prosecution, but to check it through vigorous opposition").

12   *Id.*

13   As Blackstone famously wrote, it is "better that ten guilty persons escape than that one innocent suffer," 4 William Blackstone, Commentaries 358. John Adams echoed the same basic idea, saying it is "more beneficial that many guilty persons should escape unpunished than one innocent person should suffer." 1 P. Smith, John Adams 124 (1962).

14   Jenny McEwan, Evidence and the Adversarial Process: The Modern Law 6 (1992) (emphasis in original).

15 *Id.*

16 *Id.* at 6 and 8.

17 *See id.* at 8 (speaking especially of French *juge d'instructions*).

18 *Cf.*, Raymond Li, "*Court convicts, frees waitress who killed cadre*," South China Morning Post, June 17, 2009 at 01 (reporting on the conviction of a waitress who killed a government official who tried to rape her; a law professor is quoted saying the verdict was a compromise the court had to make "to please the higher authorities with a guilty verdict and, at the same time, to heed public sentiment by letting the woman go").

19 Mike P.H. Chu, *Criminal Procedure Reform in the People's Republic of China: The Dilemma of Crime Control and Regime Legitimacy*, 18 UCLA PAC. BASIN L.J. 157, 163 (2001)

20 *See id.* at 166. 21 *Id.*

22 Norman J. Finkel, Commonsense Justice: Jurors' Notions of the Law 52 (1995)

23 *Id.*

24 *See, e.g.*, "Turkey refuses to extradite Hashemi," The Australian, Sept. 12, 2012, p. 12 (reporting Turkey's refusal to send a fugitive defendant back to Iraq after the defendant was convicted of murder and sentenced to death in absentia by an Iraqi court. The defendant pronounced that the Iraqi president's promotion of the verdict was "proof" that the defendant was innocent. Hashemi said his bodyguards were tortured into giving false statements and refused to return for a retrial in Baghdad, accusing Mr Maliki of controlling the judicial system"); Omar Al-Jawoshy and Michael Schwirtz, "Top Iraqi Leader Denounces Death Sentence," *New York Times*, Sept. 11, 2012 ("The whole thing from the beginning was a conspiracy against the Sunnis," said Sheikh Talal Hussain al-Mutar, the head of one of Iraq's main Sunni tribes. "The whole investigation and courts were fake and controlled by the government"); See also "Noose of silence - Iran hangs dissidents for protesting election result," *Daily Telegraph* (Australia), Jan. 30, 2010 (reporting that two anti-government activists were hanged for "waging war against God," try-ing to overthrow the Islamic establishment and being members of armed groups; an additional five protesters were sentenced to die for complaining about the results of an election).

25 *See* Chu, *supra*, at 187 (saying "Most inquisitorial systems, like adversarial systems, incorporate the presumption of innocence but do not invoke

the privilege of the right to remain silent") (citing Nico Jum, Steward Field & Chrisje Brants, Are Inquisitorial and Adversarial Systems Converging?, in Criminal Justice in Europe: A Comparative Study 42, 43 (Phil Fennell et al. eds., 1995).

26 See Stephen C. Thaman, *The Resurrection of Trial by Jury in Russia*, 31 Stan. J Int'l L. 61, 101(1995).

27 See id. ("The practice of supplementary investigation [in Russia] is a vestige of an inquisitorial system which presumes the defendant's guilt and gives law enforcement repeated chances to prove it"). Since the fall of Communism, Russian criminal procedure has become more fair, and trial by jury has become a prominent feature of the system. *See Id.*

28 Chu at 167.

29 Mike P.H. Chu, *Criminal Procedure Reform in the People's Republic of China: The Dilemma of Crime Control and Regime Legitimacy*, 18 UCLA PAC. BASIN L.J. 157, 188 (2001).

30 Andrew Jacobs, *Fast-Paced Trial in China Murder Leaves Shadows*, New York Times, Aug. 9, 2012 (reporting on a 7-hour murder trial hundreds of miles from the location of the alleged offense, in which the defendant was forced to accept a government-appointed lawyer who did not have a chance to review the prosecution's evidence and who called no defense witnesses; the trial was closed to the public and "shown on television only in carefully packaged snippets" providing a "captivating spectacle" aimed at distracting attention "from the political scandal surrounding [the defendant's] husband").

31 See, e.g., Berman, The Cuban Popular Tribunals, 69 COLUM. L. REV. 1317, 1341 (1969), in which a University of Havana law professor describes the role of the modern Cuban defense attorney in the following manner: "[t]he first job of a revolutionary lawyer is not to argue that his client is innocent, but rather to determine if his client is guilty and, if so, to seek the sanction which will best rehabilitate him."

In even starker contrast to our collective sense of fairness, an Iranian ayatollah who was responsible for sentencing hundreds of defendants to death gave the following rebuttal to a criticism about the apparent lack of due process in the Iranian system of justice: "[w]hen [the critic] says some of the verdicts are not based on principle, did he mean Islamic principles or Western principles? Under Western principles the criminals have to have lawyers and other matters to escape the law. Yes, it's true, I never paid attention to these principles." N.Y. Times, Dec. 8, 1980, at 15, col. 1.

32 N.Y. Times, Dec. 8, 1980, at 15, col. 1.

33 The widely publicized Italian trial of American college student Amanda Knox exposed the injustice of the Italian legal system. Ms. Knox and a codefendant were held in jail without charge for over a year before prosecutors indicted them. Adjudications in the case seemed to change with the political winds, as Knox was initially treated very severely and then saw her fortunes rise as worldwide criticism of the proceedings led ultimately to an exoneration. See Rachel Donadio, U.S. Student Delivers Appeal at End of Italian Trial, New York Times, December 3, 2009

34 See, e.g., Reporters sans Frontieres, "Senegal; Editor Jailed for Defaming President's Chief of Staff," Africa News, Aug. 28, 2010 (reporting on a six-month jail sentence imposed by a Dakar court on Abdourahmane Diallo, the editor of the Express News daily, for defaming President Abdoulaye Wade's chief of staff; "Diallo did not appear in court and some local journalists claimed that he never received a summons to appear"). This Day, Falana Petitions Army Chief Over Convicted Soldiers, Africa News, May 18, 2009 (reporting that after 27 Nigerian army officers protested delays in their pay while serving on an ocean vessel, they were prosecuted for mutiny and sentenced to life imprisonment). Reporters sans Frontières, Sudan: Court Imposes Prison Sentences On Three Rai Al Shaab Journalists, Africa News, July 16, 2010 (reporting on a Sudanese criminal court that sentenced three reporters to years of impris-onment for "publishing incorrect information" and "attacking the state with a view to undermining the constitutional system." According to the report, the defense lawyers stopped participating after five days of trial because the court refused to hear testimony from three defense witnesses).

35 Marshall M. Knappen, Constitutional and Legal History of England 317 (1942).

36 Albert K. R. Kiralfy, The English Legal System 183 (Sweet & Maxwell, 1954).

37 See Stroud F. C. Milsom, Historical Foundations of the Common Law 389 (Butterworths, 2d ed. 1981); William S. Holdsworth, A History of English Law 210-11 (1938); Charles Ogilvie, The King's Government and the Common Law 109, 156 (Basil Blackwell, 1958).

38 John H. Baker, An Introduction to English Legal History 137 (2002)

39   Frederic W. Maitland, The Constitutional History of England 263 (Cambridge, 1908).

40   *See* Jay Sterling Silver *"Truth, Justice, and the American Way: The Case Against the Client Perjury Rules,"* 47 Vand. L. Rev. 339, 352-53 (1994).

41   Of course this greatly simplifies the causes of the English Civil War. For a detailed treatment of this topic, see Michael Braddick's *God's Fury, England's Fire: A New History of the English Civil Wars* (2009) or Blair Worden's *The English Civil Wars: 1640-1660* (2010).

42   We owe many of our procedural rights to the advocacy of one man who lived during this period, John Lilburne. Lilburne was an extreme Protestant who was accused of importing "factuous" and "scandalous" (i.e., Puritan) books from Holland and brought before the Star Chamber in1637. *See* Pauline Gregg, Free-Born John: The Biography of John Lilburne 53(2000). Lilburne refused to swear an oath that he would tell the truth, and refused to plead until he was served with a bill of indictment. *Id.* at 56-61. He and another Puritan were declared "guilty of a very high contempt" and Lilburne was sentenced to be whipped through the streets of London and pilloried. *Id.* at 62. Admiration "spread like wildfire through the City." *Id.* at 63. Lilburne's sufferings helped lead the popular charge for abolition of the Star Chamber in 1640. See Jay Sterling Silver's article above.

As events played out, Lilburne came to criticize his fellow Puritans for their own despotism in the execution of justice. Lilburne found himself repeatedly imprisoned and on trial for crimes related to his pamphleteer-ing, and his sup-port among London's dissidents became unbreakable. At least three times, Lilburne faced prosecution and the threat of execution if convicted. He refused to incriminate himself, demanded counsel and copies of charging documents printed in English (not Latin) and suffered extended stays in dungeons and jails. The records of one trial report that upon the verdict of Lilburne's acquit-tal, "immediately the whole multitude of people in the hall, for joy of the Prisoner's acquittal, gave such a loud and unanimous shout as is believed was never heard in Guildhall, which lasted for about half an hour without intermis-sion: which made the judges for fear turn pale and hang down their heads."

43   For example, Camden, New Jersey and Camden Yards, where the Baltimore Orioles play baseball are named for Lord Camden.

44   Arthur H. Cash, John Wilkes: The Scandalous Father of Civil Liberty 252 (2006).

45 *Id.* at 261.
46 *Id.* at 285.
47 *Id.* at 362.
48 Quoted in Daniel R. Coquilette, *First Flower--The Earliest American Law Reports and The Extraordinary Josiah Quincy Jr. (1744-1775)*, 30 Suffolk U. L. Rev. 1, 29 (1996).
49 James Boswell, *View of Great Britain.* The Scots magazine, Volume 51, p. 635 (1789).
50 *Id.* at 634. 51 *Id.*
52 Judith K. Schafer, *Bondage, Freedom & The Constitution: The New Slavery Scholarship and Its Impact on Law and Legal Historiography: Slavery and criminal Sanctions: "Under the Present Mode of Trial, Improper Verdicts are Very Often Given": Criminal Procedure in the Trials of Slaves in Antebellum Louisiana,* 18 Cardozo L. Rev. 635, 636 (1996)
53 Leonard W. Levy, The Palladium of Justice: Origins of Trial by Jury 50-51 (1999).
54 The great sociologist Max Weber documented the power of England's system in *The Protestant Work Ethic.* By protecting property rights and rewarding individual thrift and commercial accumulation, the British rule of law produced wealth and abundance never seen before in human history.
55 There was one major exception among early states: the State of Louisiana. Louisiana was colonized by Frenchmen and Spaniards who brought with them the legal traditions of continental Europe and knew little about living in a world in which the individual was protected by adversarial law. *See* Judith K. Schafer, *Bondage, Freedom & The Constitution: The New Slavery Scholarship and Its Impact on Law and Legal Historiography,* 18 Cardozo L. Rev. 635-636 (1996). "During the Spanish colonial period in Louisiana, crimi-nal law was brutal, torture was legal, and sentences were carried out at the judge's discretion." *Id.* At 636. In 1805, shortly after Louisiana joined the United States, the territorial legislature passed the Crimes Act, mandating a mishmash of criminal procedures that loosely applied "the common law of England" upon the preexisting court procedures of Louisiana. Schafer notes, however, that slaves did not have these common law protections according to the Crimes Act. Louisiana slaves continued to be subject to Spanish court procedures. See id at 637. This was contrary to procedure in most slave states that recognized rights of

Roger I. Roots

slaves to traditional common law procedures when charged with criminal offenses.

56   Robert C. Black, *FIJA: Monkeywrenching the Justice System?*, 66 UMKC L. Rev. 11, 24 (1997) ("Of the twenty-six distinct guarantees in the first eight amendments to the Constitution, fifteen relate directly to criminal procedure").

57   Roscoe Pound, *The Causes of Popular Dissatisfaction with the Administration of Justice*, 29 RE, A.B.A. 395, 404-05 (1906), reprinted in 35 F.R.D. 273, 281 (1964), and in 40 AM. L. Rav. 729 (1906).

58   *Id.*

59   *See, e.g.*, Rex E. Lee, *The Profession Looks at Itself-The Pound Conference of 1976*, 1981 B.Y.U.. L. REV. 737, 738.

60   United States v. Garson, 291 F. 646, 649 (S.D.N.Y. 1923). 61   *Id.*

62   *See* S.J. Schulhofer, *The Future of the Adversary System, 3 Justice Quarterly 83-93 (1986). Resnick, The Declining Faith in the Adversary System*, 13 LITIGATION 1, 4 (1986) (both discussing the consensus of condemnation of pure adversarialism among modern lawyers and judges).

63   *See* Kim Eisler, The Last Liberal: Justice William J. Brennan 21 (2003); Rick Perlstein, Nixonland: The Rise of a President and the Fracturing of America 386 (2008).

64   *See* Christopher Wolfe, The Rise of Modern Judicial Review 292 (1994).

65   *See e.g.*, Warren E. Burger, *Isn't There a Better Way?*, 68 A.B.A. J. 274 (1982); Warren E. Burger, Agenda for 2000 A.D.--Need for Systematic Anticipation, 70 F.R.D. 83 (1976).

66   Warren E. Burger, *Reflections on the Adversary System*, 27 Val. U. L. Rev. 309 (1993) (condemning the adversarial system's high costs and inefficiency).

67   Speech by former Chief Justice Warren Burger before the American Bar Association (Feb. 12, 1984), reprinted in D. SCHRAGER & E. FROST, THE QUOTABLE LAWYER 7 (1986).

68   Jay Sterling Silver, *Professionalism and the Hidden Assault on the Adversarial Process*, 55 Ohio St. L.J. 855, 858 (1994) (describing Chief Justice Burger as "the individual most responsible for the development of the organized bar's present professionalism movement"). Even Burger's vision of professionalism was skewed toward a notion that allegiance to the state was more ethical than commitment to the interests of clients. As Professor Silver points out, the anti-adversarial movement toward "professionalism" masked a legal worldview that devalued individual liberties and exalted the supremacy of the state:

140

According to the ABA Commission on Professionalism, for example, "[t]he Bar should place increasing emphasis on the role of lawyers as officers of the court." Or, as a federal court of appeals judge stressed to law students in a Law Day address: judges and attorneys "must continue to be a team. . . . [A]ll of us owe our highest loyalty to the system." Or, as a state judge proposes in an ABA publication, counsel's "first duty [should be] to the law and to the court. The second duty would be to make a diligent effort to discover the truth. The third and last loyalty would be to the client." Counsel would become less the champion of the accused in the classic tradition of Lord Brougham and more a guardian of the existing social order, thus tilting the delicate adversarial balance of power between the prosecution and defense in favor of the state.

Silver at 863-65 (1994) (citations omitted).
69   While speaking before the Criminal Trial Institute of the District of Columbia Bar in the spring of 1966, Professor Monroe Freedman of Georgetown Law School said that he objected to rules which imposed a duty on a criminal defense attorney to betray his own client if he discovers the client's intention to commit perjury. When Warren Burger (at that time a judge on the D.C. Circuit) and other federal judges read an account of Freedman's remarks in a Washington newspaper the next day, Burger and the other judges instigated disciplinary proceedings against the professor for "express[ing] opinions" inconsistent with the legal profession's principles of ethical conduct. These events are recounted in Jay Sterling Silver's article, *"Truth, Justice, and the American Way: The Case Against the Client Perjury Rules,"* 47 Vand. L. Rev. 339, 352-53 (1994):

Efforts to silence Freedman intensified daily. Through private correspondence with Freedman's dean, Burger's group sought to have the young professor expelled from teaching. One of Burger's law clerks, posing as a "disinterested but incensed" member of the American Civil Liberties Union and writing on personal stationery, even sent a letter to the organization demanding that Freedman be removed as chair of its Washington, D.C. affiliate. The national bar quickly closed ranks as leaders of the profession publicly assailed Freedman's character.

Roger I. Roots

Id. at 353.

70   Bivens v. Six Unknown Narcotics Agents, 403 U.S. 388, 420 (1971) (Burger, C.J., dissenting).

71   Warren E. Burger, *Reflections on the Adversary System*, 27 Val. U. L. Rev. 309 (1993) (providing a relatively watered-down version of his anti-adversarial arguments, in Burger's retirement).

72   *See* Craig M. Bradley & Joseph L. Hoffmann, *Public Perception, Justice, and the "Search for Truth" in Criminal Cases*, 69 S. CAL. L. REv. 1267, 1296-302 (1996)

73   Evan Whitton, *America's English-Style Legal System Evolved to Conceal Truth, Not Reveal It,* The Atlantic, June 14, 2012, http://www.theatlantic. com/international/archive/2012/06/americas-english-style-legal-system-evolved-to-conceal-truth-not-reveal-it/258417/ (accessed 7/20/2012).

74   Harold J. Rothwax, Guilty: The Collapse of Criminal Justice (1996) (jacket cover).

75   Burton Katz, Justice Overruled: Unmasking the Criminal Justice System 4-5, 316 (1997).

76   *See, e.g.,* Robert H. Bork, *The Growth of Originalism*, 24 Academic Questions 135-36 (2011). Some observers credit Bork's 1971 article in the Indiana Law Journal, "Neutral Principles and Some First Amendment Problems," as "widely recognized as having launched modern originalist theory." Joel Alicea, Forty Years of Originalism, Policy Review, June 1, 2012 77   For a detailed discussion of the popularity of originalism among constitutional scholars, *see* Jack N. Rakove, Original Meanings: Politics and Ideas in the Making of the Constitution 1 (1996) (saying that the "jurisprudence of original intention" began sparking political controversy in the mid-1980s). Proponents of originalist methods have generally applied them selectively, and have sometimes justified the enlargement of government law enforcement powers rather than advocating carving them back to levels known to the Constitution's Framers. *See, e.g.,* Roger Roots, *The Originalist Case for the Fourth Amendment Exclusionary Rule*, 45 Gonzaga L. Rev. 1 (2009) (suggesting that much "originalist" scholarship has been typified by dubious pro-government, anti-civil liberties advocacy in the area of criminal justice). 78   *See, e.g.,* Akhil Reed Amar, The Constitution and Criminal Procedure: First Principles 154 (1997); Richard A. Posner, *Rethinking the Fourth Amendment*, 1981 Sup. Ct. Rev. 49, 49 (1982) (stating the premise

that the Fourth Amendment does not protect the interest of a criminal in avoiding punishment for his crime).

79 *Id.*

80 *Cf.* Thomas Y. Davies, *The Fictional Character of Law-and-Order Originalism: A Case Study of the Distortions and Evasions of Framing-Era Arrest Doctrine in Atwater v. Lago Vista,* 37 Wake Forest L. Rev. 239, 273-74 (2002) (documenting the Supreme Court's use of deceptive history to uphold an arrest for a non-jailable seat-belt violation in 2002).

81 To be fair, the originalist movement has produced research of high quality in areas such as Second Amendment law, the meaning of the Constitution's interstate commerce clause and federalism. But the movement's alignment with contemporary "conservative" politics has cast something of a shadow of suspicion over many of its assertions.

82 Many of the most important Founders and Constitutional Framers were gifted trial lawyers, and a thick book could be written of some of the grandstanding tactics they employed in their own practices. For example, in 1792, Patrick Henry and John Marshall teamed together to defend Richard Randolph from charges that Randolph had secretly fathered an infant by his wife's sister and then killed the infant by exposing it to winter weather. Henry and Marshall took advantage of Virginia's law banning Blacks from testifying, and used a combination of theatrics and noisy admonitions to the courtroom audience to win Randolph's acquittal. *See* Richard Brookhiser, Gentleman Revolutionary: Gouverneur Morris: The Rake Who Wrote the Constitution 181-82 (2003). Suffice it to say that the Founders them-selves did not share Warren Burger's view that zealous defense advocacy was unethical or that the duty of a defense lawyer was to deliver evidence smoothly to the courts.

83 *See, e.g.,* Patrick Henry, Speech at the Virginia Ratifying Convention (June 5, 1788), reprinted in The Anti-Federalist Papers and the Constitutional Convention Debates 199, 201 (Ralph Ketcham ed., 1986) (urging Americans to "suspect every one who approaches that jewel [of liberty]" by dint of government authority); Alexander White, To the Citizens of Virginia, Winchester Va. Gazette, Feb. 29, 1788, reprinted in The Origin of the Second Amendment: A Documentary History of the Bill of Rights 1787-1792, at 288 (David E. Young ed., 2d ed. 1995) ("In America it is the governors not the governed that must produce their Bills of Right: unless they can shew the charters under which they act, the people will not yield obedience ... ."); *see also* Thomas

Tredwell, Debates Before the New York Convention (July 2, 1788), reprinted in The Origin of the Second Amendment: A Documentary History of the Bill of Rights, 464, 467 (David Young ed., 2nd ed. 1995) (arguing that Federalist pleas to have faith that political leaders will not violate the rights of citizens were alarming and that "it is proved by all experience, [that suspicion of those in power] is essentially necessary for the preservation of freedom."). . Jefferson wrote in 1798: "in questions of power, then, let no more be heard of confidence in man, but bind him down from mischief by the chains of the Constitution." Adams, in 1772, put it this way: "The only maxim of a free government ought to be to trust no man living with power to endanger the public liberty." Four years later, his wife Abigail memorably echoed the same sentiment in a letter to him: "remember, all men would be tyrants if they could."

84   Leonard Levy, The Origins of the Fifth Amendment, 4-20 (1968). The Inquisitions "left a trail of mangled bodies, shattered minds, and smoking flesh" in the early thirteenth century until canon law developed procedures for dissidents–"guilty" of doctrinal disagreement--to challenge them. *See id.* at 19-21

85   See Michael S. Green, *The Privilege's Last Stand: The Privilege Against Self-Incrimination and the Right to Rebel Against the State*, 65 Brook. L. Rev. 627 (1999).

86   See Robert H. Bork, "Thomas More for Our Season." First Things 94 (June/ July 1999): 17-21 (condemning jury nullification as a "pernicious practice" and suggesting that nullification finds no sanction in original intent and is growing today.

87   That Bork's sentiments regarding jury nullification are inaccurate at least as statements of the Constitution's original meaning is easily refuted. *See* Joan L. Larsen, Originalism and the Jury: Article: Ancient Juries and Modern Judges: Originalism's Uneasy Relationship with the Jury, 71 Ohio St. L.J. 959 (2010) (discussing various dimensions of the issue).

88   *See* Lysander Spooner, An Essay on the Trial by Jury 1, 6 (Boston, Bela Marsh 1852). The constitutional purpose behind the grand jury process was likewise for the "protection of the guilty." Ric Simmons, *Re-Examining the Grand Jury: Is There Room for Democracy in the Criminal Justice System?*, 82 B.U. L. Rev. 1, 48 (2002).

89   *See* Jack N. Rackove, Original Meanings: Politics and Ideas in the Making of the Constitution 300 (1996) "When courts exercised their properly judicial

(as opposed to administrative) functions, the deci-sion-makers were juries. The most striking feature of colonial justice was the bare modicum of authority that judges actually exercised").

90 *See, e.g.*, Williams v. Florida, 399 U.S. 78, 100 (1970) (saying juries interpose the common sense of a community as a shield against overreaching prosecutors and government-inclined judges).

91 *See* Silverglate, *supra*, at 270. The dependence of modern prosecutors on the testimony of rewarded informants starkly differs from practices in early American courtrooms. At one time, an "interested" witness (e.g., a complainant) could not be a witness in that case. State v. Truss, 9 Porter's Rptr, 126 (Al. 1839). "[A]n informant's 'title to the penalty gives him such an interest in the event of the prosecution, as will incapacitate him." Id. at 128 (citing King v. Williams, 9 B.& C. 549; Tulley's case (1 Stange 316) (invalid where the same person was both informer and witness).

92 *See* Roger Rots, *Unfair Rules of Procedure: Why Does the Government Get More Time?*, 33 American Journal of Trial Advocacy 493-520 (2010) (discussing several provisions of the various Federal Rules of Procedure which allow more time for the government to file and respond to pleadings compared to private-sector parties).

93 *See* Alfredo Garcia, *"Toward an Integrated Vision of Criminal Procedure Rights" A Counter to Judicial and Academic Nihilism."* 77 Marz. L. Rev. 1, 2 (1993) (citing Bruce A. Green, *"Power, Not Reason": Justice Marshall's Valedictory and the Fourth Amendment in the Supreme Court's 1990 Term,"* 70 N.C.L. Rev. 373 (1992) (finding that the Supreme Court is inconsistent in its interpretation of the Fourth Amendment, yielding constructions of the Fourth Amendment in each case during one of its terms which benefited the state and limited the rights of individuals). *Cf.,* Wayne R. LaFave, *"The Seductive Call of Expediency": United States v. Leon, Its Rationale and Ramifications,* 1984 U. Ill. L. Rev. 895 (1984) (detailing the Burger Court's hectic push to limit the protections of the Fourth Amendment).

94 Justice John Paul Stevens noted in a1986 dissent that during the previous two and one-half years the Supreme Court had summarily reversed 19 criminal dismissals without briefing, oral argument or hearing. *Florida v. Meyers,* 466 U.S. 380, 386 & n.3 (1986) (Stevens, J., dissenting). Later, in *California v. Acevedo,* 500 U.S. 565 (1991) (Stevens, J., dissenting). Stevens (joined by Thurgood Marshall) recounted that "the Court has heard argument in thirty

Fourth Amendment cases involving narcotics. In all but one, the government was the petitioner. All save two involved a search or seizure without a warrant or with a defective warrant. And, in all except three, the Court upheld the constitutionality of the search or seizure." *Id.*

95 *Colorado v. Connelly*, 474 U.S. 1050, 1052 (1986) (Brennan, J., joined by Stevens, J., dissenting).

96 *See, e.g.,* Christopher Slobogin, *Having it Both Ways: Proof That the U.S. Supreme Court is 'Unfairly' Prosecution-oriented*, 48 Fla. L. Rev. 743 (1996) ("It is no secret that most of the United States Supreme Court's criminal procedure cases in the past two and a half decades have favored the government."). Slobogin points out six important aspects of criminal procedure in which the Supreme Court adopted a certain rationale or approach in support of a prosecution-oriented rule, and then changed the rule when the rule ended up helping the defense--thus 'having it both ways.' Slobogin postulates that 'result-oriented' approach has blatantly forsaken the Court's pretense of neutrality. Other examples: in *United States v. Turkish*, 623 F.2d 769 (2d Cir. 1980), the Second Circuit granted the prosecution a right to present testimony obtained through grants of immunity, but refused to extend immunity to potential defense witnesses; in *Perry v. Leeke*, 488 U.S. 272 (1989), the Supreme Court upheld a trial court's practice of ordering a defense attorney to have no communication with his client during a 15-minute courtroom intercession, in the same trial where at least three prosecution witnesses had been allowed to speak with the prosecutor during similar breaks. (And see also Potashnick v. Port City Construction Co., in which the Fifth Circuit held that in a civil case, a trial judge's ban on communication between defense counsel and client during a series of "breaks and recesses" violated due process. 609 F.2d 1101 (5th Cir. 1980).

97 Harvery A. Silverglate, Three Felonies A Day (2009).

98 *See id.* (discussing the trend among lawmakers of inventing virtual-strict-liability crimes and the practice of judges prohibiting defendants from even arguing they committed acts with innocent intentions.

99 Leipold, *supra,* at 1332. See also United States v. Watts, 519 U.S. 148, 157 (1997) (per curiam) (holding that "a jury's verdict of acquittal does not pre-vent the sentencing court from considering conduct underlying the acquitted charge, so long as that conduct has been proved by a preponderance of the evidence").

100   United States v. Booker, 543 U.S. 220 (2005) (holding—in general and with many conditions and limitations—that any fact that increases a defendant's sentence must be proven to the jury (or to the judge if jury trial has been waived).
101   At least one scholar has described the judicial use for sentencing purposes of acquitted conduct as "judicial nullification" of juries. *See* Fang L. Ngov, Judicial Nullification of Juries: Use of Acquitted Conduct at Sentencing, 76 Tenn. L. Rev. 235 (2009). *See also* Mark T. Doerr, *Not Guilty? Go to Jail: The Unconstitutionality of Acquitted-Conduct Sentencing*, 41 Columbia Human Rights L. Rev. 235 (2009) (detailing the history and illustrating several notorious cases of judicial use of acquitted conduct at sentencing); Farnaz Farkish, *Docking the Tail that Wags the Dog: Why Congress Should Abolish the Use of Acquitted Conduct at Sentencing and How Courts Should Treat Acquitted Conduct after United States v. Booker*, 20 Regent U. L. Rev. 101 (2007) (arguing acquitted-conduct sentencing deprives juries of their rightful role as legitimizer of criminal sanctions).
102   Of course efforts to limit habeas corpus protections had been well underway prior to the Burger Court. See George F. Longsdorf, *The Federal Habeas Corpus Acts Original and Amended*, 13 F.R.D. 407, 418 (1953) (describing various limitations and restrictions on the rules of federal habeas corpus procedure). For example, the enactment of the quasi-habeas statute, 28 U.S.C. Section 2255, altered ancient habeas corpus procedure by directing federal inmates to file post-conviction challenges not in the district where they were held but with the same district (often the same judge) who pre-sided over the inmates' convictions. This change alone has presented untold advantages for the government. "A § 2255 motion could be, in practice almost always was, and still is, handled entirely on paper."
103   Emanuel Margolis, *Habeas Corpus: The No-Longer Great Writ*, 98 Dick. L. Rev. 557, 567 (1994). Margolis continued:

In its haste to convict the "guilty," the majority in *Stone* undermined a major cornerstone of habeas corpus doctrine. It should be noted that the majority did not take issue with the fact that the habeas petitioners were convicted on the basis of unconstitutionally obtained evidence which was nevertheless admitted against them at trial. Thus, the Justices agreed that the defendants were deprived of their Fourth Amendment rights.

Id. at 568.

104   Stone, 428 U.S. at 490.

105   *Id.* at 500. *See also* Margolis, supra, at 584 ("the Supreme Court has persisted in demeaning the constitutional etiology and high purpose of the Great Writ"). It would be impolite to discuss this issue without acknowledging the great influence of yet another anti-adversarial judge, Henry Friendly of the U.S. Second Circuit Court of Appeals. In 1970, Judge Friendly authored an article entitled *"Is Innocence Irrelevant? Collateral Attack on Criminal Judgments,"* 38 U. Chi. L. Rev. 142 (1970). Like so many others, Friendly asked whether too much criminal procedure, especially in the area of habeas corpus law, was focused on procedure rather than substance. "Maximizing protection to persons suspected of crime was hardly [the Framers'] sole objective," wrote Friendly. Accordingly, habeas corpus review of state court convictions should go beyond questions of whether authorities violated the Constitution and deny the writ to those who could not claim to be innocent. The Antiterrorism and Effective Death Penalty Act enacted in 1995 is largely a codification of Friendly's suggestions.

106   The privilege to refuse such evidence to the state was widely recognized throughout American history. *See, e.g.,* Ward v. State, 228 P. 498 (Okla. Crim. App. 1924) (protecting a defendant from having to put on a coat); Turman v. State, 95 S.W. 533 (Tex. Crim. App. 1898) (holding that a defendant cannot be compelled to put a cap on his head); Blackwell v. State, 67 Ga. 76 (1881) (holding privilege from self incrimination extends to defendant refusing to show an amputated arm at trial); State v. Jacobs, 50 N.C. (5 Jones) 256 (1858) (upholding defendant's right to refuse to show himself at trial for and thereby disclose his race).

107   *See, e.g.,* Schmerber v. California, 384 U.S. 757 (1966) (upholding the warrantless taking of fingerprints, voice, and tissue evidence by split decision).

108   *See* Akhil R. Amar, The Constitution and Criminal Procedure, First Principle 67 (1997) (asking "Can anyone now imagine even a single justice voting that government may not use an arrestee by forcing him to submit to photographing, fingerprinting, and voice tests . . . ?").

109   Fiona M. Kolvek, *Search and Seizure - Police Officers Are Not Limited In Making Custodial Misdemeanor Arrests By The Need To Balance The Necessity Of The Arrest With The Individual's Protection From Unreasonable Searches and Seizure,* 12 Seton Hall Const. L.J. 291 (2001) ("Recent decisions

of the Supreme Court have leaned toward a balancing approach where the Court has weighed the government's interests for an arrest versus a citizen's expectation of privacy and the Court's decisions appear to have the scales tipped in favor of the police officer").

110 *See* Robert Dowlut, Bearing Arms in State Bills of Rights, Judicial Interpretation and Public Housing, 5 Saint Thomas L. Rev. 203, 205 (1992) ("Balancing tests and other vague, policy-oriented standards destroy the Bill of Rights as a document of law and make it a policy vehicle").

111 Amy Bach, Ordinary Injustice: How America Holds Court 259 (2009)

112 As Professor Jay Sterling Silver points out, the adversarial process more than a little ancestry to the ancient common-law ordeal of trial by battle. But "we have lost sight of the single redeeming feature of trial by battle: the principle of equality of arms." Jay Sterling Silver, Equality of Arms and the Adversarial Process: A New Constitutional Right, 1990 Wis. L. Rev. 1007 (1990).

113 The first known probation statute authorizing the hiring of a probation officer in Boston was enacted by Massachusetts in 1878. As many as one-third to one-half of all defendants on probation ultimately find themselves being accused of violating probation conditions. Upon such accusations, the defendants often find themselves imprisoned by means of truncated inquisitorial procedures that do not provide for trials by juries.

114 Drug courts, ostensibly aimed at diverting drug prosecutions into tribunals that treat drug offenses in accordance with a rehabilitation-focused "disease theory" of addiction, are increasingly popular in major population areas. Although their procedures vary widely, these courts generally require the defendant to plead guilty or no contest and to waive all legal challenges in exchange for rehabilitation opportunities. But critics such as the Norman Reimer of the National Association of Criminal Defense Lawyers, contend that drug courts offer the state opportunities to impose its will on larger numbers of defendants without the need for adversarial confrontation:

> All too often, drug courts denigrate fundamental rights, extracting broad waivers as the cost of admission, and expose even the most well-intended to dire consequences, often worse than if they avoided drug court and simply pleaded guilty. They tend to place a premium on early guilty pleas, thereby insulating questionable law enforcement

search and seizure practices, and provide a convenient means for prosecutors to shed defective cases. And some drug courts impede the
attorney-client relationship and undermine an accused person's Sixth
Amendment right to a vigorous defense. Worse, many drug courts
operate without transparent admission criteria, and most bar eligibility
to recidivists and those most in need of treatment. These factors tend
to exacerbate racial and economic disparities in the criminal justice
system.

Norman Reimer, "Addicted to a Flawed Solution: Drug Courts Revisited,"
Champion, April 2011, p. 7.
115 *See* Edward J. Epstein, Inquest: The Warren Commission and the
Establishment of Truth 89 (1966) (reporting that Dulles "attended the largest
number of hearings" while most of the Commissioners heard less than half the
testimony).
116 *Id.* at 85.
117 According to Mark Lane, of the 90 persons who were asked from where
they thought the shots that killed the President came, 58 said that they thought
the shots came from the "grassy knoll" area in front of the presidential motorcade and not from the building from where the Commission concluded Oswald
fired on Kennedy. Rush to Judgment 37 (1992). Of those who gave statements
or affidavits immediately or within two days of the assassination, 22 of 25 said
they believed the shots came from the knoll. *Id.* at 38-39. Of those who ultimately claimed the shots came from the building, almost half were members
of the motorcade. "Furthermore," noted Lane, "almost all of the dissenting
motorcade witnesses—13 out of 15—were Government officials, their wives
or aides, or local or federal police." *Id.* at 37.
118 "Pictures of the Texas School Book Depository, taken seconds before
the assassination and showing the sixth-floor window from which [Oswald]
allegedly fired, were secured by the police agencies from their owners.
Photographs of the grassy knoll taken by a witness just as the shots were
fired are also in the authorities' possession. The Commission declined to
publish any of these pictures." Mark Lane, Rush to Judgment 344 (1992).
119 *Id.* at 378.
120 *Id.* at 395. Lane continued:

When a witness had something to say that did not conform to the conclusions of the Commission, such testimony was often deemed invalid. The Commission 'could not accept important elements of [Deputy Sheriff] Craig's testimony'; Mrs. Randle was 'mistaken'; Governor Connally 'probably' was mistaken; Frazier 'could easily have been mistaken'; Daniels' testimony 'merits little credence'; Rowland was 'prone to exaggerate' and there were 'serious doubts about his credibility'; Whaley's memory was 'inaccurate', he was 'somewhat imprecise' and 'was in error'; Kantor 'was preoccupied' and 'probably did not see Ruby at Parkland Hospital'; Mrs. Tice was in error; Wade 'lacked a thorough grasp of the evidence and made a number of errors'; Weitzman was incorrect; Mrs. Helmick's reliability was 'undermined'; Ruby and Shanklin were misquoted; the doctors at Parkland Hospital were misquoted and also in error; Mrs Connally's testimony did 'not preclude' a possibility that it did preclude; Mrs Kennedy's testimony about the wounds was deleted; Mrs Rich was not mentioned in the text of the Report; and Mrs Clemons' existence was tacitly denied. In this fashion believable testimony was disposed of, while the catalyst of necessity changed Brennan and Mrs Markham into reliable witnesses.

Id.

121 To a large extent, this chapter is an amalgamation of two articles which were previously published. *If It's Not a Runaway, It's Not a Real Grand Jury*, 33 Creighton Law Review 821-42 (2000), and *Grand Juries Gone Wrong*. (2010), 14 Richmond Journal of Law & Public Interest 331 (2012).

122 U.S. CONST, amend. V.

123 Charles H. Whitebread & Christopher Slobogin, Criminal Procedure: An Analysis of Cases and Concepts 546 (1993). Historically, the grand jury was regarded as a primary security for the innocent against malicious and oppressive persecution. *See* Wood v. Georgia, 370 U.S. 375, 389-391 (1962).

124 Erskine's 1784 argument was recounted by Justice Harlan in *Hurtado v. California*, 110 U.S. 516, 543 (1884).

125 *See* 1 ORFIELD'S CRIMINAL PROCEDURE UNDER THE FEDERAL RULES 392 (Mark S. Rhodes ed., 2d ed. 1985) [hereinafter ORFIELD'S]:

Under the Constitution the grand jury may either present or indict. Presentment is the process whereby a grand jury initiates an independent investigation and asks that a charge be drawn to cover the facts if they constitute a crime. Since the grand jury may present, it may investigate independently of direction by the court or the United States Attorney. Proceeding by presentment is now obsolete in the federal courts. *Id.*

Orfield's noted that "the common law powers of a grand jury include the power to make presentments, sometimes called reports, calling attention to actions of public officials, whether or not they amounted to a crime." *Id.* at 392 n.16 (citing *In re* Grand Jury 315 F. Supp. 662 (D. Md. 1970).

126   Generally speaking, any felony is an "infamous" crime for purposes of the Amendment. *See* Marvin Zalman and Larry Siegel, CRIMINAL PROCEDURE: CONSTITUTION AND SOCIETY, 641 (2d ed. 1997). For an expanded treatment of this topic, *see* 1 Orfield's Criminal Procedure Under the Federal Rules, 482-85 (Mark S. Rhodes ed., 2d ed. 1985).

127   United States v. Smyth, 104 F. Supp. 283, 288 (N.D.Cal. 1952).

128   *See Note, Power of Federal Grand Juries*, 4 Stan. L. Rev. 68 (1951) (citations omitted).

129   *See* Arthur Train, The Prisoner at the Bar, 106 (1926) ("Of all the features of modern criminal procedure, bar only the office of coroner, the grand jury, or "The Grand Inquest," as it is called, is the most archaic.").

130   *See* Lawrence M. Friedman, A History of American Law, 90-93 (2d ed. 1985) (saying that the American colonies began using codified statu-tory law for the first time in the English legal system during the eighteenth century in order to combat the "unknowable" nature of extensive case law). 131   Hurtado v. California, 110 U.S. 232, 245 (1883) (Harlan, J., dissenting).

132   Susan W Brenner & Gregor G. Lockhart, Federal Grand Jury: A Guide to Law and Practice 4 (1996).

133   *See, e.g.*, Hale v. Henkel, 201 U.S. 43, 64 (1906) (recognizing that common law authority stood for the proposition that "none but witnesses have any business before the grand jury, and that the solicitor may not be present, even to examine them"). Although widespread practice in the federal system had been to allow a government attorney to present evidence to the grand jury, this was by no means a steadfast rule.

134 *See* WHITEBREAD & SLOBOGIN, CRIMINAL PROCEDURE: AN ANALYSIS OF CASES AND CONCEPTS at 546 (stating that the grand jury had the ability to both investigate the government and to deny a government indictment). *See also* ORFIELD'S, *supra* note 22, at 389; *In re* Special February 1975 Grand Jury, 565 F.2d 407 (7th Cir. 1977); United States v. Smyth, 104 F. Supp 283, 288 (N.D. Cal. 952). When functioning properly, the grand jury is supposed to be an ever-present danger to tyranny in government. *See* ARTHUR TRAIN, THE PRISONER AT THE BAR 128 (1926) (stating that the grand jury filled a need as a barrier between the powerful and the weak and as a tribunal before which the weak could accuse the powerful of their wrongs).

135 *See* Marvin Frankel & Gary Naftalis The Grand Jury: An Institution on Trial 10 (1977). *See also* Mark Kadish, *Behind the Locked Door of an American Grand Jury: Its History, Its Secrecy, and Its Process*, 24 FLA. ST. U. L. REV. 10-11 (1996) (saying grand juries in early Georgia, the Carolinas, Maryland, New Jersey, and Pennsylvania, all had sufficient independence to publicly announce dissatisfaction with government).

136 *See id*; Note, Powers of Federal Grand Juries, 4 STAN. L. REV. 77 (1951). [T]he grand jury developed at a time of small rural communities, when the government had not yet assumed responsibility for enforcing the criminal law. Private persons could initiate prosecutions. The grand jury ensured that privately instituted proceedings would not go forward until a representative body of men of the neighborhood had checked the facts and found a reasonable basis for prosecution.

137 *See* FRANKEL & NAFTALIS, THE GRAND JURY: AN INSTITUTION ON TRIAL, at 11.

138 Id.

139 *See id.* at 11.

140 *Id.* at 12.

141 *Id.* at 12.

142 Richard Calkins, *The Fading Myth of Grand Jury Secrecy*, 1 J. MARSHALL J. PRAC. & PROC. 18, 19 (1967).

143 2 THE WORKS OF JAMES WILSON537 (Robert Green McCloskey ed., 1967).

144 *See* FRANKEL & NAFTALIS, *supra*, at 15. 145 *See id.*

146 Federal Grand Jury, Hearing before the Subcommittee on Immigration, Citizenship, and International Law of the Committee on the Judiciary, House

of Representatives, 94th Cong., 2nd Sess., on H.J. Res. 46, H.R. 1277, June 10, July 1, 29 and Aug. 26, 1976 at 623 (statement of Rep. Mario Biaggi) ("grand juries received evidence in private, without the participation of the prosecution and defendant").

147 George J. Edwards, Jr., The Grand Jury 127 (1906) ("At common law the grand jurors conducted the examination of witnesses themselves, not permitting the attorney for the crown to enter the room"). Nor did early grand juries allow defense attorneys to be present among them. Such a proposal—though offered by many modern critics—would have been regarded with great suspicion by the American colonists who ratified the Constitution. *See* Kevin K. Washburn, *Restoring the Grand Jury*, 76 Fordham L. Rev. 2333, 2336-39 (2008) (criticizing the recurring claim that defense attorneys in grand jury proceedings would restore the independence of grand juries).

148 Anonymous, 7 Cow. (N.Y.) 563 (Albany, N.Y. Supreme Ct. 1827).

149 Remarks on Colledge's Trial, by Sir John Hawles, Solicitor-General in the Reign of King William the Third, 8 Howell State Trials 724 (1681) (statement of the King's counsel) (emphasis added).

150 Modern grand jury proceedings are normally conducted in the grand jury room, but at common law they could be conducted in private houses or other places for protection of the witnesses. See, e.g., *United States v. Smyth*, 104 F. Supp. 283, 300 (N.D. Cal. 1952); *United States v. Gilboy*, 160 P. Supp. 442, 458-59 (M.D. Pa. 1958). However, modern grand jury charges tend to limit this power, or even overtly conceal it from the grand jurors. See, e.g., Louis E. Goodman, *Charge to the Grand Jury*, 12 F.R.D. 495, 499-501 (N.D. Cal. 1952) (arguing against such freedom of movement and ordering the grand jury to "hold its meetings and conduct its investigations and deliberations in quarters provided by the Court and in no other places").

151 *See* George J. Edwards, Jr., The Grand Jury 127 (1906) ("At common law the grand jurors conducted the examination of witnesses themselves, not permitting the attorney for the crown to enter the room"). Note that grand juries were by no means bound to hold proceedings in a courthouse. Some grand juries convened at taverns or in the homes of grand jurors. *See* Roots, *supra* note.

152 *See id* ("In order that the crown officer might know what evidence was given to the grand jury," grand jurors in some states were required to hear the

evidence in open court, "although after so hearing it they were never denied the right to again hear the witnesses in private").

153   Akhil R. Amar, The Bill of Rights 85 (1998) (citing several sources).

154   William Henry Perrin, J. H. Battle, G. C. Kniffin, Kentucky: a history of the state, embracing a concise account of the origin and development of the Virginia colony; its expansion westward, and the settlement of the frontier beyond the Alleghanies; the erection of Kentucky as an independent state, and its subsequent development 306 (1888).

155   *See* Demythologizing The Grand Jury, 10 American Criminal Law Review 700, 734 (1972). The case is published as United States v. Burr, Fed. Case No. 14, 892 (C.Ct.D.Ky. 1806).

156   Michael H. Brown, Fifth Amendment Fraud: Indictment by Grand Jury: The Origin of the Clause, http://home.earthlink.net/~dlaw70/c1p2.htm (citing Proceedings against the Earl of Shaftesbury, 8 Howell State Trials 759, 773 (1681).

157   *See Ex Parte* Crittenden, 6 Fed. Cas. 822 (Superior Court, D.Ark. 1832) (holding that government attorney may be present during the sitting of the grand jury "to conduct the evidence and confer with them" and denying motion by a court attorney to bar a government attorney from the grand jury room); Charge to Grand Jury, 30 Fed. Cas. 992 (Cir. D.Cal. 1872) (holding that government lawyers but not private prosecutors may be present before grand juries); *In re* District Attorney, 7 Fed. Cas. 745 (Cir. Ct. W. D. Tenn. 1872) (holding that U.S. District Attorney may be present before grand juries and may keep minutes of grand jury evidence, and suggesting it was always this way in recent memory); *United States v. Edgerton,* 80 Fed. Rep. 374 (D. Mont. 1897) (stating district attorneys may be present in grand jury investigations); *Shattuck v. State,* 11 Ind. 473 (1858) (prosecutor may attend, examine witnesses, and advise on matters of law); Shoop v. People, 45 Ill. App. 110, 112 (1892) (state's attorney may be present, a practice "which, as we understand, generally prevails . . . [to aid] the grand jury when called upon by them to do so"); *State v. McNinch,* 12 S.C. 89, 94-95 (1879) (allowing solicitor to "go to the grand jury room, at the request of the foreman . . . and instructed him how to write the findings, but [not to be] in the room while the case . . . was under consideration"); *United States v. Cobban,* 127 Fed. Rep. 713 (Cir. Ct. D. Mont. 1904) (allowing district attorney to be present before federal grand juries).

158 *See* Edwards, THE GRAND JURY, at 127 ("In 1794 upon the indictment of Hardy and others for treason, the grand jury requested the attendance of the solicitor for the crown for the purpose of managing the evidence, for which leave of court was first obtained") (citing Growth of the Grand Jury System (J. Kinghorn), 6 Law Mag. & Rev. (4th S.) 380).

159 *See, e.g., State v. Adam*, 5 So. 30, 31 (La. 1888) ("The district attorney is the representative of the public and the legal adviser of the grand jury. They have a right to call upon him for assistance as to the mode of proceeding and on questions of law, although it is undeniable that it would be unlawful for him to participate in their counsel and express opinions on questions of fact. It would not be illegitimate for him to assist them in the examination of witnesses, so as to elicit from them the material or essential facts on which the prosecution necessarily rests").

160 *See* 3 Joseph Story, Commentaries on the Constitution of the United States: with a preliminary review of the constitutional history of the colonies and states, before the adoption of the Constitution, § 1779, p. 658 (1833) ("[a] n indictment [was] usually in the first instance framed by the officers of the government, and laid before the grand jury"). The grand jury would then hear evidence outside the presence of the government and, "if they are of opinion, that the indictment is groundless, or not supported by evidence, they used formerly to endorse on the back of the bill, 'ignoramus' or we know nothing of it." *Id.* "If the grand jury are satisfied of the truth of the accusation, then they write on the back of the bill, 'a true bill.'" *See also* State v. Adam, 5 So. 30, 31 (La. 1888) (holding grand juries "have a right to call upon [a district attorney] for assistance as to the mode of proceeding and on questions of law, although it is undeniable that it would be unlawful for him to participate in their counsel and express opinions on questions of fact" or "to assist them in the examination of witnesses. . . ."). The *Adam* court wrote in 1888 that "[t] he custom is one of long standing"). *See also* Federal Grand Jury, Hearing before the Subcommittee on Immigration, Citizenship, and International Law of the Committee on the Judiciary, House of Representatives, 94th Cong., 2nd Sess., on H.J. Res. 46, H.R. 1277, June 10, July 1, 29 and Aug. 26, 1976 at 623 (statement of Rep. Mario Biaggi) (saying the presence of prosecutors before grand juries was initially allowed only to aid grand juries in the drafting of legal documents).

161 *See* Byrd v. State, 1 How. (2 Miss.) 247 (1835) (holding that a county attorney is in effect an assistant to the attorney for the state and may lawfully conduct the examination of witnesses before a grand jury); Franklin v. Commonwealth. 48 S.W. 986 (Kentucky 1899) (holding that the district attorney may be present to assist the grand jury in disposing of township applications for bridge appropriations under the Act of April 16, 1870 (P. L. 1199)); *In re* Bridge Appropriations, 9 Kulp (Pa.) 427; State v. Mickel, 65 P. 484 (Utah 1901) (prosecutors may be present during grand jury investigation); State v. Baker, 33 W. Va. 319, 10 S.E. 639 (W.Va. 1889) (government attorneys may be present in grand jury investigations); State v. Kovolosky, 61 N.W. 223 (Iowa 1894) (district attorney or his appointee may be present before grand juries).

162 Investigations by grand juries evolved in England to weigh accusations presented by individuals other than Crown prosecutors. *See* Edgar J. McManus, Law and Liberty in Early New England: Criminal Justice and Due Process, 1620-1692, 92 (1993) (saying that in early New England, the persons bringing charges against an accused had to manage the prosecution themselves). *See also* Dongel, *Is Prosecution A Core Executive Function? Morrison v. Olson and the Framers Intent*, 99 Yale L. J. 1069 (1990). Public prosecutors were used in only a handful of cases in the seventeenth century. *Id.* Rhode Island led the colonies in providing for public prosecutors. The Rhode Island Assembly appointed William Dyre to the office of attorney general in 1650. *Id.* With a mandate to prosecute offenders anywhere in the colony, the attorney general could bring prosecutions in the town courts but conducted prosecutions primarily in the General Court of Trials. *Id.* The practice of private prosecutions continued, however, and numerous criminal cases were prosecuted by private citizens. *Id.* The practice of private prosecution continued throughout the nineteenth century. *See, e.g., In Re* Price, 83 F. 830 (C.Ct.S.D.N.Y. 1897) (criminal prosecution initiated not by government attorney but by complaint by private citizen).

163 3 Joseph Story, Commentaries on the Constitution of the United States: with a preliminary review of the constitutional history of the colonies and states, before the adoption of the Constitution, § 1779, p. 658 (1833).

164 *Id.*

165 *Id.*

166 *See, e.g.,* Franklin v. Commonwealth, 48 S.W. 986 (Ky. 1898) (district attorney may be present to assist grand jurors in processing bridge appropriations applications).

167 Edwards, THE GRAND JURY, at 128.

168 *Id.* at 129 (*citing, inter alia, In re* District Attorney, 7 Fed. Cas. 745 (No. 3925) (CC.WD Term. 1872). The U.S. Congress first waded into this issue on June 30, 1906, when it enacted a statute deliberately intended to overturn a District Court ruling that had upheld the common law right of grand jurors to exclude prosecutors from their midst. *See* Congressional Record, pp. 7913-14 (June 6, 1906) (in which members of the U.S. Senate indicated that Justice Department attorneys should be allowed to enter and address grand jury hearings despite the then-recent *United States v. Rosenthal* decision, 121 Fed. 862 (S.D.N.Y. 1903) (which quashed an indictment due to the presence of a federal prosecutor in the grand jury room). The statute purporting to overturn the *Rosenthal* ruling was codified at 28 U.S.C. § 515(a) (1906).

169 *See* Lester B. Orfield, The Federal Grand Jury, 22 F.R.D. 343, 346 (1958). The current Rule 6(d)(1) provides a list of who may be present while a grand jury is in session: "attorneys for the government," a witness being questioned, interpreters when needed, and a court reporter or "operator of a recording device."[fn] Thus, today a federal grand jury cannot call defense lawyers or judges even if it chooses to do so. The only attorney who may be present is an attorney for the government.

170 *See* Renee B. Lettow, Note, *Reviving Federal Grand Jury Presentments,* 103 Yale L.J. 1333, throughout (1994). *But see* Note, *Powers of Federal Grand Juries,* 4 Stan. L. Rev. 68, 69 (1951) (asserting that Rule 6 of the Federal Rules of Criminal Procedure permits United States Attorneys to be present at all grand jury hearings).

171 Edwards, THE GRAND JURY, at 128 (a district attorney in the grand jury room "should withdraw if requested to do so" (citing *In re* District Attorney U.S., 7 Fed. Cas. 745)). Prior to enactment of the Federal Rules of Criminal Procedure in 1946, it was not uncommon for grand juries to affirmatively expel government prosecutors from their investigations. In one famed late example, a 1935 New York state grand jury investigating the prevalence of racketeering, gangsterism and "the suspicious inability of the police and public prosecutors to cope with it" barred regular assistant district attorneys from appearing before it and sought to appoint Thomas Dewey as its "special prosecutor." Robert M.

Pitler, *Independent State Search and Seizure Constitutionalism: The New York State Court of Appeals' Quest For Principled Decisionmaking*, 62 Brook. L. Rev. 1, 64 (1996). Failing to appoint Dewey, the grand jury conducted its own investigation without the presence of a supervising prosecutor. *Id.*
172   U.S. CONST. amend. V states:

> No person shall be held to answer for a capital, or otherwise infamous crime, unless on a presentment or indictment of a Grand Jury, except in cases arising in the land or naval forces, or in the Militia, or in the Militia, when in actual service in time of War or public danger.

173   *See* ADVISORY COMMITTEE NOTE 4, FED. R. CRIM. PRO. 7(a) ("Presentment is not included as an additional type of formal accusation, since presentments as a method of instituting prosecutions are obsolete, at least as concerns the Federal courts."). A few voices in the federal judiciary, however, have ignored this language and allowed for "presentments" or unapproved statements of federal grand juries to stand public regardless of the will of federal prosecu-tors. For a discussion of this issue, *see* Phillip E. Hassman, Annotation, Authority of Federal Grand Jury To Issue Indictment Or Report Charging Unindicted Person With Crime Or Misconduct, 28 A.L.R. FED. 851 (1976).
174   *See* 1 ORFIELD'S CRIMINAL PROCEDURE UNDER THE FEDERAL RULES, 392 n.16 (Mark S. Rhodes ed., 2d ed. 1985) (noting that "[t]he common law powers of a grand jury include the power to make presentments . . . calling attention to actions of public officials, whether or not they amounted to a crime"); *See also* Hassman, 28 A.L.R. FED. at 854-57.
175   However, on occasion, grand juries have used the term "presentment" to indicate what is commonly a grand jury report, or a statement to the court regarding some matter but which neither recommends indictment nor initiates any prosecution. Id. at 853 n.2.
176   Lester B. Orfield, The Federal Grand Jury, 22 F.R.D. 343, 346 (1958).
177   Orfield, 22 F.R.D. at 346.
178   22 F.R.D. 343, 346; 1 Orfield's Criminal Procedure Under the Federal Rules, 258 (Mark S. Rhodes ed., 2d ed. 1985).
179   In re Grand Jury, 315 F. Supp. 662, 673 (D. Md. 1970) ("The Advisory Committee note does not indicate that the quoted provision was intended to change existing practice, although of course the Rule has the effect of law.").

180 *See* United States v. Cox, 342 F.2d 167 (5th Cir. 1965) (discussing the possibility of a presentment). *But see In Re* Grand Jury Proceedings, Special Grand Jury 89-2, 813 F.Supp. 1451, 1462 (D.Colo. 1992) (no federal grand jury can return an indictment without the consent and signature of a federal prosecutor).

181 *Id.*

182 Fed. R. Crim. P. 6(e)(2) provides: A grand juror, an interpreter, a stenographer, an operator of a recording device, a typist who transcribes recorded testimony, an attorney for the government, or any person to whom disclosure is made under paragraph (3)(A)(ii) of this subdivision shall not disclose matters occurring before the grand jury, except as otherwise provided for in these rules. No obligation of secrecy may be imposed on any person except in accordance with this rule. A knowing violation of Rule 6 may be punished as a contempt of court. *Id.* (emphasis added). *See, e.g., In re* Grand Jury Proceedings, Special Grand Jury 89-2 (Rocky Flats Grand Jury), 813 F.Supp. 1451 (D.Colo. 1992).

183 Fed. R. Crim. P. 6(e)(7) ("A knowing violation of Rule 6 . . . may be punished as a contempt of court"). Congress has not prescribed penalties for contempt of court, and several courts have come to competing interpre-tations of the possible sentencing ranges for criminal contempt. *Compare* United States v. Mallory, 525 F.Supp.2d. 1316 (S.D.Fla. 2007) (holding that in the absence of a specific statutory sentencing range, criminal contempt is a Class A felony that permits a sentence of up to life in prison) *with* United States v. Carpenter, 91 F.3d 1282 (9th Cir. 1996) (looking at the U.S. Sentencing Guidelines and concluding that criminal contempt is similar to the felony of obstruction of justice and punishable accordingly). At common law, criminal contempt was generally described as a misdemeanor. *See In re* Gompers, 41 Wash. L. Rep. 290, 306 (D.C.Cir. 1913) (Shepard, J., dissenting) (reviewing the history of criminal contempt under the common law). However, there are cases suggesting the common law treated criminal contempt as neither a felony nor a misdemeanor, allowing judges to use their discretion in craft-ing punishments to enforce their orders. *See Robinson v. Commonwealth*, 41 Va. App. 137 (2003); Dept. of Juvenile Justice v. State, 705 So. 2d 1048, 1049 (Fla. 2d DCA 1998) ("Contempt is neither a felony nor a misdemeanor"). 184 *See* Helene E. Schwartz, *Demythologizing the Historic Role of the Grand Jury*, 10 AM. CRIM. L. REV. 733-36 (1972) (reprinting the presentment).

185 *Id.* at 735. 186 *Id.*

187 *See* Frankel & Naftalis, *supra*, at 9.

188 *See* Mark Kadish, *Behind the Locked Door of an American Grand Jury: Its History, Its Secrecy, and Its Process*, 24 FLA. ST. U. L. REV. 12 (1996).

189 *See* State v. Hughes, 1 Ala. Rep. 655 (1840) (involving defendant who knew identities of grand jurors and sought to question them); State v. Fasset, 16 Conn. 457, 470 (1844) (stating that grand jury secrecy has long been imposed by law, but is often waived in practice by grand jurors them-selves in Connecticut and Massachusetts).

190 This rule appears to have waned around the mid-1800s, but cases announcing a relaxation of standards take notice of the original practice. *See* Edwards, *supra* note, at 136-37; Harriman v. State, 2 Greene (Iowa) 270 (1849); Andrews v. People, 7 NE 265 (Ill. 1886); Bartley v. People, 40 NE 831 (Ill. 1895). *But see* United States v. Shepard, 27 Fed. Cas. 1056; State v. Scott, 25 Ark. 107 (1867); People v. Naughton, 38 How. Pr. 430 (N.Y. 1870) (all standing for the proposition that an omission of such names on the indictment will not be fatal to be the indictment).

191 One example involves the Virginia grand jury that indicted Aaron Burr after two others had refused to indict him. Under the procedure of the period, Burr was able to scrutinize the jury list and challenge the presence of several grand jurors whom Burr claimed had shown personal animosity toward him in the past. *See* Helene E. Schwartz, *supra* note ?, at 737. This of course would be scarcely imaginable today. Also, Burr was able to insist that the grand jury considering his case consider evidence in his favor. *See id.* at 738. Today, of course, the secrecy shroud of federal grand juries prevents suspects from knowing either the composition or the nature of grand jury investigations.

192 Thomas Jefferson to Edmund Randolph, 1793. ME 9:83.

193 *See* Fred A. Bernstein, *Note, Behind the Gray Door: Williams, Secrecy, and the Federal Grand Jury*, 69 N.Y.U. L. REV. 563, 596 (1994).

194 *See* Susan W Brenner & Gregor G. Lockhart, Federal Grand Jury: A Guide to Law and Practice § 8.1 (1996) (saying that "secrecy promotes [truth-finding] by making it easier for a grand jury to elicit evidence from knowledge-able persons, and making it more difficult for interested parties to influence a grand jury's inquiries").

195 William J. Campbell, *Eliminate the Grand Jury*, 64 J. Crim. L. & Criminology, No. 2, 178, 180 (1973).

Roger I. Roots

196 *See* Kadish, 24 FLA. ST. U. L. REV. at 6; Bernstein, 69 N.Y.U. L. REV. at 594 (arguing that secrecy now protects the government's dominion over the grand jury rather than vice versa).

197 *See* Roger Roots, *Grand Juries Gone Wrong*, 14 RICHMOND JOURNAL OF LAW AND THE PUBLIC INTEREST, 227, 353-57 (discussing the adoption by federal courts of a fictional history of grand jury that emphasizes the prevention of escape of suspects and the prevention of suspects' tampering with witnesses).

198 *See* FRANKEL & NAFTALIS, supra, at 15.

199 William J. Campbell, *Eliminate the Grand Jury*, 64 J. CRIM. L. & CRIMINOLOGY 174 (1973).

200 United States v. Dioniso, 410 U.S. 19, 23 (1973) (Douglas, J., dissenting). 201 *See In re* Grand Jury Subpoena of Stewart, 545 N.Y.S.2d 974, 977 n.1 (N.Y. App. Div. 1989), modified by 548 N.Y.S.2d 679 (N.Y. App. Div. 1989) (not-ing that skepticism about the grand jury was "best summarized by the Chief Justice of this state in 1985 when he publicly stated that a Grand Jury would indict a ham sandwich."). While this observation was made about New York State grand juries, many observers have commented to the same effect about the federal grand jury. *See* Roger Roots, *Grand Juries Gone Wrong*, 14 RICHMOND JOURNAL OF LAW AND THE PUBLIC INTEREST 227 (2011) (citing numerous criticisms).

202 *See, e.g.,* Kevin K. Washburn, *Restoring the Grand Jury*, 76 Fordham L. Rev. 2333 (2008); Judith M. Beall, Note, *What Do You Do with a Runaway Grand Jury?: A Discussion of the Problems and Possibilities Opened up by the Rocky Flats Grand Jury Investigation*, 71 S. Cal. L. Rev. 617, 630-32 (1998); Susan W. Brenner, *The Voice of the Community: A Case for Grand Jury Independence*, 3 Va. J. Soc. Pol'y & L. 67 (1995); Laurie Buchan, *The Constitutional Rights of Federal and California Grand Jury Witnesses*, 10 S.W.U. L. Rev. 895 (1978); R. Michael Cassidy, *Toward a More Independent Grand Jury: Recasting and Enforcing the Prosecutor's Duty to Disclose Exculpatory Evidence*, 13 Geo. J. Legal Ethics 361, 362-63 (2000); Jay A. Christofferson, *Review of Selected 1997 California Legislation: Grand Jury Reform: Making Justice Just*, 29 McGeorge L. Rev. 516 (1998); Gregory T. Fouts, Note, *Reading the Jurors Their Rights: The Continuing Question of Grand Jury Independence*, 79 Ind. L. J. 323 (2004); Andrew Leipold, *Why Grand Juries Do Not (and Cannot) Protect the Accused*, 80 Cornell L. Rev. 260

(1995); Simmons, *supra* note 2, at 27; Benjamin E. Rosenberg, *"A Proposed Addition to the Federal Rules of Criminal Procedure Requiring the Disclosure of the Prosecutor's Legal Instructions to the Grand Jury,"* 38 Am. Crim. L. Rev. 1443 (2001); Kathryn E. White, Comment, *What Have You Done with My Lawyer?: The Grand Jury Witness's Right to Consult with Counsel*, 32 Loy. L.A. L. Rev. 907 (1999).

203   *See, e.g.,* Fouts, 79 Ind. L. J. at 324 (describing the grand jury as "an institution adrift from its historical moorings").

204   Benjamin E. Rosenberg, *A Proposed Addition to the Federal Rules of Criminal Procedure Requiring the Disclosure of the Prosecutor's Legal Instructions to the Grand Jury*, 38 Am. Crim. L. Rev. 1443, 1443 (2001) (citing various sources).

205   Federal Grand Jury hearing before the Subcommittee on Immigration, Citizenship, and International Law of the Committee on the Judiciary, House of Representatives, 94th Cong., 2nd Sess., June 10, July 1, July 29, and Aug. 26, 1976, page 643.

206   *Id.* at 646.

207   *See* statement of John B. Swainson, p. 653 in 1976 hearings.

208   Statement of Rep. Charles Rangel, p. 316 of Federal Grand Jury hearing before the Subcommittee on Immigration, Citizenship, and International Law of the Committee on the Judiciary, House of Representatives, 94th Cong., 2nd Sess., June 10, July 1, July 29, and Aug. 26, 1976.

209   *Id.* at 647 (statement of Patrick Tobin). 210   *Id.* at 335 (Statement of Rep. Mario Biaggi).

211   Stuart Taylor, Jr., *Prosecutorial Puppetry and the License to Rummage,* Conn. Law. Trib., May 18, 1992 at 24 (stating "investigations, subpoenas, and indictments . . . are, in fact, essentially unilateral decisions by prosecutors").

212   *See also* Washburn, *Restoring the Grand Jury*, 76 Fordham L. Rev. at 2333 (stating "Scholars regard the grand jury just as doctors regard the appendix: an organic part of our constitutional makeup, but not of much use").

213   In 1984, for example, federal grand juries issued 17,419 indictments, and only 68 no-bills, an indictment rate of 99.6%. Fouts, *Reading the Jurors Their Rights: The Continuing Question of Grand Jury Independence*, 79 Ind. L. J. at 329-30. According to TRAC, of 785 federal grand juries in 1991, grand jurors voted against the prosecutor in only sixteen of the 25,943 matters presented to them, a rate of 99.9% agreement. Even the remaining one tenth of one percent,

Roger I. Roots

according to legal statistician David Burnham, might exaggerate grand jury independence, due to prosecutors deliberately "throwing" a couple of prosecutions, such as the possibly disingenuous 1991 "investigation" of Virginia Senator Charles Robb on widespread alle-gations of illegal tape recording of a political rival. Andrew D. Leipold, *Why Grand Juries Do Not (and Cannot) Protect the Accused*, 80 CORNELL L. REV. 275-76 (1995); David Burnham, ABOVE THE LAW: Secret Deals, Political Fixes, and Other Misadventures of the U.S. Department of Justice 360 (1996).

214   Fouts, *Reading the Jurors Their Rights*, 79 Ind. L. J. at 330. 215   *Id.*

216   Although various congressional committees have heard testimony about subversion of the institution, each one went on to approve, sanction and ratify the same or further iniquities in grand jury practice. *See* "Federal Grand Jury," Hearings before the Subcommittee on Immigration, Citizenship, and International Law of the U.S. House Committee on the Judiciary, 94th Cong., June 10, July 1, July 29, and Aug. 26, 1976; "Reform of the grand jury system : hearing before the Subcommittee on Constitutional Rights of the Committee on the Judiciary," United States Senate, Ninety-fourth Congress, second session, September 28, 1976; "Grand Jury Reform," Hearings before the Subcommittee on Immigration, Citizenship, and International Law of the U.S. House of Representatives Committee on the Judiciary, 95th Cong., March 17, April 27, June 1 and 29, 1977.

The 1977 hearings began with proposals to carve back the powers of prosecutors before grand juries but ended with a bill that allowed government attorneys to disclose grand jury materials to authorities in other executive branch agencies. Such use of grand jury investigations had theretofore been impeded by holdings in such cases as *In re Holovachka*, 317 F.2d 834 (7th Cir. 1963), *In re April 1956 Term Grand Jury*, 239 F.2d 263 (7th Cir. 1965), and *In re Kadish*, 377 F.Supp. 951 (N.D.Ill. 1974).

The resulting rule changes gave even greater power to government. Hearings at 648 (statement of Patrick Tobin) "Congress has increased, not checked, the power of prosecutors operating before Federal grand juries."). The 2001 USA PATRIOT Act, passed in the wake of the 9/11 terrorist attacks, brought even more ability for government lawyers to transfer materials between each other.

217   Uniting and Strengthening America by Providing Appropriate Tools Required to Intercept and Obstruct Terrorism Act of 2001 (the "Patriot Act"),

Pub. L. No. 107-56, 115 Stat. 272 (2001) (codified in scattered sections of the U.S. Code).

218 Section 203(a) of the Patriot Act amended Rule 6 of the Federal Rules of Criminal Procedure to permit disclosures by government attorneys of "matters occurring before" grand juries to other government officials when the matters "involve foreign intelligence or counterintelligence" "in order to assist the official receiving that information in the performance of his official duties." The change requires that a disclosure made under the new excep-tion be revealed, under seal, to the court (although no provision gives the court any veto power over a prosecutor's disclosure).

219 Gregory T. Fouts, *Note, Reading the Jurors Their Rights: The Continuing Question of Grand Jury Independence,"* 79 Ind. L. J. 323, 325 (2004).

220 Testimony of Hon. Edward R. Becker, 28-54 at 47. 221 *Id.*

222 *See* generally, Wen Ho Lee, My Country Versus Me: The First-Hand Account by the Los Alamos Scientist Who Was Falsely Accused (2002) (detailing an outrageous federal prosecution of a scientist for allegedly trading nuclear secrets); Andrew P. Napolitano, Constitutional Chaos: What Happens When the Government Breaks Its Own Laws (2004) (describing several examples of false or meritless federal prosecu-tions); Michael Zinn, Mad Dog Prosecutors and Other Hazards of American Business (2003) (giving a chilling account of methods used by federal prosecutors and suggesting no one is safe from unfair prosecution). 223 *See* Alex Kozinski and Misha Tseytlin, You're (Probably) a Federal Criminal, Pp. 43-56 in In the Name of Justice: Leading Experts Reexamine the Classic Article "The Aims of the Criminal Law" (2009) (stat-ing that federal criminal law has become so large, confusing and all-encom-passing that federal prosecutors can and do prosecute virtually anyone they dislike at any time).

224 *See, e.g.,* United States v. Wander, 601 F.2d 1251 (3d Cir.1979) (criticiz-ing but ratifying and upholding grand jury investigation that consisted mostly of "read-backs" of earlier testimony provided to an earlier grand jury); United States v. Provenzano, 688 F.2d 1251 (3d Cir. 1979) (criticizing but approving practice of having a number of grand juries hear testimony which an indict-ing grand jury uses as a basis for indictment); United States v. Helstoski, 635 F.2d 200 (3d Cir. 1980) (criticizing but upholding indictment by grand jury which was unable to observe the demeanor of all witnesses who testified). 225 *See,*

e.g., United States v. Haynes, 216 F.3d 789, 798 (9th Cir. 2000) (no dismissal of indictment even though prosecutors failed to disclose evidence impeaching a key witness); United States v. Shane, 584 F.Supp. 364 (E.D.Pa. 1984) (defendant denied dismissal of indictment although he showed that prosecutors freely transferred material from one grand jury to another without court permission).

226   Grand jurors are far more likely than government personnel to be prosecuted and convicted of causing leaks to the news media. Examples of grand jurors prosecuted for leaking testimony abound. *See, e.g., United States v. Holloway*, 789 F. Supp. 957, 958 (N.D.Ind. 1992), aff'd, 991 F.2d 370 (7th Cir. 1993); *United States v. Peasley*, 741 F. Supp. 18, 19 (D.Me.1990). By contrast, consider the Unabomber case, in which government lawyers admitted that "government personnel" leaked details of the investigation to the media, but went unpunished. *See* Gale Holland, "Prosecutors Admit Unabomber Leaks: 'Government Personnel' Blamed," 4/19/96 USA Today 3A, 1996 WL 2052515.

227   One of the more terrifying examples of this occurred in 1995 when one of the grand jurors called to indict Timothy McVeigh for blowing up the Oklahoma City Federal Building went public with information that federal prosecutors were deliberately leading grand jurors away from suspects other than McVeigh and Terry Nichols. *See* Pat Shannan, "OKC: 10 Years Later," American Free Press, April 11, 2005 at 8. The juror, Hoppy Heidelberg, even wrote to the U.S. District Judge overseeing the grand jury with information about the prosecutorial misconduct. Instead of looking into the prosecutors' conduct, however, the judge summarily removed Heidelberg from the grand jury with a letter threatening Heidelberg with prosecution and cumulative punishment if Heidelberg disclosed his infor-mation. The letter was "hand-delivered by armed FBI agents who, with a threatening flash of their weapons, demanded that Heidelberg hand over his grand jury notes." *Id.* As McVeigh attorney Steven Jones has written, the government's wrath against Heidelberg helped cover up aspects of a case that probably involved government participation in the blast that killed 168 people in Oklahoma City on April 19, 1995. Steven Jones, Others Unknown (2001); James Ridgeway, *In Search of John Doe No. 2*, Mother Jones, July/Aug. 2007 at 54-61 (suggesting a federal grand jury "investigation" into the death of prison inmate Kent Trentadue was a vehicle for the Justice Department to cover up his murder by government

officials). For another case of a recalcitrant grand juror given the brush-off, *see* Federal Grand Jury, Hearing before the Subcommittee on Immigration, Citizenship, and International Law of the Committee on the Judiciary, House of Representatives, 94th Cong., 2nd Sess., on H.J. Res. 46, H.R. 1277, June 10, July 1, 29 and Aug. 26, 1976, p. 642 (discussing case of grand jury forewoman Harriet Mitchell, who insisted that an FBI agent be recalled to testify in 1971 to answer for his ear-lier, suspicious testimony. Ms. Mitchell later learned that the U.S. Attorney had dissolved the grand jury before the FBI agent could be recalled, and that the U.S. Attorney was convening a different grand jury—one without Mitchell—to hear the matter).

228 *See* Fred A. Bernstein, *Note, Behind the Gray Door: Williams, Secrecy, and the Federal Grand Jury*, 69 N.Y.U. L. REV. 563, 623 n.83 (1994).

229 These rates are especially high if traffic cases are counted as criminal cases. But even if traffic cases are excluded from consideration, most states report criminal cases either outnumbering civil cases or constituting at least 40 percent of total court dockets. *See* R. LaFountain, et al, Examining the Work of State Courts: An Analysis of 2008 State Court Caseloads (National Center for State Courts 2010) p. 23 (showing graphs from eight states; in only one state (Iowa) was the percentage of nontraffic criminal cases in 008 as low as half of the percentage of civil cases; in half the states the percent-age of criminal cases was greater in 2008 than the percentage of civil cases).

230 See Roger Roots, *Unfair Federal Rules of Procedure: Why Does the Government Get More Time?* 33 American Journal of Trial Advocacy Volume 33 (2010).

231 Fed. R. Appellate Procedure 29(a).

232 Toby J. Stern, Federal Judges and Fearing the "Floodgates of Litigation," 6 J. Const. Law 377 (2003) (discussing this recurring claim by judges, quite often expressed when denying theories of civil rights or habeas corpus rights to inmates and criminal defendants).

233 John H. Langbein's famed study of eighteenth century trial documents indicated that during four sessions of the Old Bailey in London during the 1750s, there were 171 trials in which defendants were charged with 179 offenses. *See* Langbein, *Shaping the Eighteenth-Century Criminal Trial: A View from the Ryder Sources*, 50 U. Chi. L. Rev. 1, 42 (1983)1754-1756.

234 Andrew D. Leipold, *How the Pretrial Process Contributes to Wrongful Convictions*, 42 Am. Crim. L. Rev. 1123, 1145-46 (2005)

235   *Id.* at 1145.
236   *Id.* 1145-46.
237   *Id.* at 1143. 238   *See id.*
239   State v. McCormack, 9 NW 916 (Iowa 1881) (holding that an indict-ment must state but a single offense, and reversing conviction for forgery and utter-ing a forged instrument because they were charged in a single indictment).
240   United States v. Alluan, 13 F.Supp. 289, 291 (N.D.Tex. 1936). 241   *Id.*
242   *Id.*
243   United States v. Alluan, 13 F.Supp. 289, 291 (N.D.Tex. 1936). 244   People v. Luciano, 14 N.E.2d 433 (N.Y. 1938).
245   United States v. Greve, 12 F.Supp. 372, 374 (E.D.N.Y. 1934). 246   *Id.*
247   *Id.* at 375. 248   Id.
249   *Id.* at 376.
250   Andrew D. Leipold, *How the Pretrial Process Contributes to Wrongful Convictions*, 42 Am. Crim. L. Rev. 1123, 1161 (2005).n198.
251   A few examples culled from appellate cases: *United States v. Razmilovic*, 419 F.3d 134 (2d Cir. 2005) (87-page indictment charging businessmen with, inter alia, securities fraud, wire fraud, mail fraud and conspiracy); *United States v. Chandler*, 388 F.3d 796 (11th Cir. 2004) (62 page indictment charg-ing 43 defendants with conspiracy to commit mail fraud); *United States v. Merlino*, 349 F.3d 144 (3rd Cir. 2003) (a series of indictments culminating in a thirty-six count, 111-page fourth superceding indictment "on which the seven defendants who had not already pled guilty went to trial"). See also United States v. Bennett, 9 F.Supp.2d 513 (E.D.Pa. 1998) (82 counts); United States v. Gotti, 9 F.Supp.2d 320 (S.D.N.Y. 1998) (mob boss and 2 codefen-dants charged with 86 counts); United States v. Mariani, 7 F.Supp.2d 556 (M.D.Pa. 1998) (a 140-count indictment against six defendants for cam-paign-finance-related allegations); United States v. Paradies, 14 F.Supp.2d 1315 N.G.Ga. 1998) (83 counts).
252   Some examples: *United States v. Nixon*, 918 F.2d 895, 895 & n. 1 (11th Cir.1990) (95 counts); *United States v. Hammond*, 781 F.2d 1536, 1537 (11th Cir.1986) (116 counts); *United States v. Kopituk*, 690 F.2d 1289, 1320 (11th Cir.1982) (12 defendants, 70 counts, 130 witnesses, 22,000 pages of trial tran-script, seven-month trial); *United States v. Martino*, 648 F.2d 367, 385 (5th Cir.1981), cert. denied, 456 U.S. 949, 102 S. Ct. 2020, 72 L. Ed. 2d 474 (1982) (20 defendants, 35 counts, more than 200 witnesses, three-month trial) (quoting

United States v. Morrow, 537 F.2d 120, 136 (5th Cir.1976)); Phillips, 664 F.2d at 1017 n. 68 (12 defendants, 407 overt acts, 36 counts, 12,000 pages of trial transcript, four-and-a-half-month trial). See also *United States v. Garner*, 837 F.2d 1404, 1413 (7th Cir.1987), cert. denied, 486 U.S. 1035, 108 S. Ct. 2022, 100 L. Ed. 2d 608 (1988) (178-page indict-ment, 348 alleged illegal acts, six-week trial); *United States v. Anderson*, 799 F.2d 1438 (11th Cir. 1986) (forty-five count, 166-page indictment against thirty defendants).

253   *United States v. Perisco*, 349 F.2d 6 (2nd Cir. 1965), involved the sixteen week trial of five defendants for robbery of merchandise in interstate com-merce and conspiracy. There were 9,595 pages of transcript. The charge took thirteen hours over a two day period plus a four hour supplemental charge, and "several hundred pages of the charge were devoted to references to portions of the testimony, either by way of summary or direct quotation, for the purpose of marshaling the evidence or explaining points of law . . .." *Id.* at 8. The court reversed, in part because of the probability, given the length and repetition of the charge, that the jury must have become confused and unable to exercise its independent recollection of all the testimony.

254   In *United States v. Crosby*, 2d Cir. 1961, 294 F.2d 928, the court rejected a challenge to the instructions based on length. Seven individual defendants and one corporate defendant were tried on a fifty-count indictment charg-ing wire fraud, mail fraud, and the sale of unregistered securities. The trial took 3 1/2 months and produced a 10,000 page transcript. The charge took eight hours, but the Second Circuit found the extended instructions to have been necessary in such a lengthy, complicated case.

255   *United States v. Kopituk*, 690 F.2d 1289 (11th Cir. 1982) (citing *United States v. Phillips*, 664 F.2d at 1016-1017 (six month trial; 36-count, 100 page indictment; 12 defendants); *United States v. Martino*, 648 F.2d 367, 385-386 (5th Cir. 1981) (20 defendants, most with Spanish or Italian surnames; 35-count indictment; three month trial; more than 200 witnesses); United States v. Morrow, 537 F.2d at 135-137 (23 defendants).

256   *See, e.g., United States v. Schlesinger*, 261 Fed. Appx. 355 (2d Cir. 2008) (no bill of particulars needed because the sheer length of the 52-page indict-ment charging 28 counts of mail fraud conspiracy, substantive mail and wire fraud, money laundering conspiracy, and substantive money laundering sup-posedly provided enough information for the defense).

257   United States v. Hickey, 580 F.3d 922, 930 (9th Cir. 2009).

258 *Id. See also* United States v. Walker, 363 F.3d 711, 715 (8th Cir. 2004) (both a superseding indictment and the original indictment remain pending and the government may go to trial on the original indictment); United States v. Vavlitis, 9 F.3d 206, 209 (1st Cir. 1993) (an original indictment remains pend-ing and can be used at trial even if a superseding indictment omits an ele-ment of a charged offense); United States v. Bowen, 946 F.2d 734, 736-37 (10th Cir. 1991) (a superseding indictment does not invalidate a preceding indictment and the government may proceed to trial on any pending indict-ment); United States v. Drasen, 845 F.2d 731, 732 n.2 (7th Cir. 1988) ("It is well established that two indictments may be outstanding at the same time for the same offense if jeopardy has not attached to the first indictment . The government may then select the indictment under which to proceed at trial."); United States v. Stricklin, 591 F.2d 1112, 1116 n.1 (5th Cir. 1979) ("Since the original indictment apparently was never dismissed, there are technically two pending indictments against Stricklin, and it appears that the government may select one of them with which to proceed to trial."); United States v. Cerilli, 558 F.2d 697, 700 n.3 (3d Cir. 1977) (both an original and superseding indict-ment may be pending at the same time and the gov-ernment may choose which to proceed to trial under).

259 "Juror's Illness Delays Longest Criminal Trial," New York Times, Sept. 1, 1989.

260 Robert Reinhold, *The Longest Trial - A Post-Mortem; Collapse of Child-Abuse Case: So Much Agony for So Little*, New York Times, January 24, 1990 (reporting that the trial of Raymond Buckey and his mother, Peggy McMartin Buckey involved lurid claims of "children being raped and sodom-ized, of dead rabbits, mutilated corpses and a horse killing, and of blood drinking, satanic rituals and the sacrifice of a live baby in a church").

261 Paul Richter, Longest Mob Trial Ends in Acquittals, LA Times, Aug. 27, 1988.

262 Paul Richter, Longest Mob Trial Ends in Acquittals, LA Times, Aug. 27, 1988.

263 Jim Herron Zamora, Henry K. Lee, Jaxon Van Derbeke, *Ex-cops cleared of 8 counts -- mistrial on 27 others / Oakland Riders acquitted of misconduct charges*, San Francisco Chronicle, October 1, 2003.

264 *United States v. Hernandez*, 921 F.2d 1569 (11th Cir. 1991) (writing of "the many cases in which we have held that split verdicts indicated that the

jury considered the evidence carefully and refuted any allegation of 'compelling prejudice'") (citing *United States v. Nixon*, 918 F.2d 895, 906 (11th Cir.1990); *Russo*, 796 F.2d at 1450; *United States v. Cole*, 755 F.2d 748, 762 (11th Cir.1985). 265 18 U.S.C. §§ 3161-62.

266 *See also* Akhil R. Amar, *Foreword: Sixth Amendment First Principles*, 84 Georgetown L.J. 641, 646 (1996) ("Because judges (rightly) see the remedy as extreme, they are loath in any given case to admit that the speedy trial right was indeed violated").

267 People v. Douglass, 4 Cow. 26 (N.Y. 1825). 268 Territory v. Nichols, 2 P. 78, 80 (N.M. Terr. 1884).

269 Most of this chapter was previously published as an article in the Seton Hall Constitutional Law Journal, at 11 Seton Hall Con. L. J. 685-757 (2001). 270 As of June, 1996, there were more than 700,000 full- and part-time professional state-sworn police in the United States. See BUREAU OF JUSTICE STATISTICS, CENSUS OF STATE AND LOCAL LAW ENFORCEMENT AGENCIES, 1996 (1998) available at <http://virlib.ncjrs.org/Statistics.asp>. Figures for earlier decades and centuries are difficult to obtain, but a few indicators suggest that the ratio of police per citizen has grown by at least four thou-sand percent. In 1816, the British Parliament reported that there was at that time one constable for every 18,187 persons in Great Britain. See Jerome Hall, *Legal and Social Aspects of Arrest Without a Warrant*, 49 HARVARD L. REV. 566, 582 (1936). Conventional wisdom would suggest that American ratios were, if anything, lower. Today there is approximately one officer for every 386 Americans.

271 The City of Los Angeles, for example, spends almost half (49.1%) of its annual discretionary budget on police but only 17.7% on fire and 14.8% on public works. *See* City of Los Angeles 1999-2000 Budget Summary (visited Dec. 2000) <http://www.cityofla.org/cao/bud9900.pdf>. The City of Chicago spends over forty percent of its annual budget on police. See Chicago Budget 1999 (visited Dec. 2000) <http://www.ci.chi.il.us/mayor/ Budgetl999/sld011.htm> (pie chart). Seattle spends more than $150 million, or 41 percent of its annual budget, on police and police pensions. See City of Seattle 2000 Proposed Budget (visited Dec. 2000) <http://www. ci.seattle.wa.us/budget>. The City of New York is one exception, due primarily to New York State's unique system for funding education. Police and the administration of justice constitute the third largest segment, or twelve percent, of the City's budget,

after education and human resources. See THE CITY OF NEW YORK, EXECUTIVE BUDGET, FISCAL YEAR 2000 1 (2000) (pie chart).

272 *See* Carol S. Steiker, Second Thoughts About First Principles, 107 HARV. L. REV. 820, 830 (1994) (saying twentieth century police and "our contempo-rary sense of 'policing' would be utterly foreign to our colonial forebears").

273 *See id.*

274 *See id.* at 831 (saying the sole monetary reward for such officers was occasional compensation by private individuals for returning stolen property).

275 *See* CHARLES SILBERMAN, CRIMINAL VIOLENCE, CRIMINAL JUSTICE 314 (1978). The City of Boston, for example, enacted an ordinance requiring drafted citizens to walk the streets "to prevent any danger by fire, and to see that good order is kept." *Id.*

276 *C.f. id.* (mentioning that cops' role of maintaining order predates their role of crime control).

277 *But see, e.g.*, Steiker, *supra*, at 824 (saying the "invention ... of armed quasi-military, professional police forces, whose form, function, and daily presence differ dramatically from that of the colonial constabulary, requires that modern-day judges and scholars rethink" Fourth Amendment remedies).

278 *See, e.g.*, ROBERT H. BORK, SLOUCHING TOWARDS GOMORRAH: MODERN LIBERALISM AND AMERICAN DECLINE 104 (1996) (criticizing Supreme Court rulings that have "steadily expanded" the rights of criminals and placed limitations upon police conduct).

279 *Cf.* E.X. BOOZHIE, THE OUTLAW'S BIBLE 15 (1988) (stating the true mission of police is to protect the status quo for the benefit of the ruling class).

280 As a textual matter, the Constitution grants authority to the federal government to define and punish criminal activity in only five instances. Article I grants Congress power (1) "[t]o provide for the Punishment of counterfeiting the Securities and current Coin of the United States," art. I, Sec. 8, cl. 6; (2) "[t]o define and punish Piracies and Felonies committed on the high Seas, and Offenses against the Law of Nations," id, cl. 10; (3) "[t]o make Rules for the Government and Regulation of the land and naval Forces," *id.* at cl. 14; (4) "[t]o exercise exclusive Legislation in all Cases whatsoever, over" the District of Columbia and federal reservations. *id.* at cl. 17; see also Cohens v. Virginia, 19 U.S. (6 Wheat.) 264, 426 (1821) ("Congress has a right to punish

murder in a fort, or other place within its exclusive jurisdiction; but no general right to punish murder committed within any of the states"). Likewise, (5) Article III defines the crime of "Treason against the United States" and grants to Congress the "Power to declare [its] Punishment...." U.S. CONST. art. III, Sec. 3.

281 Several early constitutions expressed a right of citizens "to be protected in the enjoyment of life, liberty and property," and therefore purported to bind citizens to contribute their proportion toward expenses of such protec-tion. *See* DELAWARE DEC. OF RIGHTS of Sept. 11, 1776, Sec. 10; PA. CONST. of Sept. 28, 1776, Dec. of Rights, Sec. VIII; VT. CONST. of July 8, 1777, Chap. 1, Sec. IX. Other typical provisions required that the powers of government be exercised only by the consent of the people, *see, e.g.,* N.C. CONST. of Dec. 18, 1776, Sec. V, and that all persons invested with government power be accountable for their conduct. See MD. CONST. of Nov. 11, 1776, Sec. IV. 282 The constitutions of several early states expressed the intent that citizens were obligated to carry out law enforcement duties. *See, e.g.,* DELAWARE DEC. OF RIGHTS of Sept. 11, 1776, Sec. 10 (providing every citizen shall yield his personal service when necessary, or an equivalent); N.H. CONST. of June 2, 1784, Part I, art. I, Sec. XII (providing that every member of the community is bound to "yield his personal service when necessary, or an equivalent"); VT. CONST. of July 8, 1777, Chap. 1, Sec. IX (providing every member of society is bound to contribute his proportion towards the expenses of his protection, "and to yield his personal service, when necessary").

283   *C.f.* JAMES BOVARD, LOST RIGHTS: THE DESTRUCTION OF AMERICAN LIBERTY 51 (1st ed. 1994) (discussing Revolution-era perception that the law was a means to restrain government and to secure rights of citizens).

284   Originally, all criminal procedure fell under the rule of private vengeance. A victim or aggrieved party made a direct appeal to county authorities to force a defendant to face him. See ARTHUR TRAIN, THE PRISONER AT THE BAR 120 n. (1926). From these very early times, "grand" or "accusing" juries were formed to examine the accusations of private individuals. *Id.* at 121 n. Although the accusing jury frequently acted as a trial jury as well, it eventually evolved into a separate body that took on the role of accuser on behalf of aggrieved parties. It deliberated secretly, acting on its members' own personal information and upon the application of injured parties. *Id.* at 124 n.

285   In the early decades of American criminal justice, criminal cases were hardly different from civil actions, and could easily be confused for one another if "the public not being joined in it." Clark v. Turner, 1 Root 200 (Conn. 1790) (holding action for assault and battery was no more than a civil case because the public was not joined). It was apparently not unusual for trial judges themselves to be confused about whether a case was criminal or civil, and to make judicial errors regarding procedural differences between the two types of cases. See Meacham v. Austin, 5 Day 233 (Conn. 1811) (upholding lower court's dismissal of criminal verdict because the case's process had been consistent with civil procedure rather than criminal procedure).

286   See Respublica v. Griffiths, 2 Dall. 112 (Pa. 1790) (involving action by private individual seeking public sanction for his prosecution).

287   See, e.g., Smith v. State, 7 Tenn. 43 (1846) (using the term prosecutor to describe a private person); Plumer v. Smith, 5 N.H. 553 (1832) (same); Commonwealth v. Harkness, 4 Binn. 193 (Pa. 1811) (same).

288   See Harold J. Krent, Executive Control Over Criminal Law Enforcement: Some Lessons From History, 38 AM. U. L. REV. 275, 281-90 (1989) (saying that any claim that criminal law enforcement is a 'core' or exclusive executive power is historically inaccurate and therefore the Attorney General need not be vested with authority to oversee or trigger investigations by the independent counsel).

289   See Respublica v. Griffiths, 2 Dall. 112 (Pa. 1790) (holding the Attorney General must allow his name to be used by the prosecutor).

290   Private prosecutors generally had to pay the costs of their prosecutions, even though the state also had an interest. See Dickinson v. Potter, 4 Day 340 (Conn. 1810). Government attorneys general took over the prosecutions of only especially worthy cases and pursued such cases at public expense. See Waldron v. Turtle, 4 N.H. 149, 151 (1827) (stating if a prosecution is not adopted and pursued by the attorney general, "it will not be pursued at the public expense, although in the name of the state").

291   See State v. Bruce, 24 Me. 71, 73 (1844) (stating a threat by crime victim to prosecute a supposed thief is proper but extortion for pecuniary advan-tage is criminal).

292   See Plumer v. Smith, 5 N.H. 553 (1832) (holding promissory note invalid when tendered by a criminal defendant to his private prosecutor in exchange for promise not to prosecute).

293 Shaw v. Reed, 30 Me. 105, 109 (1849).

294 See *In re April 1956 Term Grand Jury*, 239 F.2d 263 (7th Cir. 1956). 295 *See* Goodman v. United States, 108 F.2d 516 (9th Cir. 1939).

296 *See* Krent, 38 AM. U. L. REV. 275, at 293.28 C.f. Ellen D. Larned, 1 History of Windham County, Connecticut 272-73 (1874) (recounting attempts by Windham County authorities in 1730 to arrest a large group of rioters who broke open the Hartford Jail and released a prisoner).

297 C.f. Ellen D. Larned, 1 History of Windham County, Connecticut 272-73 (1874) (recounting attempts by Windham County authorities in 1730 to arrest a large group of rioters who broke open the Hartford Jail and released a prisoner).

298 *Id.* at 273.

299 *See* Buckminster v. Applebee, 8 N.H. 546 (1837) (stating the sheriff has a duty to raise the posse to aid him when necessary).

300 *See* Waterbury v. Lockwood, 4 Day 257, 259-60 (Conn. 1810) (citing English cases).

301 *See* Jerome Hall, *Legal and Social Aspects of Arrest Without A Warrant*, 49 HARV. L. REV. 566, 579 (1936).

302 Barrington v. Yellow Taxi Corp., 164 N.E. 726, 727 (N.Y. 1928). 303 *See* Eustis v. Kidder, 26 Me. 97, 99 (1846).

304 By the early 1900s, courts held that civilians called into posse service who were killed in the line of duty were entitled to full death benefits. *See* Monterey County v. Rader, 248 P. 912 (Cal. 1926); Village of West Salem v. Industrial Commission, 155 N.W. 929 (Wis. 1916).

305 United States v. Rice, 27 Fed. Cas. 795 (W.D.N.C. 1875).

306 The Constitution is not without provisions for criminal procedure. Indeed, much of the Bill of Rights is an outline of basic criminal procedure. *See* LAWRENCE M. FRIEDMAN, A HISTORY OF AMERICAN LAW 118 (2d ed. 1985). But these provisions represent enshrinements of individual liberties rather than government power. The only constitutional provisions with regard to criminal justice represent barriers to governmental power, rather than provisions for that power. Indeed, the Founders' intent to protect individual liberties was made clear by the language of the Ninth Amendment and its equivalent in state constitutions of the founding era. The Ninth Amendment, which declares that "[t]he enumeration in the Constitution, of certain rights, shall not be construed to deny or disparage others retained by the people," provides

Roger I. Roots

a clear indication that the Framers assumed that persons may do whatever is not justly prohibited by the Constitution rather than that the government may do whatever is not justly prohibited to it. *See* Randy E. Barnett, Introduction: James Madison's Ninth Amendment, in THE RIGHTS RETAINED BY THE PEOPLE 43 (Randy E. Barnett ed., 1989).

307 *See* JAMES S. CAMPBELL ET AL., LAW AND ORDER RECONSIDERED: REPORT OF THE TASK FORCE ON LAW AND LAW ENFORCEMENT TO THE NATIONAL COMMISSION ON THE CAUSES AND PREVENTION OF VIOLENCE 450 (1970) (discussing survey by the President's Commission on Law Enforcement and Administration of Justice).

308 The term "policing" originally meant promoting the public good or the community life rather than preserving security. See Rogan Kersh et al., "*More a Distinction of Words than Things*": The Evolution of Separated Powers in the American States, 4 ROGER WILLIAMS U. L. REV. 5, 21 (1998).

309 *See, e.g.*, N.C. CONST. of Dec. 18, 1776, Dec. of Rights, Sec. II (providing that people of the state have a right to regulate the internal government and police thereof); PA. CONST. of Sept. 28, 1776, Dec. of Rights, art. III (stating that the people have a right of "governing and regulating the internal police of [the people]").

310 *See* Police Jury v. Britton, 82 U.S. (15 Wall.) 566 (1872). The purpose of such juries was 1) to police slaves and runaways, (2) to repair roads, bridges, and other infrastructure, and (3) to lay taxes as necessary for such acts. *Id.* at 568. *See also* BLACK'S LAW DICTIONARY 801 (abridged 6th ed. 1991).

311 When Blackstone wrote of offenses against "the public police and economy" in 1769, he meant offenses against the "due regulation and domestic order of the kingdom" such as clandestine marriage, bigamy, ren-dering bridges inconvenient to pass, vagrancy, and operating gambling houses. 4 WILLIAM BLACKSTONE, COMMENTARIES 924-27 (George Chase ed., Baker, Voorhis& Co. 1938) (1769).

312 *See, e.g.*, Wolf v. Colorado, 338 U.S. 25,27-28 (1948) (proclaiming that "security of one's privacy against arbitrary intrusion by the police" is at the core of the Fourth Amendment (clearly a slight misstatement of the Founders' original perception)).

313 *See* Roger Lane, Urbanization and Criminal Violence in the 19th Century: Massachusetts as a Test Case, in NATIONAL COMMISSION ON THE CAUSES AND PREVENTION OF VIOLENCE, VIOLENCE IN AMERICA:

HISTORICAL AND COMPARATIVE PERSPECTIVES 445, 451 (Graham & Gurr dir., 1969) (saying citizens were traditionally supposed to take care of themselves, with help of family, friends, or servants "when available").
314 *See, e.g.*, Kennard v. Burton, 25 Me. 39 (1845) (involving collision between two wagons).
315 *See* Roger Lane, Urbanization and Criminal Violence, *supra*, at 451. 316 ALEXIS DE TOCQUEVILLE, DEMOCRACY IN AMERICA 96 (J.P. Mayer ed., Harper Perennial Books 1988) (1848).
317 *Id.* 318 *See id.*
319 *See* Pauline Maier, *Popular Uprisings and Civil Authority in Eighteenth-Century America*, 27 WM. & MARY Q. 3-35 (1970).
320 DE TOCQUEVILLE, *supra*, at 72.
321 Roger Lane, Urbanization, *supra*, at 450. 322 *Id.*
323 *See id.* at 451.
324 *See, e.g.*, Lamb v. Day, 8 Vt. 407 (1836) (involving suit against constable for improper execution of civil writ); Tomlinson v. Wheeler, 1 Aik. 194 (Vt. 1826) (involving sheriff's neglect to execute civil judgment); Stoyel v. Edwards, 3 Day 1 (1807) (involving sheriffs execution of civil judgment).
325 If the modern police profession has a father, it is Sir Robert Peel, who founded the Metropolitan Police of London in 1829. *See* SUE TITUS REID, CRIMINAL JUSTICE: BLUEPRINTS 58 (5th ed. 1999) (attributing the founding of the first modern police force to Peel). Peel's uniformed officers — nick-named 'Bobbies' after the first name of their founder — operated under the direction of a central headquarters (Scotland Yard, named for the site once used by the Kings of Scotland as a residence), walking beats on a full-time basis to prevent crime. *See id.* Less than three decades later, Parliament enacted a statute requiring every borough and county to have a London-type police force. *See id.* The 'Bobbie' model of policing caught on more slowly in the United States, but by the 1880s most major American cities had adopted some type of full-time paid police force. *See id.* at 59 (noting that the county sheriff system continued in rural areas).
326 *See* LAWRENCE M. FRIEDMAN, CRIME AND PUNISHMENT IN AMERICAN HISTORY 151-52 (1993) (citation omitted).
327 *See* LAWRENCE M. FRIEDMAN, CRIME AND PUNISHMENT IN AMERICAN HISTORY 151 (1993).

328 *See id.* at 152 (describing early police use of station houses as homeless shelters for the poor). This same type of public problem-solving still remains a large part of police work. Police are called upon to settle landlord-tenant disputes, deliver emergency care, manage traffic, regu-late parking, and even to respond to alleged haunted houses. See id. at 151 (recounting 1894 alleged ghost incident in Oakland, California). Police continue to provide essential services to communities, especially at night and on weekends when they are the only social service agency. *See* Charles Silberman, Criminal Violence, Criminal Justice 321 (1978).

329 *See* GARRY WILLS, A NECESSARY EVIL: A HISTORY OF AMERICAN DISTRUST OF GOVERNMENT 248(1999) (citation omitted).

330 *See* SUE TITUS REID, CRIMINAL JUSTICE: BLUEPRINTS, at 65 (5th ed. 1999).

331 *See* JEROME H. SKOLNICK & JAMES J. FYFE, ABOVE THE LAW: POLICE AND THE EXCESSIVE USE OF FORCE 129 (1993).

332 *See id.*

333 *See id.* at 130.

334 *See* E.X. BOOZHIE, THE OUTLAW'S BIBLE 15 (1988).

335 Private prosecution was not without costs to taxpayers. The availability of free courtrooms to air grievances tended to promote litigation. In 1804, the Pennsylvania legislature acted to allow juries to make private prosecutors pay the costs of prosecution in especially trifling cases. Act of Dec. 8, 1804 PL3, 4 Sm L 204 (repealed 1860). Private persons were thereafter liable for court costs if they omitted material exculpatory information from a grand jury, thereby causing a grand jury to indict without knowledge of potential defenses. *See* Commonwealth v. Harkness, 4 Binn. 194 (Pa. 1811). This pro-tection, like many others, was lost when police and public prosecutors took over the criminal justice system in the twentieth century. *See* United States v. Williams, 504 U.S. 36 (1992) (holding prosecutor has no duty to present exculpatory evidence to grand jury).

336 In the American constitutional scheme, the states have 'general jurisdiction,' meaning they may regulate for public health and welfare and enact whatever means to enforce such regulation as is necessary and con-sti-tutionally proper. *See, e.g.*, Garcia v. San Antonio Metro. Transit Auth., 469 U.S. 528 (1985), National League of Cities v. Usery, 426 U.S. 833 (1976) (both standing for the general proposition that states have constitutional power to provide for protection, health, safety, and quality of life for their citizens).

See also Lawrence Tribe, American Constitutional Law, Sec. 6-3, 7-3 (2d ed. 1988). State and municipal police forces can therefore be viewed as constitutional to the extent they actually carry out the lawful enactments of the state.

337 *See* Silas J. Wasserstrom, *The Incredible Shrinking Fourth Amendment,* 21 AM. CRIM. L. REV. 257, 347 (1984).

338 *See* Jerome Hall, *Legal and Social Aspects of Arrest Without A Warrant,* 49 HARV. L. REV. 566, 567 (1936).

339 *See id.*

340 *See id.* at 567-71 (discussing earliest scholarly references to the distinction). A 1936 Harvard Law Review article suggested the distinction is a false one owed to improper marshalling of scholarship. *See id.* (writing of "the general misinterpretation" resulting from a 1780 case in England).

341 *See id.* at 575 n.44 (citing the case of Beckwith v. Philby, 6 B. & C. 635 (K. B. 1827)).

342 *See id.* at 571-72. Although official right was apparently considered somewhat greater than that of private citizens during much of the 1700s, the case law enunciates no support for any such distinction until Rohan v. Sawin, 59 Mass. (5 Cush.) 281 (1850). It was apparently already the common practice of English constables to arrest upon information from the public in the 1780's. *See id.* at 572. The "earlier requirement of a charge of a felony had already been entirely forgotten" in England by the early nineteenth century. *Id.* at 573. According to Hall, the only real distinction in practice in the early nineteenth century was that officers were privileged to draw their suspi-cions from statements of others, whereas private arrestors had to base their cause for arrest on their own reasonable beliefs. *See id.* at 569.

343 *See* Rohan v. Sawin, 59 Mass. (5 Cush.) 281, 285 (1850).

344 *See* 18 U.S.C. Sec. 925 (a)(l) (2000) (exempting government officers from federal firearm disabilities).

345 *See, e.g.,* CAL. PENAL CODE Sec. 468 (West 1985) (releasing police from liability for possession of sniper scopes and infrared scopes).

346 *See, e.g.,* FLA. STAT. CH. 338. 155 (1990).

347 *See, e.g.,* FLA. STAT. CH. 320.025 (1990) (allowing confidential auto reg-istration for police).

348 *See* ARK. CODE ANN. Sec. 20-22-703 (Michie 2000).

349 *See* 18 U.S.C. Sec. 1114 (amended 1994) (providing whoever murders a federal officer in first degree shall suffer death).

350 *See* CAL. PENAL CODE Sec. 832.9 (West 1995).

351 *See, e.g.*, CAL. HEALTH & SAFETY CODE Sec. 199.95-199.99 (West 1990) (mandating HIV testing for persons charged with interfering with police officers whenever officers request).

352 *See* Electronic Communications Privacy Act, 18 U.S.C. 2511 (2000); United States v. Leon, 104 S. Ct. 3405 (1984).

353 *See* Williams v. Poulos, 11 F.3d 271 (lst Cir. 1993).

354 *See, e.g.*, People v. Curtis, 450 P.2d 33, 35 (Cal. 1969) (speaking of the "[g]eneral acceptance" by courts of the elimination of the right to resist unlawful arrest).

355 *See* HERBERT J. STORING, WHAT THE ANTI-FEDERALISTS WERE FOR: THE POLITICAL THOUGHT OF THE OPPONENTS OF THE CONSTITUTION 53 (1981). The statements of James Madison when introducing the proposed amendments to the Constitution before the House of Representatives, June 8, 1789, also support such a reading of the Bill of Rights. House of Representatives, June 8, 1789 Debates, reprinted in THE ORIGIN OF THE SECOND AMENDMENT: A DOCUMENTARY HISTORY OF THE BILL OF RIGHTS 1787-1792 647, 657 (David E. Young, ed.) (2d ed. 1995) (stating "the great object in view is to limit and qualify the powers of Government").

356 *See* STORING, *supra*, at 48.

357 *See, e.g.*, MD. CONST. of 1776, art. I (declaring that "all government of right originates from the people, is founded in compact only, and instituted solely for the good of the whole"); MASS. CONST. of 1780, art. I ("All men are born free and equal, and have certain natural, essential, and unalien-able rights"); N.H. CONST. of 1784, art. I ("All men are born equally free and independent").

358 *See* Coyle v. Hurtin, 10 Johns. 85 (N.Y. 1813). 359 *See* Bad Elk v. United States, 177 U.S. 529 (1900).

360 *See* Rex v. Gay, Quincy Mass. Rep. 1761-1772 91 (Mass. 1763) (acquitting assault defendant who beat a sheriff when sheriff attempted to arrest him pursuant to invalid warrant).

361 *See* Wolf v. Colorado, 338 U.S. 25, 30 n. 1, 31 n. 2 (1948) (citing cases upholding right to resist unlawful search and seizure).

362 *See* Adams v. State, 48 S.E. 910 (Ga. 1904).

363 *See* MD. CONST. of 1776, art. IV; N.H. Const. of 1784, art. X.

364 *See, e.g.*, State v. Kutchara, 350 N.W.2d 924, 927 (Minn. 1984) (saying Minnesota law does not recognize right to resist unlawful arrest or search); People v. Curtis, 450 P.2d 33, 36 (Cal. 1969) (holding California law prohibits forceful resistance to unlawful arrest).

365 *See, e.g.*, CAL. PENAL CODE Sec. 243 (criminalizing the resistance, delay or obstruction of an officer in the discharge of "any duty of his office"). CAL. PENAL CODE Sec. 834(a) (1957) ("If a person has knowledge ... that he is being arrested by a peace officer, it is the duty of such person to refrain from using force or any weapon to resist such arrest").

366 *See, e.g.*, United States v. Charles, 883 F.2d 355 (5th Cir. 1989) (excusing as harmless error the failure of officers executing warrant to have the warrant in hand during raid); United States v. Cafero, 473 F.2d 489, 499 (3d Cir. 1973) (holding failure to deliver copy of warrant to the party being searched or seized does not invalidate search or seizure in the absence of prejudice); Willeford v. State, 625 S.W.2d 88, 90 (Tex. App. 1981) (upholding validity of search and seizure before arrival of warrant). Not only has the requirement that officers show their warrant before executing it been eliminated, but the requirement that officers announce their authority and purpose before executing search warrants has been all but eliminated. *See* Richards v. Wisconsin, 570 U.S. 385 (1997) (eliminating requirement that officers be refused admittance before using force to enter the place to be searched in many cases).

367 *See* William A. Schroeder, *Warrantless Misdemeanor Arrests and the Fourth Amendment*, 58 MO. L. REV. 771 (1993) (discussing the erosion of requirements for arrest warrants in many jurisdictions).

368 *See, e.g.,* Polk v. State, 142 So. 480, 481 (Miss. 1932) (striking down statute allowing warrantless arrest for misdemeanors committed out-side an officer's presence); Ex Parte Rhodes, 79 So. 462, 462-63 (Ala. 1918) (holding statute unconstitutional which allowed for warrantless arrest for out-of-presence misdemeanors).

369 *See* Schroeder, 58 MO. L. REV. at 793.

370 *See* Thor v. Superior Court, 855 P.2d 375, 380 (Cal. 1993) (saying the developing consensus "uniformly recognizes" a patient's right to control his own body, stemming from the "long-standing importance in our Anglo-American legal tradition of personal autonomy and the right of self-determination.") (citations omitted). "For self-determination to have any meaning,

it cannot be subject to the scrutiny of anyone else's conscience or sensibilities." *Id.* at 385.

371 *See* Michael v. Hertzler, 900 P.2d 1144, 1145 (Wyo. 1995) (stating if a statute reaches a fundamental interest, courts are to employ strict scrutiny in making determination as to whether enactment is essential to achieve compelling state interest).

372 "[Only] the gravest abuses, endangering paramount interests, give occasion for permissible limitation." Thomas v. Collins, 323 U.S. 516, 530 (1945). A "compelling state interest" is defined as "[o]ne which the state is forced or obliged to protect." BLACK'S LAW DICTIONARY 282 (6th ed. 1990) (citing Coleman v. Coleman, 291 N.E.2d 530, 534 (1972)).

373 The American constitutional order grants to every individual a privilege to stand his ground in the face of a violent challenger and meet violence with violence. A "duty to retreat" evolved in some jurisdictions, however, where a defender contemplates the use of deadly force. *See* WAYNE R. LAFAVE & AUSTIN W. SCOTT, CRIMINAL LAW 461 (2d ed. 1986). But with police, the courts have never imposed a duty to retreat. See id. This, combined with the recurring police claim that an attacker might get close enough to grasp the officer's sidearm, has meant, in practical terms, that an officer may repel even a minor physical threat with deadly force.

The effect of this exception for law enforcement officers has been to grant an almost absurd advantage to police in 'self-defense' incidents. Not only do cops have no duty to retreat, but they seem privileged to kill when-ever a plausible threat of any injury manifests itself. Cops — unlike the general public — appear excused whenever they open fire on an individual who threatens any harm — even utterly nonlethal — against them, such as a verbal threat to punch the officer combined with a step forward.

374 *See* James J. Fyfe, Police Use of Deadly Force: Research and Reform, in THE CRIMINAL JUSTICE SYSTEM: POLITICS AND POLICIES 134-40 (George F. Cole & Mare G. Gertz eds., 7th ed. 1998).

375 *Id.* at 135 (quoting Chapman and Crocket).

376 *See* People v. Klein, 137 N.E. 145, 149 (Ill. 1922) (reporting that "numerous" peace officers testified that shooting was the customary method of arrest-ing speeders during trial of peace officer accused of murder).

377 *See id.*; Miller v. People, 74 N.E. 743 (Ill. 1905) (involving village marshal who shot and killed speeding carriage driver).

378 *See* Fyfe, in THE CRIMINAL JUSTICE SYSTEM: POLITICS AND POLICIES, at 137.

379 *See id.* at 140.

380 *See id.* at 141 (table showing fatal shootings per 1,000 police officers, Philadelphia). A study of Philadelphia P.D. firearm discharges from 1970 through 1978 found only two cases that resulted in departmental dis-cipline against officers on duty. *See id.* at 147 n.2. One case involved an officer firing unnecessary shots into the air; the other involved an officer who shot and killed his wife in a police station during an argument over his paycheck. *See id.*

381 *See* Tennessee v. Garner, 471 U.S. 1 (1985). 382 471 U.S. 1 (1985).

383 *See* Fyfe, *supra*, at 136.

384 The *Garner* decision has been interpreted in different ways by different courts and law-making bodies. *See* Michael R. Smith, *Police Use of Deadly Force: How Courts and Policy-Makers Have Misapplied Tennessee v. Garner*, 1 KAN. J. L. & PUB. POL'Y, 100, 100-01 (1998). Smith argues that many of these interpretations stem from inaccurate readings of *Garner* and that lower courts have failed to hold police officers liable according to the standard required by the Supreme Court. *See id.*

385 On behalf of modern police, courts have adopted a qualified immunity defense to police misconduct claims. Essentially, where cops can justify by plausible explanation that their conduct was within the bounds of their occupational duties, there is a "good faith" defense. *See* Harlow v. Fitzgerald, 457 U.S. 800 (1982); Procunier v. Navarette, 434 U.S. 555 (1978); Imbler v. Pachtman, 424 U.S. 409 (1976); Wood v. Strickland, 420 U.S. 308 (1975). But as David Rudovsky points out, the "good faith" defense is an arti-ficial ingredient to normal tort liability. "The standard rule," notes Rudovsky, "is that a violation of another's rights or the failure to adhere to prescribed standards of conduct constitutes grounds for liability." David Rudovsky, The Criminal Justice System and the Role of the Police, in THE POLITICS OF LAW: A PROGRESSIVE CRITIQUE, 242, 248 (David Kairys ed., 1982). The "good faith" defense for police is thus an artificial layer of tort immunity protection not normally available to other types of litigants. Under the standard rules of tort law, after all, a defendant's good faith, intent, or knowledge of the law are irrelevant. *See id.* at 248.

386 *See* Smith, 1 KAN. J. L. & PUB. POL'Y, 100, at 117. 387 *See id.* at 106.

388 Idaho v. Horiuchi, 215 F.3d 986 (9th Cir. 2000) (Kozinski, J., dissenting).

389 OCTOBER 22 COALITION TO STOP POLICE BRUTALITY ET AL., STOLEN LIVES: KILLED BY LAW ENFORCEMENT 307 (2d. ed. 1999) (hereinafter "STOLEN LIVES") (saying officer shot and killed victim after victim 'made a move' following a foot chase).

390 *See id.* at 207 (listing a 1993 Michigan case).

391 *See id.* at 262 (reporting 1990 Brooklyn case in which cop had shot unarmed teenage suspect in back of head for allegedly reaching into jacket).

392 *See id.* at 250 (reporting 1996 New York case in which man was shot 24 times by police while sitting in car with his hands in the air); *id.* at 252 (reporting shooting of alleged car thief after motion 'as if they were going for a gun').

393 *See id.* at 262 (reporting 1990 Bronx shooting precipitated by the decedent turning toward an officer as officer opened door of decedent's cab). 394 *See id.* at 263 (reporting 1988 New York case initiated when a driver made illegal turn and ending with police pumping 16 bullets into her).

395 *See id.* at 262 (reporting 1990 Brooklyn case in which decedent was shot nine times while standing and twice in back while lying on ground). 396 *See id.* at 240 (reporting a 1998 New York case).

397 *See id.* at 232 (reporting 1991 New Mexico case). 398 *See id.* at 220 (reporting 1998 Nevada case). 399 *See id.* at 29.

400 *Id.* at 44.

401 *Id.* at 46. The possession of a wooden stick has cost more than one person his life at the hands of police. *See also id.* at 68.

402 *Id.* at 53.

403 *Id.* at 53.

404 *See* Detroit Police Kill Mentally Ill Deaf Man, BOSTON GLOBE, Aug. 31, 2000 at A8.

405 *See* STOLEN LIVES, *supra*, at 57. 406 *See id.* at 60.

407 *See id.* at 62.

408 *See id.* at 206 (listing a 1993 Michigan case). In another Michigan case, a cop shot someone who merely had a VCR remote control in his pocket, claiming he mistook it for a gun. *See id.* at 205.

409 *See id.* at 305 (saying Houston police surrounded truck and fired 59 times at victim as he sat in truck holding can opener). No civilian witnesses saw the "shiny object" (can opener) police claimed they saw. *See id.*

410 Police use of throwdown guns has been alleged across the country. Guns which are introduced without a suspect's fingerprints when they should have fingerprints, and guns that are found by police officers after an initial, supposedly complete, search of a crime scene by other detectives, can be said to raise questions about police use of throw-down guns. *C.f.* Joe Cantlupe & David Hasemyer, Pursuit of Justice: How San Diego Police Officers Handled the Killing of One of Their Own. It Is a Case Flawed by Erratic Testimony and Questionable Conduct, SAN DIEGO UNION-TRIBUNE, Sept. 11, 1994, at A1 (raising the issue in a San Diego case).

411 *See* Webster v. City of Houston, 689 F.2d 1220, 1227 (5th Cir. 1982).

412 *Id.* at 1222.

413 *See id.* at 1221-23 (describing "damning" evidence of official cover-up and police vindication as a matter of policy).

414 *See* STOLEN LIVES, *supra*, at 72. In one 1987 Los Angeles case, a man was shot four times and killed when he picked up a discarded pushbroom to deflect police baton blows. *See id.* 72.

415 *See id.* at iv. In one particularly egregious case, a police killing was upheld as beyond liability where officers shot a speeding trucker who refused to stop. *See* Cole v. Bone, 993 F.2d 1328 (8th Cir. 1993). But *see, e.g.,* Gutierrez-Rodriquez v. Cartagena, 882 F.2d 553 (1st Cir. 1989) (affirming verdict against plainclothes officers who shot driver who drove away); Sherrod v. Berry, 827 F.2d 195 (7th Cir. 1987) (affirming verdict against officers who shot driver as driver reached into jacket pocket during questioning); Moody v. Ferguson, 732 F. Supp. 176 (D.S.L. 1989) (rendering judgment against officers who shot driver fleeing in vehicle from traffic stop).

416 *See* Zuchel v. City and County of Denver, Colorado, 997 F.2d 730 (10th Cir. 1993).

417 *See* Alison L. Patton, *The Endless Cycle of Abuse: Why 42 U.S.C. § 1983 Is Ineffective in Deterring Police Brutality*, 44 HASTINGS L. J. 753, 754 (1993) (saying plaintiffs rarely win absent independent witnesses or physical evidence).

418 *See* Peter L. Davis, *Rodney King and the Decriminalization of Police Brutality in America*, 53 MD. L. REV. 271, 288 (1994). Prior to the 1900s, it was not uncommon for law enforcers who killed suspects during confrontations to be placed on trial for their lives even when they reacted to violent resisters. *See* United States v. Rice, 27 F. Cas. 795 (C.C.N.C. 1875)

(No. 16,153) (involving deputy United States Marshall on trial for murder of tax evasion suspect); State v. Brown, 5 Del. (5 Harr.) 505 (Ct. Gen. Sess. 1853) (fining peace officers for assault and false imprisonment); Conner v. Commonwealth, 3 Bin. 38 (Pa. 1810) (involving a constable indicted for refusing to execute arrest warrant). Even justices of the peace could be criminally indicted for dereliction of duties. *See* Respublica v. Montgomery, Dall. 419 (1795) (upholding validity of a criminal charge against a justice of the peace who failed to suppress a riot).

419   *See* Davis, 53 MD. L. REV., at 290 (noting the hopeless conflict of interest in handling police violence complaints).

420   *See* Steiker, *Second Thoughts About First Principles*, 107 HARV. L. REV., at 836 (saying police excesses such as beatings, torture, false arrests and the third degree arc well documented).

421   *See* STOLEN LIVES, *supra*, at vii.

422   *See* International Secretariat of Amnesty International, News Release, From Alabama to Wyoming: 50 Counts of Double Standards — The Missing Entries in the US Report on Human Rights, Feb. 25, 1999.

423   *See* STOLEN LIVES at iv. 424   *See id.* at v.

425   Certain examples demonstrate. FBI agents in Elizabeth, New Jersey shot 38 times inside an apartment to kill an unarmed man who they first tried to say had fired first. *See id.* at 226. In February 1999, Bronx police fired 41 bullets at an unarmed African immigrant in his apartment doorway. *See id.* at 234. After this unlawful killing, cops unlawfully searched the decedent's apartment to justify shooting, failing to find any evidence of drugs. See id. In August 1999, Manhattan cops fired a total of 35 shots at alleged robber (who probably did not fire), injuring bystander and sending crowds fleeing. *See id.*

426   Most states that allow the death penalty require that aggravating factors exist before imposition of capital punishment. *See, e.g.,* IDAHO CODE Sec. 19-2515 (1997) (allowing death penalty for crimes involving "especially heinous, atrocious or cruel, [or] manifesting exceptional depravity" or showing "utter disregard for human life"); TEX. CRIM. P. ANN. 37.071 (West 1981) (listing factors such as whether the crime was "unreasonable in response to the provocation"); WYO. STAT. ANN. Sec. 6-2-102 (Michie 1999) (allowing death penalty only upon a finding of aggravating factors such as a creation of great risk of death to two or more persons or for "especially atrocious or cruel" conduct).

427   The earliest attempts at professionalization of constables failed in the United States due to insufficiency of public funds. See Steiker, *Second Thoughts About First Principles*, 107 HARV. L. REV., at 831. Some of the earliest U.S. Supreme Court decisions regarding police forces involve disputes over municipal police spending. *See, e.g.,* Louisiana ex rel. Hubert v. New Orleans, 215 U.S. 170 (1909) (resolving dispute over debts run up by municipal police district); New Orleans v. Benjamin, 153 U.S. 411 (1894) (involving dispute over unbudgeted debts run up by New Orleans police board); District of Columbia v. Hutton, 143 U.S. 18 (1891) (dealing with salary dispute involving District of Columbia police force).

428   *See* LAWRENCE M. FRIEDMAN, CRIME AND PUNISHMENT IN AMERICAN HISTORY 362 (1993). Dallas police, for example, arrested 8,526 people in 1929 "on suspicion" but charged less than five percent of them with a crime. *See id.* 429   The infamous case of Brown v. Mississippi, 297 U.S. 278 (1936), provides a grim reminder of the torture techniques that have been employed upon suspects during the past century. In *Brown*, officers placed nooses around the necks of suspects, temporarily hanged them, and cut their backs to pieces with a leather strap to gain confessions. *Id.* at 281-82.

430   LAWRENCE M. FRIEDMAN, CRIME AND PUNISHMENT IN AMERICAN HISTORY 151 (1993). at 151 n.20 (quoting George S. McWatters, who studied New York detectives in the 1870s).

431   *See* TITUS REID, CRIMINAL JUSTICE: BLUEPRINTS, at 122 (citations omitted).

432   *See* Peter B. Kraska & Victor E. Kappeler, *Militarizing American Police: The Rise and Normalization of Paramilitary Units*, 44 SOC. PROBS. 1, 11 (1997). 433   One-hundred-seventeen federal, state, and local officers were killed feloniously in 1996 — the lowest number since 1960. See SUE TITUS REID, CRIMINAL JUSTICE: BLUEPRINTS, at 123 (5th ed. 1999).

434   *See* National Institute for Occupational Safety and Health, Violence in the Work Place, June 1997.

435   *See id.*

436   Approximately 40 percent of police deaths are due to accidents. *See* TITUS REID, *supra*, at 123.

437   *See* National Institute for Occupational Safety and Health, Fatal Injuries to Workers in the United States, 1980-1989: A Decade of Surveillance 14 (April 15, 1999); Robert Rockwell, Police Brutality: More than Just a Few

Bad Apples, REFUSE & RESIST, Aug. 14, 1997 (describing the "cultivation of the myth of policing as the most dangerous occupation").
438   *See id.* at 13.
439   *See* JEROME H. SKOLNICK & JAMES J. FYFE, ABOVE THE LAW: POLICE AND THE EXCESSIVE USE OF FORCE 93 (1993).
440   *See* Jerome Hall, *Legal and Social Aspects of Arrest Without A Warrant,* 49 HARV. L. REV. 566, 582-83 (1936) (describing early constables as "[a] bomina-bly paid").
441   OCTOBER 22 COALITION TO STOP POLICE BRUTALITY ET AL., STOLEN LIVES: KILLED BY LAW ENFORCEMENT v (2d. ed. 1999) (hereinafter "STOLEN LIVES") at v (saying when police arrive on the scene, they often escalate the situation rather than defuse it).
442   *See id.* at vi.
443   *See, e.g.,* Brandon v. City of Providence, 708 A.2d 893 (R.I. 1998) (finding municipality immune from liability when cops prevented relatives of injured shooting victim from taking victim to the hospital before victim died). *See also* Stolen Lives, *supra,* at 305 (saying Tennessee police prevented fire fighters from saving victim of fire in 1997 case). Other notorious examples can be cited, including the 1993 Waco fire (in which fire trucks were held back by federal agents) and the 1985 MOVE debacle in Philadelphia in which police dropped a bomb on a building occupied by women and children and then held back fire fighters from rescuing bum victims. *See* WILLIE L. WILLIAMS, TAKING BACK OUR STREETS: FIGHTING CRIME IN AMERICA 16 (1996) (saying investigative hearings revealed cops had held back rescuers as a 'tactical decision').
444   *See* JEROME H. SKOLNICK & JAMES J. FYFE, ABOVE THE LAW: POLICE AND THE EXCESSIVE USE OF FORCE 75 (1993) (citing U.S. Civil Disorder Commission study).
445   *See id.* at 83 (describing police riots at Columbia University and Los Angeles).
446   *See* RIGHTS IN CONFLICT: THE OFFICIAL REPORT TO THE NATIONAL COMMISSION ON THE CAUSES AND PREVENTION OF VIOLENCE xxiii, xxvi (1968).
447   *See* John D. Bessler, *The Public Interest and the Unconstitutionality of Private Prosecutors,* 47 ARK. L. REV. 511 (1994) (attacking private prosecution as unfair, arbitrary, and not in the public interest).

448 *See* Richard M. Brown, *Historical Patterns of Violence in America,* in NATIONAL COMMISSION ON THE CAUSES AND PREVENTION OF VIOLENCE, VIOLENCE IN AMERICA: HISTORICAL AND COMPARATIVE PERSPECTIVES 57 (Graham & Gurr, ed. 1969).
449 *See* State v. Walker, 32 Me. 195 (1850) (upholding actions of the private group).
450 *See* United States v. Whittier, 28 F. Cas. 591 (C.C.E.D. Mo. 1878).
451 *See* Richard Maxwell Brown, The American Vigilante Tradition, in NATIONAL COMMISSION ON THE CAUSES AND PREVENTION OF VIOLENCE, VIOLENCE IN AMERICA: HISTORICAL AND COMPARATIVE PERSPECTIVES 57 (Graham & Gurr, dir. 1969).
452 *See* JAMES S. CAMPBELL, ET AL., LAW AND ORDER RECONSIDERED: REPORT OF THE TASK FORCE ON LAW AND LAW ENFORCEMENT 441 (1970) (discussing successes of citizen auxiliary units in Queens, New York and other areas).
453 *See id.* 437-54 (1970) (discussing successes of citizen involvement in law enforcement).
454 American frontier vigilantism generally targeted serious criminals such as murderers, coach robbers and rapists as well as horse thieves, counterfeiters, outlaws, and 'bad men.' *See* NATIONAL COMMISSION ON THE CAUSES AND PREVENTION OF VIOLENCE, VIOLENCE IN AMERICA: HISTORICAL AND COMPARATIVE PERSPECTIVES 97 (Graham & Gurr, dir. 1969). Arguably, such offenders qualified as felons and would have faced the death penalty under the common law even if more conventional court processes were followed. That such vigilante movements often followed rudimentary due process of law is attested by historians such as Richard Maxwell Brown, who recounts that "vigilantes' attention to the spirit of law and order caused them to pro-vide, by their lights, a fair but speedy trial." Richard Maxwell Brown, *supra,* at 164. The northern Illinois Regulator movement of 1841, for example, pro-vided accused horse thieves and murderers with a lawyer, an opportunity to challenge jurors, and an arraignment. *See id.* at 163. At least one accused murderer was acquitted by a vigilante court on the Wyoming frontier. *See* Joe B. Frantz, The Frontier Tradition: An Invitation to Violence, in NATIONAL COMMISSION ON THE CAUSES AND PREVENTION OF VIOLENCE, VIOLENCE IN AMERICA: HISTORICAL AND COMPARATIVE PERSPECTIVES 129-30 (Graham & Gurr, dir. 1969). Many accused were let off with whipping and

expulsion rather than execution in the early decades of vigilante justice. See Brown, supra note 189, at 164. Less than half of all vigilante groups ever killed any-one. See id. Ironically, the move by vigilante groups toward killing convicted suspects began in the 1850s, — corresponding closely with the meteoric rise of professional policing. *See id.*
Vigilante movements occasionally developed to rescue the law from corrupt public officials who were violating the law. The case of the vigilantes who arrested and hanged Sheriff Henry Plummer of Virginia City, Montana in 1864 is such an example. See LEW L. CALLAWAY, MONTANA'S RIGHTEOUS HANGMEN (1997) (arguing the vigilantes had no choice but to take the law into their own hands).

455 "[T]he Western frontier developed too swiftly for the courts of justice to keep up with the progression of the people." Joe B. Frantz, The Frontier Tradition: An Invitation to Violence, at 128. Vigilante movements did little more than play catch-up to what can only be described as rampant frontier lawlessness. Five-thousand wanted men roamed Texas in 1877. *See id.* at 128. Major crimes often went totally unprosecuted and countless offenders whose crimes were well known lived openly without fear of arrest on the western frontier. *See id.* Vigilantes filled in only the most gaping holes in court jurisdiction, generally (but not always) intervening to arrest only the perpetrators of serious crimes. See id. and at 130 (saying "improvised group action" was the only resort for many on the far frontier).

456 David H. Bayley & Clifford D. Shearing, The Future of Policing, in THE CRIMINAL JUSTICE SYSTEM: POLITICS AND POLICIES 150, 150 (George F. Cole & Marc G. Gertz, eds., 7th ed. 1998).

457 *See id.* at 151, 154.

458 Tucker Carlson, *Washington's Inept Police Force*, WALL ST. J., Nov. 3, 1993, at A19.

459 *See* Charles Silberman, Criminal Violence, Criminal Justice at 297. Silberman points out that New York City police solved only two percent of robbery cases in which a witness could not identify an offender or the offender was not captured at the scene. *See id.*

460 *See id.* at 296 (saying clearance rate dropped precipitously between 1960 and 1976 as proportion of crimes committed by strangers increased). 461 *See id.* (citing figures registered between 1960 and 1976).

462 *See id.* at 296.

463 *See* Laura Parker & Gary Fields, *Unsolved Killings on Rise: Percent of Cases Closed Drops From 86% to 69%*, USA TODAY, Feb. 22, 2000, at A1.

464 *See id.*

465 *See* BARRY SCHECK, ET AL., ACTUAL INNOCENCE 175 (2000).

466 428 U.S. 153 (1976) (finding death penalty constitutional so long as adequate procedures are provided to a defendant).

467 *See* SCHECK, *supra*, at 218.

468 *See* Illinois Governor Orders Execution Moratorium, USA TODAY, Feb. 1, 2000, at 3A.

469 *See* SCHECK, *supra*, at 218 (noting an average of 4.6 condemned people per year have been set free after 1996, while only 2.5 death row inmates per year were freed between 1973 and 1993).

470 *See id.* at xv (noting these 5,000 exonerations came from only the first 18 thousand results of DNA testing at crime laboratories — a rate of almost 30% exonerated).

471 *C.f. id.* at 180 (detailing indictment of four officers for perjury and obstruction of justice in the wake of one DNA exoneration).

472 DNA testing has proven that at least 67 people were sent to prison or death row for crimes they did not commit. *See id.* at xiv. This number grows each month. *See id.*

473 *C.f.* Morgan Cloud, *The Dirty Little Secret*, 43 EMORY L. J. 1311, 1311 (1994) (saying "[p]olice perjury is the dirty little secret of our criminal justice system"). 474 *See* BURTON S. KATZ, JUSTICE OVERRULED: UNMASKING THE CRIMINAL JUSTICE SYSTEM 77-86 (1999).

475 *See* Charles Silberman, Criminal Violence, Criminal Justice, at 308 (describing interrogation techniques of police as "an art form in its own right."). Lying or bluffing can often persuade a suspect to admit crimes to the police which would not otherwise be proven. *See id.*

476 *C.f. id.* (recounting that an officer under observation would simply lie on the stand if challenged in court about whether Miranda warnings were given before questioning a suspect).

477 *See* Joe Cantlupe & David Hasemyer, *Pursuit of Justice: How San Diego Police Officers Handled the Killing of One of Their Own. It Is a Case Flawed by Erratic Testimony and Questionable Conduct*, SAN DIEGO UNION-TRIBUNE, Sept. 11, 1994, at A1 (exposing that some officers gave false testimony in case of suspected cop-killers).

478   Andrew Horwitz, *Taking the Cop Out of Copping a Plea: Eradicating Police Prosecution of Criminal Cases*, 40 ARIZ. L. REV. 1305, 1321 (1998) (quoting Jerome H. Skolnick).

479   *See* Daniel B. Wood, *One precinct stirs a criminal-justice crisis*, CHRISTIAN SCIENCE MONITOR, Feb. 18, 2000, at 1.

480   *See* SUE TITUS REID, CRIMINAL JUSTICE: BLUEPRINTS, at 120 (5th ed. 1999).

481   *See* Charles Silberman, Criminal Violence, Criminal Justice, AT 231.

482   *See* Gary Fields, *New Orleans' Crime Fight Started With Police*, USA TODAY, Feb. 1, 2000, at 6A.

483   *See* Tucker Carlson, *Washington's Inept Police Force*, WALL ST. J., Nov. 3, 1993, at A19.

484   *See* Abuse of Power, DETROIT NEWS, May 3, 1996.

485   *See* Lawrence W. Sherman, *Becoming Bent: Moral Careers of Corrupt Policemen*, IN "ORDER UNDER LAW": READINGS IN CRIMINAL JUSTICE 96, 104-06 (1981) (discussing police burglary scandals of the 1960s).

486   *See* Wood, *One precinct stirs a criminal-justice crisis*, at 5 (citing critics). 487   *See* LAWRENCE M. FRIEDMAN, CRIME AND PUNISHMENT IN AMERICAN HISTORY 154 (1993). The Lexow Committee of 1894 was perhaps the first to probe police misconduct in New York City. The Committee found that the police had formed a "separate and highly privileged class, armed with the authority and the machinery of oppression." *See id.*. Witnesses before the Committee testified to brutal beatings, extortion and perjury by New York police. *See id.* at 154-55.

488   In April 1994, for example, thirty-three New York officers were indicted and ultimately convicted of perjury, drug dealing and robbery. *See* James Lardner, *Better Cops. Fewer Robbers*, N.Y. TIMES MAG., Feb. 9, 1997, pp. 44-52. The following year, sixteen Bronx police officers were indicted for robbing drug dealers, beating people, and abusing the public. *See id.*

489   *See* Jerome H. Skolnick, A Sketch of the Policeman's "Working Personality," in THE CRIMINAL JUSTICE SYSTEM: POLITICS AND POLICIES 116, 123 (George F. Cole & Marc G. Gertz 7th ed. 1998).

490   *See* Wood, *One precinct stirs a criminal-justice crisis*, at 5 (quoting critics). 491   *C.f.* SUE TITUS REID, CRIMINAL JUSTICE: BLUEPRINTS, at 117-119 (5th ed. 1999) (describing police subculture).

492 *See* FRIEDMAN, CRIME AND PUNISHMENT IN AMERICAN HISTORY, at 154 (saying New York police of the 1890s engaged in routine extortion of businesses, collecting kickbacks from push-cart vendors, corner groceries, and businessmen whose flag poles extended too far into the street). In Chicago, police historically sought "contributions" from saloonkeepers. See id. at 155.

493 *See, e.g.*, PATRICK J. BUCHANAN, RIGHT FROM THE BEGINNING 283-84 (1990) (detailing police favoritism toward one St. Louis newspaper and antagonism toward its competitor); Jonathan D. Rockoff, Comment Costs Kennedy Police Backing, PROVIDENCE J., April 21, 2000, at 1B (describing police unions' threats to drop their support for Rep. Kennedy due to Kennedy's public remarks).

494 *See* Davis, 53 MD. L. REV., at 355.

495 *See* Silas J. Wasserstrom, *The Incredible Shrinking Fourth Amendment,* 21 AM. CRIM. L. REV. 257, 293-94 (1984) (stating no one has ever been convicted under the statute, 18 U.S.C. Section 2236).

496 *See* U.S. Dep't of Justice, Office of Inspector General, The FBI Laboratory: An Investigation into Laboratory Practices and Alleged Misconduct in Explosives-Related and Other Cases (April 1997) (detailing Justice Department's findings of impropriety at the FBI Crime Lab).

497 *Cf.* Charles Silberman, Criminal Violence, Criminal Justice SILBERMAN, at 211-14 (observing the behavior of cops on patrol).

498 *See id.* at 215-16 (citing study conducted in Kansas City in the 1970s).

499 *C.f. id.* at 215 (pointing to mounting criticism of traditional approach). Studies of police pull-overs and sidewalk stops invariably demonstrate patterns of economic, racial, and social discrimination as well. *See, e.g.,* Bruce Landis, *State Police Records Support Charges of Bias in Traffic Stops,* PROVIDENCE J., Sept. 5, 1999 at 1A (reporting Rhode Island traffic stop statistics demonstrate racial bias by state police).

500 The United States' 'war on drugs' is a perfect illustration of the difficulties of implementing broad-ranging social policy through police enforcement mechanisms. "Not since Vietnam ha[s] a national mission failed so miser-ably." JIM MCGEE & BRIAN DUFFY, MAIN JUSTICE: THE MEN AND WOMEN WHO ENFORCE THE NATION'S CRIMINAL LAWS AND GUARD ITS LIBERTIES 43 (1996). The federal drug control budget increased from $4.3 billion in 1988 to $11.9 billion in 1992, yet national drug

supply increased greatly and prices dropped during the same period. See id. at 42. The costs of enforce-ment in 1994 ranged from $79,376 per arrestee by the DEA to $260,000 per arrestee by the FBI, with no progress made at all toward decreasing the drug trade. See id.

501   See JOHN R. LOTT, JR., MORE GUNS, LESS CRIME: UNDERSTANDING CRIME AND GUN CONTROL LAWS 213 n.3 (1998) (citing forthcoming paper). 502   See JOHN PHILLIP REID, IN DEFIANCE OF THE LAW: THE STANDING-ARMY CONTROVERSY, THE Two CONSTITUTIONS, AND THE COMING OF THE AMERICAN REVOLUTION (1981) (recounting the history and consti-tutional background of the standing-army controversy that preceded the Revolution).

503   THE DECLARATION OF INDEPENDENCE paras. 12, 13, 14 (U.S. 1776). The duties of such troops were in no way military but involved the keeping of order and the suppression of crime (especially customs and tax violations). 504   See JOHN P. REID, supra, at 79.

505   See id. at 79.

506   See id. at 50 (citation omitted).

507   See id. at 29 (quoting the orations of Hancock).

508   In Edinburgh in 1736, a unit of town guards maintaining order during the execution of a convicted smuggler was pelted with stones and mud until some soldiers began firing weapons at the populace. See JOHN P. REID, supra, at 114-15 (recounting the history and constitutional background of the standing-army controversy which preceded the Revolution). After nine citizens were found dead, the captain of the guard was tried for murder, convicted, and him-self condemned to be hanged. See id. When officers of the crown indicated a willingness to pardon the captain, a mob of civilians "rescued" the captain from prison and hanged him. See id. 509   See Jerome Hall, Legal and Social Aspects of Arrest Without A Warrant, 49 HARV. L. REV. 566, 587-88 (1936).

510   Id. at 587.

511   Ben C. Roberts, On the Origins and Resolution of English Working-Class Protest, in NATIONAL COMMISSION ON THE CAUSES AND PREVENTION OF VIOLENCE, VIOLENCE IN AMERICA: HISTORICAL AND COMPARATIVE PERSPECTIVES 238, 252 (Graham & Gurr, dir. 1969).

512   JOHN P. REID, supra, at 80.

513   See id. at 95 (quoting from a 1770 issue of the New Hampshire Gazette).

514 Analogies might also be drawn between military occupation and policing in slave states throughout the eighteenth and early nine-teenth centuries impacted the manner in which criminal justice was imposed regionally. Frederick Law Olmsted wrote before the Civil War that slavery bred habits of "bullies and ruffians" among slave states. In Charleston, South Carolina, wrote Olmsted, an observer could see "police machinery, such as you never find in towns under free government: citadels, sentries, passports, grape-shotted cannon, and daily public whippings." *See* Adam Goodheart, 1861: The Civil War Awakening 122 (2008). As Goodheart noted, the police station in early Charleston was actually a barracks with all the accoutrements of a fortress in an occupied country.

515 *See* Peter B. Kraska & Victor E. Kappeler, *Militarizing American Police: The Rise and Normalization of Paramilitary Units*, 44 SOC. PROBS. 1, 2-3 (1997) (citing National Institute of Justice report detailing "partnership" between Defense and Justice Departments in equipping personnel to "engage the crime war").

516 *See* William Booth, *The Militarization of 'Mayberry,'* WASH. POST, June 17, 1997, at A1.

517 *See id.* 518 *See id.*

519 *See id.* (quoting Kraska).

520 *See* Kraska & Kappeler, *supra*, at 10.

521 *See* Roger Roots, The Approaching Death of the Collective Right Theory of the Second Amendment, 39 DUQUESNE L. REV. 71 (2000).

522 *See id.* 523 *C.f. id.*

524 *See* JOHN R. LOTT, JR., MORE GUNS, LESS CRIME: UNDERSTANDING CRIME AND GUN CONTROL LAWS (1998) (supporting a proposition con-sistent with the title); GARY KLECK, POINT BLANK: GUNS AND VIOLENCE IN AMERICA (1991).

525 *Id.* (KLECK), at 111-116, 148.

526 *See* George F. Will, *Are We a Nation of Cowards?*, NEWSWEEK, Nov. 15, 1993, at 93. The error rate is defined as the rate of shootings involving an innocent person mistakenly identified as a criminal. *See id.*

527 See ANTHONY J. PINIZZOTTO, ET AL., U.S. DEP'T OF JUSTICE, NAT'L INST. OF JUSTICE, IN THE LINE OF FIRE: A STUDY OF SELECTED FELONIOUS ASSAULTS ON LAW ENFORCEMENT

OFFICERS 8 (1997) (table showing 41 percent accuracy by police as opposed to 91 percent accuracy by their assailants with handguns).

528 *See, e.g.*, Morgan v. California, 743 F.2d 728 (9th Cir. 1984) (involving drunk officers who backed their car into innocent civilian couple and then brandished guns to threaten them).

529 *See* Shapiro v. New York City Police Dept., 595 N.Y.S.2d 864 (N.Y. Sup. Ct. 1993) (upholding revocation of pistol license of cop who threatened drivers with gun during two traffic disputes); Matter of Beninson v. Police Dept., 574 N.Y.S.2d 307 (N.Y. Sup. Ct. 1991) (involving revocation of pistol permit of cop based on two displays of firearms in traffic situations).

530 *See* JOSHUA DRESSLER, UNDERSTANDING CRIMINAL LAW 255 n. 34 (2d ed. 1995) (citing review of nearly 700 shootings).

531 *See* Tucker Carlson, *Washington's Inept Police Force*, WALL ST. J., Nov. 3, 1993, at A19.

532 U.S. CONST. amend. III ("No Soldier shall, in time of peace be quartered in any house, without the consent of the Owner, nor in time of war, but in a manner to be prescribed by law").

533 *See* Morton J. Horwitz, *Is the Third Amendment Obsolete?*, 26 VALPARAISO U. L. REV. 209, 214 (1991) (stating the Third Amendment might have produced a constitutional bar to standing armies in peace-time if public antipathy toward standing armies had remained intense over time).

534 3 JOSEPH STORY, COMMENTARIES ON THE CONSTITUTION OF THE UNITED STATES 747-48 (1833) (emphasis added).

535 For a well-written local history of this conflict, see HENRY BLACKMAN PLUMB, HISTORY OF HANOVER TOWNSHIP 121-140 (1885).

536 *See id.*

537 *See id.* at 125-26. 538 *See id.* at 130.

539 *See id.* at 138 (adding that those convicted "were allowed easily to escape, and no fines were ever attempted to be collected").

540 *See, e.g.*, JAMES BOVARD, FREEDOM IN CHAINS: THE RISE OF THE STATE AND THE DEMISE OF THE CITIZEN (1999) (presenting a thesis in line with the title); JAMES BOVARD, LOST RIGHTS: THE DESTRUCTION OF AMERICAN LIBERTY (1994) (detailing America's loss of freedom).

541 *See* Olmstead v. United States, 277 U.S. 438, 478 (1928) (Brandeis, J., dissenting) (saying the right to be let alone is "the most comprehensive of rights and the right most valued by civilized man.").

542   *C.f.* Stephen D. Mastrofski, et al., The Helping Hand of the Law: Police Control of Citizens on Request, 38 CRIMINOLOGY 307 (2000) (detailing study finding officers are likely to use their power to control citizens at mere request of other citizens).

543   U.S. CONST. amend. IV.

544   *See, e.g.,* Maryland Minority, Address to the People of Maryland, Maryland Gazette, May 6, 1788, reprinted in THE ORIGIN OF THE SECOND AMENDMENT, supra note 89, at 356, 358 (stating that an amendment protecting people from unreasonable search and seizure was considered indispensable by many who opposed the Constitution).

545   *See, e.g.,* AKHIL R. AMAR, THE CONSTITUTION AND CRIMINAL PROCEDURE: FIRST PRINCIPLES 1-45 (1997). Amar argues that the Amendment lays down only a few "first principles"— namely "that all searches and seizures must be reasonable, that warrants (and only war-rants) always require probable cause, and that the officialdom should be held liable for unreasonable searches and seizures." Id. at 1.

546   *See, e.g.,* Richard A. Posner, Rethinking the Fourth Amendment, 1981 SUP. CT. REV. 49 (arguing that the Fourth Amendment should not provide a guilty criminal with any right to avoid punishment).

547   *See* AMAR, THE CONSTITUTION AND CRIMINAL PROCEDURE, at 3-17 (arguing the Framers intended no warrant requirement).

548   *See id.*

549   *See* California v. Acevedo, 500 U.S. 565, 581 (1991) (Scalia, J., concurring) (referencing Amar's claims for support). Ten years earlier, in Robbins v. California, 453 U.S. 420 (1981), Justice Rehnquist cited a 1969 book by Professor Telfred Taylor — Amar's predecessor in the argument that the Fourth Amendment's text requires only an ad hoc test of reasonableness — for the same proposition. Id. at 437 (Rehnquist, J., dissenting).

550   *See, e.g.,* Hulit v. State, 982 S.W.2d 431, 436 (Tex. Crim. App. 1998) (citing Amar for proposition that Fourth Amendment requires no warrants).

551   *See, e.g.,* Max Boot, Out of Order: Arrogance, Corruption, and Incompetence on the Bench 66 (1998) (reciting the Amar/Taylor thesis without reservation).

552   Since the addition of Justice Rehnquist to the Supreme Court, the Court has traveled far down the road toward ejecting the warrant requirement. *See* generally Silas J. Wasserstrom, *The Incredible Shrinking Fourth Amendment,*

21 AM. CRIM. L. REV. 257 (1984). The Court has increasingly tended to adopt a balancing test pitting the citizen's "Fourth Amendment interests" (rather than his "rights") against "legitimate governmental interests." *See, e.g.,* Delaware v. Prouse, 440 U.S. 648, 654 (1979).

553   In United States v. Chadwick, 433 U.S. 1, 6 (1977), the United States Justice Department mounted a "frontal attack" on the warrant requirement and argued that the warrant clause of the Fourth Amendment protected only "interests traditionally identified with the home." Accordingly, the Justice Department would have eliminated warrants in every other setting. 554 Compare Howard v. Lyon, 1 Root 107 (Conn. 1787) (involving constable-who obtained "escape warrant" to recapture an escaped prisoner and even had the warrant "renewed" in Rhode Island where prisoner fled), and Bromley v. Hutchins, 8 Vt. 68 (1836) (upholding damages against a deputy sheriff who arrested an escapee without warrant outside the deputy's jurisdiction), with United States v. Watson, 423 U.S. 411 (1976) (allowing warrantless arrest of most suspects in public so long as probable cause exists).

555   *See* Morgan Cloud, *Searching through History; Searching for History,* 63 U. CHI. L. REV. 1707, 1713 (1996) (citing the exhaustive research of William Cuddihy for the proposition that specific warrants were required at Founding).

556   AMAR, THE CONSTITUTION AND CRIMINAL PROCEDURE, at 5.

557   1 Conn. 40 (1814).

558   *See id.* at 44.

559   3 Day 1, 3 (Conn. 1807).

560   1761-1772 Quincy Mass. Reports (1763). Perhaps Amar's statement can be read as a commentary on the dearth of originalist scholarship among those who support strong protections for criminal suspects and defendants. "Originalism" as a means of constitutional interpretation is not always definable in a single way, and "originalists" may often contradict each other as to their interpretation of given cases. *See* Richard S. Kay, *"Originalist" Values and Constitutional Interpretation,* 19 HARV. J.L. & PUB. POL'Y 335 (1995). Professor Kay has identified four distinct interpretive methods as being "origi-nalist"— any two of which might produce differing conclusions: 1) original text, 2) original intentions, 3) original understanding, and 4) original values. *See id.* at 336. This being conceded, originalism has generally been the domain of "conservative" jurists for the past generation, fueled by reactions to the methods of adjudication employed by the Warren Court. *See id.* at 335.

561   9 N.H. 239 (1838).
562   3 Bin. 38, 43 (Pa. 1810).
563   Admittedly, two of Amar's cited cases present troubling statements of the law. The rule of Amar's first case, *Jones v. Root*, 72 Mass. 435 (1856), is somewhat difficult to discern. Although the case may be read as a total rejection of required warrants (as Amar contends, *supra*, at 4-5 n.10), it may also be read as an adoption of the "in the presence" exception to the war-rant requirement known to the common law. The court's opinion is no more than a paragraph long and merely upholds the instruction of a lower court that a statute allowing warrantless seizure of liquors was constitutional. Jones, 72 Mass. at 439. The opinion also upheld the use of an illustration by the trial judge that suggested the seizure was similar to a seizure of stolen goods observed in the presence of an officer. *See id.* at 437.
A second case may also be read to mean that the government may search and seize without warrant, but might also be read as enunciating the "breach of peace" exception to the warrant requirement. *Mayo v. Wilson*, 1 N.H. 53 (1817) involved a town tythingman who seized a wagon and horses of an apparent teamster engaged in commercial delivery on the Sabbath, in violation of a New Hampshire statute. Amar quotes *Mayo*'s pronouncement that the New Hampshire Fourth-Amendment equivalent "does not seem intended to restrain the legislature ..." But elsewhere in the opinion, the New Hampshire Supreme Court stated that an arrest required a "warrant in law" — either a magistrate's warrant, or excusal by the commission on the basis of a felony or breach of peace. Mayo, 1 N.H. at 56. "[B]ut if the affray be over, there must be an express warrant." *Id.* (emphasis added). Not much support for Amar's thesis there.
Mayo was decided only fourteen years after the dawn of judicial review in *Marbury v. Madison*, 5 U.S. 137 (1803), during an era when the constitutional interpretations of legislatures were thought to have equal weight to the interpretations of the judiciary. *Cf.* HENRY J. ABRAHAM, THE JUDICIAL PROCESS 335-40 (7th ed. 1998) (describing the slow advent of the concept of judicial review). Indeed, the first act of a state legislature to be declared unconstitutional came only seven years earlier, *see* Fletcher v. Peck, 10 U.S. 87 (1810), and the first state court decision invalidated by the Supreme Court had come only one year earlier. *See* Martin v. Hunter's Lessee, 14 U.S. 304 (1816). The very heart of the *Mayo* decision that Amar relies on (the proposition that

state legislatures have concurrent power of constitutional review with the judiciary) was so thoroughly discredited soon afterward that Amar's extrapolation that Founding era courts did not require warrants seems exceedingly far-fetched.

As judicial review gathered sanction, the doctrine apparently enunciated in *Mayo* became increasingly discredited. *See* Ex Parte Rhodes, 79 So. 462 (Ala. 1918) (saying "[t]here is not to be found a single authority, decision, or textbook, in the library of this court, that sanctions the doctrine that the legisla-ture, a municipality, or Congress can determine what is a 'reasonable' arrest"). 564 Amar cites six cases (all referred to in *United States v. Watson*, 423 U.S. 411 (1976)), as standing for the proposition that state Fourth Amendment equivalents did not presume a warrant requirement. AMAR, *supra*, at 5 n. 11. The first case, *State v. Brown*, 5 Del. (5 Harr.) 505 (Ct. Gen. Sess. 1853), is difficult to reconcile with Amar's thesis that antebellum courts recognized no warrant requirement. *Brown* upheld a criminal verdict against a night watchman who entered a residence in pursuit of a fleeing chicken thief and instead falsely arrested — without warrant — the proprietor. The sec-ond case cited by Amar, *Johnson v. State*, 30 Ga. 426 (1860), simply upheld a guilty verdict against a man who shot a policeman during a warrantless arrest for being an accomplice to a felony. The Georgia Supreme Court repeated the common law exception allowing that an officer may arrest fel-ons without warrant. The third case, *Baltimore & O. R.R. Co. v. Cain*, 81 Md. 87, 31 A. 801 (1895), merely reversed a civil jury verdict for an arrestee on grounds that the appellant railroad company was entitled to a jury instruction allowing for a breach-of-peace exception to the warrant requirement. The fourth case, *Reuck v. McGregor*, 32 N.J.L. 70 (Sup. Ct. 1866), reversed a civil verdict on grounds of excessive damages — while upholding civil liability for causing warrantless arrest of an apparently wrongly-accused thief. *Holley v. Mix*, 3 Wend. 350 (N.Y. Sup. Ct. 1829), Amar's fifth case, offers little support for Amar's thesis. *Holley* upheld a civil judgment against a private person and an officer who arrested a suspect pursuant to an invalid warrant. Finally, *Wade v. Chaffee*, 8 R.I. 224 (1865), simply held that a constable was not bound to procure a warrant where he had probable cause to believe an arrestee was guilty of a felony, even though no fear of escape was present. 565 Amar cites four cases as standing for the proposition that state courts interpreted their state constitutional predecessors of the Fourth Amendment's text as requiring no warrants for searches or seizures.

AMAR, *supra*, at 5 n.10. *Jones v. Root*, 72 Mass. (6 Gray) 435 (1856), upheld a Massachusetts "no-warrant" statute in a one-paragraph opinion explained in the footnote above. In *Rohan v. Sawin*, 59 Mass. (5 Cush.) 281 (1850), Massachusetts' highest court found that a warrantless arrest qualified under the "felon" exception to the warrant requirement. Mayo v. Wilson, 1 N.H. 53 (1817), is described in the footnote above.

Finally, the 1814 Pennsylvania case of *Wakely v. Hart*, 6 Binn. 316 (Pa. 1814), resolved a civil suit brought by an accused thief (Wakely) against his arresters upon grounds that the arrest had been warrantless and Wakely had been guilty only of a misdemeanor. The Pennsylvania Supreme Court upheld a jury's verdict for the arresters, upon the rather-fudged finding that Wakely had fled from the charges against him and had been guilty of at least "an offence which approaches very near to a felony," if not an actual felony. *Wakely*, 6 Binn. at 319-20.

566   *See* Eric Schnapper, *Unreasonable Searches and Seizures of Papers*, 71 VA. L. REV. 869, 874 (1985) (saying the search and seizure clause of the Fourth Amendment "embodies requirements independent of the warrant clause" but which were more strict at Founding than warrant requirement).

567   *See* Wilkes v. Wood, 19 Howell's State Trials 1153, 1167 (c.p. 1763) (stating "a jury have it in their power to give damages for more than the injury received").

568   *See* Schnapper, *supra*, at 917 (referring to *Boyd v. United States*, 116 U.S. 616 (1886)). *Boyd*'s proposition was slowly watered down and distinguished until the case of *Andresen v. Maryland* finished it off. Andresen v. Maryland, 427 U.S. 463 (1976) (holding that business documents evidencing fraudulent real estate dealings could be constitutionally seized by warrant).

569   *See* Gouled v. United States, 255 U.S. 298 (1921) (pronouncing "mere evidence" rule, which stood for more than 45 years).

570   *See* Schnapper, *supra*, at 923-29.

571   *See* Warden v. Hayden, 387 U.S. 294 (1967) (holding that police can obtain even indirect evidence by use of search warrants). Hayden overturned at least five previous Supreme Court decisions by declaring that "privacy" rather than property was the "principle object of the Fourth Amendment." *Id.* at 296 n.1, 304.

572   *See* Frisbie v. Butler, 1 Kirby 213 (Conn. 1787).

573   *See, e.g.*, Stevens v. Fassett, 27 Me. 266 (1847) (involving defendant who had obtained two arrest warrants against plaintiff without officer

assistance); State v. McAllister, 25 Me. 490 (1845) (involving crime victim who swore out warrant affidavit against alleged assailant); State v. J.H., 1 Tyl. 444 (Vt. 1802) (quashing criminal charge gained by unsworn complaint of private individual).

574 *See* Humes v. Taber, 1 RI. 464 (1850) (involving search by sheriff accompanied by private persons).

575 *See* Kimball v. Munson, 2 Kirby (Conn.) 3 (1786) (upholding civil damages against two men who arrested suspect without warrant to obtain reward).

576 *See* Wasserstrom, *The Incredible Shrinking Fourth Amendment*, 21 AM. CRIM. L. REV. 257, 289 (1984).

577 The Framers regarded private persons acting under color of "public authority" to be subject to constitutional constraints like the proscription against double jeopardy..*See* Stevens v. Fassett, 27 Me. 266 (1847) (holding private prosecutors were prohibited from twice putting a defendant in jeopardy for the same offense).

578 256 U.S. 465 (1921).

579 *Burdeau v. McDowell* involved a corporate official (McDowell) who was fired by his employer for financial malfeasance at work. After McDowell's termination, company representatives raided his office, opened his safe, and rifled through his papers. *See id.* at 473. Upon finding incriminating evidence against McDowell, company representatives alerted the United States Justice Department and turned over certain papers to the govern-ment. A district judge ordered the stolen papers returned to McDowell before they could be seen by a grand jury. The Supreme Court reversed, stating the Fourth Amendment "was intended as a restraint upon the activi-ties of sovereign authority, and was not intended to be a limitation upon other than governmental agencies." *Id.* at 475.

580 *See* Cloud, *Searching through History; Searching for History*, at 1716 (discussing transition during early 1700s from concept that 'a man's house is his castle (except against the government)' to the legal adage that 'a man's house is his castle (especially against the government)').

581 Massachusetts and Vermont apparently required that only public officers execute search warrants in the early nineteenth century. *See* Commonwealth v. Foster, 1 Mass. 488 (1805) (holding justice of peace had no authority to issue a warrant to a private person to arrest a criminal suspect); State v. J.H., 1 Tyl. 444 (Vt. 1802).

582 *See* Bissell v. Bissell, 3 N.H. 520 (1826).

583 *See* Kimball v. Munson, which upheld civil damages against two men who arrested an alleged horse thief without warrant in response to a constable's reward offer. 2 Kirby 3 (Conn. 1786). Kimball suggested the two private persons would have been protected from liability had they secured a warrant soon after their arrest of the suspect. *See also* Frisbie v. Butler, 1 Kirby 213 (Conn. 1787) (applying specificity requirement to search warrant issued to private person).

584 *See* Del Col v. Arnold, 3 U.S. (3 Dall.) 333 (1796) (holding that "privateers" on the open seas who capture illegal vessels under the auspices of government authority act at their own peril and may be held liable for all damages to the captured vessels — even where the captured vessels are engaged in crimes on the high seas).

585 Walter v. United States, 447 U.S. 649, 656 (1979). *See also* United States v. Jacobsen, 466 U.S. 109, 113 (1984) (saying "This Court has also consistently construed this protection as proscribing only governmental action; it is wholly inapplicable to a private individual not acting as an agent of the Government or with the participation or knowledge of any government official.").

586 *See* Humes v. Taber, 1 R.I. 464 (1850)

587 *See* Melvin v. Fisher, 8 N.H. 406, 407 (1836) (saying "he who causes another to be arrested by a wrong name is a trespasser, even if the process was intended to be against the person actually arrested").

588 *See* Holley v. Mix, 3 Wend. 350 (N.Y. 1829).

589 *See* Kimball v. Munson, 2 Kirby 3 (Conn. 1786) (faulting two arrestors for failing to obtain a proper warrant immediately after their warrantless arrest of a suspected felon); Knot v. Gay, 1 Root 66, 67 (Conn. 1774) (stating warrantless arrest is permitted "where an highhanded offense had been committed, and an immediate arrest became necessary, to prevent an escape").

590 *See* Wade v. Chaffee, 8 R.I. 224 (R.I. 1865) (holding a constable is not bound to procure a warrant before arresting a felon even though there may be no reason to fear the escape of the felon).

591 *See, e.g.*, Oleson v. Pincock, 251 P. 23, 25 (Utah 1926); Burroughs v. Eastman, 59 N.W. 817 (Mich. 1894); Minnesota v. Cantieny, 24 N.W. 458 (Minn. 1885); William A. Schroeder, *Warrantless Misdemeanor Arrests and the Fourth Amendment*, 58 Mo. L. REV. 790-91 (1993).

592 *See id.* (Schroeder), at 784 n.14-16 (listing eight jurisdictions allowing such arrests).

593 *But see id.* at 791 n.39 (listing four cases that have held warrantless arrests for crimes committed outside an officer's presence unconstitutional). 594 *See id.* at 779-81 n.13 (providing two pages of statutory provisions allowing warrantless arrest for domestic violence and other specific misdemeanors).

595 *See* Welsh v. Wisconsin, 466 U.S. 740 (1984) (requiring warrant to forcibly enter a home to arrest someone inside for a misdemeanor traffic offense); Payton v. New York, 445 U.S. 573, 589 (1980) (requiring warrant to forcibly enter a home to arrest a suspected felon unless exigent circumstances prevail).

596 *See* United States v. Watson, 423 U.S. 411, 412 (1976). *Watson* represents one of the starkest redrawings of search and seizure law ever pronounced by the Supreme Court. Essentially, the Court declared that officers may arrest without warrant wherever they have probable cause. Justice Thurgood Marshall released a blistering dissent accusing the majority of betraying the "the only clear lesson of history" that the common law "considered the arrest warrant far more important than today's decision leaves it." *Id.* at 442 (Marshall, J., dissenting).

597 United States v. Hensley, 469 U.S. 221, 229 (1985).

598 *See* Conner v. Commonwealth, 3 Bin. 38, 42-43 (Pa. 1810) (insisting that public safety alone justifies exceptions to the warrant requirement).

599 *See* Tennessee v. Garner, 471 U.S. 1, 14 (1985). The number of crimes considered felonies varied greatly according to location and period. Plymouth Colony knew only seven in 1636: treason, willful murder, willful arson, conversing with the devil, rape, adultery, and sodomy. *See* Julius Goebel, Jr., *King's Law and Local Custom in Seventeenth Century New England*, 31 COLUM. L. REV. 416, n.43 (1931). In general, the American colo-nists considered far fewer crimes to be felonies than did the people of England. C.f. Thorp L. Wolford, The Laws and Liberties of 1648, reprinted in ESSAYS IN THE HISTORY OF EARLY AMERICAN LAW 147, 182 (David H. Flaherty, ed. 1969) (saying there were far more felonies in English than in Massachusetts law).

600 JOSHUA DRESSLER, UNDERSTANDING CRIMINAL LAW 253 (2d ed. 1995).

601 United States v. Rabinowitz, 339 U.S. 56, 70 (1950) (Frankfurter, J. dissenting).

602 *See* United States v. Watson, 423 U.S. 411, 439-440 (1976).

603 But see id. at 438 (Marshall, J., dissenting) ("[T]he fact is that a felony at common law and a felony today bear only slight resemblance, with the result that the relevance of the common-law rule of arrest to the modern interpretation of our Constitution is minimal").

604 *See* WAYNE R. LAFAVE & JEROLD H. ISRAEL, CRIMINAL PROCEDURE 20 (2d ed. 1992).

605 *See* Amar, supra at 12.

606 *See* Wasserstrom, *The Incredible Shrinking Fourth Amendment*, 21 AM. CRIM. L. REV. 289 (1984) (saying false arrest was subject to strict liability in colonial times).

607 *See* Amar, *supra* at 12.

608 *See* Clarke v. Little, 1 Smith 100, 101 (N.H. 1805) (addressing liabilities of deputy to debtor's creditors).

609 Hall v. Brooks 8 Vt. 485 (1836) (holding constable liable for refusing to serve court process).

610 *See* Shewel v. Fell, 3 Yeates 17, 22 (Pa. 1800) (holding sheriff liable to prisoner's creditor for entire debt of prison escapee).

611 *See* Chapman v. Bellows, 1 Smith 127 (N.H. 1805). 612 *See* Morse v. Betton, 2 N.H. 184, 185 (1820).

613 *See* Lamb v. Day, 8 Vt. 407 (1836) (holding constable liable for allowing mare in his custody to be used); Bissell v. Huntington, 2 N.H. 142. 146-47 (1819).

614 *See* Webster v. Quimby, 8 N.H. 382, 386 (1836).

615 *See* Administrator of Janes v. Martin, 7 Vt. 92 (Vt. 1835). 616 *See* Kittredge v. Bellows, 7 N.H. 399 (1835).

617 *See* Herrick v. Manly, 1 Cai. R. 253 (N.Y. Sup. Ct. 1803). 618 *See* Bromley v. Hutchins, 8 Vt. 194, 196 (Vt. 1836). 619 *See* Hazard v. Israel, 1 Binn. 240 (Pa. 1808).

620 *See* Fullerton v. Mack, 2 Aik. 415 (1828).

621 *See* Rex v. Gay, Quincy, Mass. Rep. 1761-1772 (1763) (acquitting defendant who battered sheriff when sheriff attempted arrest with warrant irregular on its face).

622 *See* Percival v. Jones, 2 Johns. Cas. 49, 51 (N.Y. 1800) (holding justice of peace liable for issuing arrest execution against person privileged from imprisonment).

623 *See id.*

624 *See* Preston v. Yates, 24 N.Y. 534 (1881) (involving sheriff who obtained indemnity bond from private party).

625 *See* Grinnell v. Phillips, 1 Mass. 530, 537 (1805) (involving Massachusetts statute requiring officers to be bonded).

626 *See* Tilley v. Cottrell, 43 A. 369 (R.I. 1899) (holding constable liable for damages against him for which his indemnity bond did not cover).

627 *C.f.* White v. French, 81 Mass. 339 (1860) (involving officer arrested when his obligor failed to pay for officer's liability); Treasurer of the State v. Holmes, 2 Aik. 48 (Vt. 1826) (involving sheriff jailed for debt in Franklin County, Vermont).

628 At the time of Founding, juries remedied improper searches and seizures by levying heavy damages from officers who conducted them. *See* AMAR, *supra*, at 12. The ratification debates made it clear that no method of curbing "the insolence of office" worked as well as juries giving "ruinous damages whenever an officer has deviated from the rigid letter of the law, or been guilty of any unnecessary act of insolence or oppression." Maryland Farmer, Essays by a Farmer (1), reprinted in THE COMPLETE ANTI-FEDERALIST 5, 14 (Herbert J. Storing ed., 1981). Punitive damages were apparently com-mon in search and seizure trespass cases, and provided "an invaluable maxim" for securing proper and reasonable conduct by public officers. Today, however, municipalities never have to pay out punitive damages. *See* Newport v. Fact Concerts, Inc., 453 U.S. 247, 271 (1981).

629 *See* Johnson v. Georgia, 30 Ga. 426 (1860) (holding that a policeman is as much under protection of the law as any public officer).

630 Many Founding-Era constitutions contained statements declaring a right of remedy for every person. *See, e.g.,* DEL. CONST. of 1776, Sec. 12 (providing that "every freeman for every injury done him in his goods, lands or person, by any other person, ought to have remedy by the course of the law of the land"); MASS. CONST. of 1780, art. I, Sec. XI (providing "Every subject of the commonwealth ought to find a certain remedy, by having recourse to the laws, for all injuries or wrongs"); N.H. CONST. of 1784, part I, Sec. XIV (stating "Every subject of this state is entitled to a certain remedy"). Some early proposals for the national Bill of Rights also included such remedy pro-visions. *See, e.g.,* Proposed Amended Federal Constitution, April 30, 1788, reprinted in THE ORIGIN OF THE SECOND AMENDMENT: A DOCUMENTARY HISTORY OF THE BILL OF RIGHTS 1787-1792 790, 791 (David E. Young,

ed.) (2d ed. 1995) (providing that "every individual... ought to find a certain remedy against all injuries, or wrongs").

631 *C.f.* THE DECLARATION OF INDEPENDENCE para. 11 (U.S. 1776) ("He has erected a multitude of New Offices, and sent hither swarms of Officers to harass our people, and eat out their substance").

632 A small history lesson regarding the early development of officer immunity is provided in Seaman v. Patten, 2 Cai. R. 312 (N.Y. Sup. Ct. 1805). Early tax and custom enforcement agents were unsworn volunteers, having "generally received a portion of the spoil." *Id.* at 315. Corresponding to this system, such agents acted at their own peril and were civilly liable for their every impropriety. This "hard rule" of high officer liability was still in force a generation after the Constitution was ratified, although courts began to hold officers less accountable for their mistakes when officers became sworn to perform certain ever-more-difficult duties. *See id.*

633 *See* Seaman, 2 Cai. R. at 317; Bissell v. Huntington, 2 N.H. 142, 147 (1819) (declaring that sheriffs good faith acts should receive "most favourable construction."). "[N]either the court, the bar, nor the public should favor prosecutions against them for petty mistakes." *Id.* at 147.

634 *See* Diana Hassel, *Living a Lie; The Cost of Qualified Immunity*, 64 Mo. L. REV. 123, 151 n. 122.

635 State v. Dunning, 98 S.E. 530, 531 (N.C. 1919).

636 *See, e.g.,* Stinnett v. Commonwealth, 55 F.2d 644, 647 (4th Cir. 1932) (reversing jury verdict against officer on grounds that "courts should not lay down rules which will make it so dangerous for officers to perform their duties that they will shrink and hesitate from action"); State v. Dunning, 98 S.E. 530 (N.C. 1919) (reversing criminal verdict against officer who shot approaching man on grounds that the officer enjoyed a privilege to use deadly force instead of retreating).

637 The Supreme Court's recent jurisprudence has offered a more relaxed definition of "probable cause" as a "fluid concept" of "suspicion" rather than a fixed standard of probability. *See* Wasserstrom, *The Incredible Shrinking Fourth Amendment*, 21 AM. CRIM. L. REV. 257, 337 (1984) (analyzing Justice Rehnquist's opinion in Illinois v. Gates).

638 *See* Grau v. United States, 287 U.S. 124, 128 (1932), overturned by Brinegar v. United States, 338 U.S. 160 (1949).

639 Wasserstrom, *The Incredible Shrinking Fourth Amendment*, 21 AM. CRIM. L. REV. 257, 274 (1984).

640 *See* AMAR, *supra*, at 20. Judges of the Founding era appear to have been somewhat more reluctant than modern judges to issue search and seizure warrants. For an early example of judicial scrutiny of warrant applications, *see* United States v. Lawrence, 3 U.S. 42 (1795) (upholding refusal of district judge to issue warrant for arrest of French deserter in the face of what government claimed was probable cause). Today, search warrant applications are rarely denied. The "secret wiretap court" established by Congress to process wiretap applications in 1978, has rejected only one wiretap request in its 22-year life. *See* Richard Willing, Wiretaps sought in record numbers, USA TODAY, June 5, 2000, at A1 (saying the court approved 13,600 wiretap requests in the same period). 641 Private persons were liable if, for example, their complaint was too vague as to the address to be searched, *see* Humes v. Taber, 1 R.I. 464 (1850); misspelled the name of the accused, *see* Melvin v. Fisher, 8 N.H. 406, 407 (1836) (saying "he who causes another to be arrested by a wrong name is a trespasser, even if the process was intended to be against the person actu-ally arrested); or called for the execution of a warrant naming a "John Doe" as a target, *see* Holley v. Mix, 3 Wend. 350 (N.Y. 1829).

642 *See* Hervey v. Estes, 65 F.3d 784 (9th Cir. 1995) (involving challenge to search warrant wrongfully obtained through false references to anonymous sources).

643 *See* Hummel-Jones v. Strope, 25 F.3d 647 (8th Cir. 1994) (involving police officer's failure to disclose to judge that an undercover deputy sheriff was the "confidential informant" referred to in a search warrant application).

644 *See* David B. Kopel & Paul H. Blackman, *The Unwarranted Warrant: The Waco Search Warrant and the Decline of the Fourth Amendment*, 18 HAMLINE J. PUB. L & POL'Y 1, 13 (saying Waco warrant was filled with statements irrelevant to Koresh's alleged firearm violations).

645 *See id.* at 21 (noting ATF agent's false claims that various spare parts were machine gun conversion kits).

646 *See* ALAN M. DERSHOWITZ, THE ABUSE EXCUSE AND OTHER COP-OUTS, SOB STORIES, AND EVASIONS OF RESPONSIBILITY 235 (1994).

647 *Id.* at 233.

648 The 1920's saw an explosion of police privilege to oversee two separate— but often interrelated — elements of American life: Prohibition and the auto-mobile. *See* FRIEDMAN, CRIME AND PUNISHMENT IN AMERICAN

HISTORY, at 300 (saying search and seizure became a particularly salient issue during Prohibition). In 1925, the Supreme Court, by split decision, released an opinion that would grow within the next 75 years into an immense expan-sion of police prerogatives while at the same time representing an enor-mous loss of personal security for American automobile travelers. *Carroll v. United States* upheld a warrantless search of an automobile for liquor as valid under the infamous Volstad Act, enacted to breathe life into the Eighteenth Amendment. 267 U.S. 137 (1925). The *Carroll* opinion led lower courts to more than one interpretation, *see* Francis H. Bohlen & Harry Shulman, *Arrest With and Without a Warrant*, 75 U. Pa. L. Rev. 485, 488-89 (1927), but slowly became recognized as a pronouncement of an "automobile exception" to the warrant requirement. *See* United States v. Ross, 456 U.S. 798, 822 (1982). Two decades after *Carroll*, Justice Robert H. Jackson tried in earnest to force the genie back into the bottle by narrowing the automobile exception to cases of serious crimes, but a 7-2 majority outnumbered him. *See* Brinegar v. United States, 338 U.S. 160, 180-81 (1949) (Jackson, J., dissent-ing). Since *Brinegar*, the ""automobile exception" has been a fixture of Fourth Amendment jurisprudence, and has greatly expanded. The automobile excep-tion now accounts for the broadest umbrella of warrant exceptions. *See, e.g.,* California v. Acevedo, 500 U.S. 565 (1991) (allowing warrantless search of containers in automobiles even without probable cause to search the vehicle as a whole). Indeed, the automobile exception has expanded so far that it has made a mockery of Fourth Amendment doctrine. As Justice Scalia pointed out in his Acevedo concurrence, an anomaly now exists protecting a brief-case carried on the sidewalk from warrantless search but allowing the same briefcase to be searched without warrant if taken into a car. Acevedo at 581 (Scalia, J., concurring).

649 Police surveillance of American roadways has brought the bar of justice far closer to most Americans than ever before. Few accounts of the sheer scale of traffic stops are available, but anecdotal evidence suggests traffic encoun-ters with police number in the hundreds of millions annually. In North Carolina alone, more than 1.2 million traffic infractions were recorded in a single year. *See* FRIEDMAN, CRIME AND PUNISHMENT IN AMERICAN HISTORY, at 279. Of actual traffic stops, no reliable estimate can be made.

650 *See* SKOLNICK & FYFE, ABOVE THE LAW: POLICE AND THE EXCESSIVE USE OF FORCE, at 99.

Roger I. Roots

651 In Delaware v. Prouse, 440 U.S. 648 (1979), the Supreme Court actually considered, but stopped short of, allowing cops to randomly stop any traveler without any particularized reason — with one justice (Rehnquist) argu-ing that cops may do so. Prouse, 440 U.S. at 664 (Rehnquist, J., dissenting).
652 *See* Flanders v. Herbert, 1 Smith (N.H.) 205 (1808) (finding constable who stopped a driver and horse team pursuant to an invalid writ of attachment liable for trespass). Private tort principles rather than state licensing programs governed highway travel at the time of the Framers. See Kennard v. Burton, 25 Me. 39 (1845).
653 *See* David Rudovsky, The Criminal Justice System and the Role of the Police, in THE POLITICS OF LAW: A PROGRESSIVE CRITIQUE, 242, 247 (David Kairys, ed. 1982).
654 Prior to the imposition of the exclusionary rule in *Mapp v. Ohio*, 367 U.S. 643 (1961), the Cincinnati police force rarely applied for search warrants. In 1958, the police obtained three warrants. In 1959 the police obtained none. *See* Bradley C. Canon, *Is the Exclusionary Rule in Failing Health?: Some New Data and a Plea Against a Precipitous Conclusion*, 62 KENTUCKY L. J. 681, 709 (1974). Similarly, the use of search warrants by the New York City Police Department prior to Mapp was negligible, but afterward, over 5000 warrants were issued. *See* Wasserstrom, *The Incredible Shrinking Fourth Amendment*, 21 AM. CRIM. L. REV. 257, 297 n.203 (1984).
655 Brinegar v. United States, 338 U.S. 160, 181 (1949) (Jackson, J., dissenting) (expressing belief that many unlawful searches are never revealed because no evidence is recovered).
656 *See* U.S. CONST. amend. V (providing no person "shall be compelled in any criminal case to be a witness against himself").
657 *See* Miranda v. Arizona, 384 U.S. 436 (1966).
658 *See* SKOLNICK & FYFE, ABOVE THE LAW: POLICE AND THE EXCESSIVE USE OF FORCE, at 61.
659 Perhaps the most extreme example of lopsided investigative resources occurred in the Oklahoma City bombing case in 1995. Defense attorneys complained that "the resources of every federal, state, and local agency in the United States" were at the government's disposal — including a 24-hour FBI command center with 400 telephones to coordinate evidence-gathering for the prosecution. *See* Petition For Writ of Mandamus of Petitioner-Defendant, Timothy James McVeigh at 13, McVeigh v. Matsch (No. 96-CR-68-M)

(10th Cir. Mar. 25, 1997). In contrast, the defense complained that "without subpoena power, without the right to take depositions, and without access to national intelligence informa-tion, the McVeigh defense can go no further." *Id.* at 4.

660   *See* Brady v. Maryland, 373 U.S. 83 (1963) (finding that suppression of evidence favorable to defense violates due process). Prosecutors are required by the Brady doctrine to reveal exculpatory evidence in their possession or in the possession of the investigating agency. *See* United States v. Zuno-Arce, 44 F3d 1420 (9th Cir. 1995). Only one federal court of appeals has held that prosecutors are imputed to hold knowledge of information "readily avail-able" to them and require such knowledge to be transferred to the defense. *See* Williams v. Whitley, 940 F2d 132 (5th Cir. 1991). However, nothing in the law mandates that police look for exculpatory evidence.

661   *See, e.g.,* STOLEN LIVES, *supra,* at 248 (reporting 1997 New York City case in which officers closed off scene of shooting by police for a half an hour after the shooting). Upon being allowed to enter the shooting scene, observers noticed that police had moved large kitchen table to the side of room to make police claim that victim (who had apparently been on other side of the table from officers) had lunged at them more plausible. *See id.*

662   *See* PAUL MARCUS, THE ENTRAPMENT DEFENSE 3 (2d ed. 1995).

663   *See id.* at 3-4.

664   *See* Blaikie v. Linton, 18 Scot. Law Rep. 583 (1880).

665   *See* Regina v. Bickley, 2 Crim. App. R. 53, 73 J.P.R. 239 (C.A. 1909).

666   Brannan v. Peek, 2 All E.R. 572, 574 (Q.B. 1947).

667   *Id.*

668   223 F. 412 (9th Cir. 1915).

669   Rivera v. State, 846 P.2d 1, 11 (Wyo. 1993).

670   SKOLNICK & FYFE, ABOVE THE LAW: POLICE AND THE EXCESSIVE USE OF FORCE, at 102 (quoting Paul Chevigny)

671   *See id. See also* STOLEN LIVES, *supra,* at 302. Kevin McCoullough, who was suing the City of Chattanooga for unjust imprisonment, was shot dead by police at his workplace after he allegedly threw or ran at police with a metal object. McCoullough had predicted his own murder by police in state-ments to co-workers. *See id.*

672   *See id.* (citing President's Commission on Law Enforcement and Administration of Justice study).

673 *See* FRIEDMAN, CRIME AND PUNISHMENT IN AMERICAN HISTORY, at 154 (citations omitted).

674 JEFFREY REIMAN, THE RICH GET RICHER AND THE POOR GET PRISON: IDEOLOGY, CLASS, AND CRIMINAL JUSTICE 166 (5th ed. 1997).

675 *See* HERBERT MITGANG, DANGEROUS DOSSIERS (1988). The FBI kept a 207-page file on cartoonist Bill Mauldin, a 153-page file on book publisher Alfred A. Knopf, and a 23-page file on Lincoln biographer Carl Sandburg, for example. *See id.* at 249, 195, and 81.

676 The Fraternal Order of Police (FOP), the largest police organization in the United States, has over 270,000 members and has been named one of the most powerful lobbying groups in Washington. *See* National Fraternal Order of Police, Press Release, Sept. 17, 1997, available at <http://www. mofop.org/power>.

677 An example of the police lobby's power is its ability to scuttle asset forfeiture reform. The International Association of Chiefs of Police (IACP) managed to keep congressional leaders from attaching forfeiture reform to budget legislation in 1999. See IACP, End of Session Report for the 1st Session of 106th Congress: FY 2000 Funding Issues, Jan. 17, 2000. *See also* Peter L. Davis, *Rodney King and the Decriminalization of Police Brutality in America,* 53 MD. L. REV. 271, 281 n.40 (1994). Police unions in many juris-dictions successfully thwart efforts to establish civilian review boards. *See id.* at 282.

678 See Richard Willing, *High Court Restricts Police Power to Frisk,* USA TODAY, Mar. 29, 2000, 4A.

679 Much of this chapter was previously published in volume 45 of the Gonzaga Law Review (2009). Thanks are owed to the students and staff at Gonzaga University and the *Gonzaga Law Review.*

680 *See* Weeks v. United States, 232 U.S. 383, 398 (1914).

681 *See* Mapp v. Ohio, 367 U.S. 643, 655 (1961) (extending the federal exclu-sionary rule to state court practice under the Fourteenth Amendment).

682 *See* generally Yale Kamisar, *The Writings of John Barker Waite and Thomas Davies on the Search and Seizure Exclusionary Rule,* 100 Mich. L. Rev. 1821 (2002) (discussing the history of criticism of the exclusionary rule).

683 Jerry E. Norton, *The Exclusionary Rule Reconsidered: Restoring the Status Quo Ante,* 33 Wake Forest L. Rev. 261, 264 (1998) (writing of the "newly discovered exclusionary rule").

The Conviction Factory

684 *See* generally Akhil Reed Amar, *Fourth Amendment First Principles*, 107 Harv. L. Rev. 757 (1994) [hereinafter Amar I]; Akhil Reed Amar, The Constitution and Criminal Procedure: First Principles (1997) [hereinafter Amar II]; Akhil Reed Amar, The Bill of Rights: Creation and Reconstruction (1998) [hereinafter Amar III]; Akhil Reed Amar, *Against Exclusion (Except to Protect Truth or Prevent Privacy Violations)*, 20 Harv. J. L. & Pub. Pol'y 457 (1997) [hereinafter Amar IV].

685 Even a partial list of articles discussing this debate would take up many pages. *See, e.g.,* Randy E. Barnett, *Resolving the Dilemma of the Exclusionary Rule: An Application of Restitutive Principles of Justice*, 32 Emory L.J. 937, 941-42 (1983) (calling for an alternative to the exclusionary rule); Donald Dripps, *Akhil Amar on Criminal Procedure and Constitutional Law: "Here I Go Down that Wrong Road Again"*, 74 N.C. L. Rev. 1559, 1563 (1996) (detailing the long history of criticisms of the exclusionary rule and other criminal procedure protections); Yale Kamisar, *In Defense of the Search and Seizure Exclusionary Rule*, 26 Harv. J. of L. & Pub. Pol'y 119, 119 n.1 (2003) (citing dozens of articles); Randall R. Rader, *Legislating a Remedy for the Fourth Amendment*, 23 S. Tex. L.J. 585, 606-07 (1982) (discussing the abolition or replacement of the exclusionary rule); William J. Stuntz, *Warrants and Fourth Amendment Remedies*, 77 Va. L. Rev. 881, 897-918 (1991) (dis-cussing remedies for warrant violations); Malcolm R. Wilkey, *Constitutional Alternatives to the Exclusionary Rule*, 23 S. Tex. L.J. 531, 539 (1982) (criticiz-ing the exclusionary rule and recommending alternatives); Jeffrey Gittins, *Comment, Excluding the Exclusionary Rule: Extending the Rationale of Hudson v. Michigan to Evidence Seized During Unauthorized Nighttime Searches*, 2007 BYU L. Rev. 451, 451 (2007) (discussing the exclusionary rule controversy); Matt J. O'Laughlin, *Comment, Exigent Circumstances: Circumscribing the Exclusionary Rule in Response to 9/11*, 70 UMKC L. Rev. 707, 708 (2002); Aloysius T. Webster, *Comment, Protecting Society's Rights While Preserving Fourth Amendment Protections: An Alternative to the Exclusionary Rule*, 23 S. Tex. L.J. 693, 706 (1982) (advocating abandonment of the modern exclu-sionary rule).

686 Of course, rules of exclusion also apply in Fifth and Sixth Amendment jurisprudence, but are less controversial in those contexts. In a broader sense, the law of evidence is riddled with "exclusionary rules" that govern such mat-ters as hearsay and unauthenticated records.

687   *See* Amar II, at 156 ("The exclusionary rule rewards the guilty man, and only the guilty man, precisely because he is guilty.").

688   *See* Patrick Tinsley et al., *In Defense of Evidence and Against the Exclusionary Rule: A Libertarian Approach*, 32 S.U. L. Rev. 63, 64 (2004).

689   *See id.* at 68. 690   *Id.* at 64.

691   Amar IV, at 459.

692   Akhil Reed Amar, The Constitution and Criminal Procedure: First Principles (1997) [hereinafter Amar II] at 91 (saying the exclusion-ary rule "creates what I shall call an upside-down effect, providing the guilty with more protection than, and often at the expense of, the innocent.").

693   *See, e.g.*, Michael J. Zydney Mannheimer, *Coerced Confessions and the Fourth Amendment*, 30 Hastings Const. L.Q. 57, 61 (2002) (arguing in support of the exclusionary rule as a result of a relationship between the Fourth and Fifth Amendments, but making "no pretense that [this opinion] is supported by an originalist view ... .To the contrary, I readily concede that it might not have occurred to the Framers that coerced confessions are a Fourth Amendment issue."). But see Thomas Y. Davies, *Recovering the Original Fourth Amendment*, 98 Mich. L. Rev. 547, 663-66 (1999). Although Davies touched upon various overstatements made by modern anti-exclusion scholars regarding Founding-era Fourth Amendment remedies, he did not delve deeply into them. *Id.*

694   *Cf.* Thomas Y. Davies, *The Fictional Character of Law-and-Order Originalism: A Case Study of the Distortions and Evasions of Framing-Era Arrest Doctrine in Atwater v. Lago Vista*, 37 Wake Forest L. Rev. 239, 273-74 (2002) (documenting the Supreme Court's use of deceptive history to uphold an arrest for a non-jailable seat-belt violation in 2002); Roger Roots, *Are Cops Constitutional?*, 11 Seton Hall Const. L.J. 685, 722-24 (2001) (comparing the admiration of policing by modern "conservatives" with the dearth of support for modern-style law enforcement in early America).

695   *See, e.g.*, Mapp v. Ohio, 367 U.S. 643, 648 (1961) (majority opinion) (saying without the exclusionary rule, the Fourth Amendment "might as well be stricken from the Constitution" (quoting Weeks v. United States, 232 U.S. 383, 393 (1914))); *see* also Wolf v. Colorado, 338 U.S. 25, 44 (1949) (Murphy, J., dissenting) (saying that the conclusion is "inescapable that but one remedy exists to deter violations of the search and seizure clause," namely, "the rule which excludes illegally obtained evidence"); William C. Heffernan, *On*

Justifying Fourth Amendment Exclusion, 1989 Wis. L. Rev. 1193, 1224 (1989) (concluding that the exclusionary rule is implicitly required by the text and history of the Fourth Amendment).

696   Justice Hugo Black, widely known as the arch-textualist of his era, expressed the opinion this way: "The federal exclusionary rule is not a command of the Fourth Amendment but is a judicially created rule of evidence which Congress might negate." Wolf, 338 U.S. at 39-40 (Black, J., concurring).

697   Mapp, 367 U.S. at 660. *Mapp* was actually a plurality decision with two concurrences, one dissent and one memorandum aligned with the dissent. Justice Harlan's dissent summed up the crude alliance that was forged among the five victorious justices: "For my Brother Black is unwilling to subscribe to [the four-member plurality's] view that the *Weeks* exclusionary rule derives from the Fourth Amendment itself, but joins the majority opinion on the premise that its end result can be achieved by bringing the Fifth Amendment to the aid of the Fourth." *Id.* at 685 (Harlan, J., dissenting) (citation omitted).

698   *See* Herring v. United States, 129 S.Ct. 695, 699-701 (2009) (discussing *United States v. Leon*, 468 U.S. 897 (1984)); *see also* L. Timothy Perrin et al., *It Is Broken: Breaking the Inertia of the Exclusionary Rule*, 26 Pepp. L. Rev. 971, 979-87 (1999) (suggesting the exclusionary rule should be abandoned upon reevaluating its costs and impacts).

699   *See* Heather A. Jackson, *Arizona v. Evans: Expanding Exclusionary Rule Exceptions and Contracting Fourth Amendment Protection*, 86 J. Crim. L. & Criminology 1201, 1218 (1996).

700   *See* generally The Jury and the Search for Truth: The Case Against Excluding Relevant Evidence at Trial: Hearing on S.3 Before the S. Comm. on the Judiciary, 104th Cong. 104-724 (1995) (debating bill proposing to eliminate the exclusionary rule in federal courts entirely).

701   *See, e.g.*, Hernandez v. State, 60 S.W.3d 106, 112-14, 115 (Tex. Crim. App. 2001) (Keller, J., dissenting) (contending that the states are not bound by Mapp v. Ohio because it was a mere plurality opinion and because "mod-ern cases have rejected the notion that the Fourth Amendment requires exclusion and have instead described the rule as a judicially created prophylactic").

702   *See* Adam Liptak, *Supreme Court Edging Closer to Repeal of Evidence Ruling*, N. Y. Times, Jan. 31, 2009, at A1 (naming Justices Roberts, Alito, Scalia and Thomas as justices willing to abolish the exclusionary rule entirely).

703 *See, e.g.*, 1 Wayne R. LaFave, Search and Seizure: A Treatise on the Fourth Amendment § 1.2 (1978); Fletcher N. Baldwin, Jr., *Due Process and the Exclusionary Rule: Integrity and Justification*, 39 U. Fla. L. Rev. 505, 539 (1987); Donald Dripps, *The Case for the Contingent Exclusionary Rule*, 38 Am. Crim. L. Rev. 1 (2001); Jackson, 86 J. Crim. L. & Criminology 1201, at 1221-24; Yale Kamisar, *Does (Did) (Should) the Exclusionary Rule Rest on a "Principled Basis" Rather than an "Empirical Proposition"?*, 16 Creighton L. Rev. 565, 620-21 (1983); Yale Kamisar, *Wolf and Lustig Ten Years Later: Illegal State Evidence in State and Federal Courts*, 43 Minn. L. Rev. 1083, 1145-50 (1959); Thomas S. Schrock & Robert C. Welsh, *Up From Calandra: The Exclusionary Rule as a Constitutional Requirement*, 59 Minn. L. Rev. 251, 308-09 (1975); Potter Stewart, *The Road to Mapp v. Ohio and Beyond: The Origins, Development and Future of the Exclusionary Rule in Search-and-Seizure Cases*, 83 Colum. L. Rev. 1365, 1392 (1983).

704 Sanford E. Pitler, *Comment, The Origin and Development of Washington's Independent Exclusionary Rule: Constitutional Right and Constitutionally Compelled Remedy*, 61 Wash. L. Rev. 459, 466 (1986).

705 Boyd v. United States, 116 U.S. 616, 633 (1886). 706 *Amar* IV, at 459.

707 *See Amar* II, at 91 (saying that "nothing in the text, history, or structure of the Fourth Amendment supports" the exclusionary rule).

708 116 U.S. at 634-35.

709 232 U.S. 383, 398 (1914). *See* D. Shane Jones, *Application of the "Exclusionary Rule" to Bar Use of Illegally Seized Evidence in Civil School Disciplinary Proceedings*, 52 Wash. U. J. Urb. & Contemp. L. 375, 376 (1997) (claiming the Supreme Court created the exclusionary rule in *Weeks*); James Stribopoulos, *Lessons From the Pupil: A Canadian Solution to the American Exclusionary Rule Debate*, 22 B.C. Int'l & Comp. L. Rev. 77, 94 (1999) (claiming the Supreme Court "introduced the exclusionary rule to American law through its 1914 decision in Weeks"); Captain Douglas R. Wright, *How to Improve Military Search and Seizure Law*, 116 Mil. L. Rev. 157, 171 (1987) (stating Weeks "originated" the exclusionary rule); Christopher A. Harkins, Note, *The Pinocchio Defense Witness Impeachment Exception to the Exclusionary Rule: Combating a Defendant's Right to Use with Impunity the Perjurious Testimony of Defense Witnesses*, 1990 U. Ill. L. Rev. 375, 378 (1990) (saying the Supreme Court announced the Fourth Amendment exclusionary rule in *Weeks*).

710   *See, e.g.,* Amar I, at 788; Amar II,, at 22; Amar IV, at 460-61.

711   *See, e.g.,* Virginia v. Moore, 128 S.Ct. 1598, 1603-04 (2008) (citing Akhil Reed Amar, Fourth Amendment First Principles, 107 Harv. L. Rev. 757, 764 (1994), for the proposition that warrantless arrests were "taken for granted" by early judges); Atwater v. City of Lago Vista, 532 U.S. 318, 332 n.6 (2001) (citing Amar's Fourth Amendment commentary as authoritative); City of West Covina v. Perkins, 525 U.S. 234, 247 n.2 (1999) (Thomas, J., concurring) (citing Amar's Fourth Amendment scholarship); Dubbs v. Head Start, Inc., 336 F.3d 1194, 1212 (10th Cir. 2003) (citing Akhil Reed Amar, The Constitution and Criminal Procedure: First Principles 7-19 (1997), for the proposition that "not all searches lacking warrants or consent are unconstitutional under the Fourth Amendment").

712   *Cf.* Amar III, at 71. 713   *See id.* at 69.

714   *See* Davies, *Recovering the Original Fourth Amendment*, 98 Mich. L. Rev. 547, at 573-74 (criticizing Amar's claims that early courts applied a "generalized reasonableness" test for determining Fourth Amendment violations). Amar's argument that the Framers of the Fourth Amendment did not intend to require warrants in any circumstances has also been thoroughly undermined by countervailing scholarship. *See, e.g.,* Donald Dripps, *Akhil Amar on Criminal Procedure and Constitutional Law: "Here I Go Down that Wrong Road Again"*, 74 N.C. L. Rev. 1559, at 1603-08 (1996) (criticizing Amar's claims). No scholar familiar with Founding-era law would support Amar's claims that warrants were not required for early searches and seizures. Dozens of published antebellum decisions refute this claim alone. The citizens of early America were known to be so insistent upon the warrant requirement that they would occasionally stop an officer in the act of executing an arrest and demand to see his warrant. The 1820 South Carolina case of *City Council v. Payne*, 11 S.C.L. (2 Nott & McC.) 475 (S.C. 1820), is illustrative of a common attitude of the citizenry regarding the warrant requirement. In *City Council*, a private citizen physically rescued a suspect from a city guard, vowing that "whilst he drew the breath of life, no guard should carry a citizen to the guard-house" without a warrant. *Id.* at 476. The rescuer (Payne) was convicted of obstructing an officer only because the officer had arrested the suspect pursuant to a recognized exception to the warrant requirement. *Id.* at 478-79.

715   One published Founding-era case that appears to give partial support to Amar's thesis is *Wrexford v. Smith*, 2 Root 171 (Conn. 1795). In *Wrexford,*

a thief who stole tobacco from a store and ran off was pursued and arrested without warrant by a person responding to an "advertisement from the owner of the store." *Id.* at 171. (From the given facts, it is not clear how much time elapsed between the theft and the pursuit.) When the thief sued for assault and battery and false imprisonment (after being "prosecuted and convicted of the theft"), the arrestor was found not liable. *Id.* An arrestor, wrote the court, "will be excusable provided the person taken is found guilty." *Id.* "Stealing is a crime so odious in itself and so destructive to the well being of society, that every good citizen ought to assist in arresting the thief in his flight." *Id.*

In general, warrants immunized searchers and seizers from civil liability. *See, e.g.,* Horn v. Boon, 34 S.C.L. (3 Strob.) 307 (S.C. 1848) (refusing to hold complainants liable for initiating a prosecution against a woman accused of selling liquor without a license). But even facially valid warrants did not immunize authorities who carried out searches or seizures in an improper manner. *See, e.g.,* McElhenny v. Wylie, 34 S.C.L. (3 Strob.) 284 (S.C. 1848) (holding searcher civilly liable for search carried out late at night in which sleeping couple were awakened in their bed, and a home was searched by a citizen posse unnecessarily). An otherwise lawful search would be "a mere naked trespass, under color but without the sanction of law," if executed with unnecessary harshness and disruptiveness. *Id.* at 288.

716 In fact, early American law imposed much greater civil liability upon actors in the criminal justice system than does contemporary law. Founding-era law made even judges liable for search and seizure violations. *See, e.g.,* Taylor v. Alexander, 6 Ohio 144, 147 (1833) ("And if the magistrate proceed unlawfully in issuing the process, he, and not the executive officer, will be liable for the injury."). Indeed, warrants offered no protection from civil lia-bility in certain cases. *See* Duckworth v. Johnston, 7 Ala. 578, 580, 582 (1845) (a warrant issued pursuant to an accusation that did not constitute a crime exposed the constable, the court, and the complainant to liability; even the original complainants were liable for the execution of some improper warrants); Randall v. Henry, 5 Stew. & P. 367 (Ala. 1834) (involving a pros-ecutor held liable for a defective complaint); Scott v. McCrary, 1 Stew. 315 (Ala. 1828) (civil suit against arrestors); Backus v. Dudley, 3 Conn. 568 (1821) (upholding judgment in favor of pauper who was arrested without warrant by town selectmen); Pearce v. Atwood, 13 Mass. 324, 353 (1816) (uphold-ing judgment against officer who unnecessarily executed arrest warrant on the Sabbath); Holley

v. Mix, 3 Wend. 350, 353-55 (N.Y. 1829) (upholding judgment and award against constable and complainant for arresting an accused felon pursuant to a warrant that did not specifically name the party to be arrested); State v. Curtis, 2 N.C. (1 Hayw.) 543, 543 (1797) (stating officer is liable if executing a warrant beyond his jurisdiction).

717   See Lawson v. Buzines, 3 Del. (3 Harr.) 416, 416 (1842); Boggs v. Vandyke, 3 Del. (3 Harr.) 288, 288 (1840); Hall v. Hall, 6 G. & J. 386, 409 (Md. 1834) (hold-ing that "the constable in execution of a warrant to arrest a party, breaks another's house at his peril").

718   *Cf.* United Public Workers of America v. Mitchell, 330 U.S. 75, 95-96 (1947) (treating both the Ninth and Tenth Amendments as mere truisms without substantive power to limit Congress); United States v. Darby, 312 U.S. 100, 124 (1941) (in which the Supreme Court dismissed the Tenth Amendment as "but a truism"); *see also* Kurt T. Lash, *James Madison's Celebrated Report of 1800: The Transformation of the Tenth Amendment*, 74 Geo. Wash. L. Rev. 165, 192-94 (2006) (describing the Supreme Court's occasional treatment of the Ninth and Tenth Amendments as "mere truisms," *i.e.*, statements of the existing relationships among the states, the people, and the national government, without any distinct authority to limit government).

719   It seems axiomatic that the Framers intended the Fourth Amendment to enshrine the body of search and seizure protections, which were glorified in the most illustrious decisions and statements of the period, rather than continuing practices that were widely criticized in common discourse. *Cf.* Andrew E. Taslitz, Reconstructing the Fourth Amendment: A History of Search and Seizure 1789-1868, at 41 (2006) ("The Fourth Amendment ultimately embodied therefore a repudiation rather than a celebration of colonial search and seizure precedent."). Post-Founding juris-prudence also made clear that the Fourth Amendment (or, more properly speaking, constitutional protections against unreasonable searches and seizures at both state and federal levels) offered greater protection than the law of trespass. For example, in the 1854 Alabama case of Thompson v. State, a defendant convicted of assault for invading the home of a slave without a warrant argued that the slave owner's ratification of the warrantless search should make the search legal in case of criminal prosecution. 25 Ala. 41, 44 (1854). "If the search was unlawful, [the slave owner]'s acquiescence in and approval of it made it lawful, as in the beginning it was a mere civil trespass; and [the slave owner] being the

Roger I. Roots

prosecutor, whatever affects him affects the State." *Id.* Thus, the argument was that just as after-the-fact consent by the slave owner was a good defense to a civil action, "so it is to an indictment" for "if, upon the facts, [the slave owner] could not recover damages, the State ought not to convict upon the same facts, because the State would get an advantage of its citizen if it were otherwise." *Id.* Yet, the Alabama Supreme Court held that it made "not the slightest difference[] that the owner of the premises consented to or acquiesced in the search." *Id.* at 48.

720 *See* Findlay v. Pruitt, 9 Port. 195, 200 (Ala. 1839) (upholding liabilityof arrestor for trespass and assault for arrest with insufficient cause); Braveboy v. Cockfield, 27 S.C.L. (2 McMul.) 270, 273 (S.C. 1841) (holding that words on the arrest warrant were insufficient to justify an arrest, thus placing liability on constable); Colvert v. Moore, 17 S.C.L. (1 Bail.) 549, 549 (S.C. 1830) (action against arrestor for assault and false imprisonment); Garvin v. Blocker, 4 S.C.L. (2 Brev.) 157, 158 (S.C. 1807) (successful suit against constable and justice of the peace). During the early 1800s, there was virtual strict liability for every search and seizure violation. *See* Randall v. Henry, 5 Stew. & P. 367 (Ala. 1834) (suggesting that someone - the magistrate, the complainant or the arrestor - was liable for every false arrest); Reed v. Legg, 2 Del. (2 Harr.) 173, 176 (1837) (holding that complainants are liable for procuring a search warrant that turns up nothing, even if an executing officer is protected by the warrant); Simpson v. Smith, 2 Del. Cas. 285 (1817) (holding person who swore out search warrant application liable, regardless of the existence of probable cause and the procedural propriety of his claims, when the arrestee was found innocent); State v. McDonald, 14 N.C. (3 Dev.) 468, 471-72 (1832) (officer and other defendants liable for searching a house upon inaccurate search warrant); Harmon v. Gould, Wright 709, 710 (Ohio 1834) (all parties responsible for invalid process were liable). Warrants were illegal if they lacked formal seals, but the lack of such seals was no defense for a complainant who instigated the issuance of a warrant. See, e.g., Kline v. Shuler, 30 N.C. (8 Ired.) 484, 486 (1848) (upholding liability of complainant even though constable should not have served the defective warrant).

In contrast to the legal regime of today, even the magistrates who signed invalid warrants were held liable in the civil courts of the nineteenth century. *See* Hall v. Hall, 6 G. & J. 386, 412 (Md. 1834) ("The law anxiously regards the security of a ministerial officer in serving process directed to him ... [but]

a magistrate issuing a warrant may act illegally and subject him-self to an action or to a prosecution ... ."); Miller v. Grice, 31 S.C.L. (2 Rich.) 27 (S.C. 1845) (holding a magistrate liable for false arrest if he knowingly signs arrest warrant for a crime committed outside his jurisdiction); Perrin v. Calhoun, 4 S.C.L. (2 Brev.) 248, 250 (S.C. 1808) (holding magistrate liable for aiding in a trespass for wrongly endorsing an out-of-state warrant); *see also* Roots, supra note 16, at 698-99 (discussing gradual abandonment of the rule of strict liability for false arrest). If an officer was immunized from suit by a valid warrant, a victim had recourse against those who swore out a fruitless affidavit upon which the warrant was based. *See, e.g.*, Reed, 2 Del. (2 Harr.) at 175.

721   *See, e.g.*, Hall v. Hall, 6 G. & J. 386 (Md. 1834) (involving appeal of civil suit for trespass by constable and posse, with little mention of what happened in underlying prosecution); Price v. Graham, 48 N.C. (3 Jones) 545, 546 (1856) (saying only that the arrestee was "brought before two justices of the peace [and] discharged").

722   *See* generally Hans-Hermann Hoppe, Democracy: The God That Failed (2001) (describing growth of government as a component of democratization).

723   *Id.* at 687 & n.5.

724   *See, e.g.*, Hallett v. Lee, 3 Ala. 28, 29 (1841) (holding it is the duty of a sheriff to gather as many citizen deputies as it takes to execute court man-dates); McElhenny v. Wylie, 34 S.C.L. (3 Strob.) 284, 286 (S.C. 1848) (stating that a sheriff or deputy has power to call out a posse "whenever he is resisted, or has reasonable grounds to suspect and believe that such assistance will be necessary").

725   *See* Randall v. Henry, 5 Stew. & P. 367 (Ala. 1834) (involving private prosecutor who launched complaint).

726   *See* generally Leonard W. Levy, Origins of the Fifth Amendment (1968) (indicating that the distinction between civil and criminal cases grew steadily between the sixteenth and eighteenth centuries).

727   *See, e.g.*, State v. Evans, 1 Del. Cas. 251 (1800).

728   *See also* Donald A. Dripps, *Reconstruction and the Police: Two Ships Passing in the Night?*, 24 Const. Comment. 533, 535 (2007) (book review) (discussing the book's argument that "modern law's tolerance of broad police powers conflicts with founding-era values" (citing Andrew E. Taslitz, Reconstructing the Fourth Amendment: A History of Search and Seizure, 1789-1868 (2006)).

Roger I. Roots

729 *See, e.g.*, Reed v. Legg, 2 Del. (2 Harr.) 173, 173, 176 (1837) (complainant liable for swearing out an affidavit for a search warrant which turned up no stolen goods; complainant accompanied officers on the search); Simpson v. Smith, 2 Del. Cas. 285 (1817) (complainant was sued for seeking search warrant which uncovered no stolen goods; the complaining citizen actu-ally accompanied the officer during the search); State v. McDonald, 14 N.C. (3 Dev.) 468, 469 (1832).

730 *See* State v. Dean, 48 N.C. (3 Jones) 393, 395 (1856).

731 *See* Reed v. Legg, 2 Del. (2 Harr.) 173, 173, 176 (1837) (indicating that a private individual sought out and then accompanied the execution of a search warrant); State v. Hancock, 2 Del. Cas. 249 (1802). The search and seizure provisions of early state constitutions and the federal constitution were intended to apply to private individual searchers and seizers as well as government actors.

732 Davies, *Recovering the Original Fourth Amendment*, 98 Mich. L. Rev. 547, at 660 ("The Framers likely perceived the threat to the right to be secure in house and person in very specific terms - they feared the possibility that future legislatures might authorize the use of general warrants for revenue searches of houses.").

733 *Id.*

734 *See* Russell W. Galloway, Jr., *The Intruding Eye: A Status Report on the Constitutional Ban Against Paper Searches*, 25 How. L.J. 367, 377 n.44 (1982) ("The *Boyd* case was the first Supreme Court case to discuss the issue of paper searches because between 1790 and the Civil War, federal statutes did not authorize such searches."). The *Boyd* Court addressed the rarity of the seizure in its consideration: "The act of 1863 was the first act...in this country or in England, so far as we have been able to ascertain, which authorized the search and seizure of a man's private papers ... ." Boyd v. United States, 116 U.S. 616, 622-23 (1886).

735 *See* Davies, *Recovering the Original Fourth Amendment*, 98 Mich. L. Rev. 547, at 660.

736 *See id.* at 663.

737 *See* Bradford P. Wilson, The Fourth Amendment as More Than a Form of Words: The View from the Founding, in The Bill of Rights: Original Meaning and Current Understanding 151, 154 (Eugene W. Hickock, Jr. ed., 1991).

738   U.S. Const. amend. V ("Nor shall [any person] be compelled in any criminal case to be a witness against himself...").

739   The Federalist No. 83, at 563 (Alexander Hamilton) (Jacob E. Cooke ed., 1961).

740   *Id.*; *see also* Taslitz, Reconstructing the Fourth Amendment, at 57.

741   *See* State v. Wagstaff, 105 S.E. 283, 283-84 (S.C. 1920) (holding official criminally liable in a prosecution for assault); State v. Armfield, 9 N.C. (2 Hawks) 246, 246-47 (1822) (finding constable criminally liable for being too forceful and going beyond the scope of a warrant).

742   State v. Brown, 5 Del. (5 Harr.) 505, 506 (1854) (involving an officer who was criminally indicted and convicted for entering an occupied dwelling at night without warrant while chasing a fleeing felon); State v. Mahon, 3 Del. (3 Harr.) 568, 569 (1841) (finding arrestor lacked sufficient authority and was unduly forceful); Long v. State, 12 Ga. 293, 295-96 (1852) (involving vigilantes who were criminally charged with theft for wrongly taking property from a suspected criminal without warrant).

743   Jones v. Commonwealth, 40 Va. (1 Rob.) 748, 753 (1842) (upholding criminal liability for the informer and the constable, but overturning conviction of magistrate who issued invalid warrant).

744   . 4 William Blackstone, Commentaries 218.

745   *See* Bivens v. Six Unknown Named Agents of Fed. Bureau of Narcotics, 403 U.S. 388, 413 (1971) (Burger, C.J., dissenting) (writing that society pays a high price "for such a drastic remedy").

746   Thus, John H. Wigmore (author of the foremost treatise on evidence) complained that the remedy of exclusion "rests on a reverence for the Fourth Amendment so deep and cogent that its violation will be taken notice of, at any cost of other justice, and even in the most indirect way." John H. Wigmore, *Using Evidence Obtained by Illegal Search and Seizure*, 8 A.B.A. J. 479, 482 (1922).

747   *Cf.* David E. Steinberg, *The Original Understanding of Unreasonable Searches and Seizures*, 56 Fla. L. Rev. 1051, 1072 (2004) ("Prior to *Boyd v. United States*, constitutional search and seizure provisions probably were discussed in fewer than fifty opinions.").

748   Frederick Schauer, *On the Supposed Jury-Dependence of Evidence Law*, 155 U. Pa. L. Rev. 165, 168 (2006).

749   *Id.*

Roger I. Roots

750 *See* Commonwealth v. Carver, 26 Va. (5 Rand.) 660, 661-62 (1827) (holding that decisions of higher courts are binding on lower courts).

751 *See, e.g.,* Ellis v. White, 25 Ala. 540, 541-42 (1854).

752 *See* Roger Roots, *When the Past is a Prison: The Hardening Plight of the American Ex-Convict,* 1 Just. Pol'y J., Fall 2004, at 8, http://www.cjcj. org/jpj/2007/08/justice/policy/journal/3 (offering some early American anecdotes).

753 Bernard Schwartz, A History of the Supreme Court 7 (1993) (saying "no meaningful reporting of cases in the modern sense existed" during the late eighteenth or early nineteenth centuries). *See* Ephraim Kirby, Reports of Cases Adjudged in the Superior Court of the State of Connecticut from the Year 1785, to May, 1788, with Some Determinations in the Supreme Court of Errors (1789) (the first full-fledged official case reporter published in the colonies); John H. Langbein, *Chancellor Kent and the History of Legal Literature,* 93 Colum. L. Rev. 547, 573 (1993) (referring to Kirby's Reports as America's first case reports). Kirby's Reports published rulings from 1785 to 1788, an important period. Aside from Kirby's Reports, only a handful of ratification-era lawyers' journals have been preserved, and collections of reports of trials reported in early newspapers or books are found here and there. *See, e.g.,* The Superior Court Diary of William Samuel Johnson 1772-1773 (John T. Farrell ed., 1942) (published diary of a judge and authentic Framer of the Constitution).

754 *See* Marc M. Arkin, *Rethinking the Constitutional Right to a Criminal Appeal,* 39 UCLA L. Rev. 503, 503 (1992) (conventional wisdom is that "criminal appeals did not exist at the time of the Founding").

755 *See, e.g., id.;* 6 Del. (1 Houst.) intr. n. (1920) (stating that Delaware offered no appeal whatsoever from its criminal courts until the late nineteenth century).

756 *See, e.g.,* Ned v. State, 7 Port. 187, 201 (Ala. 1838) (stating appellate jurisdiction is reserved for civil cases); Humphrey v. State, Minor 64, 65 (Ala. 1822) (holding that the Alabama Supreme Court has no general criminal appellate jurisdiction without passage of a specific act granting such jurisdiction by the state legislature).

757 Steinberg, 56 Fla. L. Rev. 1051, at 1072 ("Prior to *Boyd v. United States,* constitutional search and seizure provisions probably were discussed in fewer than fifty opinions.").

758 *See* Amar II, *supra,* at 146.

759 Davies, *Recovering the Original Fourth Amendment*, 98 Mich. L. Rev. 547, at 627 ("In the late eighteenth century, searches were still of limited utility to criminal law enforcement. The principal possessory offense was possession of stolen property. In the absence of forensic science, items other than stolen property would usually have been of limited evidentiary value."). Nor is this proposition only of recent notice. *See* 2 James Wilson, The Works of James Wilson 163 (James DeWitt Andrews ed., Chicago, Callaghan & Co. 1896) (authored circa 1790) ("The principal species of evidence, which comes before juries, is the testimony of witnesses.").

760 Consider the example of *Reed v. Legg*, 2 Del. (2 Harr.) 173, 173-74 (Del. 1837), where the facts indicate that allegedly stolen goods recovered during a search were immediately returned to their alleged rightful owner.

761 Sources of law known to the Framers themselves consisted primarily of treatises by English jurists such as Hale and Blackstone. In colonial America "the reporting of any decision was unusual," and "this state of affairs lasted well into the early national period." Langbein, 93 Colum. L. Rev. 547, at 572-73 (citation omitted).

762 Pitler, 61 Wash. L. Rev. 459, at 466. 763 Amar I, at 786.

764 *See* Davies, *Recovering the Original Fourth Amendment*, 98 Mich. L. Rev. 547, *supra*, at 627.

765 *See id.*

766 *See* Langbein, 93 Colum. L. Rev. 547, at 573 (referring to Kirby's Reports as the first American case reporter).

767 Frisbie v. Butler, 1 Kirby 213, 213 (Conn. 1787).

768 Constitutional search and seizure provisions require warrants to state with specificity "the place to be searched, and the persons or things to be seized." U.S. Const. amend. IV. However, the warrant in *Frisbie v. Butler* gave searchers authority to "search all suspected places and persons that the complainant thinks proper" and to arrest unnamed perpetrators. 1 Kirby at 213-14.

769 Frisbie, 1 Kirby at 213-14. 770 *Id.* at 214.

771 *Id.*

772 The opinion states it was issued "by the whole Court," although it is not clear how many judges participated. *Id.* at 215.

773 *Id.*

774 *Id.*

775 *See* Pitler, 61 Wash. L. Rev. 459, at 466 n.36 ("The earliest statement of the common law rule came in *Commonwealth v. Dana*, 43 Mass. 329 (2 Met. 1841)...."); Davies, *Recovering the Original Fourth Amendment*, 98 Mich. L. Rev. 547, supra note 15, at 664 n.318 (identifying the 1841 case of *Commonwealth v. Dana* as the first American appearance of a court holding suggesting that courts may admit illegally seized evidence).

776 *See, e.g.*, Sturdevant v. Gaines, 5 Ala. 435, 436 (1843) (upholding judgment for malicious prosecution where a criminal suspect had been arrested without probable cause and released by pretrial habeas corpus).

777 *See* generally Robert J. Pushaw, Jr., *The Inherent Powers of Federal Courts and the Structural Constitution*, 86 Iowa L. Rev. 735 (2001).

778 Grumon v. Raymond, 1 Conn. 40, 41 (1814). 779 *Id.*

780 *Id.* at 40-41. 781 *Id.* at 40-41, 54.

782 *See* George E. Hinman, Zephaniah Swift, in Founders and Leaders of Connecticut 1633-1783, at 293, 294 (Charles Edward Perry ed., 1934) (describing Zephaniah Swift's's early political career).

783 Lewis Henry Boutell, The Life of Roger Sherman 165 (Chicago, A.C. McClurg & Co. 1896).

784 The Connecticut Wits: John Trumbull (1750-1831), Timothy Dwight (1752-1817), Joel Barlow (1754-1812), in American Literature Survey: Colonial and Federal to 1800, at 483, 484 (Milton R. Stern & Seymour L. Gross eds., 1968).

785 *See* generally Marian C. McKenna, Tapping Reeve and the Litchfield Law School (1986).

786 William A. Beers, A Biographical Sketch of Roger Minott Sherman (Bridgeport, J.H. Cogswell 1882).

787 John Adams was overseas serving as Ambassador to England during the Constitutional Convention. However, the Fourth Amendment contains language originally drafted by Adams which first appeared in the 1780 Massachusetts Constitution. *See* Davies, *Recovering the Original Fourth Amendment*, 98 Mich. L. Rev. 547, supra, at 566 n.25 (stating that "virtually all of the language in the Fourth Amendment, including 'unreasonable searches and seizures,' had appeared as of the 1780 Massachusetts provision" drafted by Adams).

788 Pitler, 61 Wash. L. Rev. 459, at 466.

789   Allen E. Shoenberger, *The Not So Great Writ: The European Court of Human Rights Finds Habeas Corpus an Inadequate Remedy: Should American Courts Reexamine the Writ?*, 56 Cath. U. L. Rev. 47, 56 (2006) ("The ambit of the writ has been greatly limited - some would say to the virtual vanishing point.").

790   . *See* Arkin, *Rethinking the Constitutional Right to a Criminal Appeal*, 39 UCLA L. Rev. 503, at 535, 536 (finding that "habeas corpus was primarily a pretrial remedy" during the early 1800s); Rollin C. Hurd, A Treatise on the Right of Personal Liberty, and on the Writ of Habeas Corpus and the Practice Connected with It: With a View of the Law of Extradition of Fugitives 182 (Albany, W.C. Little & Co. 1858) (quoting In re Carlton, 7 Cow. 471 (1827)) ("Any person illegally detained has a right to be discharged, and it is the duty of this court to restore him to his liberty.").

791   *See* James Robertson, *Lecture, Quo Vadis, Habeas Corpus?*, 55 Buff. L. Rev. 1063, 1080 (2008) (saying that after 1920, habeas corpus "began its transition into what it mostly is today - a legal tool for bringing post-conviction, collateral challenges in criminal cases.").

792   Akhil Reed Amar, *Of Sovereignty and Federalism*, 96 Yale L.J. 1425, 1509 n.329 (1987).

793   U.S. Const. art. I, § 9, cl. 2.

794   William S. Church, A Treatise on the Writ of Habeas Corpus § 87 (2d ed., San Francisco, Bancroft-Whitney 1893).

795   *See, e.g.*, Porter v. Porter, 53 So. 546, 547 (Fla. 1910) ("The writ of habeas corpus is a common-law writ of ancient origin designed as a speedy method of affording a judicial inquiry into the course of any alleged unlawful custody of an individual or any alleged unlawful actual deprivation of personal liberty."); *Ex parte* Sullivan, 138 P. 815, 821 (Okla. Crim. App. 1914) (saying the writ is granted to inquire into all cases of illegal imprisonment); *see also* Sims v. M'Lendon, 34 S.C.L. (3 Strob.) 557, 557 (S.C. 1849) (involving suspect released from jail without indictment after a defective arrest).

796   *See* Caroline Nasrallah Belk, Note, *Next Friend Standing and the War on Terror*, 53 Duke L.J. 1747, 1750-54 (2004) (discussing the history of so-called next-friend standing in habeas corpus cases).

797   *See* People *ex rel.* McCanliss v. McCanliss, 175 N.E. 129, 129 (N.Y. 1931) ("By immemorial tradition the aim of habeas corpus is a justice that is swift and summary.").

Roger I. Roots

798 *See* Porter v. Porter, 53 So. 546, 547 (Fla. 1910) ("The writ requires the body of the person alleged to be unlawfully held in custody or restrained of his liberty to be brought before the court that appropriate judgment may be rendered upon judicial inquiry into the alleged unlawful restraint.").

799 *See Ex parte* Tong, 108 U.S. 556, 559 (1883) (the purpose of a habeas inquiry "is not to inquire into the criminal act which is complained of, but into the right to liberty notwithstanding the act"); 20 Am. Jur. Trials § 3, at 13 (1973) ("Moreover, the guilt or innocence of the petitioner is in no way brought into question ... .").

800 *See* 1 Joseph Chitty, A Practical Treatise on the Criminal Law 119 (2d ed., London, Samuel Brooke 1826). As stated by Chitty:

> Indeed whenever a person is restrained of his liberty, by being confined in a common gaol [jail], or by a private person, whether it be for a criminal or civil cause, and it is apprehended that the imprisonment is illegal, he may regularly by habeas corpus have his body, and the proceedings under which he is detained, removed to some superior jurisdiction, having authority to examine the legality of the commitment; and on the return, he will be either discharged, bailed, or remanded.

Id.

801 *See* Ex parte Beatty, 12 Wend. 229, 231-33 (N.Y. 1834) (involving suspect discharged due to irregular process); Nelson v. Cutter, 17 F. Cas. 1316, 1316 (C.C.D. Ohio 1844) (No. 10,104) (discharging defendants due to defect in arrest affidavit); Commonwealth v. Alexander, 6 Binn. 176, 176-77 (Pa. 1813) (discharging debtor due to wrongful arrest).

802 *See* Lutterloh v. Powell, 2 N.C. (1 Hayw.) 307, 307-08 (1796). 803 *Id.* at 307, 308.

804 *See* Arkin, *Rethinking the Constitutional Right to a Criminal Appeal*, 39 UCLA L. Rev. 503, at 535-36 ("The difficulty in ascertaining state habeas practice in the antebellum period partly results from the fact that habeas decisions were reported sporadically at best, especially by the lower courts where petitions for the writ were entertained most frequently."); *see also* In re Reynolds, 20 F. Cas. 592, 595 (N.D.N.Y. 1867) (No. 11,721) ("During my own service as judge in a state court, I exercised the power of discharging minors held under

228

invalid enlistments in repeated instances ... In most of these instances not even a newspaper notice of the case was ever published.").

805 *See* Sims v. M'Lendon, 34 S.C.L. (3 Strob.) 557, 557 (S.C. 1849) (involving suspect released from jail without indictment after a defective arrest); M'Clintic v. Lockridge, 38 Va. (11 Leigh) 253, 253, 258 (1840) (upholding issuance of habeas corpus writ for a prisoner arrested pursuant to an invalid escape warrant).

806 *See* Miller v. Grice, 30 S.C.L. (1 Rich.) 147, 147 (S.C. 1844) (describing habeas corpus discharge of defendant arrested on a South Carolina warrant for a crime committed in North Carolina; defendant later sued and recovered against the magistrate who signed the warrant, Miller v. Grice, 31 S.C.L. (2 Rich.) 27, 31-32, 36 (S.C. 1845)).

807 *See* Green v. Garrett, 17 Va. (3 Munf.) 339 (1812). 808 *Id.* at 343 (argument of Wickham).

809 *Id.* at 344.

810 40 Va. (1 Rob.) 748 (1842). 811 *Id.* at 750.

812 *Id.*

813 Hemphill v. Coats, 4 Stew. & P. 125 (Ala. 1833) (quashing and dismissing case after judgment on ground that underlying arrest warrant was irregular and defective).

814 *Id.* at 128.

815 *See, e.g.,* In re Stacy, 10 Johns. 328, 334 (1813) (per curiam) (releasing civilian arrested for treason by military authorities due to lack of jurisdiction); Miller v. Grice, 30 S.C.L. (1 Rich.) 147, 147-48 (S.C. 1844) (describing habeas corpus discharge of defendant arrested by warrant outside the jurisdiction where the alleged crime was committed).

816 For example, in 1850, the Georgia Supreme Court reversed the murder conviction of an African-American slave because no evidence of a valid charging warrant was admitted into evidence during the prosecution's case at trial. Judge v. State, 8 Ga. 173 (1850). Although a valid warrant charging murder existed, the warrant was not introduced until after the defense moved for a directed verdict after the closing of the prosecution's case. *Id.* at 176. The trial court admitted the warrant; the Supreme Court reversed. *Id.* at 176-77.

817 Ex parte Burford, 7 U.S. (3 Cranch) 448 (1806).

818 *Id.* at 449-50. The opinion provides few specific details of Burford's allegedly objectionable conduct; however, the Court at one point addresses

Roger I. Roots

the issue of how authorities should properly deal with a "person of ill fame."
Id. at 452-53.

819   *Id.* at 450-52. 820   *Id.* at 453. 821   *Id.* at 451.

822   The panel of justices that decided *Burford* included William Cushing, William Paterson, Bushrod Washington, Samuel Chase, John Marshall and William Johnson. Cushing had been a Massachusetts judge during the Revolutionary and ratification periods. Paterson actually signed the Constitution as a convention delegate from New Jersey. Chase had been a member of the Continental Congress during the Revolution and signed the Declaration of Independence. Bushrod Washington was George Washington's nephew. John Marshall had been a member of the Virginia Convention that ratified the Constitution. William Johnson was the son of a Revolutionary War hero and studied law in the office of Charles Cotesworth Pinckney, an influential delegate at the Constitutional Convention of 1787. *See* generally Gustavus Myers, History of the Supreme Court of the United States (1912).

823   That the Marshall Court assumed Burford may have been a real offender is clear from the penultimate sentence in the opinion: "If the prisoner is really a person of ill fame, and ought to find sureties for his good behavior, the [lower court] justices may proceed de novo, and take care that their proceedings are regular." Burford, 7 U.S. at 453.

824   547 U.S. 586 (2006).

825   129 S.Ct. 695 (2009). 826   Hudson, 547 U.S. at 591.

827   8 U.S. (4 Cranch) 75 (1807).

828   *See* generally Eric M. Freedman, Habeas Corpus: Rethinking the Great Writ of Liberty 20-35 (2001) (providing detailed analysis of the proceedings in *Bollman*).

829   *See id.*

830   Bollman, 8 U.S. (4 Cranch) 75. It was a practice in early American criminal litigation for defendants to "demur" to the charges against them rather than tendering a plea when challenging warrants or charging instruments. Upon a defendant's demur, a court would inquire into the validity of the complaint and other documents and conduct whatever proceedings were necessary to examine the propriety of the accusations. In the case of *Grumon v. Raymond*, for example, the demurrals of five arrested suspects apparently led to a summary discharge of the suspects as a consequence of an illegal general

warrant. 1 Conn. 40, 41 (1814) (describing a pretrial discharge after the five suspects demurred to the charges).

831 *See* Bollman, 8 U.S. (4 Cranch) at 125 ("If ... upon this inquiry it manifestly appears that no such crime has been committed, or that the suspicion entertained of the prisoner was wholly groundless, in such cases only is it lawful totally to discharge him.") (quoting a "very learned and accurate commentator") (internal quotation marks omitted).

832 *Id.* at 109-10 (argument of C. Lee).

833 . *Id.* at 136.

834 It should be noted that in earlier proceedings in the *Bollman* case, the D.C. Circuit Court, also represented by bona fide Founding Fathers such as William Cranch, a nephew of John Adams, had written that the issuance of arrest warrants against the men was inconsistent with the Fourth Amendment. *See* United States v. Bollman, 24 F. Cas. 1189, 1190, 1192-93 (C.C.D.C. 1807) (No. 14,622).

835 Even those Fourth Amendment scholars who are aware of *Burford* and *Bollman* don't seem to find their words to be as significant as I do. *See* Wayne R. LaFave, *Pinguitudinous Police, Pachydermatous Prey: Whence Fourth Amendment "Seizures"?,* 1991 U. Ill. L. Rev. 729, 764 (1991) (saying "the very first Fourth Amendment case of any consequence to reach the Supreme Court" was *Boyd v. United States* in 1886). Davies discusses *Burford* and *Bollman* in a lengthy footnote but doesn't seem to regard the cases as making any important statements about the Fourth Amendment or the exclusionary rule. *See* Davies, *Recovering the Original Fourth Amendment,* 98 Mich. L. Rev. 547, at 613 n.174. Certainly, statesmen of the nineteenth cen-tury regarded *Bollman* as an important precedent, which supported exclu-sionary remedies for illegal seizures of persons. *See, e.g.,* James Asheton Bayard, Executive Usurpation: Speech of Hon. James A. Bayard, of Delaware, in the Senate of the United States 15 (July 19, 1861) (transcript available in the Harvard College Library) (addressing Fourth Amendment law). Bayard stated that:

There must be probable cause of guilt, and without that supported by oath, the court will discharge. There must also be authority for the arrest and commitment, or the court will discharge. If an offense be not charged, if there is no oath, or the oath does not show prob-able cause in support of the charges, as in the case of Swartout [sic] and Bollman, the court will discharge.

Id.

836   After the Court's decision in *Burford*, but before the Court's decision in *Bollman*, Justice Paterson died. His seat was taken by Henry Brockholst Livingston, another Founder who had been a Revolutionary War officer.

837   Robertson, *Quo Vadis, Habeas Corpus?*, 55 Buff. L. Rev. 1063, at 1074.

838   *See* generally Walter Flavius McCaleb, Ph.D., The Aaron Burr Conspiracy (New York, Wilson-Erickson 1936) (1903).

839   *See* 1 J.F.H. Claiborne, Mississippi, As a Province, Territory and State 284 (La. State Univ. Press 1964) (1880) (reprinting the grand jury's presentment). Burr was later rearrested on essentially the same charges, tried, and acquitted. *See* McCaleb, The Aaron Burr Conspiracy.

840   *See, e.g.,* Treadaway v. Finney (Conn. Super. Ct. 1773), in American Historical Association, Superior Court Diary of William Samuel Johnson, 1772-1773, at 206 (1942) (conceding that plaintiff recovering damages for false arrest "does not say what has been the Event or is become of the information").

841   *Cf.* Sims v. M'Lendon, 34 S.C.L. (3 Strob.) 557, 557 (S.C. 1849) (involving suit over defective prosecution; the underlying charge was dismissed with-out clear procedural narrative); Cleek v. Haines, 23 Va. (2 Rand.) 440, 440 (1824) (involving false arrest case over an arrest which was discharged by justice of the peace without prosecution). *Taylor v. Alexander*, 6 Ohio 144 (1833), an 1833 Ohio Supreme Court decision, provides an example of a case in which exclusion may have gone unrecorded. Taylor was arrested after a flawed search warrant was executed on his residence. *Id.* The war-rant was flawed in that the underlying affidavit claimed the alleged crime - stealing buckwheat - was committed by either Taylor or his wife, but the warrant required that only Taylor answer for the crime if the goods were found. *Id.* at 145-46. The allegedly stolen items sought by the search warrant were found in Taylor's possession, and he was arrested and brought before a magistrate. *Id.* at 144, 148. Little further is known of the criminal prosecution (if any). Taylor later sued his arrestors for trespass, assault and battery, and false imprisonment based on the flawed warrant, but he did not recover. *Id.* at 144-45. From the reported facts on appeal we know: (1) Taylor was found in possession of purportedly stolen goods sought by the (invalid) search warrant; (2) any

criminal case against Taylor ended in Taylor's exoneration (perhaps because of the invalidity of the search warrant); and (3) Taylor later sued his arrestors for torts arising from the invalid search warrant. *Id.* at 144-45, 148. Consider also the case of State v. Brown, 5 Del. (5 Harr.) 505, 505 (1854), involving criminal charges against a town watchman who illegally entered a home without warrant while chasing a chicken thief. The case mentions the underlying arrests of "three negroes" who were "taken before the Mayor next morning and discharged" due to the illegality of the warrantless arrests. *Id.* at 506.

842   *See* Reed v. Legg, 2 Del. (2 Harr.) 173, 174 (1837) (stating only that "the prosecution of course failed" after the suspect's possession of allegedly stolen goods was found to have an innocent explanation, "and these actions were brought ... for the alledged trespass"); Johnson v. Chambers, 32 N.C. (10 Ired.) 287, 290 (1849) (saying only that "magistrate had dismissed the warrant, on which the plaintiff had been arrested"); Murray v. Lackey, 6 N.C. (2 Mur.) 368, 368-69 (1818) (involving malicious prosecution suit where evidence of underlying discharge was not recorded).

843   Pitler, 61 Wash. L. Rev. 459, at 466.

844   *See* Price v. Graham, 48 N.C. (3 Jones) 545, 546-47 (1856) (suggesting that man arrested under an invalid warrant and immediately discharged upon appearance was released apparently because of the invalidity of the warrant; the accused murderer later sued the complainant for malicious prosecution).

845   Pitler, 61 Wash. L. Rev. 459, at 466.

846   The discussion on this topic is dominated by voices calling for one Fourth Amendment remedy exclusive of all others: "With respect to Fourth Amendment remedies, almost all commentators take for granted that either liquidated damages or exclusion will be exclusively applied." Alan Dalsass, *Note, Options: An Alternative Perspective on Fourth Amendment Remedies,* 50 Rutgers L. Rev. 2297, 2298 n.8 (1998).

847   *Cf., e.g.,* Letter from Charles Francis Adams to Hon. William H. Seward (Feb. 25, 1864), in Papers Relating to Foreign Affairs, Accompanying the Annual Message of the President to the Second Session Thirty-Eighth Congress (1864 pt. 1) 230-31 (1865) (quoting "Sir H. Cairns" as saying, "The moment you arrest [a criminal suspect] you have made the seizure, and the law also says in the interests of justice that the magistrate may remand him within certain limits ... and, moreover, there are safeguards in the habeas corpus

against the abuse of authority there.... It is no answer to say that the individual may have his action for damages where there has been a breach of the law.") (emphasis added).

848   McCall v. McDowell, 15 F. Cas. 1235 (C.C.D. Cal. 1867) (No. 8,673).

849   *Id.* at 1242 (emphasis added).

850   21 Ind. 370, 372, 383 (1863). 851   *Id.* at 373.

852   *Id.*

853   *See* Ex parte Field, 9 F. Cas. 1, 9 (C.C.D. Vt. 1862) (No. 4,761) (releasing inmate charged with discouraging enlistment and fining a marshal for failing to produce the inmate upon receipt of the habeas corpus writ).

854   *Id.* at 3-4. Judge Smalley drew a clear conceptual nexus between habeas corpus as a remedy for search and seizure violations and the paper seizures condemned in the English decision of *Wilkes v. Wood* that guided the Framers who drafted the Fourth Amendment. *See Wilkes v. Wood*, (1763) 98 Eng. Rep. 489 (K.B.). "If the arrest and detention in this case be sustained," wrote Judge Smalley, "it strikes a much more deadly and fatal blow to civil liberty, than did the general warrants which the British cabinet ordered to be issued against the printers and publishers of the North Briton, number 45 .... ." Ex parte Field, 9 F. Cas. at 6 (citing the search of the residence of House of Commons member John Wilkes in 1763).

855   *See* Bennett L. Gershman, *The Gate is Open But the Door is Locked - Habeas Corpus and Harmless Error*, 51 Wash. & Lee L. Rev. 115, 124 (1994) ("Each Term [of the Supreme Court] seems to bring several new decisions that further restrict the availability of the writ."); Robertson, *Quo Vadis, Habeas Corpus?*, 55 Buff. L. Rev. 1063, at 1084 (remarking that federal judges now "expend a lot more energy" dismissing habeas petitions by applying the numerous statutory and doctrinal limitations of contemporary habeas practice than they would if they ever reached the merits of such petitions). 856   *See, e.g.*, Lacey v. Palmer, 24 S.E. 930, 931 (Va. 1896) ("The...writ of habeas corpus is not to determine the guilt or innocence of the prisoner."). 857   U.S. Const. amend. IV ("The right of the people to be secure in their persons, houses, papers, and effects, against unreasonable searches and seizures, shall not be violated, and no Warrants shall issue, but upon prob-able cause, supported by Oath or affirmation, and particularly describing the place to be searched, and the persons or things to be seized.").

858   Amar II, *supra*, at 113.

859 Malcolm Richard Wilkey, *The Exclusionary Rule: Why Suppress Valid Evidence?*, 62 Judicature 214, 215-32 (1978).
860 Malcolm Richard Wilkey, Why Suppress Valid Evidence?, as reprinted in Taking Sides: Clashing Views on Controversial Legal Issues 264, 269 (M. Ethan Katsh ed., 5th ed. 1993).
861 *Id.*
862 Ker v. Illinois, 119 U.S. 436, 445 (1886). 863 127 U.S. 700, 715 (1888).
864 342 U.S. 519, 522-23 (1952).
865 Professor Amar has made the same assertion as Wilkey. *See* Amar II at 108 (citing *Frisbie v. Collins* for the claim that "an exception for unconstitutional seizures of persons was always recognized").
866 *See, e.g.*, Miller v. Grice, 30 S.C.L. (1 Rich.) 147, 147-48 (S.C. 1844) (describing habeas corpus discharge of a defendant arrested by warrant outside the jurisdiction where the alleged crime was committed); In re Stacy, 10 Johns. 328, 333-34 (N.Y. Sup. Ct. 1813) (Kent, C.J.) (releasing civilian arrested for treason by military authorities due to lack of jurisdiction).
867 Frisbie, 342 U.S. at 522 (citing *Ker*, 119 U.S. at 444).
868 *See* Adams v. New York, 192 U.S. 585, 596 (1904) (saying *Ker* established that an illegal arrest "would not prevent the trial of the person thus abducted in the state wherein he had committed an offense").
869 *Ker*, 119 U.S. at 444; *see also* Annotation, Right to Try One Brought within Jurisdiction Illegally or as a Result of a Mistake as to Identity, 165 A.L.R. 947, 948 (1946). Only Kansas, it was said, adhered to precedents "contrary to the general rule." 165 A.L.R. at 950.
870 The case of *In re Pleasants*, 11 Am. Jurist & L. Mag. 257 (1834), almost directly contradicted the ruling in Ker. In *Pleasants*, an inmate arrested upon a warrant issued in the D.C. Circuit but executed in the Eastern District of Virginia was ordered discharged, on grounds that the warrant was without validity in Virginia. *Id.* at 257-59.
871 In re May, 1 N.W. 1021, 1021, 1024 (Mich. 1879) (ordering release of prostitute arrested without warrant).
872 *Id.* at 1024.
873 People v. Crocker, 1 Mich. 31, 31 (1869). 874 18 P. 177, 178-79 (Kan. 1888).
875 Id. at 178.

876   John E. Theuman, *Annotation, Modern Status of Rule Relating to Jurisdiction of State Court to Try Criminal Defendant Brought within Jurisdiction Illegally or as a Result of Fraud or Mistake*, 25 A.L.R. 4th 157 (1983) (emphasis added).

877   *Annotation, Right to Try One Brought within Jurisdiction Illegally or as a Result of Mistake as to Identity*, 18 A.L.R. 509, 512 (1922) (citing State v. Simmons, 18 P. 177 (Kan. 1888); State v. Garrett, 45 P. 93 (Kan. 1896); In re Robinson, 45 N.W. 267 (Neb. 1890)).

878   Judge Wilkey's argument often recurs in anti-exclusion scholarship. *See, e.g.*, Amar II, *supra*, at 108 (citing *Frisbie v. Collins* for the proposition that "even at the height of the exclusionary rule, an exception for unconstitutional seizures of persons was always recognized").

879   *See* David B. Kopel, *The Self-Defense Cases: How the United States Supreme Court Confronted a Hanging Judge in the Nineteenth Century and Taught Some Lessons for Jurisprudence in the Twenty-First*, 27 Am. J. Crim. L. 293, 302 (2000) (footnotes omitted) ("At common law, it was well-settled that if a person was attacked by a peace officer, and the person did not know that the attacker was a peace officer acting with a proper warrant, the per-son could resist the attack. If necessary, deadly force was permitted."). Even fugitive criminals who jumped bail were privileged to shoot to kill officers who employed improper force against them. *See id.* at 302-03.

880   *See* Starr v. United States, 153 U.S. 614, 623, 628 (1894) (overturning murder conviction of bail jumper Henry Starr on grounds that the jury had not been instructed on the privilege to resist a false arrest).

881   *See* Adams v. State, 48 S.E. 910, 911-12 (Ga. 1904) (indicating third-party intermeddlers were privileged to forcibly liberate wrongfully arrested persons from unlawful custody).

882   *See* 1 William Hawkins, A Treatise of the Pleas of the Crown 103-04 (John Curwood ed., 8th ed., London, S. Sweet 1824); *see also* Roberts v. State, 14 Mo. 138 (1851) (reversing murder conviction on grounds that a person killing an officer who is arresting him illegally is guilty of only man-slaughter). When a posse of marshals attempted to arrest a suspected train robber near Checotah, Oklahoma Territory in 1895, the suspect shot and killed a Cherokee Indian policeman. Glenn Shirley, Law West of Fort Smith: A History of Frontier Justice in the Indian Territory, 1834-1896, at 73 (1957). At the suspect's trial for murder, Judge Isaac Parker instructed the jury to acquit the defendant of

the murder charge, based on an unlawful arrest attempt without a warrant. *Id.* No verdict on the robbery charge was reported. *Id.*

883 City Council v. Payne, 11 S.C.L. (2 Nott & McC.) 475, 476 (S.C. 1820).

884 *See id.* at 477-79.

885 *See* Andrew P. Wright, *Resisting Unlawful Arrests: Inviting Anarchy or Protecting Individual Freedom?*, 46 Drake L. Rev. 383, 388 (1997) (discussing the states' gradual departure from recognizing the right to resist unlawful arrests).

886 Cf. State v. M'Lain, 4 S.C.L. (2 Brev.) 443, 443-44 (S.C. 1810) (quashing indictment of a purported pig thief because the word pig does not appear in the statute criminalizing hog stealing).

887 The Magna Carta's due process clause recognized the importance of procedural sequence as early as 1215. Authorities could move on the people only after strictly following the law of the land; otherwise, the people had every right to resist authority and demand restoration of the status quo ante. See Magna Carta, para. 39 (1215), available at http://www.bl.uk/trea-sures/magna-carta/translation/mc_trans.html (last visited Dec. 1, 2009) ("No free man shall be seized or imprisoned, or stripped of his rights or posses-sion, or outlawed or exiled, or deprived of his standing in any other way, nor will we proceed with force against him, or send others to do so, except by the lawful judgment of his equals or by the law of the land.") (British Library translation).

888 Entick v. Carrington, 19 How. St. Tr. 1029, 1042 (1765) (argument of plaintiff's counsel).

889 *See* Bad Elk v. United States, 177 U.S. 529, 537 (1900) (holding that an arrestee, in some circumstances, may shoot to kill an officer who displays a gun with intent to commit a warrantless arrest based on insufficient cause).

890 *Cf.* Noles v. State, 26 Ala. 31, 40 (1855) (defense counsel citing more than a dozen cases). The court stated that:

Every arrest of a freeman without warrant, unless it be under a charge of felony, is unlawful, and he may use as much force as is necessary either to prevent the arrest, or to effect his escape if arrested; and if he cannot prevent this unlawful arrest, or regain his liberty, but by slaying the aggressor, he has the right to do so ... . *Id.*; *see also* Woodruff v. Woodruff, 22 Ga. 237, 241, 245-46 (1857) (standing for the general proposition that an individual may display a firearm upon the approach of investigators and threaten to shoot the investigators if they continue forward unless the investigators have some lawful authority to do so).

891   The doctrines imposed by modern courts to immunize prosecutors, police and judges were unheard of in early America. *See, e.g.*, Burlingham v. Wylee, 2 Root 152, 152-53 (Conn. Super. Ct. 1794) (holding both the justice who issued a capias warrant and the constable who arrested a Connecticut resident without proper jurisdiction civilly liable for trespass, false imprisonment and assault and battery); Percival v. Jones, 2 Johns. Cas. 49, 49 (N.Y. 1800) (holding justice of the peace liable for ordering imprisonment without taking proper steps, despite the justice's claims of good faith). If an arrest warrant varied from its underlying affidavit (or alleged a crime not justified by facts stated in the affidavit), the issuing magistrate was liable. See Randall v. Henry, 5 Stew. & P. 367 (Ala. 1834); Bennett v. Black, 1 Stew. 494 (Ala. 1828) (involving magistrate held liable for warrant charging offense different from offense alleged in affidavit); Grumon v. Raymond, 1 Conn. 40, 47-48 (1814) (upholding liability of the justice of the peace who issued an imprecise warrant and the constable who executed it); Morgan v. Hughes, 2 T.R. 225, 100 Eng. Rep. 123 (K.B. 1788) (involving magistrate held liable for issuing a defective warrant).

892   *See* Galloway, *The Intruding Eye*, 25 How. L.J. 367, at 372 ("The mere evidence rule...prohibited government seizure of objects merely because of their evidentiary value in proving an individual guilty of a crime.").

893   *See, e.g.*, Cohoon v. Speed, 47 N.C. (2 Jones) 133, 135 (1855) (search warrants are valid only when larceny is charged, and such warrants cannot be used to search for other evidence); State v. McDonald, 14 N.C. (3 Dev.) 468, 470 (1832) ("A search warrant in this state, is to be granted only where a larceny is charged to have been committed."); *see also* Father of Candor, A Letter Concerning Libels, Warrants, and the Seizure of Papers; With a View to Some Late Proceedings, and the Defence of Them by the Majority 47 (2d ed., London, J. Almon 1764) [hereinafter A Letter Concerning Libels] ("Nothing, as I apprehend, can be forcibly taken from any man, or his house entered, without some specific charge under oath... .
It must either be sworn that I have certain stolen goods, or such a particular thing that is criminal in itself ... . Without these limitations, there is no liberty or free enjoyment of person or property ... .").

894   *See* Galloway *The Intruding Eye: A Status Report on the Constitutional Ban Against Paper Searches*, 25 How. L.J. 367at 390, 390 n.100 (discussing the long history of the constitutional ban on the seizure of private papers).
895   Chitty's Treatise on the Criminal Law, published in various editions at the beginning of the nineteenth century, enunciated the mere evidence rule as described in *Entick v. Carrington. See* 1 Joseph Chitty, A Practical Treatise on the Criminal Law: Comprising the Practice, Pleadings, and Evidence, which Occur in the Course of Criminal Prosecutions, Whether by Indictment or Information: with a Copious Collection of Precedents 65 (London, n. pub., 2d ed., corr., enlrg. 1826) (citing 11 St. Tr. 313, 321) ("But a search warrant for libels and other papers of a suspected party is illegal; for ... the difference between seizing stolen goods and private papers of the party accused is apparent. In the one, I am permitted to seize my own goods ... . In the other, the party's own property would be seized ... .").
896   *See* Warden v. Hayden, 387 U.S. 294, 298-301 (1967).
897   *See* Thomas M. Cooley, A Treatise on the Constitutional Limitations Which Rest Upon the Legislative Power of the States of the American Union 365 (Boston, Little, Brown & Co., 5th ed. 1883) (1874) (stating that the common law "secures to the citizen immunity in his home against the prying eyes of the government, and protection in person, property, and papers, against even the process of the law, except in a few specified cases") (emphasis added); *see also* Jeter v. Martin, 4 S.C.L. (2 Brev.) 156, 157 (S.C. 1807) (saying that account books of common citizens were considered inadmissible due to lack of reliability).
898   It appears that Professor Davies and this author disagree over the definition of the term "mere evidence rule." In Davies' seminal Fourth Amendment article, he suggested that the mere evidence rule was first articulated in *Boyd v. United States* in 1886. *See* Davies, *Recovering the Original Fourth Amendment*, 98 Mich. L. Rev. 547, at 727, 726 n.511. Davies seems to define the mere evidence rule as something akin to the exclusionary rule itself. The distinction may not be important, except our differing views of the *Boyd* decision flow from it. In my reading, the mere evidence rule was alive and well in 1791 when the Fourth Amendment was ratified, leading American jurists down a clear path toward the *Boyd* and *Weeks* decisions; while in the view of Davies (as I read it), *Boyd* repre-sented more of a "novel and sweeping" departure from the jurisprudence which preceded it. *Id.*, at 726.

Roger I. Roots

899   Amar, The Constitution and Criminal Procedure (Amar II), at 23.
900   *See id.* at 6.
901   *See* Amar, *Fourth Amendment First Principles*, 107 Harv. L. Rev. 757
(1994) (Amar I), at 772 (describing *Wilkes v. Wood* as the case "whose lessons
the Fourth Amendment was undeniably designed to embody"); *see also* Berger
v. New York, 388 U.S. 41, 49 (1967) (citation omitted) ("Almost a century
thereafter this Court took specific and lengthy notice of *Entick v. Carrington*,
finding that its holding was undoubtedly familiar to and "in the minds of
those who framed the Fourth Amendment....'" (quoting Boyd v. United States,
116 U.S. 616, 626-27 (1886))); Stanford v. Texas, 379 U.S. 476, 484 (1965)
(describing *Entick* as a "wellspring of the rights now protected by the Fourth
Amendment"); Lopez v. United States, 373 U.S. 427, 454 (1963) (Brennan, J.,
dissenting) (citation and footnote omitted):

> In the celebrated case of *Entick v. Carrington*, Lord Camden laid
> down two distinct principles: that general search warrants are unlaw-
> ful because of their uncertainty; and that searches for evidence are
> unlawful because they infringe the privilege against self-incrimina-
> tion. Lord Camden's double focus was carried over into the structure
> of the Fourth Amendment.

Marcus v. Search Warrant, 367 U.S. 717, 728 (1961) (discussing "the great
case of *Entick*"); Frank v. Maryland, 359 U.S. 360, 363 (1959) (citation
omitted) ("In 1765, in England, what is properly called the great case of Entick
v. Carrington announced the principle of English law which became part of
the Bill of Rights...."); United States v. Lefkowitz, 285 U.S. 452, 466 (1932)
(stating "Lord Camden declared that...the law of England did not authorize a
search of private papers to help forward conviction even in cases of most atrocious crime... The teachings of that great case were cherished by our statesmen
when the Constitution was adopted."); Boyd v. United States, 116 U.S. 616,
626 (1886) (calling *Entick* "one of the landmarks of English liberty" and holding that the Fourth Amendment was intended to incorporate its rulings).
902   *See* Otis H. Stephens & Richard A. Glenn, Unreasonable Searches and
Seizures: Rights and Liberties Under the Law 32-34 (2006) (providing an
overview of Wilkes v. Wood).

903   Horace Bleakley, Life of John Wilkes 94 (1917) (describing the investigation as "a perfect orgy of arrest" as authorities apprehended "no fewer than
forty-nine persons, mostly journeymen printers, in the space of three days").
904   A general warrant is a warrant that does not sufficiently specify by name
or other details the person or persons to be arrested or the places and things
to be searched or seized. See Coolidge v. New Hampshire, 403 U.S. 443, 467
(1971) (saying a general warrant authorizes "a general exploratory rummag-
ing" through a person's property).
905   See generally Peter D.G. Thomas, John Wilkes: A Friend to Liberty
(1996) (detailing the litigation, the politics and much of the evidence involved
in the Wilkes prosecution).
906   See generally Wilkes v. Wood, 98 Eng. Rep. 489 (K.B.) (1763); see also
Davies, Recovering the Original Fourth Amendment, 98 Mich. L. Rev. 547, at
562-64 (describing the travels of Wilkes' case).
907   See Taslitz, Reconstructing the Fourth Amendment, at 21. 908   See, e.g.,
Amar I, at 772 (describing Wilkes v. Wood as the "paradigm search and seizure
case" for the Founding generation). The Wilkes case has been cited by the
Supreme Court as providing guidance for interpreting the Fourth Amendment
on many occasions. See, e.g., Atwater v. City of Lago Vista, 532 U.S. 318, 332
n.6 (2001).
909   Amar I, at 772 n.54.
910   Galloway, The Intruding Eye: A Status Report on the Constitutional Ban
Against Paper Searches, 25 How. L.J. 367 supra, at 369. Lord Camden, whose
name was originally Charles Pratt, authored both the Wilkes v. Wood and Entick
v. Carrington decisions in his capacity as Chief Justice of Common Pleas.
911   Amar I, at 772 n.54.
912   See Timothy Lynch, In Defense of the Exclusionary Rule, 23 Harv. J. L.
& Pub. Pol'y 711, 723 n.67 (2000).
913   This phrase is attributable to the eminent Fourth Amendment scholar
Thomas Y. Davies. See Davies, The Fictional Character of Law-and-Order
Originalism: A Case Study of the Distortions and Evasions of Framing-Era
Arrest Doctrine in Atwater v. Lago Vista, 37 Wake Forest L. Rev. 239, 273-74
(2002) (documenting how the Supreme Court used false and distorted history
to uphold an arrest for a non-jailable seatbelt violation).
914   See, e.g., Amar I, at 786.

Roger I. Roots

915 *See* Taslitz, Reconstructing the Fourth Amendment, at 21 (pointing out that Lord Camden drew a link between search and seizure principles and the right against self-incrimination in *Entick v. Carrington*).
916 A footnote is in order here to point out some oddities in the writing, editing and publication of the *Entick* opinion. Francis Hargrave, editor of the "long version" of the *Entick* opinion that was published in Volume 11 of State Trials in 1781, reconstructed the opinion from Lord Camden's written notes. "It was not without some difficulty," Hargrave wrote in his introduction to the case, "that the copy of this judgment was obtained by the editor." 11 Francis Hargrave, State Trials 313 (London, T. Wright 1765). "He has reason to believe," wrote Hargrave, "that the original, most excellent and most valuable as its contents are, was not deemed worthy of preservation by its author [Camden] but was actually committed to the flames." He continued: "Fortunately, the editor remembered to have formerly seen a copy of the judgment in the hands of a friend; and upon application to him, it was immediately obtained, with liberty to the editor to make use of it at his discretion." *Id.*
917 Entick v. Carrington, 19 How. St. Tr. 1029, 1073 (1765) (emphasis added). 918 Wilkes v. Wood, 98 Eng. Rep. 489, 490 (K.B. 1763).
919 Entick, 19 How. St. Tr. at 1073.
920 Davies has questioned whether the Framers of the Fourth Amendment actually read the language in *Entick*, which linked search and seizure protections to silence rights. *See* Davies, *Recovering the Original Fourth Amendment*, 98 Mich. L. Rev. 547, supra note 15, at 727. According to Davies, the Entick opinion referenced by the Boyd Court was a longer ver-sion (Entick v. Carrington, 11 State Trials 313 (decided in 1765 but published in 1781)) of the *Entick* opinion first circulated in the American colonies (2 Wils. 275, 95 Eng. Rep. 807) (published in 1770) that the Framers were more likely to have read. *See id.* Only the longer version contained Lord Camden's pronouncement that "the law obligeth no man to accuse himself ... . and it should seem, that search for evidence is disallowed upon the same principle." Entick v. Carrington, 11 Harg. St. Tr. 313, 323 (1765) (emphasis added).
For this reason, Davies argues that the Fourth Amendment's Framers and ratifiers did not have Entick's coupling of search and seizure protections with silence rights in mind when they approved the Fourth Amendment. In fact, Davies suggests that the intent behind the Fourth Amendment was essentially the same as that behind the Massachusetts Fourth Amendment

corollary - drafted by John Adams in 1780 - since the wording of the two provisions is quite similar. *See* Davies, *Recovering the Original Fourth Amendment*, 98 Mich. L. Rev. 547, at 566 n.25 ("Virtually all of the language in the Fourth Amendment, including "unreasonable searches and seizures,' had appeared as of the 1780 Massachusetts provision; hence, it is unlikely that Camden's statements in the longer version of *Entick* influenced the Framers' views.").

Such a problem of temporal order, if valid, does indeed undermine the long-held view that the Framers in Philadelphia relied on *Entick* as their wellspring of principles behind the Fourth Amendment. But Davies' argument relies on the notion that the Framers of the Fourth Amendment were oblivious to a famous English opinion that had been published and circulated in 1781, more than five years before the constitutional debates in Philadelphia and ten years before ratification of the Fourth Amendment. We know that many American Founding-era lawyers kept fairly up-to-date libraries of English cases and even spent much of their time hand-copying legal rulings and statutes. *See* generally Mary Sarah Bilder, The Transatlantic Constitution: Colonial Legal Culture and the Empire (2004) (documenting the informal system of copying and transcribing laws applicable to the Colonies beginning in the 1600s). Moreover, the set of books containing the longer version (Hargrave's *A Complete Collection of State-Trials and Proceedings For High-Treason, and other Crimes and Misdemeanours* (known as State Trials, 4th edition (1781)) was a fixture of late-eighteenth-century law libraries. Over a hundred of these sets survive in the rare book collections of American libraries today, and several libraries (e.g., Yale's and Harvard's) hold more than one complete set. The notion that all of these book sets, published in 1781, crossed the Atlantic only after the Fourth Amendment was proposed and ratified (between September 1787 and December 1791) seems highly unlikely.

In any case, there is no denying that the conceptual link between silence rights and search and seizure protections was enunciated in documents other than the *Entick* opinion and featured in the most widely circulated pre-ratification texts that addressed search and seizure issues in any depth. The *Wilkes v. Wood* opinion itself, which was printed in Wilson's Reports (1770) as well as widely republished and discussed in newspa-pers on both sides of the Atlantic, associated silence rights and search and seizure protections. *See* Wilkes v. Wood, 98 Eng. Rep. 489, 490 (K.B. 1763) (referring specifically to the seizure of

Wilkes' papers: "Nothing can be more unjust in itself, than that the proof of a man's guilt shall be extracted from his own bosom.").
921   Commonwealth v. Dana, 43 Mass. (2 Met.) 329, 335-36 (1841) (admitting lottery evidence on grounds that the principles of Entick "have but little bearing on the present case" and "the warrant in this case is in conformity with all the ... [Massachusetts] declaration of rights").
922   See 3 Encyclopedia of American Civil Liberties 1749 (Paul Finkelman ed., 2006) (calling the Father of Candor letter "one of the more remarkable documents in all of English political and legal thought"). "The book went through several editions," Finkelman continued, "was read on both sides of the Atlantic," and was "well-known to Patriot leaders by the time the Continental Congress met in Philadelphia." Id.; see also Leonard W. Levy, Origins of the Bill of Rights 163 (1999) (saying Americans of the Founding period knew well the arguments in the Father of Candor pamphlet); William James Smith, 3 Grenville Papers clviii (William J. Smith ed., London, Woodfall & Kinder 1853) ("The letter concerning Libels, Warrants, &c., was one of the most important of the political pamphlets which were written in that very pamphlet-writing age....").
923   A Letter Concerning Libels, *supra*, at 44-45. Father of Candor also made the point that:

The laws of England are to tender to every man accused, even of capital crimes, that they do not permit him to be put to torture to extort a confession, nor oblige him to answer a question that will tend to accuse himself. How then can it be supposed, that...any common fellows under a general warrant...[may] seize and carry off all his papers; and then at his trial produce these papers...in evidence against himself... This would be making a man give evidence against and accuse himself, with a vengeance. And this is to be endured, because the prosecutor wants other sufficient proof, and might be traduced for acting groundlessly, if he could not get it; and because he does it truly for the sake of collecting evidence.

Id.
924   Sir William Meredith, A Reply to the Defence of the Majority, on the Question Relating to General Warrants 21-22 (1764) (emphasis added and capitalization altered).

925 Amar II, *supra*, at 25 (speaking of a "universal law against exclusion" that allegedly prevailed prior to the *Boyd* decision).

926 That Founding-era observers of search and seizure debates were well-versed in *Entick*'s and *Wilkes*'s subtle dimensions is shown by recurring references to the *Entick* and *Wilkes* cases when search and seizure prin-ciples were discussed. Whenever nineteenth-century courts interpreted the Fourth Amendment (and its state corollaries), they invariably looked to *Entick* and *Wilkes* for guidance. For example, in the case of *Ex parte Field*, the court explicitly linked *Wilkes*' treatment of illegally seized papers to the exclusionary application of habeas corpus discharge of persons ("If the arrest and detention in this case be sustained, it strikes a much more deadly and fatal blow to civil liberty, than did the general warrants [in *Wilkes v. Wood*]."). *Id.* at 6.

927 Boyd v. United States, 116 U.S. 616, 630, 633 (1886).

928 Anti-exclusion scholars claim that *Boyd*'s "fusion" of Fourth Amendment protections and Fifth Amendment silence principles was a "landmark" holding in 1886. *See* Pitler, 61 Wash. L. Rev. 459, at 467 n.43 (stating *Boyd*'s "convergence of the two amendments resulted in exclusion").

929 *See, e.g.,* Pitler, 61 Wash. L. Rev. 459, at 467 n.43 (referring to *Boyd*'s recognition of an intimate relationship between the Fourth and Fifth Amendments as "convergence theory").

930 It may be argued that the Supreme Court briefly separated the wedded Fourth and Fifth Amendments in *Adams v. New York*, 192 U.S. 585 (1904), where the Court upheld the admission of illegally seized evi-dence in a state trial. While the holding of *Adams* rejected arguments for applying the Fourth Amendment exclusionary rule, *id.* at 597-99, its basis for distinguishing *Boyd* has been widely debated. Did *Adams* merely decline to incorporate the Fourth Amendment rule into state practice under the Fourteenth Amendment? Or did Adams make deeper cuts into the oper-ability of exclusion? In either case, *Adams* turned out to be a "wild turn in the exclusionary rule roller coaster track," according to Supreme Court Justice Potter Stewart. Stewart, *The Road to Mapp v. Ohio and Beyond: The Origins, Development and Future of the Exclusionary Rule in Search-and-Seizure Cases*, 83 Colum. L. Rev. 1365, 1374 (1983).

931 The law-and-order originalists' interpretations of the Fifth Amendment Self-Incrimination Clause are so plainly irreconcilable with the known prac-tices and interpretations of earlier courts that such scholars must resort to

tricks of rhetoric to sustain them. Amar, for example, introduces the Clause as "an unsolved riddle of vast proportions, a Gordian knot in the middle of [the] Bill of Rights." Amar II, *supra*, at 46. While acknowledging early precedents excluding all manner of compelled out-of-court statements, Amar paints them as the product of confusion and illogic. See id. Much more logical, according to this view, are interpretations that severely limit the protections of the Self-Incrimination Clause in a manner consistent with prosecution advocacy.

932 4 John H. Wigmore, A Treatise on the System of Evidence in Trials at Common Law § 2264, at 3126 (1904) ("the radical fallacy of the [*Boyd*] opinion lies in its attempt to wrest the Fourth Amendment to the aid of the Fifth").

933 Burger drew from anti-exclusion "originalists" of his era and referred to the Fourth Amendment exclusionary rule as a "Draconian, discredited device" and a "judicially contrived doctrine." Stone v. Powell, 428 U.S. 465, 500, 501 (1976) (Burger, C.J., concurring).

934 *Id.* at 496, 497.

935 Akhil Reed Amar & Renee B. Lettow, *Self-Incrimination and the Constitution: A Brief Rejoinder to Professor Kamisar*, 93 Mich. L. Rev. 1011, 1013 (1995).

936 Pitler, 61 Wash. L. Rev. 459, at 467. Pitler claimed that "the common law rule of nonexclusion remained unchallenged until 1886 when the United States Supreme Court reached its landmark decision in *Boyd v. United States*." *Id.* at 466.

937 Amar II at 23 (referencing Telford Taylor's Two Studies in Constitutional Interpretation: Search, Seizure, and Surveillance (1969)).

938 As Richard A. Nagareda points out, "the most plausible construction of the phrase 'to be a witness' [in the Fifth Amendment] is as the equivalent of the phrase "to give evidence" found in contemporaneous state sources." Richard A. Nagareda, *Compulsion "To Be a Witness" and the Resurrection of Boyd*, 74 N.Y.U. L. Rev. 1575, 1605 (1999). The Framers' use of the word witness elsewhere in the Constitution likewise indicates a general evidentiary con-struction rather than one limited to mere oral witnessing. See id. at 1609-15 (discussing the meaning of the word "witness" in the Confrontation Clause, the Treason Clause and the Compulsory Process Clause - each of which suggests an analogy to "providing evidence" rather than mere testifying).

939 Entick v. Carrington, 19 How. St. Tr. 1029, 1066 (1765). 940 Entick, 19 How. St. Tr. at 1063, 1066.

941 *Id.* at 1064; see also Galloway, *The Intruding Eye: A Status Report on the Constitutional Ban Against Paper Searches*, 25 How. L.J. 367, at 422.
942 William A. Alderson, A Practical Treatise Upon the Law of Judicial Writs and Process in Civil and Criminal Cases 611 (New York, Baker, Voorhis & Co., 1895); Galloway at 335 (quoting Commonwealth v. Dana, 2 Mass. (2 Met.) 329, 334 (1841)).
943 *See* Galloway at 411-13 (describing the view that papers are essentially extensions of a person and his private thoughts).
944 Amar IV, at 465. 945 *Id.*
946 *See* Galloway *The Intruding Eye: A Status Report on the Constitutional Ban Against Paper Searches*, 25 How. L.J. 367 at 367.
947 *Id.* at 418 ("There can be little doubt that the framers of the fourth amendment intended the amendment's first clause to ban all searches of private papers.").
948 Entick v. Carrington, 19 How. St. Tr. 1029, 1073 (emphasis added).
949 *See* McCormick on Evidence § 72(a), at 130 (Kenneth S. Broun ed., 6th ed. 2006) ("Rules of privilege...are not designed or intended to facilitate the fact-finding process or to safeguard its integrity. Their effect instead is clearly inhibitive; rather than facilitating the illumination of truth, they shut out the light."); *see also id.* § 87, at 151 ("None can deny the [attorney-client] privilege's unfortunate tendency to suppress the truth...."). Wigmore famously said of the attorney-client privilege that "its benefits are all indi-rect and speculative; its obstruction is plain and concrete." *Id.* (quoting 8 Wigmore on Evidence § 2291, at 554 (McNaughton rev. 1961)).
950 *See, e.g.,* Pitler, 61 Wash. L. Rev. 459, at 466 (claiming the "doctrine of nonexclusion developed from the common law courts' paramount concern with truth-seeking and punishing the guilty").
951 *See* McCormick, § 71, at 126 (suggesting that evidentiary privileges and disqualifications have waned over time); *id.* § 78, at 142 (indicating that the "older branches" of the "ancient tree" of spousal privilege were more protective of secrecy than the privilege's "late offshoot").
952 *See, e.g.,* John F. Archbold, The Practice of Country Attornies and their Agents, in the Courts of Law at Westminster 102 (1838) (saying clergymen were privileged from arrest while going to and coming from church for religious duties); 1Thomas Coventry & Samuel Hughes, An analytical digested index to the common law reports: from the time of Henry III to the

commencement of the reign of George III 97 (Philadelphia, R.H. Small, 1832) (collecting English cases privileging certain persons from arrest while attending and traveling to and from court); James F. Oswald, Contempt of Court, Committal, and Attachment and Arrest Upon Civil Process, in the Supreme Court of Judicature (London, W. Clowes and Sones 1895) (discussing the long history of various privileges from arrest while going to and coming from English courts).

953 *See* Richards v. Goodson, 4 Va. (2 Va. Cas.) 381 (1823) (discharging prisoner because he was privileged from arrest while attending court in his own case); Ex parte M'Neil, 6 Mass. (4 Tyng) 245 (1810) (releasing debtor who was arrested while attending court); *see also* Hurd, A Treatise on the Right of Personal Liberty, at 270 (discussing privilege from arrest on Sunday, while under civil process, etc.).

954 Ohio Rev. Code Ann. § 2331.11(A)(2) (LexisNexis 2005) (Stating that "electors, while going to, returning from, or in attendance at elections" are privileged from arrest); *see also* Hargis v. Vaughan, 1 Del. Cas. 241, 241 (1799) (ordering discharge of a man arrested while returning from the general election on grounds he was privileged to go to and return from an election polling station).

955 *See* Hargis, 1 Del. Cas. at 241; Swift v. Chamberlain, 3 Conn. 537, 538-39 (1821) (upholding discharge of arrestee who had been seized while await-ing election returns and allowing an additional civil action for malicious prosecution).

956 As a member of Parliament, John Wilkes was "privileged from arrests in all cases except treason, felony, and ACTUAL breach of the peace...." King v. Wilkes, (1763) 95 Eng. Rep. 737, 740 (K.B.) (argument of Wilkes' counsel). Wilkes was ordered discharged from the Tower. *Id.*

957 *See* U.S. Const. art. I, § 6, cl. 1.

958 *See* Commonwealth v. Keeper of the Jail of Philadelphia, 4 Serg. & Rawle 505, 506 (Pa. 1818) (construing the 1802 statute).

959 The spousal privilege alone has existed since at least 1628, when Lord Coke wrote that "A wife [for they are two souls in one flesh], and it might be a cause of implacable discord and dissention betweene the husband and the wife, and a meane of great inconvenience." 1 Edward Coke, The First Part of the Institutes of the Laws of England; or, A Commentary upon Littleton: Not the Name of the Author Only, but of the Law Itself xcii (16th ed., rev.,

corr.1809) (Latin translation in brackets)). 960 Pitler, 61 Wash. L. Rev. 459, at 466.

961 *See* Amar II at 66.

962 *See, e.g.*, Thomas D. Morris, *Slaves and the Rules of Evidence in Criminal Trials*, 68 Chi.-Kent L. Rev. 1209 (1993) (discussing the trend toward allowing Blacks and Indians to provide testimony in American courts of the nineteenth century); Jonathan L. Entin, *Symposium: The Ohio Constitution - Then and Now: An Examination of the Law and History of the Ohio Constitution on the Occasion of its Bicentennial: An Ohio Dilemma: Race, Equal Protection, and the Unfulfilled Promise of a State Bill of Rights*, 51 Clev. St. L. Rev. 395 (2004) (discussing the history of Ohio's rules prohibiting Blacks from testifying against Whites in Ohio courts).

963 *See* Davis v. Dinwoody, (1792) 100 Eng. Rep. 1241, 1241 (K.B.). 964 Funk v. United States, 290 U.S. 371, 376 (1933).

965 *Id.* at 376.

966 *See id.* ("But the last fifty years have wrought a great change in these respects, and to-day the tendency is to enlarge the domain of competency....") (quoting *Benson v. United States* 146 U.S. 325, 336 (1892)).

967 *See* Mason Ladd, *Credibility Tests - Current Trends*, 89 U. Pa. L. Rev. 166, 174-76 (1940) (discussing the common law rule that a criminal defendant could not testify in his own defense because his motive to lie was so strong).

968 Brief for the Petitioner at 7, Hawkins v. United States, 358 U.S. 74 (1958) (No. 20).

969 Pitler, 61 Wash. L. Rev. 459, at 466.

970 *See* Stephen A. Siegel, *The Federal Government's Power to Enact Color -Conscious Laws: An Originalist Inquiry*, 92 Nw. U. L. Rev. 477, 479 (1998) (discussing the long history of legal impediments to blacks and other minorities imposed by early legal systems).

971 *See, e.g.*, Amar II at 154 (describing the "commonsensical point" that "the essence of our Constitution's rules about criminal procedure" is that they "seek[] to protect the innocent" and "lawbreaking, as such, is entitled to no legitimate expectation of privacy"); Richard A. Posner, *Rethinking the Fourth Amendment*, 1981 Sup. Ct. Rev. 49, 49 (1982) (stating the premise that the Fourth Amendment does not protect the interest of a criminal in avoiding punishment for his crime).

972 Wilkey, Why Suppress Valid Evidence?, *supra*, at 267.

Roger I. Roots

973 *Cf.* Ex parte Richardson, 16 S.C.L. (Harp.) 308, 308 (S.C. 1824) (granting motion for prohibition against lower court's convening without proper procedure, prohibiting trial court from retrying defendant because of gross procedural errors in initiation of the prosecution); The Superior Court Diary of William Samuel Johnson 1772-1773, reprinted in 4 American Legal Records 98 (John T. Farrell ed., 1942) (discussing a "guilty" thief who sued his arrestor over the manner of his arrest).

974 Warden v. Hayden, 387 U.S. 294, 304 (1967). 975 *See id.* at 296 n.1.

976 *See* Weeks v. United States, 232 U.S. 383, 393, 398 (1914). 977 *See id.* at 389, 398.

978 *See* Pitler, 61 Wash. L. Rev. 459, at 466.

979 *See, e.g.,* Norton, *supra,* at 262 (justifying the exclusionary rule on restitution grounds); accord Heffernan, *On Justifying Fourth Amendment Exclusion,* 1989 Wis. L. Rev. 1193, 1217 (1989).

980 *Id.* at 861, 867. The opinion is somewhat confusing on the question of whether the liquor was contraband, indicating that the "liquor was purchased by Youman or his wife at a time when and a place where it was lawful to sell and buy intoxicating liquor, but it was unlawful to have it in possession for purposes of sale, as charged in the warrant." *Id.* at 861.

981 "The people of the States, during the existence of the confederation, suffered from the violation of private property by their governments. In reconstituting their political system ... they protected property from unrea-sonable searches and seizures, and the title from detriment, except in the due course of legal proceeding." Dodge v. Woolsey, 59 U.S. (18 How.) 331, 378 (1855) (Campbell, J., dissenting).

982 The recurring use of quotation marks around the terms innocent and guilty stems from the author's cynicism toward the notion that any gov-ernment authority is capable of determining criminal guilt independent of a jury in each given case. Of course, the Framers generally believed in the theory that every individual possesses natural rights, which are presumed superior to the rights of the state and the power of positive law. *See, e.g.,* Andrew P. Napolitano, A Nation of Sheep 1-9 (2007) (describing the gradual movement of American legal philosophy from natural-rights orien-tations toward more instrumentalist principles); Robert P. George, Natural Law, the Constitution, and the Theory and Practice of Judicial Review, in Vital Remnants: America's Founding and the Western Tradition 151, 152 (Gary L. Gregg II ed., 1999) ("Most modern

commentators agree that the American founders were firm believers in natural law" and viewed the state's role as presumptively inferior by comparison). Under the Framers' construction of criminal procedure, determination of criminal liability was the sole province of juries, who could pronounce a defendant innocent even if the state proved him to be unquestionably "guilty" in fact. *See, e.g.*, William E. Nelson, *The Eighteenth-Century Background of John Marshall's Constitutional Jurisprudence*, 76 Mich. L. Rev. 893, 904 (1979) ("Juries rather than judges spoke the last word on law enforcement in nearly all, if not all, of the eighteenth-century American colonies.").

983 *See* Wilkes v. Wood, (1763) 98 Eng. Rep. 489, 493-94, 497-99 (K.B.).

984 Wells v. Jackson, 17 Va. (3 Munf.) 458, 468 (1814) (Roane, J., concurring). 985 *Id.* at 468.

986 Two curious cases illustrate this point. *Long v. State* involved a buggy-wheel thief who was apprehended in 1850 by private persons purporting to act under the authority of law. 12 Ga. 293 (1852). The thief begged for release and promised to pay his arrestors a slave, some blacksmith tools, a wagon and some other goods (in addition to the stolen buggy wheels) in exchange for release from prosecution. *See id.* at 295-98. Later, the thief lodged a complaint against his arrestors for robbery, and a Georgia grand jury indicted five men for criminal theft of the goods in excess of the buggy wheels. *See id.* at 295-96. The Georgia Supreme Court upheld robbery convictions of the vigilantes, stating that, although the buggy-wheel thief was plainly guilty of stealing the wheels, his guilt was immaterial. See id. at 326, 328, 332. What mattered was that the non-deputized law enforcers had failed to secure a proper warrant or take the thief to a magistrate. *See id.* at 326.

The 1837 North Carolina case of *Mead v. Young*, 19 N.C. (2 Dev. & Bat.) 521 (1837), is another bona fide example of a guilty man taking advantage of constitutional protections from unreasonable search and seizure. *Mead* involved a complainant (Young) who obtained a warrant from a magistrate for the arrest of Mead for beating and wounding one of Young's slaves. *Id.* at 521-22. The warrant commanded a man named Boyd (who was not a public officer) "to apprehend the said company, and them safely keep." *Id.* at 522. Boyd gathered a posse and went searching for Mead. *Id.* Seeing the posse, Mead surrendered. *Id.* Subsequent conversations between Mead and Young resulted in a payment by Mead to Young of $ 150, possibly to compensate for injuries to the slave but also likely intended as satisfaction of an impend-ing criminal prosecution

Roger I. Roots

(which never commenced). *See id.* Mead later sued both Young and Boyd for trespass and false imprisonment. *Id.* The North Carolina Supreme Court held that the warrant afforded no protection for Young and Boyd because it failed to identify Mead by name, stating that "by the best established principles of the common law - principles deemed so important, as to be embodied in our Constitution, and placed beyond the reach even of legislation - certainty of the person so to be seized, is "an essential matter required,' in every warrant to apprehend a man for an imputed crime." *Id.* at 526; *see also* Flanders v. Herbert, 1 Smith 205, 210-11 (N.H. 1808) (upholding jury's award of damages to plaintiff who was a "wrong-doer" but who suffered an illegal seizure by constables).

987   *See, e.g.,* Patrick Henry, Speech at the Virginia Ratifying Convention (June 5, 1788), reprinted in The Anti-Federalist Papers and the Constitutional Convention Debates 199, 201 (Ralph Ketcham ed., 1986) (urging Americans to "suspect every one who approaches that jewel [of liberty]" by dint of government authority); Alexander White, To the Citizens of Virginia, Winchester Va. Gazette, Feb. 29, 1788, reprinted in The Origin of the Second Amendment: A Documentary History of the Bill of Rights 1787-1792, at 288 (David E. Young ed., 2d ed. 1995) ("In America it is the governors not the governed that must produce their Bills of Right: unless they can shew the charters under which they act, the people will not yield obedience ... ."); *see also* Thomas Tredwell, Debates Before the New York Convention (July 2, 1788), reprinted in The Origin of the Second Amendment: A Documentary History of the Bill of Rights, 464, 467 (David Young ed., 2nd ed. 1995) (arguing that Federalist pleas to have faith that political leaders will not violate the rights of citizens were alarming and that "it is proved by all experience, - [that suspicion of those in power] is essentially necessary for the preservation of freedom.").

988   See Lysander Spooner, An Essay on the Trial by Jury 1, 6 (Boston, Bela Marsh 1852). The constitutional purpose behind the grand jury process was likewise for the "protection of the guilty." Ric Simmons, *Re-Examining the Grand Jury: Is There Room for Democracy in the Criminal Justice System?*, 82 B.U. L. Rev. 1, 48 (2002).

989   Levy, Origins of the Fifth Amendment, at 4-20. The Inquisitions "left a trail of mangled bodies, shattered minds, and smoking flesh" in the early thirteenth century until canon law developed procedures for dissidents– "guilty" of doctrinal disagreement - to challenge them. *See id.* at 19-21. 990   *See* Michael

S. Green, *The Privilege's Last Stand: The Privilege Against Self-Incrimination and the Right to Rebel Against the State*, 65 Brook. L. Rev. 627 (1999).

991 *E.g.*, Amar II at 25.

992 The strong constitutional foundations of the exclusionary rule also seem to be supported by legal developments in other countries whose court systems evolved from English common law. It was once common for anti-exclusion scholars to state that the United States was alone in the world in its adoption of exclusion. Chief Justice Burger, for example, claimed so in his famous dissent in *Bivens v. Six Unknown Named Agents of Fed. Bureau of Narcotics*, 403 U.S. 388, 415 (1971) (Burger, C.J., dissenting) ("This evidentiary rule is unique to American jurisprudence."). Of course, the unique nature of American constitutional sovereignty - being held by the individual rather than the state - makes comparisons between America's constitutional order and that of other countries somewhat inappropriate. Even so, it is evident that Burger's argument has been undermined in recent decades. English, Scottish, Canadian and Australian courts have all independently applied versions of the exclusionary rule in the past 30 years, although not consistently. *See* Stribopoulos, *supra*, at 87, 89-92, 118-19 (describing Britain's tortured application and prohibition of the rule). At present, England, Scotland, Canada and Australia all use exclusion at the discretion of judges in various circumstances. *See id.* Scotland has adopted something of a rule of discre-tionary exclusion, generally admitting inadvertently seized evidence and excluding evidence seized with deliberate illegality. *Id.* at 89-90. These foreign systems have adopted exclusion - by court discretion in specific circumstances rather than by rule - upon general principles of fundamental fairness. *See id.* at 87, 89, 120 (describing the justification for a discretionary exclusion rule in England, Scotland, and Canada). The law of Great Britain never did have a fully settled common law rule of nonexclusion as anti-exclusion scholars sometimes allege. Telford Taylor pointed out in 1969 that "English case law in this field is sparse, but in both of the only two important post-*Entick* decisions, seizures of purely evidentiary documents were sustained." Telford Taylor, Two Studies in Constitutional Interpretation: Search, Seizure, and Surveillance and Free Trial and Fair Press 61 (1969). Going back in time yields English cases of habeas corpus discharge for search and seizure violations similar to early decisions in the United States. *See* 3 The Legal Guide 122-23 (London, Richards & Co. 1840) (reporting a case in which inmates arrested unlawfully were discharged from custody and

granted damages); The King v. White, 20 How. St. Tr. 1376, 1380-81 (1771) (order-ing inmate discharged on grounds that he had no other remedy under the impressment [statute).

993 For a detailed discussion of apposite state cases immediately preceding the *Boyd* decision, *see* Donald E. Wilkes, Jr., *A Critique of Two Arguments Against the Exclusionary Rule: The Historical Error and the Comparative Myth*, 32 Wash. & Lee L. Rev. 881, 891-92 (1975).

994 *See* Michael Bentley, Modern Historiography: An Introduction ix (1999).

995 *See* generally Arthur Best, Wigmore on Evidence (4th ed. 1995). 996 *See* Donald E. Wilkes, Jr., *A Critique of Two Arguments Against the Exclusionary Rule: The Historical Error and the Comparative Myth*, 32 Wash. & Lee L. Rev. 881, 896-97 (1975).

997 Wigmore, *Using Evidence Obtained by Illegal Search and Seizure*, 8 A.B.A. J. 479 (1922) (claiming "it has long been established that the admis-sibility of evidence is not affected by the illegality of the means through which the party has been enabled to obtain the evidence").

998 Anti-exclusion scholars occasionally cite dicta in an 1822 federal circuit case, *United States v. La Jeune Eugenie*, 26 F. Cas. 832 (C.C.D. Mass. 1822) (No. 15,551), as supporting the proposition that a common law rule of nonex-clusion prevailed in the early Republic. *See, e.g.,* O'Laughlin,
Exigent Circumstances: Circumscribing the Exclusionary Rule in Response to 9/11, 70 UMKC L. Rev. 707, at 708 (footnote omitted) (claiming "*La Jeune Eugenie* is illustrative of the state of the exclusionary rule in the antebel-lum era."). *La Jeune Eugenie* was an admiralty case involving the capture of a French slave ship (La Jeune Eugenie) by an American-flagged vessel on the high seas. 26 F. Cas. at 833. The case had ramifications in many areas of law, including admiralty law, international law and the law of the slave trade, and it ultimately led to a ruling by the Supreme Court, in 1825, that the United States government had no authority to intervene in slave shipments under the flags of other nations. *See* The Antelope, 23 U.S. (10 Wheat.) 66, 101-02 (1825).

The opinion in *La Jeune Eugenie* states that "the right of using evidence does not depend, nor, as far as I have any recollection, has ever been supposed to depend upon the lawfulness or unlawfulness of the mode, by which it is obtained." 26 F. Cas. at 843. While this language does appear to support the alleged "doctrine of nonexclusion," it hardly illustrates "the state of the exclu-sionary rule in the antebellum era." Compare *La Jeune Eugenie*, 26 F. Cas.

at 833 with O'Laughlin, *supra*, at 708. For one thing, the court in *Le Jeune Eugenie* addressed the law of tort in admiralty jurisdictions rather than making pronouncements about the scope of the Fourth Amendment. *See* Davies, *Recovering the Original Fourth Amendment*, 98 Mich. L. Rev. 547, *supra*, at 664 n.320 (discussing the "widespread misperception that Justice Story addressed and rejected exclusion under the Fourth Amendment in dicta in his 1822 circuit court opinion" in *La Jeune Eugenie*). In Davies's words, "all Story's dictum stands for is the unexceptional proposition that exclusion is not appropriate when evidence has been obtained through an unlawful private arrest and search - a view which has never been seriously challenged." *Id.* at 665 n.320.

999   Dana, 43 Mass. (2 Met.) at 336.

1000   *Id.* at 337. There is contradictory language in the *Dana* opinion. On one hand, the decision held that the warrant and seizure in the case were lawful. *See id.* On the other hand, there is language in the opinion, "admitting that the lottery tickets and materials were illegally seized...." *Id.* This author reads this language as offering the hypothetical scenario that an illegal search and seizure occurred for purposes of speculating as to the admissibility of evidence. Wigmore apparently interpreted the same language as a holding and consequently construed *Dana* as establishing an exclusionary ruling. *See* Wigmore, *Using Evidence Obtained by Illegal Search and Seizure*, 8 A.B.A. J. 479, 479 & n.1 (1922). Professor Donald Wilkes has suggested that the *Dana* Court meant "assuming" rather than "admitting." *See* Donald E. Wilkes, *supra*, at 894. Readers are urged to consult the opinion and form their own conclusions.

1001   State v. Flynn, 36 N.H. 64 (1858).

1002   *Id.* at 68-69. The facts in *Flynn* are described without much detail, and, apparently, the officer saw liquor or evidence of liquor but did not seize it. *Id.* at 68 (counsel for the State said "there was no seizure"). Moreover, the court apparently sustained the legality of the search and seizure (if any), meaning *Flynn* (like the *Dana* case in Massachusetts) offered mere dicta in favor of nonexclusion: "The objection made in this case ... is, rather, that information obtained by means of a search-warrant ... is not competent to be given in evidence, because it has been obtained by compulsion ... ." *Id.* at 70. While the court apparently did not rule on whether there had been any search and seizure violation (or held that any search or seizure was lawful), it held that the objection was unsustainable. *See id.*

1003   *Id.* at 72. *Flynn* also cited a previous New Hampshire case, *State v. McGlynn*, 34 N.H. 422 (1857), for support. *Id.* at 66-67. In *McGlynn*, the court found "upon general principles" that a constable who assisted in an arrest and search of a suspect and a search of his premises need not swear before testifying in court that the "proceedings had been legal and regular." McGlynn, 34 N.H. at 425, 424.

1004   State v. Agalos, 107 A. 314 (N.H. 1919) (citing Flynn, 36 N.H. 64). 1005 110 Mass. 359, 360 (1872) (citing a civil forfeiture case, *Commonwealth v. Intoxicating Liquors*, 4 Allen 593 (1862)).

1006   *See* Commonwealth v. Tibbetts, 32 N.E. 910, 911 (Mass. 1893) (citing *Dana, Certain Lottery Tickets, Certain Intoxicating Liquors*, and *Taylor* for proposition that "evidence which is pertinent to the issue is admissible, although it may have been procured in an irregular or even illegal manner"); Commonwealth v. Henderson, 5 N.E. 832, 833 (Mass. 1885) (upholding admission of evidence obtained by officer pursuant to search and stating "it is immaterial whether the proceedings of the officer in serving the search warrant were regular and lawful or not"); Commonwealth v. Taylor, 132 Mass. 261, 262-63 (1882) (stating that testimony of medical examiner who performed autopsy without authority admissible); Commonwealth v. Welsh, 110 Mass. 359, 360 (1872) (citing Certain Intoxicating Liquors for proposition that evidence found under erroneous warrant "would not thereby be rendered incompetent as evidence"); Commonwealth v. Certain Intoxicating Liquors, 86 Mass. (4 Allen) 593, 597-600 (1862) (citing Dana and upholding civil forfeiture of liquor seized pursuant to flawed and fabricated paperwork); Certain Lottery Tickets, 59 Mass. (5 Cush.) 369, 374 (1850); Commonwealth v. Dana, 43 Mass. (2 Met.) 329, 337 (1841).

1007   After much searching, the author has identified only two pre-*Boyd* decisions that plainly upheld the admission of illegally seized physical evidence (or at least officer testimony that such evidence had been found) in criminal prosecutions over objections based on constitutional search and seizure protections. *See* Commonwealth v. Welsh, 110 Mass. 359, 360 (1872) (upholding the admission into evidence of seized liquor in a criminal trial and citing Intoxicating Liquors for the proposition that any defects in the search would not render the evidence inadmissible); Commonwealth v. Henderson, 5 N.E. 832, 833 (Mass. 1885) (upholding conviction and stating "it is immaterial whether the proceedings of the officer in serving the search-warrant were regular and

lawful or not"). The other pre-1886 cases cited by Wigmore and mentioned in this discussion either were not criminal cases (e.g., *Certain Lottery Tickets, supra*), involved only questions of testimony as opposed to physical evidence (e.g., *McGlynn* and *Flynn, supra*), or offered mere dicta as opposed to actual holdings (e.g., *Dana*, supra). Even *Welsh* did not state that its seizure had been illegal, but assumed hypothetically that it was. *See* Welsh, 110 Mass. at 360.
1008   Williams v. State, 28 S.E. 624, 625 (Ga. 1897). 1009   State v. Madison, 122 N.W. 647, 650-51 (S.D. 1909).
1010   *See, e.g.,* State v. Sheridan, 96 N.W. 730, 731 (Iowa 1903) (excluding goods unlawfully taken); Blum v. State, 51 A. 26, 28-30 (Md. 1902) (holding illegally seized evidence inadmissible); People ex rel. Ferguson v. Reardon, 90 N.E. 829, 833 (N.Y. 1910) (closely following Boyd and upholding habeas corpus discharge of a businessman arrested for refusing to show his stock transfer record books upon demand); State v. Slamon, 50 A. 1097, 1098-99 (Vt. 1901) (following Boyd).
1011   John H. Wigmore, A Treatise on the System of Evidence in Trials at Common Law § 2183, at 2956-57 n.1 (1905).
1012   *Id.* § 2264, at 3125-26. 1013   *Id.* § 2264, at 3124-25 n.2.
1014   Wigmore, 8 A.B.A. J., at 479-83 n.1.
1015   John H. Wigmore, Using Evidence Obtained by Illegal Search and Seizure, 7 Mass. L.Q., Aug. 1922, at 33, 36 (reprinting essentially the same citations).
1016   *See, e.g.,* Chastang v. State, 3 So. 304, 304 (Ala. 1887) (allowing admission of a gun seized during a search-incident-to-arrest by warrant - and explicitly distinguishing its holding from Boyd while agreeing with *Boyd*'s analysis).
1017   *See id.*; State v. Laundy, 204 P. 958, 974-76 (Ore. 1922); State v. Mausert, 95 A. 991, 992-93 (N.J. 1915); Younger v. State, 114 N.W. 170, 172 (Neb. 1907). 1018   *See* Faulk v. State, 90 So. 481, 481 (Miss. 1922); State v. Fuller, 85 P. 369, 370-71 (Mont. 1906) (holding that defendant had consented to a comparison of his shoes with shoe prints found at the crime scene and had thus waived his objection); State v. Fowler, 90 S.E. 408, 410-11 (N.C. 1916).
1019   *See* Wood v. McGuire, 21 Ga. 576, 582 (1857).
1020   *See* State v. Gorham, 65 Me. 270, 271-73 (1876) (erroneously cited in Wigmore, 8 A.B.A. J. 479, 481 n.1 (1922)).
1021   *See* Commonwealth v. Taylor, 132 Mass. 261, 262-3 (1882). 1022   *See* Faunce v. Gray, 38 Mass. (21 Pick.) 243, 245-46 (1838).

Roger I. Roots

1023 *See, e.g.*, Stevison v. Earnest, 80 Ill. 513, 516-17 (1875) (upholding the admission of loose papers over a party's objection); State v. Sawtelle, 32 A. 831, 833 (N.H. 1891) (involving a telegram, claimed by a company to be privileged, which was ordered to be produced).
1024 *See* People v. Margelis, 186 N.W. 488, 489 (Mich. 1922) (excluding a pint of whiskey which fell out of a suspect's pocket during an illegal arrest).
1025 Wigmore collected his set of precedents in a traveling footnote that was published in various publications, including several editions of his evidence treatise and a 1922 ABA Journal article, *Using Evidence Obtained by Illegal Search and Seizure*. Wigmore, *supra*, 479-83 n.1. This citation string first appeared in Wigmore's 1904 treatise and remained essentially unchanged, except for the addition of new cases as they developed. Wigmore, *supra*, § 2183, at 295-57 n.1.
1026 Even some fairly populous states with well-developed case law, such as Florida, Ohio, Virginia and Wisconsin, had no published cases on the question. *See* Wigmore, 8 A.B.A. J., at 479 n.1.
1027 For example, Wigmore cited Utah as one jurisdiction supportive of a rule of nonexclusion. *See* Wigmore, 8 A.B.A. J., at 483 n.1 ("search without a warrant, held admissible; the offense being committed in [the officers'] presence"). Yet, the Supreme Court of Utah actually declined to rule on the issue at all and suggested that exclusion would be the appropriate remedy if the question were presented. *See* Salt Lake City v. Wight, 205 P. 900, 903 (Utah 1922). The Court stated that:

> It may well be that under some circumstances, in a proper case, the trial court would be justified in making an order suppressing evidence ... so as to preclude its being used as evidence against one who is criminally accused, but no such case is presented upon this record for our consideration and determination.

Id.
Wigmore's footnote omitted one jurisdiction with an exclusionary rule, Wyoming, even though he must have come across references to its cases in *Wight*, which he cited. *See* State v. Peterson, 194 P. 342, 344, 350, 354 (Wyo. 1920) (imposing the rule of exclusion for search and seizure violations); Wight, 205 P. at 903; Wigmore, 8 A.B.A. J., at 483 n.1.

1028   Compare Blum v. State, 51 A. 26, 28-30 (Md. 1902), with Lawrence v. State, 63 A. 96, 102-03 (Md. 1906). *Blum* reversed a trial court's admission of books and papers on grounds that the introduction of such evidence violated Maryland's Fourth and Fifth Amendment corollaries. Blum, 51 A. at 28-30. The Lawrence decision (upholding admission of illegally seized evidence) overturned earlier precedents on Maryland's books (e.g., *Blum*), which had recognized an exclusionary rule. Lawrence, 63 A. at 102-03. Wigmore cited the *Lawrence* case in his search and seizure footnote but did not mention *Blum*. Wigmore, 8 A.B.A. J., at 481 n.1.

1029   In his notes on Michigan cases alone, Wigmore failed to list several cases supporting exclusion, which were referenced in cases he did cite. *See, e.g.,* People v. Halveksz, 183 N.W. 752, 753 (Mich. 1921) (excluding evi-dence and discharging defendant on grounds that "no power exists at com-mon law to make a search and seizure without a warrant"); People v. Le Vasseur, 182 N.W. 60, 61 (Mich. 1921) (excluding evidence and discharging defendant); People v. Vander Veen, 182 N.W. 61, 62 (Mich. 1921) (uphold-ing exclusion); People v. Woodward, 183 N.W. 901, 901-02 (Mich. 1921) (upholding exclusion). Wigmore's Michigan citations make it appear that Michigan had started with a strict nonexclusionary rule and then moved toward an exclusionary rule in the wake of the unsound reasoning of *Boyd* and *Weeks. See* Wigmore, 8 A.B.A. J., at 481 n.1 (citing Cluett v. Rosenthal, 100 Mich. 193, 197 (1894) as Michigan's first case validating the admission of testimony regarding the contents of an illegally seized book). In fact, Michigan courts had been discharging illegally seized persons for generations. *See, e.g.,* In re May, 1 N.W. 1021, 1021-24 (Mich. 1879) (ordering release of improperly arrested vagrant and stating it is irrelevant whether she is guilty); People v. Crocker, 57 Mich 31 (1869) (order-ing discharge of suspect who was arrested by an unsigned warrant). Moreover, the court in *Rosenthal v. Muskegon Circuit Judge*, which preceded the *Cluett* ruling and was not cited by Wigmore, ordered civil plaintiffs in pos-session of illegally seized books and papers to surrender them immediately to their owners (the defendants) and not to "use such original books and papers, or use or disclose the contents of such cop-ies, in any manner whatsoever...." 57 N.W. 112, 115 (Mich. 1893) (quoting Hergman v. Dettlebach, 11 How. Pr. 46, 48 (N.Y. 1855)). Wigmore also failed to mention another early Michigan exclusion case, Newberry v. Carpenter, 65 N.W. 530, 531-32 (Mich. 1895) (holding that government agents may not seize an entire building with a search warrant solely for purposes of seeking evidence against a criminal defendant, and releasing the building to its owner and recognizing the mere evidence rule of *Hibbard v. People*, 4 Mich. 125 (1856)). Michigan's true exclusion-rule history is almost precisely the opposite of the history told by Wigmore and later described in *Wolf v. Colorado*'s famous tables of state cases. *See* 338 U.S. 25, 33-34, 36 (1949) (listing Michigan as a state that "opposed the *Weeks* doctrine before the *Weeks* case had been decided," and which, after *Weeks*, "overruled or distinguished prior contrary decisions"). In reality, Michigan can be viewed as a jurisdiction that originally recognized exclusion but moved toward nonexclusion in the wake of Wigmore's "research" and then flip-flopped to follow *Weeks*, perhaps after Michigan judges scrutinized Wigmore's citations.

1030   Compare State v. Strait, 102 N.W. 913, 913-15 (Minn. 1905) (holding that parties have no right of exclusion before grand juries, thus distinguish-ing its facts from those of *Boyd* while implicitly following it), with State v. Hoyle, 107 N.W. 1130, 1130 (Minn. 1906) (upholding admission of evidence from a warrantless search).

Other state courts also flip-flopped on the issue. Compare State v. Harley, 92 S.E. 1034, 1035 (S.C. 1917) (admitting illegally seized articles on grounds that illegality was immaterial), and State v. Atkinson, 18 S.E. 1021, 1024-25 (S.C. 1894) (stating papers were admissible regardless of how they were found so long as the defendant was not made to produce them), with Blacksburg v. Beam, 88 S.E. 441, 441 (S.C. 1916) (excluding liquor obtained illegally).

1031   Wigmore, 8 A.B.A. J. 481.

1032   Compare Blum, 51 A. at 30 (following *Boyd* and excluding evidence of an inspection of business records), with Lawrence, 63 A. at 102-03 (citing "the recent and valuable work on Evidence of Professor Wigmore" and its "exhaustive and discriminating review of the authorities" and stating that evidence will be admitted regardless of the legality of its seizure). The "valu-able work on Evidence of Professor Wigmore" language continues to justify Maryland's nonexclusionary "rule" (which is actually an abandonment of Maryland's original exclusionary rule described in *Blum*) to this day. *See* Ford v. State, 967 A.2d 210, 230 (Md. Ct. Spec. App. 2009) (citing the language as support for the proposition that Maryland recognizes no exclusionary rule); Marshall v. State, 35 A.2d 115, 117 (Md. 1943) (citing Wigmore's "valuable work" to show that illegally taken evidence may be admitted); Meisinger v. State, 141

A. 536, 537-38 (Md. 1928) (citing Wigmore's "valuable work" for the proposition that "when evidence offered in a criminal trial is otherwise admissible, it will not be rejected because of the manner of its obtention"); Archer v. State, 125 A. 744, 749-50 (Md. 1924) (citing Wigmore's "valuable work"); *see also* Cohn v. State, 109 S.W. 1149, 1150-51 (Tenn. 1908) (citing 4 Wigmore on Evidence §§2183, 2264 and a dozen of Wigmore's inclu-sionary cases for the proposition that although evidence was produced by illegal spying, "it would not be rejected by the court as relevant to the issue"). *Cf.* State v. Anderson, 174 P. 124 (Idaho 1918) (split decision with majority upholding admission of liquor seized without warrant). Wigmore cited *Anderson* with the claim that it "flatly approved the orthodox principle, and [did not take] the trouble to notice *Weeks v. U.S.*" Wigmore, 8 A.B.A. J., at 480-81 n.1. Yet, Wigmore failed to report that the *Anderson* decision was so close that three justices on the Idaho Supreme Court each held sepa-rate positions, and that the case was originally decided in favor of exclusion. Anderson, 174 P. at 126. A lengthy dissent by Justice Morgan revealed the conflict among the panelists:

> Some time ago I was assigned the task of preparing the opinion of the court in this case. A draft of an opinion was prepared, but my utmost efforts have not convinced the other justices of the sound-ness of my logic, nor of the wisdom of the decisions of the Supreme Court of the United States, ably expressed, in similar cases.

See id. (Morgan, J., dissenting). Wigmore's exaggerated claims may have played a role in altering the outcome of the decision during its drafting stage. *See id.* at 125 (the majority citing Wigmore as support for the false claim that the "doctrine [of nonexclusion] has received the approval of the courts of a majority of the states").

Morgan's dissent also questioned the notion that the nonexclusion cases cited by Wigmore were not merely procedural. Morgan pointed out that some of the holdings, presented as being on the merits of exclusion, were in fact rulings on the appropriate procedure for challenging illegally seized evidence. *See id.* at 126 (Morgan, J., dissenting) ("Some of the decisions above cited," wrote Morgan, "announce the rule that a court will not pause in the trial of a crimi-nal case to frame and try a collateral issue to determine the means by which evidence against the defendant was obtained."). According to Morgan, even

Roger I. Roots

Adams v. New York, 192 U.S. 585 (1904), can be read as merely holding that a suppression motion should not be made during a criminal trial, but should be a pretrial motion. *See* Anderson, 174 P. at 128.

1033   Amar II, at 25 (speaking of a "universal law against exclusion" that allegedly prevailed in the nineteenth century).

1034   Professor Davies observes that neither of the two English cases cited by the Dana Court, Legatt v. Tollervey, (1811) 104 Eng. Rep. 617 (K.B.), and Jordan v. Lewis, (1740) 104 Eng. Rep. 618 (K.B.), "were germane to an alleged violation of a constitutional standard[]" because "they each involved an attempt by a defendant officer to prevent a plaintiff-victim in a false prosecution case from admitting unofficially obtained court records as evidence of the false prosecution - the reverse of the setting involved in the constitutional argument for exclusion." See Davies, *Recovering the Original Fourth Amendment*, 98 Mich. L. Rev. 547, supra note 15, at 664 n.318.

1035   *See* Wilson Huhn, *The Stages of Legal Reasoning: Formalism, Analogy, and Realism*, 48 Vill. L. Rev. 305, 305 (2003) (suggesting that stare decisis develops chronologically through the stages of formalism, analogy, and realism, especially in resolving difficult questions of law, and roughly corresponding to the stages of cognitive and moral development).

1036   Amar II, at 25 (speaking of a "universal law against exclusion" that allegedly prevailed in the nineteenth century).

1037   Wigmore, 8 A.B.A. J., at 479. 1038   *See id.*

1039   *See* Donald E. Wilkes, *A Critique of Two Arguments Against the Exclusionary Rule*, 32 Wash. & Lee L. Rev. 881, at 884 (saying defenders of the exclusionary rule were caught unprepared in the 1970s by Chief Justice Burger's claim that the exclusionary rule was without constitutional support).

1040   *See* Osmond K. Fraenkel, *Concerning Searches and Seizures*, 34 Harv. L. Rev. 361, 367 & n.35 (1921) (criticizing Wigmore's assertions).

1041   People v. Marxhausen, 171 N.W. 557, 560-1 (Mich. 1919) (emphasis added) (citations omitted).

1042   Fraenkel, *supra*, at 367. 1043   *Id.* at 367 n.35.

1044   *See* Note, *Evidence Obtained by Illegal Search and Seizure*, 14 Colum. L. Rev. 338, 338 (1914) (stating "it seems clear that the Fourth Amendment was intended" to "impede prosecutions irrespective of the guilt or innocence of the accused").

1045   Stewart, *supra*, at 1372.

1046   Pitler, 61 Wash. L. Rev. 459, at 479; *cf.* Donald A. Dripps, *Justice Harlan on Criminal Procedure: Two Cheers for the Legal Process School,* 3 Ohio St. J. Crim. L. 125, 136 (2005) ("Justice Harlan's dissent in *Mapp* is as noteworthy for what it did not say as for what it did say. Harlan did not invoke the original under-standing of either the Fourth Amendment or the Fourteenth."). A caveat is merited here because the Supreme Court's opinion in *Adams v. New York* did state that a vast majority of cases on the issue went against exclusion. *See* 192 U.S. 585, 598 (1904) ("But the English and nearly all of the American cases have declined to extend this doctrine to the extent of excluding tes-timony which has been obtained by such means, if it is otherwise compe-tent"). Yet, *Adams* stopped short of claiming that nonexclusion was a settled rule of the common law, as many anti-exclusionists claim today. And the decision in *Adams* was likely influenced by the ascending "scholarship" of John H. Wigmore.

1047   *See, e.g.,* California v. Minjares, 443 U.S. 916, 920 (1979) (Rehnquist, J., dissenting from denial of stay) (criticizing the Weeks Court for its "almost casual[]" holding that exclusion was required by the Fourth Amendment); Stone v. Powell, 428 U.S. 465, 497 (1976) (Burger, C.J., concurring) (in which Chief Justice Burger referred to the Court's exclusionary rule regime as a "remarkable situation - one unknown to the common-law tradition"); Bivens v. Six Unknown Named Agents of Fed. Bureau of Narcotics, 403 U.S. 388, 415-16 (1971) (Burger, C.J., dissenting) (criticizing the application of the exclusionary rule).

1048   See, e.g., Wesley W. Horton, The Connecticut State Constitution: A Reference Guide 50 (1993) (stating that Connecticut search and seizure law is still "mostly virgin territory" except for a handful of decisions).

1049   *See* Ex parte Burford, 7 U.S. (3 Cranch) 448, 451 (1806); Ex parte Bollman, 8 U.S. (4 Cranch) 75, 110-11 (1807).

1050   *See* Boyd v. United States, 116 U.S. 616, 638 (1886). 1051   *See* Frisbie v. Butler, 1 Kirby 213, 215 (Conn. 1787).

1052   This chapter is drawn from an article of the same name previously pub-lished in Volume 8 of the Seton Hall Circuit Review (2011). A version of this paper was presented as an address before the National Libertarian Party Convention in Denver, Colorado on May 24, 2008.

1053   *See* Akhil R. Amar, The Bill of Rights: Creation & Reconstruction 83 (1998); U.S. Const. art. III § 2 ("The Trial of all Crimes, except in Cases of

Roger I. Roots

Impeachment, shall be by Jury . . ."); U.S. Const. amend. VI ("In all criminal prosecutions, the accused shall enjoy the right to a speedy and public trial, by an impartial jury . . ."); U.S. Const. amend. VII ("the right of trial by jury [in civil cases] shall be preserved . . .").

1054 U.S. Const. amend. V ("No person shall be held to answer for a capital, or otherwise infamous crime, unless on a presentment or indictment of a Grand Jury . . .").

1055 Amar, THE BILL OF RIGHTS, at 83. Many thanks are owed to the scholarship of Professor Amar on this subject. I criticize some of Amar's conclusions on Fourth Amendment law extensively in the chapters above. However, I regard Amar's research into the original intent behind the jury trial provisions of the Constitution as extremely insightful. I highly recommend Amar's The Bill of Rights: Creation & Reconstruction (1998) (but not for its claims regarding the Fourth Amendment exclusionary rule).

1056 Amar, THE BILL OF RIGHTS: CREATION & RECONSTRUCTION 83 (1998). 1057 Id.

1058 Id. (citing Leonard W. Levy, The Emergence of a Free Press 227 (1985).

1059 See, e.g., Andrew E. Taslitz, Reconstructing the Fourth Amendment: A History of Search and Seizure, 1789-1868 (2006) (detailing the American colonists' outrage at Parliament's enactments creating vice admiralty courts to adjudi-cate cases stemming from the Crown's increasingly draconian enactments).

1060 The Declaration of Independence para. 14 (U.S. 1776).

1061 See Amar, THE BILL OF RIGHTS: CREATION & RECONSTRUCTION 83 (1998) (citing the 1774 Declaration of Rights of the First Continental Congress ("the respective colonies are entitled to . . . the great and inesti-mable privilege of being tried by their peers of the vicinage"); and the 1775 Declaration of the Causes and Necessity of Taking Up Arms (invoking the "inestimable privilege of trial by jury")).

1062 Cohen v. Hurley, 366 U.S. 117, 139–40 (1961) (Black, J., dissenting) (recounting the history of the colonists' promotion of the right to jury trial).

1063 Jack N. Rackove, Original Meanings: Politics and the Ideas in the Making of the Constitution 303 (1996) (reprinting excepts from Adams' excla-mations). 1064 Cohen, 366 U.S. at 139–40 (1961) (Black, J., dissenting).

1065 Id.

1066 AKHIL R. AMAR, THE BILL OF RIGHTS: CREATION & RECONSTRUCTION 97 (1998).

1067 The same trend that stripped the jury of its law-reviewing power has also led to the creation of the so-called "petty offense" exception. The Constitution's founders intended that the government must submit all criminal prosecutions to jury trials. The petty offense exception to the right to trial by jury was spawned as dicta in an 1888 opinion of the Supreme Court. *See* Callan v. Wilson, 127 U.S. 540, 555 (1888) (holding that a charge of criminal conspiracy triggered the constitutional right to jury trial but lesser crimes might not). Supreme Court rulings since the end of the 1800s have confined the right to jury trial to cases of only "serious" rather than "petty" crimes (i.e., punishable by less than six months imprisonment). *See id.* at 542. Despite the Sixth Amendment's clear language ("all criminal pros-ecutions"), the Supreme Court held that the guarantee does not apply to "petty offenses," meaning crimes punishable by less than sixth months. *See* Blanton v. City of N. Las Vegas, 489 U.S. 538 (1989). Even a fine of $5,000 in conjunction with a possible six-month jail sentence was held not seri-ous enough to warrant the expense of the right to trial by jury. United States v. Nachtigal, 507 U.S. 1, 5–6 (1993). This distinction exists nowhere in constitutional text, which explicitly guarantees a jury trial "[i]n *all* crimi-nal prosecutions" in the Sixth Amendment and for "*all* crimes" in Article III, Section 2. Justices Black and Douglas observed in a 1970 concurrence that the Supreme Court, "without the necessity of an amendment . . . decided that 'all crimes' did not mean 'all crimes,' but meant only 'all serious crimes.'" Baldwin v. New York, 399 U.S. 66, 75 (1970) (Black, J., concurring). Black and Douglas observed that the Court's lax treatment of the Constitution's plain language was for the government's benefit only: "This decision is reached by weighing the advantages to the defendant against the administrative inconvenience to the State inherent in a jury trial and magically concluding that the scale tips at six months imprisonment." *Id.* "Those who wrote and adopted our Constitution and Bill of Rights engaged in all the balancing necessary . . . . They decided that the value of a jury trial far outweighed its costs for "all crimes" and "[i]n all criminal pros-ecutions." *Id.* The aban-donment of the Constitution's plain language repre-sented "little more than judicial mutilation of our written Constitution." *Id.* Because misdemeanor prosecutions outnumber felony prosecutions in most

Roger I. Roots

American courts of general jurisdiction, the Supreme Court has stripped the right to jury trial from the majority of criminal cases.

1068 A detailed treatment of this topic would require a wholly separate book. Since 1966, federal criminal procedure has allowed the federal criminal justice system to consolidate federal litigation at large, mostly-urban centers within large geographic court districts. In practice, this has meant that many rural defendants are made to defend themselves in distant metropolitan areas and are tried before more urban juries drawn from areas where the alleged offense is not alleged to have occurred. I have litigated a couple of cases challenging this practice (*e.g.*, United States v. Stanko, 528 F.3d 581, 582 (8th Cir. 2008)) and presented papers on this topic at academic meetings. Some day in the future I hope to author an in-depth review of this topic.

1069 This article emphasizes the changes imposed upon the criminal law by the modern trend of no-nullification jury instructions. It must also be said that the Seventh Amendment's protection of the right to jury trial in civil cases has also been truncated and limited in ways not intended by the Framers and Founders. Consider tax cases, where judges have ruled that defendants are not entitled to jury trials because tax cases were litigated in non-jury chancery courts at the time of the founding. However, there were many voices of the framing era who demanded jury trials in tax cases and interpreted the Seventh Amendment as protecting a jury trial right in such cases. *See* Alan H. Scheiner, *Judicial Assessment of Punitive Damages, the Seventh Amendment, and the Politics of Jury Power*, 91 Colum. L. Rev. 142, 145–55 (1991) (citing founding-era sources which called for the right to jury trials in tax, asset forfeiture and other civil cases).

1070 *See* Erwin Chemerinsky, *The Supreme Court, 1988 Term: Foreword: The Vanishing Constitution*, 103 Harv. L. Rev. 43, 57 (1989) (stating the Rehnquist Court's jurisprudence overwhelmingly favored the government); Ward Farnsworth, *Signatures of Ideology: The Case of the Supreme Court's Criminal Docket*, 104 Mich. L. Rev. 67, 69–72 (2005) (demonstrating the Supreme Court's bias in favor of the government in criminal cases).

1071 It has been largely forgotten that the colonial judges known to the Founding generation were no more educated in the law than their contemporary fellows they met while strolling the streets. *See* Rackove, Original Meanings: Politics and the Ideas in the Making of the Constitution, at 299

("[F]ew justices brought anything resembling legal expertise to their duties . . . . legal expertise was irrelevant to many of the routine duties of courts"). 1072 *See* F. Mullett, Fundamental Law and the American Revolution 1760-1766 8 (1966). 1073 *Id.*

1074 The very notion that law and the courts are the domain of professional lawyers was alien to the founding generation, who sometimes viewed the "practice of law" by attorneys with derision and contempt. *See, e.g.,* Kevin R. C. Gutzman, The Politically Incorrect Guide to the Constitution 49 (2007); *see also The Changing Role of the Jury in the Nineteenth Century*, 74 Yale L. J. 172 (1964) ("Underlying the conception of the jury as a bulwark against the unjust use of governmental power were the distrust of 'legal experts' and a faith in the ability of the common people").

1075 *See* Jeffrey R. Pankratz, *Neutral Principles and the Right to Neutral Access to the Courts*, 67 Ind. L.J. 1091, 1103 n.70.

1076 *Id.*

1077 *Id.*

1078 *Id.*

1079 Rackove, *supra*, at 300 (emphasis added).

1080 There was widespread disdain and contempt for lawyers throughout the American colonies in the eighteenth and nineteenth centuries. *See* Pankratz, *supra*, at 1103 (writing of "a general hostility toward the legal profession" in early America). Pankratz quotes a founding-era anti-federalist, Benjamin Austin, as speaking of "a danger of lawyers becoming formidable as a combined body." *Id.* If this danger were not checked, said Austin, lawyers "might subvert every principle of law and establish a perfect aristocracy." *Id.*

1081 *See* Rackove, *supra*, at 298 (discussing Founders' view that "as members of a cohesive ruling elite, judges were unlikely to challenge either Crown or Parliament"); Alan H. Scheiner, *Judicial Assessment of Punitive Damages, the Seventh Amendment, and the Politics of Jury Power*, 91 Colum. L. Rev. 142, 150 (1991) (saying early Antifederalists feared that judges "would tend to favor the prerogatives of the executive branch"); *see also* State v. Croteau, 23 Vt. 14, 21 (1849) (stating that the principle reason for juries was the protection against "the consequences of the partiality and undue bias of judges in favor of the prosecution").

Roger I. Roots

1082   3 The Complete Anti-Federalist 49 (H. Storing ed. 1981) (An Old Whig). 1083   *Id.* at 61 (A Democratic Federalist).
1084   The Framers intense distrust of government was registered on hundreds of occasions and documents. *See, e.g.,* letter from Jefferson to Madison, Dec. 20, 1787 reprinted in Saul K. Padover, The Living U.S. Constitution, 29 (1953) ("energetic government . . . is always oppressive"); Thomas Tredwell, statement at New York Constitutional Convention, June 1788, reprinted *ibid.* at 20 ("government is like a mad horse," and only "a mad man [who] deserve[s] to have his neck broken . . . should trust himself on this horse without any bridle at all").
1085   Akhil R. Amar, America's Constitution: A Biography 207 (2005).
1086   *See* Ira Stoll, Samuel Adams: A Life 42–44 (2008) (detailing the atmosphere among colonial Bostonians during the period).
1087   Notably, early Americans were not contemptuous of all judges. For example, they named several American cities and towns after Lord Camden, the libertarian judge in England whose rulings inspired genera-tions of freedom-loving Americans. Camden, New Jersey, for example, was named for Camden. Camden Yards, where the Baltimore Orioles play baseball, is also named for Lord Camden. Akhil Reed Amar, *The Bill of Rights as a Constitution,* 100 Yale L.J. 1131 (1991).
1088   U.S. Const. art. III § 2 ("The Trial of all Crimes, except in Cases of Impeachment, shall be by Jury . . .").
1089   *See, e.g.,* Kevin R. C. Gutzman, The Politically Incorrect Guide to the Constitution 49 (2007) ("What does the Constitution say about the courts? Not much.").
1090   AKHIL R. AMAR, THE BILL OF RIGHTS: CREATION & RECONSTRUCTION 94 (1998).
1091   *Id.*
1092   *See* AKHILR.AMAR, THEBILLOFRIGHTS:CREATION&RECONS TRUCTION 94 (1998) (referencing John Taylor, An Inquiry into the Principles and Policy of the Government of the United States 209 (W. Stark ed., 1950 (1814)). 1093   Amar THE BILL OF RIGHTS, at 94.
1094   *See, e.g.,* Gary Lawson, *Response: On Reading Recipes . . . and Constitutions,* 85 Geo. L.J. 1823, 1835 n.37 (1997) ("Anyone who thinks that the Constitution designates the Supreme Court as the final, definitive expositor of the Constitution simply has not read the Constitution very carefully. The Supreme Court, through the Article III Vesting Clause, has the power and duty

to interpret the Constitution in the course of resolving disputes, but that is a far cry from a power to fix the Constitution's meaning or to bind other interpreters (including future Supreme Courts)").

1095 *See* Amar, THE BILL OF RIGHTS, at 94; Bernard Schwartz, The Bill of Rights: A Documentary History 1174 (1971) reprinting clauses from Massachusetts Governor John Hancock's speech to the state legislature: indicating that the jury trial provisions of the proposed Bill of Rights "appear to me to be of great consequence. In all free governments, a share in the administration of the laws ought to be vested in, or reserved to the people . . . .").

1096 Sullivan v. Louisiana, 508 U.S. 275, 277 (1993) ("The right [to jury trial] includes, of course, as its most important element, the right to have the jury, rather than the judge, reach the requisite finding of 'guilty'").

1097 U.S. Const. art. III, § 2.

1098 *See* Saul Cornell, The Other Founders (1999) (describing the intense advocacy for fully informed juries among the Anti-Federalists).

1099 *See, e.g.,* The Federalist No. 78, 439 (Alexander Hamilton) (Isaac Kranmick ed., 1987).

1100 *Id.*

1101 Amar, THE BILL OF RIGHTS, at 96 (discussing the unstated centrality of the jury on the First, Fourth, and Eighth Amendments).

1102 *Id.*

1103 *Id.* at 97 ("If a properly instructed jury voted to convict, a judge could set aside the conviction, but if that jury voted to acquit, reexamination was barred.").

1104 Sparf v. United States, 156 U.S. 51, 144 (1895) (Gray, J., dissenting) (citing 2 Elliot's Debates 94).

1105 U.S. Const. art. III, § 2 (emphasis added).

1106 U.S. Const. amend. VI ("In all criminal prosecutions, the accused shall enjoy the right to a speedy and public trial, by an impartial jury . . .").

1107 The Constitution includes "a right of the defendant to be given the chance to be acquitted, even though such acquittal conflicts with both the facts and the judge's instructions on the law." Alan W. Scheflin, *Jury Nullification: The Right to Say No*, 45 S. Cal. L. Rev. 168, 219 (1972).

1108 For two cases dealing with this scenario, *see* Mason v. Commonwealth, 419 S.E.2d 856, 858 (Va. App. 1992); and Bryant v. Georgia, 296 S.E.2d 168, 169 (Ga. Ct. App. 1982).

Roger I. Roots

1109   Thomas P. Bruetsch, *The Legislature "Caps" the Jury: Damage Caps and the Michigan Constitution,* 1 J.L. Soc'y 151, 151 (1999).
1110   *See* Jackson v. Virginia, 443 U.S. 307, 317 n.10 (1979) ("To be sure, the factfinder in a criminal case has traditionally been permitted to enter an unassailable but unreasonable verdict of 'not guilty. This is the logical corollary of the rule that there can be no appeal from a judgment of acquittal, even if the evidence of guilt is overwhelming.").
1111   Gregg v. Georgia, 428 U.S. 153, 199 n.50 (1976).
1112   *See, e.g.,* United States v. North, 910 F.2d 843, 910–11 (D.C. Cir. 1990) (describing the "judicial distaste" for special verdicts in criminal cases); United States v. Wilson, 629 F.2d 439, 443 (6th Cir. 1980) (holding that criminal juries have a "general veto power" and need never justify their decisions after the fact); United States v. McCracken, 488 F.2d 406, 418–19 (5th Cir. 1974) (collecting cases).
1113   Joseph Towers, Observations on the Rights and Duty of Juries in Trials for Libels 32–33 (1785) ("English juries have been in possession, time immemorial, of the right of giving a general verdict, of determining both the law and the fact, in every criminal case brought before them").
1114   *Wilson,* 629 F.2d at 443.
1115   This chapter will not restate the English pre-Revolutionary underpinnings of trial by jury, a long history ably recounted elsewhere. *See, e.g.,* Leonard W. Levy, The Palladium of Justice: Origins of Trial by Jury (1999). Associate U.S. Supreme Court Justice William O. Douglas wrote that the right to jury trial was among the most important natural rights recognized by the English colonists who came to America in the 1600s. The famed trial of printer William Bradford in colonial Pennsylvania in 1692 illustrates that colonial judges sometimes violated almost every other protection in the zeal to convict dissidents, including denial of the prohibition against double jeopardy, denial of speedy trial, denial of the right to know the charges, but nonetheless recognized the right of jurors to judge both the law and the facts in criminal cases. *See* William O. Douglas, An Almanac of Liberty 55 (1954) (describing Bradford's arguments with the judge).
1116   *See, e.g.,* Stettinius v. United States, 5 D.C. (5 Cranch) 573 (D.C. Cir. 1839) (allowing legal arguments to be made to the jury); United States v. Fenwick, 4 D.C. (4 Cranch) 675 (D.C. Cir. 1836) (sustaining the right to make legal arguments to the jury).

1117 *See* William H. Rehnquist, Grand Inquests: The Historic Impeachments of Justice Samuel Chase and President Andrew Johnson (1992).

1118 *See, e.g.*, William E. Nelson, *The Eighteenth-Century Background of John Marshall's Constitutional Jurisprudence,* 76 Mich. L. Rev. 893, 904 (1978) ("juries rather than judges spoke the last word on law enforcement in nearly all, if not all, of the eighteenth-century American colonies").

1119 Georgia v. Brailsford, 3 U.S. (3 Dall.) 1 (1794). 1120 *Id.* at 4.

1121 *Id.*

1122 *See* Nelson, The Eighteenth-Century Background, *supra.*

1123 *See* Amar, THE BILL OF RIGHTS, *supra,* at 94 ("Unable to harbor any realistic expectations of serving in the small House of Representatives or the even more aristocratic Senate, ordinary citizens could nevertheless participate in the application of national law through their service on juries.").

1124 SAUL CORNELL, THE OTHER FOUNDERS (1999) (discussing the advocacy of Anti-Federalists such as William Findley)

1125 *See, e.g.*, JACK N. RACKOVE, ORIGINAL MEANINGS: POLITICS AND THE IDEAS IN THE MAKING OF THE CONSTITUTION (1996) (discussing the Framers' view that the jury was intended to be a protector of rights). *See also*
Herbert J. Storing, What the Anti-Federalists Were For 19 (1981) (citing and quoting from various founding-era writers). John Adams famously remarked that "the common people . . . should have as complete a control, as decisive a negative, in every judgment of a court of judicature' as they have, through the legislature, in other decisions of government." *See supra* note 1074.

1126 Letters from the Federal Farmer (XV) (Jan. 18, 1788), reprinted in 2 The Complete Anti-Federalist 190–93 (Herbert J. Storing ed. 1981).

1127 Letters from the Federal Farmer (XV), reprinted in 2 The Complete Anti-Federalist 315, 320 (Herbert J. Storing ed., 1981).

1128 Alexis De Tocqueville, Democracy in America 293–94 (Phillips Bradley ed.) (1945).

1129 *See* Amar, THE BILL OF RIGHTS, *supra,* at 101.

1130 *See* Gutzman The Politically Incorrect Guide to the Constitution 172 (2007).

1131 *See* Cornell, THE OTHER FOUNDERS 59 (1999) (discussing Martin's emphasis on jury trials to protect liberty).

1132 *Id.* at 60.

1133   *See, e.g.*, the Anti-Federalist pamphlet, An Old Whig (VIII), reprinted in 3 THE COMPLETE ANTI-FEDERALIST 46, 49 (Herbert J. Storing ed., 1981) ("Judges, unencumbered by juries, have been ever found much better friends to government than to the people. Such judges will always be more desireable than juries to [tyrants]"). *See* George Billias, Elbridge Gerry, Founding Father and Republican Statesman (1976). Gerry—for whom the term "gerrymandering" is named—was a signer of the Articles of Confederation and the Declaration of Independence and served as Vice President under Madison.

1135   J. Madison, *Debates in the Federal Convention*, in 2 Records of the Federal Convention of 1787, 587 (M. Farrand ed. 1937).

1136   Alexander Hamilton, The Federalist No. 83 563 (J. Cooke ed., 1961).

1137   Nancy S. Marder, *The Myth of the Nullifying Jury*, 93 Nw. U. L. Rev. 877, 957 n.358 (1999) (alteration in original) (quoting Mark DeWolfe Howe, *Juries as Judges of Criminal Law*, 52 Harv. L. Rev. 582, 605 (1939) (quoting 2 Life and Works of John Adams 253-55 (C.F. Adams ed., 1856))).

1138   "The Federal Farmer" was the pseudonym of an Anti-Federalist writer who authored two influential pamphlets during the ratification period. His criticisms can be said to represent the most recurring complaints of the Anti-Federalists who objected to the pre-Bill-of-Rights Constitution on grounds that it represented a consolidation of the states into a central government and failed to explicitly lay out the natural rights and freedoms of the people. The Federal Farmer's identity has been debated by historians for genera-tions; however several scholars have suggested that he was Richard Henry Lee or Melancton Smith. *See* 14 The Documented History of the Ratification of the Constitution 6. (John P. Kaminski and Gaspare J. Saladino eds., 1981); Gordon S. Wood, *The Authorship of the Letters from the Federal Farmer*, 3 The William and Mary Quarterly 299–308 (1974).

1139   Letters from the Federal Farmer (XV), reprinted in 2 The Complete Anti-Federalist, *supra*, note 1126 at 320.

1140   The federal courts are virtually uniform on the issue. *See, e.g.*, United States v. Manning, 79 F.3d 212, 219 (1st Cir. 1996) ("a district judge may not instruct the jury as to its power to nullify"); United States v. Walling, No. 94-1175 1995 U.S. App. LEXIS 18130, at *4 (10th Cir. Apr. 7, 1995); United States v. Sepulveda, 15 F.3d 1161, 1190 (1st Cir. 1993) (upholding a conviction in a case in which a judge instructed jurors that they "should" convict if the government meets its burden of proof but "must" acquit if it does not);

United States v. Powell, 955 F.2d 1206, 1213 (9th Cir. 1991); United States v. Trujillo, 714 F.2d 102, 105–06 (11th Cir. 1983); United States v. Drefke, 707 F.2d 978, 982 (8th Cir. 1983). State courts are similarly uniform; *see, e.g.*, Mouton v. Texas, 923 S.W.2d 219, 222 (Tex. Ct. App. 1996); People v. Goetz, 532 N.E.2d 1273, 1273 (N.Y. 1988) (upholding an instruction that the jury "must" find a defendant guilty if the jury finds that each element beyond a reasonable doubt). Some judges, perhaps self-conscious of this improper assumption of power, use the phrase "should convict." Jones v. City of Little Rock, 862 S.W.2d 273, 275 (Ark. 1993); Farina v. United States, 622 A.2d 50, 60 (D.C. 1993); Michigan v. Demers, 489 N.W.2d 173, 174 (Mich. Ct. App. 1992); Davis v. Mississippi, 520 So. 2d 493, 494–95 (Miss. 1988); Montana v. Pease, 227 Mont. 424, 431, 740 P.2d 659, 663 (Mont. 1987); State v. Haas, 596 A.2d 127, 131 (N.H. 1991) (upholding instructions that the jury "should find the defendant guilty" if the prosecution proves all of the ele-ments of the crime). Pattern, or model, jury instructions in many jurisdictions also tell juries they are not to question a judge's interpretation of the law. *See, e.g.*, New York State Office of Court Administration, *Criminal* Jury Instructions *New York* (2d ed. 1995-2001) at http://www.nycourts.gov/cji/5-SampleCharges/SampleCharges.html (last visited Dec. 3, 2011) (providing language in the New York Model Jury Instructions which states that a trial jury "must" convict a defendant if all the elements are proven beyond a reasonable doubt).
1141   *See, e.g.*, United States v. Muse, 83 F.3d 672, 677 (4th Cir. 1996); United States v. Calhoun, 49 F.3d 231, 236 n.6 (6th Cir. 1995); Illinois v. Moore, 171 Ill.2d 74, 109–10, 662 N.E.2d 1215, 1231–32 (Ill. 1996); People v. Weinberg, 631 N.E.2d 97, 100 (N.Y. 1994); State v. Bjerkaas, 472 N.W.2d 615 (Wis. Ct. App. 1991).
1142   *See, e.g.*, Ratzlaf v. United States, 510 U.S. 135, 149 (1994) (noting the "venerable principle that ignorance of the law generally is no defense to a criminal charge").
1143   For a fascinating overview of the internal disagreements and politics among judges on the Supreme Court, *see* Tonja Jacobi, *Competing Models of Judicial Coalition Formation and Case Outcome Determination,* 1 J. Legal Analysis 411 (2009).
1144   *The Changing Role of the Jury in the Nineteenth Century*, 74 Yale L.J. 170, 173–74 (1964) ("There is much evidence of the general acceptance of this principle in the period immediately after the Constitution was adopted."

Roger I. Roots

"During the first third of the nineteenth century . . . judges frequently charged juries that they were the judges of law as well as the fact and were not bound by the judge's instructions . . . . [C]ounsel had the right to argue the law— its interpretation and its validity—to the jury."); *see also* William E. Nelson, The Americanization of the Common Law: The Impact of Legal Change on Massachusetts Society, 1760-1830 3 (1975) ("juries rather than judges regularly decided the law" in the early colonies and in the first two generations of the United States"); Joseph Towers, Observations on the Rights and Duty of Juries, in Trials for Libels 32–33 (1785) ("English juries have been in possession, time immemorial, of the right of giving a general verdict, of determining both the law and the fact, in every criminal case brought before them"). James Wilson, the leading legal theoretician of the constitutional debates and one of six original justices appointed by George Washington to the Supreme Court, regarded jurors as "the ultimate interpreters of the law." 2 The Works of James Wilson 541 (Robert Green McCloskey ed., 1967). Wilson authored his famous *Lectures on Law* in 1791—the very year the Bill of Rights was ratified. *Lectures on Law* was the most authoritative source of legal interpretation contemporary to the Founding period.

1145 United States v. Morris, 26 F. Cas. 1323, 1331–36 (C.C.D. Mass. 1851).

1146 Amar, THE BILLL OF RIGHTS, *supra*, at 342 n.65.

1147 Pierce v. State, 13 N.H. 536 (1843).

1148 Clay S. Conrad, Jury Nullification: The Evolution of a Doctrine 69 (1998).

1149 *See* Commonwealth v. Porter, 51 Mass. (10 Met.) 263 (Mass. 1845).

1150 *See, e.g.,* Towers, Observations on the Rights and Duty of Juries *s* (discussing and criticizing the notion (which must have been raised by others of the period) that judges and not juries should be the sole deciders of the law).

1151 *See* Rackove, ORIGINAL MEANINGS, at 298 (adding that judges who advocate the restriction of juries "had few admirers in America").

1152 *Id.* at 301.

1153 *See* United States v. Battiste, 24 F.Cas. 1042 (Mass. 1835) (reprinting Justice Story's instructions to a jury suggesting that "the jury are no more judges of the law in a capital case or other criminal case . . . than they are in every civil case"). Conrad, Jury Nullification: The Evolution of a Doctrine, at 65–67 (discussing in some detail the background of Justice Story's instructions in *Battiste*).

1154 *The Changing Role of the Jury in the Nineteenth Century*, 74 Yale L.J. 170, 180, n.63 (1964).

1155 *See, e.g.,* N. Sec. Co. v. United States, 193 U.S. 197, 400 (1904) (Holmes, J. dissenting) (repeating the ancient saying).

1156 Justice Holmes' comments are worth repeating: "For great cases are called great, not by reason of their real importance in shaping the law of the future, but because of some accident of immediate overwhelming interest which appeals to the feelings and distorts the judgment. These immediate interests exercise a kind of hydraulic pressure which makes what previously was clear seem doubtful, and before which even well settled principles of law will bend." *Id.* at 400–01.

1157 *See* St. Clair v. United States, 154 U.S. 134 (1894). 1158 *Id.* at 144 (1894).

1159 *Id.*

1160 *Id.*

1161 *Id.* at 184. 1162 *Id.*

1163 *St. Clair*, 154 U.S. at 184.

1164 Sparf v. United States, 156 U.S. 51, 59 (1895). 1165 *Id.* at 62.

1166 *Id.* at 61, n.1. 1167 *Id.*

1168 The *St. Clair* trial occurred in June 1893 and its judgment was upheld by the Supreme Court on May 26, 1894. *See St. Clair*, 154 U.S. 134. The *Sparf* decision was rendered by the Supreme Court on January 21, 1895. *See Sparf*, 156 U.S. at 59.

1169 *Sparf*, 156 U.S. at 64.

1170 *Id.* at 107 (Jackson, J., concurring).

1171 The *Sparf* plurality discussed these precedents at length, *see id.* at 103–05, but went far beyond them.

1172 *Sparf*, 156 U.S. at 84.

1173 Justice Harlan repeated with favor a claim by Justice Field in *United States v. Greathouse*, 26 F. Cas. 18, 21 (N.D. Cal. 1863), that "[t]here prevails a very general, but an erroneous, opinion that in all criminal cases the jury are the judges as well of the law as of the fact . . ." *Sparf*, 156 U.S. at 78.

1174 For example, the plurality dissects Chief Justice John Jay's jury instruction in *Georgia v. Brailsford*, 3 U.S. 1, 4 (1794) (discussed *supra*) by suggesting it may have been misreported, noting "the different parts of the charge conflict with each other." *Sparf*, 156 U.S. at 65.

Roger I. Roots

1175 *Sparf*, 156 U.S. at 63–64.
1176 *Id.* at 107 (Jackson, J., concurring).
1177 *Id.* at 107 (Brewer, J., dissenting) ("I concur in the views expressed in the opinion of the court as to the separate functions of court and jury, and in the judgment of affirmance against Hansen; but I do not concur in hold-ing that the trial court erred in admitting evidence of confessions, or in the judgment of reversal as to Sparf").
1178 *Id.* at 110–82 (Gray, J., dissenting).
1179 *Evidence Against St. Claire*, S.F. Call, Aug. 30, 1895, p. 4, Col. 1. 1180 *Hanged For Murder on the High Seas*, N.Y. Times, Oct. 19, 1895.
1181 The trial judge had in fact instructed the jury that "*it may be in the power of the jury*, under the indictment by which these defendants are accused and tried, of finding them guilty of a less crime than murder, to wit, man-slaughter, or an attempt to commit murder; yet, as I have said in this case, if a felonious homicide has been committed at all, of which I repeat you are the judges, there is nothing to reduce it below the grade of murder." *Sparf*, 156 U.S. at 60 (emphasis added).
1182 *Sparf*, 156 U.S. at 80.
1183 Depending on one's interpretation, it may be said that the role-of-the-jury discussion by Justice Harlan represented the views of his own plurality plus those of Justices Jackson, Brewer, and Brown. However, the awkward separations of the opinions in *Sparf* do not make this clear. Harlan's opinion was not pared into separate sections on the different issues of law, and Brewer's and Brown's opinion was designated a dissent rather than a partial concurrence and partial dissent.
1184 Julie Seaman, *Black Boxes: fMRI Lie Detection and the Role of the Jury*, 42 Akron L. Rev. 931, 935 (2009) ("the Supreme Court settled the ques-tion more than 100 years ago [in *Sparf*] by holding that a criminal jury has the power, but not the right, to acquit against the law"); Ran Zev Schijanovich, *The Second Circuit's Attack On Jury Nullification In* United States v. Thomas: *In Disregard of the Law and the Evidence*, 20 Cardozo L. Rev. 1275, (1999) ("[t]he battle line in the jury nullification debate in federal criminal cases had been clearly drawn and stable for the last 100 years" after *Sparf*); *id.* at 1324 n.2 ("In 1895 the United States Supreme Court in *Sparf v. United States*, 156 U.S. 51 (1895), put to rest any doubts that in federal criminal cases it is the

province of the court to state what the law is and that the jury's duty is confined to applying the facts to the law.").

1185   In practice, judges exercise wide latitude and in many jurisdictions openly tolerate nullification arguments made to juries by defense attorneys. Johnny Cochran's closing arguments in the 1995 O.J. Simpson murder trial, for example, contained explicit statements to the jury about the jury's power to punish police misconduct by acquitting Simpson:

> This is what this is about. That is why we love what we do, an opportunity to come before people from the community, the consciences of the community. You are the consciences of the community. You set the standards. You tell us what is right and wrong. You set the standards. You use your common sense to do that.

> Who then polices the Police? You . . . police the Police. You police them by your verdict. You are the ones to send the message. Nobody else is going to do it in this society. They don't have the courage. Nobody has the courage. They have a bunch of people running around with no courage to do what is right, except individual citizens. You . . . are the ones in war, you are the ones who are on the front line. These people set policies, these people talk all this stuff; you implement it. You are the people. You are what makes America great, and don't you forget it.

John T. Reed, *Penn, Zenger, and O.J.: Jury Nullification -- Justice or the "Wacko Fringe's" Attempt to Further Its Anti-Government Agenda?*, 34 Duq. L. Rev. 1125, 1125 (1996) (quoting People v. Simpson, No. BA097211 (Cal. Super. Ct. 1995), Reporter's Transcript of Proceedings, Sept. 28, 1995, Vol. 232, at 47793–8036, 9:01 a.m., available in LEXIS, Cal library, OJTRAN file).

1186   *See, e.g.*, Honorable Judge Frederic Block, *Reflections on Guns and Jury Nullification*, Champion Magazine, July 2009, at 12 (discussing the differing instructions he gives compared to those given by his fellow District Judge Jack Weinstein).

1187   *See id.* (discussing Judge Weinstein's tendency not to inform jurors of their nullification options).

Roger I. Roots

1188 *See, e.g.,* Teresa L. Conaway, Carol L. Mutz & Joann M. Ross, *Jury Nullification: A Selective, Annotated Bibliography,* 39 Val. U.L. Rev. 393 (2004) (outlining the massive commentary and jurisprudence on the topic).
1189 United States v. Dougherty, 473 F.2d 1113 (D.C. Cir. 1972). 1190 *Id.*
1191 *Id.*
1192 According to the LexisNexis Academic search engine, 333 separate decisions have referenced the *Dougherty* case since 1972 (Dec. 3, 2011).
1193 An exhausting (but not exhaustive) compilation of articles is available in the annotated bibliography of Teresa L. Conaway, Carol L. Mutz and Joann M. Ross. *See* Conaway, et al, *Survey: Jury Nullification: A Selective, Annotated Bibliography,* 39 Val. U.L. Rev. 393 (2004); *infra,* Appendix A. These scholarly articles seem (from my own imperfect interpretation of the authors' descriptions) to generally agree that jury independence or nullification is a beneficial, lawful, commendable, and laudable feature of jury trials in at least some cases. The articles come to differing conclusions regarding how jury nullification applies or should apply but conclude that jury nullification is a legitimate component of trial by jury, consistent with the Constitution's original intent.
1194 My article "The Rise and Fall of the American Jury," 8 *Seton Hall Circuit Review* 1 (2011), from which most of this chapter is drawn, contains appendices listing the titles of a few dozen published articles which criticize jury nullification and suggest various methods to censure and limit it.
1195 *See, e.g.,* Honorable Donald M. Middlebrooks, *Reviving Thomas Jefferson's Jury:* Sparf *and* Hansen v. United States *Reconsidered,* 46 Am. J. Legal Hist. 353 (2004); Honorable Jack B. Weinstein, *Considering Jury 'Nullification': When May and Should a Jury Reject the Law to Do Justice?,* 30 Am. Crim. L. Rev. 239 (1993) (arguing that some jury nullification stems from idealism that is "good for the American soul"); Honorable Jack B. Weinstein, *The Many Dimensions of Jury Nullification,* 81 Judicature 169 (1998) (saying nullifying juries do so to be fair, not because of disaffection with established law); Honorable Robert D. Rucker, *The Right to Ignore the Law: Constitutional Entitlement Versus Judicial Interpretation,* 33 Val. U. L. Rev. 449 (1999) (celebrating Indiana's history of jury nullification).
1196 *See, e.g.,* Jeffrey Abramson, We, the Jury: The Jury System and the Ideal of Democracy (1994); Clay S. Conrad, Jury Nullification: The Evolution of a Doctrine (1998); William L. Dwyer, In the Hands of the People: The

Trial Jury's Origins, Triumphs, Troubles, and Future in American Democracy (2001); Godfrey Lehman, Is This Any Way To Run A Jury? (2001); Norman J. Finkel, Commonsense Justice: Jurors' Notions of the Law (1995); Thomas Andrew Green, Verdict According to Conscience: Perspectives on the English Criminal Trial Jury, 1200–1800 (1985); Mortimer R. Kadish & Sanford H. Kadish, Discretion to Disobey: A Study of Lawful Departures from Legal Rules (1973); Godfrey D. Lehman, We the Jury: The Impact of Jurors on Our Basic Freedoms (1997); Lysander Spooner, An Essay on the Trial by Jury (Project Gutenberg 1998) (1852). Anyone knowing of a published scholarly book focusing solely on trial by jury or its history which concludes that juries should be instructed that they must follow a judge's interpretation of the law is urged to contact the author.

1197   Duncan v. Louisiana, 391 U.S. 145, 156 (1968).

1198   United States v. Booker, 543 U.S. 220, 238 (2005) (trial by jury is necessary to thwart "judicial despotism" that could arise from "arbitrary punishments upon arbitrary convictions") (citing The Federalist No. 83, p. 499 (Alexander Hamilton) (C. Rossiter ed., 1961)).

1199   Apprendi v. New Jersey, 530 U.S. 466, 477 (2000) ("To guard against a spirit of oppression and tyranny on the part of rulers," trial by jury is the "great bulwark of [our] civil and political liberties") (citations omitted).

1200   The Supreme Court has repeatedly stated that the common law known to the Framers must be consulted whenever specific questions arise from the provisions of the Constitution. Thus, for the meaning of "trial by jury," we are supposed to look at the common law of 1789-1791 for specific details. *See, e.g.*, United States v. Bailey, 444 U.S. 394, 415 n.11 (1980).

1201   *See, e.g.*, Alan W. Scheflin & Jon Van Dyke, *Jury Nullification: The Contours of a Controversy*, Law & Contemp. Probs., 51, 55 (Autumn 1980) (say-ing "[t]he critical issue in recent years has become whether the defendant has the right to have the jury instructed as to its universally-recognized power."); Eleanor Tavris, *The Law of an Unwritten Law: A Common Sense View of Jury Nullification*, 11 W. St. U. L. Rev. 97, 98 (1983) ("Since it is an undeniable fact of judicial life that juries need explain their acts of nullification to no one, the controversy exists—and rages—as to whether juries may be prop-erly instructed as to the existence of this power."); Steven M. Warshawsky, Note, *Opposing Jury Nullification: Law, Policy, and Prosecutorial Strategy*, 85 Geo. L.J. 119, 234–35 (1996) ("The contemporary debate over jury nullification focuses . . . on whether jurors should be informed of their nullification power at trial.").

1202 *See generally* Andrew D. Leipold, *Rethinking Jury Nullification*, 82 Va. L. Rev. 253 (1996).

1203 *Id.*

1204 *Id.*

1205 James Joseph Duane, *Jury Nullification: The Top Secret Constitutional Right*, 22 No. 4 Litig. 6, 8 (1996).

1206 United States v. Dougherty, 473 F.2d 1113, 1139 (D.C. Cir. 1972) (Bazelou, C.J., dissenting).

1207 United States v. Krzyske, 836 F.2d 1013, 1021 (6th Cir. 1988). 1208 *Id.*

1209 *Id.* at 1021–22.

1210 *See* Duane, *Jury Nullification: The Top Secret Constitutional Right*, 22 No. 4 Litig. 6, 10 (1996). at 10 (describing the "widespread myth popular among judges" that the law "requires juries to convict every man shown to be technically guilty beyond a reasonable doubt").

1211 Consider also the observation of James Wilson, one of the eminent Framers of America's Founding documents. "[E]very one who is called to act, has a right to judge" the constitutionality of acts and actions of government, wrote Wilson. The Works of James Wilson 186 (Robert Green McCloskey ed., 1967). 1212 United States v. Powell, 955 F.2d 1206, 1213 (9th Cir. 1991) ("anarchy would result from instructing the jury that it may ignore the require-ments of the law").

1213 *See, e.g.*, United States v. Dougherty, 473 F.2d 1113, 1136 (D.C. Cir. 1972) ("To assign the role of mini-legislature to the various petit juries, who must hang if not unanimous, exposes criminal law and administration to paral-ysis, and to a deadlock that betrays rather than furthers the assump-tions of viable democracy.").

1214 This was the crux of the two-judge majority's holding in *Dougherty*, 473 F.2d 1113. For years, this argument has been a mainstay of anti-informed-jury advocates.

1215 Numerous books in recent years have exposed the capricious and selec-tive nature of modern criminal law. *See, e.g.*, Gene Healy, Go Directly to Jail: The Criminalization of Almost Everything (2007) (discussing various examples of how the criminal laws have become unknowable and unpredictable); Douglas

N. Husak, Overcriminalization (2008) (addressing the increasing size, scope and randomness of modern criminal law); Andrew P. Napolitano, Constitutional Chaos: What Happens When the Government Breaks its
Own Laws (2004) (describing the erosion of natural rights by the imposition of increasingly pervasive government criminal laws); Paul Craig Roberts & Lawrence M. Stratton, The Tyranny of Good Intentions: How Prosecutors and Law Enforcement Are Trampling the Constitution in the Name of Justice (2008) (describing how instrumentalism among the three branches of government has eroded the rule of law); Harvey Silvergate, Three Felonies A Day: How the Feds
Target the Innocent (2009) (suggesting an average American unknowingly commits three felonies a day).
1216   *See* Jerome Pohlen, Oddball Texas: A Guide to Some Really Strange Places 6 (2006) (discussing the case and the impact on Oprah Winfrey); David J. Bederman, *Food Libel: Litigating Scientific Uncertainty in a Constitutional Twilight Zone*, 10 DePaul Bus. L.J. 191 (1998) (discussing the Oprah Winfrey case in the context of a general discussion of the "constitutional twilight zone" of so-called food disparagement statutes).
1217   *See* Matt Bartosik, *Kids Arrested for Food Fight*, NBC Chicago (Nov. 10, 2009), http://www.nbcchicago.com/news/local-beat/Kids-Arrested-for-Food-Fight-69575092.html.
1218   *See Knife at Lunch Gets 10-Year-Old Girl Arrested at School*, WFTV.com
(Dec. 14, 2007), http://www.wftv.com/news/14858405/detail.html.
1219   *See Desk Doodling Arrest: Alexa Gonzalez, 12-Year-Old, Handcuffed for Drawing on School Desk*, Huffington Post (Feb. 5, 2010), http://www. huffing-tonpost.com/2010/02/05/desk-doodling-arrest-alex_n_450859.html.
1220   See Zach Smith, *Report: Martin County student arrested for pass-ing gas, turning off classmate's computer*, TCPalm (Nov. 21, 2008), http:// www.tcpalm. com/news/2008/nov/21/report-martin-county-student-arrested-passing-gas-/.
1221   *See* Angie Goff, *Boy Booked for Opening Christmas Present*, WIS News 10 (Oct. 6, 2006), http://www.wistv.com/Global/story.asp?S=5774586&nav=0RaPXRrw.
1222   *See Rough Justice*, The Economist, July 2, 2010, *available at* http:// www. economist.com/node/16640389.

Roger I. Roots

1223 *See* Sara Israelsen, *Defense Grows in Orem Lawn Case*, Deseret News (Sept. 19, 2007), http://www.deseretnews.com/article/695211283/Defense-grows-in-Orem-lawn-case.html.

1224 One of the more depressing articles I have read on the growth of the American police and prosecution state is Craig Horowitz, *The Defense Rests—Permanently*, New York Magazine (Mar. 4, 2002) http:// nymag.com/nymetro/news/crimelaw/features/5730/. This depressing article describes a criminal justice system that has become so lopsided in favor of the state that its results are wholly disproportionate, unfair, and almost random. Many criminal defense lawyers, the article sug-gests, are leaving the filed of criminal defense entirely due to the system's lopsidedness.

1225 *See* Amar II, *supra* note 34 (discussing the commonly held view among the Framers that jury trial was as much of a right of jurors—rep-resenting the community—as it was a right of defendants).

1226 Saul Cornell, The Other Founders 134 (1999) (discussing the arguments of Anti-Federalist William Findley of Pennsylvania).

1227 Jefferson was writing to Tom Paine in 1789, recommending that France adopt trial by jury. *See* Letter from Thomas Jefferson to Thomas Paine (July 11, 1789), in 15 The Papers of Thomas Jefferson 269 (Julian P. Boyd ed., 1958).

1228 Douglas N. Husak, Overcriminalization (2008) (discussing numerous examples of silly and oppressive criminal laws); Elbert Hubbard & Bert Hubbard, Selected writings of Elbert Hubbard: His Mintage of Wisdom, Coined from a Life of Love, Laughter and Work 199 (1922) ("Very few bad laws are ever repealed . . . The law-books are filled with silly laws that no lawyer dare cite . . .").

1229 *See, e.g.*, Encyclopedia of New Jersey 295 (Maxine N. Lurie & Marc Mappen, eds. 2004).

1230 Steven N. Gofman, *Car Cruising: One Generation's Innocent Fun Becomes the Next Generation's Crime*, 41 Brandeis L.J. 1 (2002) (discussing "cruising" ordinances nationwide).

1231 Lists of stupid laws are frequently circulated on the internet and on email discussion lists. *See, e.g.*, www.idiotlaws.com; www.dumblaws.com.

1232 *See, e.g.*, Harvey A. Silvergate, Three Felonies A Day: How the Feds Target the Innocent (2009) (the increased complexity of criminal statutes now expose the average American to prosecution for three felonies per day).

1233   See Peter J. Smith, *New Legal Fictions*, 95 Geo. L.J. 1435, 1438 (2007) ("Members of Congress often do not read the bills on which they are asked to vote, let alone consider the meaning of statutory terms in light of dictionary definitions and canons of construction."); Susan Freiwald, *Online Surveillance: Remembering the Lessons of the Wiretap Act*, 56 Ala. L. Rev. 9, 45 (2004) (referring to a statutory scheme that "is so confusing and intricate that it is nearly impossible to determine which provisions apply to which practices"); *Id.* at 75 ("Commentators have complained about the limited deliberation that preceded the USA PATRIOT Act, which was passed despite the fact that members of Congress did not have a chance to view the actual text.").

1234   *See, e.g.*, Sheryl Lindsell-Roberts & Myron Miller, Loony Laws & Silly Statutes (1994) (collecting numerous nationwide examples of ludicrous and silly laws); Sandra B. Zellmer, *The Devil, the Details, and the Dawn of the 21st Century Administrative State: Beyond the New Deal*, 32 Ariz. St. L.J. 941, 995, 996 (2000) (Discussing appropriations riders often attached to bills in ways that allow "only minimal opportunity for review and assessment by con-gressional members outside of the appropriations committees, let alone by members of the interested public," in a process that is "often shielded from public review and critique, is especially vulnerable to manipulation by special interests." New laws tend to grant extensive powers to government agencies while insulating government action "from complying with other-wise applicable legal standards. As a result, the judiciary's role is impaired, because reviewing courts have virtually no means to assess whether agency action taken pursuant to a rider's directive is arbitrary and capricious."); *see also* Thomas J. Maroney, *Fifty Years of Federalization of Criminal Law: Sounding the Alarm or 'Crying Wolf?'*, 50 Syracuse L. Rev. 1317, 1327 (2000) ("It is not just their numbers that are significant. Much of the legislation takes the form of the omnibus crime bill, which 'can be hundreds of pages long and contain an infinite number of provisions defining new crimes . . .'").

1235   Respublica v. Oswald, 1 U.S. 319, 328–29 (1788).

1236   *Id.* (citing argument of William Findley, a Pennsylvania Anti-Federalist).

1237   Note, *The Changing Role of the Jury in the Nineteenth Century*, 74 Yale L.J. 172 (1964).

1238   Amar, THE BILL OF RIGHTS, *supra*, at 99 (citing 1 The Works of James Wilson 186 (Robert Green McCloskey ed., 1967)). As Amar notes, Wilson's invocation of all actors who perform constitutional duties must surely

Roger I. Roots

have meant jurors as well as judges and legislators, although Wilson "did not single out juries by name."
1239 *Id.*
1240 The Federalist No. 62 (James Madison) (Publius).
1241 John Adams, diary entry of February 12, 1771, *reprinted in* Rackove, Original Meanings: Politics and Ideas in the Making of the Constitution 301 (1996).
1242 *See* United States v. Dougherty, 473 F.2d 1113, 1135 (D.C. Cir. 1972) ("The jury knows well enough that its prerogative is not limited to the choices articulated in the formal instructions of the court.").
1243 Duane, *Jury Nullification: The Top Secret Constitutional Right*, 22 No. 4 Litig. 6, 10 (1996).
1244 *See id.*
1245 *See id.* (emphasis added) (citing the Federal Judicial Center, Pattern Jury Instructions 21 (1987).
1246 Several courts have formally approved similar instructions telling the jury they "must" convict. *See* Farina v. United States, 622 A.2d 50, 61 (D.C. 1993); People v. Bernhard Goetz, 532 N.E.2d 1273 (N.Y. 1988); *see also* United States v. Fuentes, 57 F.3d 1061 (1st Cir. 1995) (telling a jury they "must" convict is not plain error); Miller v. Georgia, 391 S.E.2d 642, 647 (Ga. 1990) (permissible to tell jury their verdict "would be guilty" if they found proof of guilt beyond a reasonable doubt).
1247 *See Legislation Declared Unconstitutional, in* Congress A to Z the Encyclopedia of American Government (D.R. Tarr & A. O'Connor eds., 2003). 1248 For books detailing the terrifying growth of America's contemporary police and prosecution empire, *see* Harvey Silverglate, Three Felonies A Day: How the Feds Target the Innocent (1st ed. 2009) (suggesting an average American unknowingly commits three felonies a day); Cato Institute, Go Directly to Jail: The Criminalization of Almost Everything (Gene Healy ed., 2006) (detailing the increasing ambiguity in criminal statutes).
1249 See generally, Marc Galanter, *The Vanishing Trial: An Examination of Trials and Related Matters in Federal and State Courts*, 1 J. Empirical Legal Studies 459-570 (2004).
1250 Id. at 460.

1251 *Mowry v. Whipple*, 8 R.I. 360, 363 (1866). "It seems manifest that, under such a rule, there would be no proper security from false accusations and arrests").

1252 *See* Percival v. Jones, 2 Johns. Cas. 49, 51 (N.Y. 1800) (holding justice of peace liable for issuing arrest execution against person privileged from imprisonment).

1253 *See* Fullerton v. Mack, 2 Aik. 415 (S.C. 1828). 1254 *See* Wise v. Withers, 7 U.S. (3 Cranch) 331 (1806). 1255 *Id.*

1256 For a discussion of the development of immunities for prosecutors, *see* Margaret Z. Johns, *Reconsidering Absolute Prosecutorial Immunity*, 2005 B.Y.U.L. Rev. 53, 53 (2005). Johns notes that "the doctrine of abso-lute immunity [is] unsupported by history and contrary to public policy." *Id.* at 56.

1257 , "[A] charge of crime should not be lightly made . . ." Lee v. Jones, 44 R.I. 151, 158, 116 A. 201 (R.I. 1922).

1258 *See, e.g.*, State v. McDonald, 6 N.E. 607, 611 (Indiana 1886) ("The judgment is reversed at appellee's costs"). Many state jurisdictions also had statutes on the books imposing civil and criminal penalties almost immediately upon anyone who filed a meritless complaint. The Nebraska criminal code, for example, like many others, contained a provision that required a magistrate, "on the examination, shall be satisfied that there is no just cause for the complaint, it shall be his duty to discharge the accused and render judgment in the name of the state against the party complaining, for the costs of the prosecution." Errickson v. State, 7 NW 333, 334 (Neb. 1880) (quoting from Section 270 of the Nebraska Criminal Code).

1259 *See, e.g.*, Graff v. Motta, 748 A.2d 249, 252 (R.I. 2000) (saying that in "*Graff* I on the counts of malicious prosecution . . . , we necessarily upheld a jury finding that there was no probable cause to support the charge . ..")'; Graff v. Motta, 695 A.2d 486, 491 (R.I. 1997) ("Given the evidence presented at the trial below, a reasonable jury could have concluded that the. . . charge was resurrected and filed without probable cause and in retaliation"); Soares v. Ann & Hope of Rhode Island, Inc., 637 A.2d 339, 345 (R.I. 1994) ("Therefore, with respect to the malicious-prosecution claim, the jury was left to consider whether Ann & Hope had probable cause to institute the criminal proceeding and whether it instituted the proceeding with "mal-ice"); Johnson v. Palange, 406 A.2d 360, 372 (R.I. 1979) ("We emphasize that the dispositive issue here

is . . . whether there were sufficient facts to give Lieutenant Palange probable cause . . . to believe that they had violated the statute. That question, as we have already said, was properly submitted to the jury for resolution"); Desimone v. Carmenuch, 87 R.I. 95, 99; 139 A.2d 81, 83 (R.I. 1958) (involving a case for malicious prosecution and a decision by a trial judge sitting without a jury; the Supreme Court held that it would not disturb the trial judge's determination, as the trial judge "saw and heard the witnesses . . . . [and h]is findings depended to a great extent upon the cred-ibility of the witnesses and the weight of the testimony"); Quinlan v. Breslin, 61 R.I. 327, 331; 200 A. 989, 991 (1938) (overturning a lower court judgment of nonsuit on grounds that "[t]he existence or want of probable cause was. . . an issue of fact" rather than an issue of law to be decided by a judge); Beaumier v. Provensal, 58 R.I. 472, 475; 193 A. 521, 522 (R.I. 1937) (uphold-ing judgment for a plaintiff in a malicious-prosecution case because "[t] here was evidence here on which the jury reasonably could have found that there was lack of probable cause for charging the plaintiff with larceny"); Kitchen v. Rosenfeld, 44 R.I. 399; 117 A. 537 (1922) ("Whether the prosecutor acted upon advice of counsel [prior to prosecuting] and whether he made a complete disclosure of all the facts and circumstances are questions of fact for the jury"); Smith v. Markensohn, 29 R.I. 55, 57; 69 A. 311 (R.I. 1908) ("The verdict of the jury is in effect that the payment was made under duress and protest, and that there was want of probable cause. I think that the jury might properly so find upon the evidence"); Mowry v. Whipple, 8 R.I. 360, 363 (1866) ("the [trial] Court instructed the jury that both malice and want of probable cause must be proved, to the satisfaction of the jury. . . . This ruling was in accordance with the best authorities, and, as we think, was correct") (emphasis added throughout the paragraph above).
1260   Quinlan v. Breslin, 200 A. 989, 990 (R.I. 1938).
1261   *Hill v. Rhode Island State Employees' Retirement Board*, 935 A.2d 608, 613 (2007) ("Whether defendants in a malicious-prosecution action had prob-able cause to initiate a criminal action is a question of law to be determined by the court").

INDEX

Roger I. Roots

Made in the USA
San Bernardino, CA
24 October 2016